AF708398

Language Policy and Conflict Prevention

Language Policy and Conflict Prevention

Edited by

Iryna Ulasiuk
Laurenţiu Hadîrcă
William Romans

BRILL
NIJHOFF

LEIDEN | BOSTON

Library of Congress Cataloging-in-Publication Data

Names: Ulasiuk, Iryna, editor. | Hadîrcă, Laurenţiu, editor. | Romans, William, editor.
Title: Language policy and conflict prevention / edited by Iryna Ulasiuk, Laurenţiu Hadîrcă, William Romans.
Description: Leiden ; Boston : Brill Nijhoff, 2018. | Includes bibliographical references and index.
Identifiers: LCCN 2018008380 (print) | LCCN 2018010444 (ebook) | ISBN 9789004357754 (E-book) | ISBN 9789004357747 (hardback : alk. paper)
Subjects: LCSH: Linguistic minorities--Legal status, laws, etc.--Europe. | OSCE High Commissioner on National Minorities. Oslo Recommendations regarding the Linguistic Rights of National Minorities.
Classification: LCC KJC5146.L36 (ebook) | LCC KJC5146.L36 L36 2018 (print) | DDC 342.2408/7--dc23
LC record available at https://lccn.loc.gov/2018008380

Typeface for the Latin, Greek, and Cyrillic scripts: "Brill". See and download: brill.com/brill-typeface.

ISBN 978-90-04-35774-7 (hardback)
ISBN 978-90-04-35775-4 (e-book)

Copyright 2018 by Koninklijke Brill NV, Leiden, The Netherlands.
Koninklijke Brill NV incorporates the imprints Brill, Brill Hes & De Graaf, Brill Nijhoff, Brill Rodopi, Brill Sense and Hotei Publishing.
All rights reserved. No part of this publication may be reproduced, translated, stored in a retrieval system, or transmitted in any form or by any means, electronic, mechanical, photocopying, recording or otherwise, without prior written permission from the publisher.
Authorization to photocopy items for internal or personal use is granted by Koninklijke Brill NV provided that the appropriate fees are paid directly to The Copyright Clearance Center, 222 Rosewood Drive, Suite 910, Danvers, MA 01923, USA. Fees are subject to change.

This book is printed on acid-free paper and produced in a sustainable manner.

Contents

PART 2
Language Rights and Evolving Standards and Practice

Preface

In response to concern about language policies within participating States, and the impact which they could have upon minority-majority relations, in 1998 the then High Commissioner Max Van der Stoel launched the 'Oslo Recommendations regarding the Linguistic Rights of National Minorities'. He intended it to be a reference tool for the development of state policies and laws which would contribute to an effective implementation of the language rights of persons belonging to national minorities, particularly in the public sphere. Language was identified both as a personal matter closely connected with identity and as an essential tool of social organization which in many situations becomes a matter of public interest. This remains entirely true today, and all holders of my office have been confronted on a regular basis with the tensions which can arise between groups, when one or both of these aspects is mismanaged, creating an unnecessary conflict between the two. The Recommendations and Guidelines of the HCNM are designed to be a key resource for OSCE participating States in the management of diverse societies. All eight are based upon a synthesis of knowledge and experience gathered by the Institution, and developed through a partnership forged with external practitioners and academic experts.

Crises stemming from language policies are never inevitable, and where the key principles in the Oslo Recommendations are followed, they are eminently avoidable. As disputes arise, and where the political will exists, my Institution assists governments to find constructive solutions acceptable to both majority and minority populations. This is fully in line with my responsibility to act as "an instrument of conflict prevention at the earliest possible stage". Sometimes such diplomatic work must be done quietly, without attendant publicity, since experience shows that this is the more effective method of achieving results.

I wholeheartedly welcome the present volume, and I particularly welcome the substantial contributions to it by a number of current and former staff of my Office, which ensures that HCNM experience and lessons learned in the implementation of the Recommendations are fully taken into account. In fact this publication covers, with a conflict prevention perspective, many issues arising from implementation of language policies, including respect for linguistic rights, relevant to states with diverse societies. It also provides an insight into the work that many international organisations do in this area, in partnership with governments. Moreover, it includes the contributions of a wide variety of independent experts, thus successfully showcasing the importance of co-operation between the HCNM, leading academics working in the field of language policy, and some of our partner organisations within the United Nations, the Council of Europe, and the European Union.

Investment in implementing balanced language policies pays off with increased political stability, greater engagement from all members of society, and better productivity. This book is timely, and I hope that it will stimulate debate, and serve as a resource for actors involved in managing diversity, as well as those looking to better understand the different aspects of the role of the OSCE and its partner organisations working to reduce the risk of conflict.

Lamberto Zannier,
OSCE High Commissioner on National Minorities

Notes on Contributors

Lamberto Zannier
is currently the OSCE High Commissioner on National Minorities. Before taking up this position, Ambassador Zannier served as the OSCE Secretary General for two consecutive terms, from July 2011 until June 2017. An Italian career diplomat since 1978, Zannier has specialized in multilateral diplomacy and international security. He has authored several publications on security, conflict prevention and crisis management issues. Zannier holds a law degree and an honorary degree in International and Diplomatic Sciences from the University of Trieste, Italy.

Bob Deen
is a Senior Adviser to the High Commissioner on National Minorities (HCNM) and Head of the Section covering Eastern Europe, the Caucasus and Central Asia. He holds a MSc in Nationalism and Ethnicity from the London School of Economics and Political Science and a MA in International Relations from the University of Groningen. Prior to joining the OSCE Bob worked as a Political Adviser for the European Union in the South Caucasus, as a Research Fellow for the Dutch Institute for International Relations 'Clingendael' and as an aid worker and field researcher in Kyrgyzstan and Tajikistan.

William Romans
is a Senior Legal Adviser at the HCNM. Previous positions include Human Rights Expert with EULEX Kosovo, Chief of the Human Rights Section at the OSCE Mission to Kosovo, Senior Legal Officer at the Special Court for Sierra Leone, and Judgement Coordinator at the United Nations International Criminal Tribunal for Rwanda. He holds an LL.B. (Hon) from the University of Edinburgh, an LL.M. from Stellenbosch University, and is qualified as an attorney in New York.

Laurenţiu Hadîrcă
has worked as Senior Legal Adviser to the OSCE HCNM since March 2014. Prior to that, in 2010–2014 he served as Legislative Support Officer for the OSCE ODIHR, reviewing the legislation of various countries, often jointly with experts from the UN and Venice Commission. In 2007–2010 he served as Legal Analyst for the OSCE Mission in Kosovo, and in 2005–2007 he was National Coordinator of the OSCE Trial Monitoring Programme in Moldova. In 2004–2007, he was also a university lecturer in Moldova. Laurenţiu Hadîrcă holds master's

degrees in Comparative Constitutional Law (LL.M.) and in International Relations (M.Litt.).

Iryna Ulasiuk
is a Senior Legal Adviser at the HCNM. She previously worked for the Robert Schuman Center for Advanced Studies, at the European University Institute (EUI) (Florence, Italy) where she was engaged in various research projects. She holds a doctorate in law from the EUI. Her main areas of specialization are in comparative constitutional law (especially fundamental rights and freedoms related aspects), citizenship law, European, international and comparative legal regulation of culture, media, education and language use, and the protection of minorities.

Jennifer Croft
is currently the Deputy Head of the Human Rights Department at the OSCE Office for Democratic Institutions and Human Rights (ODIHR). From 2010–2017 she worked as a Senior Adviser to the OSCE High Commissioner on National Minorities. Previously she held a number of headquarters and field-based positions with the U.S. State Department and the U.S. Agency for International Development. She holds a MA in Law and Diplomacy from the Fletcher School of Law and Diplomacy at Tufts University.

Asa Solway
is a Senior Legal Adviser for the OSCE High Commissioner on National Minorities. An international lawyer, he has expertise in access to justice, international human rights law and international criminal and humanitarian law, and has worked with the United Nations, OSCE and national governments in various countries including Kosovo, Ukraine and Sierra Leone. He also serves as a part-time Lecturer at UC Berkeley School of Law.

Alessandro Rotta
is Senior Adviser to the OSCE High Commissioner on National Minorities since November 2015. Prior to that he worked as Senior Political Advisor to the EU Special Representative in Kosovo (2011–2015), as Political Advisor in the EULEX Kosovo Mission (2008–2011) and as a Political Advisor to the Special Coordinator of the Stability Pact for South Eastern Europe in Brussels (2006–2008). Previously, he was coordinator of studies and researcher on South Eastern Europe at the Centro Studi di Politica Internazionale-CeSPI, a Rome-based think tank, from 2000 to 2006. Alessandro holds a degree in Political Science from the University of Florence.

Sarah Stephan
is a Project Officer at the HCNM and a PhD candidate at Åbo Akademi University. Before joining the HCNM she worked as a researcher and project manager at the Åland Islands Peace Institute where her research focused on territorial autonomy regimes. Sarah holds an LL.B. in European and Comparative Law from the Hanse Law School and an LL.M. in Public International Law from Helsinki University.

Dmitry Nurumov
served as Special Adviser on Ukraine for the HCNM from 2015–2016. He joined HCNM in 2011 as a Legal Adviser. Prior to that, he worked at the ODIHR Rule of Law Unit as Rule of Law Programme Coordinator. He has also worked as Legal Expert for the OSCE Centre in Almaty as well as for the International Organisation for Migration and for a local NGO in Kazakhstan. In 2000, he defended a PhD in International Public Law at Moscow State Institute (University) of International Relations. He has written and edited publications on criminal procedure, human rights and constitutional law.

Michael Angermann
has been a project officer for the OSCE HCNM since 2013. While the regional focus of his work is on Central Asia and the South Caucasus, thematically he has been extensively involved in educational projects. Prior to joining the OSCE HCNM, he worked for different institutions within the German Development Cooperation in and on Central Asia. Mr. Angermann holds an M.A. in Central Asian Studies, East European Studies and Macroeconomics from Humboldt University and the Free University Berlin.

Atanasia Stoianova
has been collaborating with the OSCE HCNM as an educational expert for MLE promotion in the countries of Central Asia since 2008, having prior experience as a school director, public official, teacher trainer, project manager and researcher, as well as an internship in MLE at the Teachers' College, Columbia University, USA. Ms. Stoianova is the author of evaluation studies for international agencies and public authorities. Her publications in the field are addressed to teachers, school directors, public authorities, as well as researchers.

Fernand de Varennes
is Dean of the Faculty of Law at the Université de Moncton (Canada), Extraordinary Professor at the Faculty of Law of the University of Pretoria (South Africa), and from 2019 Cheng Yu Tung Visiting Professor at the Faculty of Law

of the University of Hong Kong (China). He is also United Nations Special Rapporteur on Minority Issues and is renowned as one of the world's leading experts on the international human rights of minorities and was one of the experts involved in the drafting of the Oslo Recommendations regarding the Linguistic Rights of National Minorities.

Elżbieta Kuzborska

is an expert on national minorities, a human rights lecturer and author. She was Senior Minorities Fellow at the OHCHR in 2014. She has cooperated with the European Foundation of Human Rights where she provided legal training for members of minorities. She was previously a Lecturer at the University of Białystok in Vilnius, where the teaching is conducted in the mother tongue of the Polish minority. As a Board Member of the Association of Polish Academics in Lithuania she has supported young people of a minority background. She is also an active member of the Association of Polish Lawyers in Lithuania.

Francesco Palermo

is Professor for comparative constitutional law at the School of Law, University of Verona and Director of the Institute for Comparative Federalism at Eurac Research in Bolzano/Bozen. Former Senior Legal Adviser to the OSCE High Commissioner on National Minorities, former member and President of the Council of Europe's Advisory Committee on the Framework Convention for the Protection of National Minorities.

Petra Roter

is Associate Professor of International Relations at the University of Ljubljana and a Senior Research Fellow at the Centre of International Relations in Ljubljana. She received her Ph.D. at the University of Cambridge. She is presently a Visiting Scholar at the University of Cambridge (2017). She co-ordinates the MA in International Relations and is a national director of the E.MA – European Master in Human Rights and Democratisation. Her research includes international regimes on diversity management and minority protection, international conflict management and post-conflict reconstruction, nation-building and state-formation processes. She is the President of the Advisory Committee (2016–2018).

Brigitta Busch

is an applied linguist at the Department of Linguistics at the University of Vienna. In 2009 she was granted a Berta-Karlik research professorship for excellent scientists by the University of Vienna. She has also been working for many years as an expert for the Council of Europe, where she was first involved in the Confidence-Building Measures Programme in Eastern and South-Eastern Europe. She was a member of the Advisory Committee from 2009 to 2010 and from 2014 to 2018.

Vesna Crnić-Grotić
is chair of the Committee of Experts of the European Charter for regional or minority languages. Professor of International Law and Dean of the Faculty of Law, University of Rijeka, Croatia. Former chair of the Main Commission for Law of the National Council for Science in Croatia and a member of the panel for legal science of the Croatian Science Foundation. She was the Agent for Croatia at the International Court of Justice Genocide Case (Croatia v. Serbia). She was a member of the Main Commission of the SEE University in Tetovo, Macedonia, within the OSCE HCNM project.

Rita Izsák-Ndiaye
is a human rights expert from Hungary who has been working with various civil society and multilateral organizations as well as with the Government of Hungary on such issues as social inclusion, discrimination, racism, minority rights and other related subjects. She is a former UN Special Rapporteur on minority issues and currently a member of the UN Committee on the Elimination of Racial Discrimination until 2021. She is married with two children and is based in Dakar, Senegal.

Bruno De Witte
is Professor of European Union law at Maastricht University and Co-director of the Maastricht Centre for European Law. He is also a part-time Professor at the European University Institute in Florence. His research covers European Union constitutional law, as well as the legal regulation of culture, languages and minorities.

Jennifer Jackson-Preece
is Associate Professor of Nationalism and Deputy Head of the European Institute, LSE. Dr. Jackson-Preece is the author of two leading academic monographs in the area of minority rights, *National Minorities and the European Nation-States System*, and *Minority Rights: Between Diversity and Community*. She regularly acts as an expert advisor to international organisations, including on the OSCE HCNM *Ljubljana Guidelines on Integration of Diverse Societies* (2012) and the Council of Europe's *Fourth Thematic Commentary on the*

Scope of Application of the Framework Convention for the Protection of National Minorities (2016).

Joseph Marko
is Full Professor of comparative public law and political sciences at the University of Graz/Austria. He served as international judge at the Constitutional Court of Bosnia and Herzegovina from 1997 to 2002 and as member of the Advisory Committee established under the Framework Convention for the Protection of National Minorities between 1998 and 2007. Since 1998 he is director of the Institute for Minority Rights at the European Academy Bozen/South Tyrol. From June 2016 to July 2017 he served as legal advisor for the UN in the Cyprus re-unification negotiations. His research focuses on the study of nationalism, ethnic conflict, power sharing in divided societies, minority protection and immigrant integration.

Roberta Medda-Windischer
(LL.M, PhD), Senior Researcher and Group Leader for National Minorities, Migration and Cultural Diversity at the Eurac Research Institute for Minority Rights, is an international lawyer specialised in human rights and minority protection. Dr. Medda-Windischer worked as Legal Officer for various international organisations, including ECHR- CoE, UNHCR, OSCE/ODIHR, and UN OHCHR. At Eurac Research, her research focuses on the protection of minorities in international law and on new minorities stemming from migration, on which she has authored and edited monographs and multi-authored volumes, and published numerous articles and chapters in edited volumes both in Italy and abroad.

PART 1

Language, Integration of Societies and Conflict Prevention

CHAPTER 1

Introduction: Shaping Language Policies to Promote Stability

Bob Deen and William Romans

1 Introduction

For states with diverse societies, a balanced language policy should be considered an essential element in maintaining internal cohesion and promoting regional security. This introductory chapter aims to set out why this is the case by exploring the links between language, ethnicity, and conflict. We look at how European and other states have, since the end of the First World War, understood and reacted to minority-related disputes, such as those touching upon language and ethnicity. One such reaction, further outlined in the following sections, is the internationalisation of rights through treaties and the creation of multilateral political and legal instruments to help accommodate the challenges of ethnic and linguistic diversity, including, the creation of the institution of the OSCE High Commissioner on National Minorities (HCNM) a quarter of a century ago.

We shall also introduce readers to themes developed later in the book, where contributing authors will explore some of the elements which might be found in a balanced language policy. This includes the relevant binding legal standards and their enforcement, as well as the Recommendations and Guidelines issued by successive High Commissioners.[1] Contributing authors will further consider the diversity of work that states and international actors take in promoting, implementing and monitoring the linguistic rights of national minorities. Finally, the book turns towards more contemporary challenges, such as the inclusion of minority languages in the online world, as well as Europe's rapidly evolving demographics, and considers how we might better manage the inevitable process of change.

---

* The views expressed in this chapter are those of the authors, and do not necessarily represent those of the High Commissioner on National Minorities.

1 Most relevantly, the OSCE HCNM *Oslo Recommendations on the Linguistic Rights of National Minorities& Explanatory Note* (February 1998) as well as the OSCE HCNM *Ljubljana Guidelines on Integration of Diverse Societies* (November 2012).

© KONINKLIJKE BRILL NV, LEIDEN, 2018 | DOI 10.1163/9789004357754_002

2 Language, Ethnicity and Conflict

It should not come as a surprise that language policy is a contentious subject within diverse societies. Language politics are part of identity politics, and in many states across Europe, as well as the wider region covered by the Organization for Security and Co-operation in Europe ('from Vancouver to Vladivostok'), language means so much more than its primary function as a means of communication.[2] It is one of the key components of national or ethnic identity. As such, it features prominently in the ideology of ethnic nationalism, or the exclusionary creed of 'one people, one language, one State' with 'people' defined along ethno-linguistic lines.[3] Nationalist doctrine regularly emphasizes language as a core test of nationality, as an outward sign of a group's peculiar identity, and a significant means of ensuring its community.[4]

The survival of a language is often seen as essential to the survival of a people. Since languages are passed on at home by the family, they are also linked to the idea of ethnicity as kinship, as embodied in concepts such as 'mother tongue'. Threats to the use of language by a group, and its sustainability, can be perceived as existential. Such threats frequently evoke a visceral response that goes beyond regular competition for power or influence. This means that language can be and often is instrumentalised and even securitised. It is elevated beyond the regular realm of politics, declared a vital interest, and extraordinary measures are called for in order to protect it.[5]

Language securitisation is not an abstract concept or a matter of the distant past; it remains a matter for great concern across Europe today. The cancellation of the controversial *2012 Law 'on Principles of the State Language Policy'* by the Ukrainian Parliament, in the days after the ousting of President Yanukovych in March 2014, contributed to the crisis in and around Ukraine because it was perceived and presented as a threat to the country's minority Russian-speaking population. A provision on 'linguistic self-determination' is

---

2 The Conference for Security and Co-operation in Europe ('CSCE') as it was originally called, was renamed the Organization for Security and Co-operation in Europe ('OSCE') at the Budapest Summit in 1994, taking effect on 1 January 1995. As the Budapest document specifically noted, the change had "no effect on the character of its commitments nor the status of the CSCE and its institutions". For simplicity, the acronym 'OSCE' will be used throughout.

3 The historian Eric Hobsbawm has characterised such phenomena as "linguistic nationalism centered on the vernacular". *See* A.D. Smith, *Nationalism and Modernism* (London, 1998), p. 123.

4 E. Kedourie, *Nationalism* (Hutchinson, 1985), p. 66.

5 *See* B. Buzan, O. Waever and J. de Wilde, *Security: A Framework for Analysis* (London, 1998).

even included in a footnote of the Minsk agreements.[6] Language issues regularly become matters of international concern, as states raise matters related to linguistic rights both in bilateral and multilateral diplomacy. Language can also become a rallying flag around which groups can mobilize, and conflicts can erupt. Experience has shown that, fortunately, it also works the other way around. Guarantees regarding the use of language can be employed to avert or end conflict. Language concessions granted to minorities were an essential element within the Ohrid Framework Agreement that formally ended the short conflict in the country in 2001.[7] Such conflicts are often started by militant groups who use anger over perceived repressive state policies, including language policies, as their rallying call.

It would be a misconception however to conclude from this that language policies are a cause of conflict in and of themselves. Language has great symbolic power and thus is open to manipulation. As others before him, the first High Commissioner concluded early on in his mandate that national or ethnic arguments often mask interests of power, prestige or legitimacy.[8] Instead, cultural rights such as the right to use one's language are tools around which a constituency can be rallied to stake a claim of entitlement; groups are not fighting *about* culture but rather *with* culture, because it is perceived as an authentic justification of the group's distinctiveness.[9] Over time, as a conflict regarding political, economic or other resources evolves, language takes up much more importance than it had at the start of the conflict. This has been called a 'language-oriented surface syndrome' that obscures the more deeply rooted, structural causes.[10] A conflict over linguistic rights may not start about language, but it cannot be sustainably resolved without addressing both the 'surface syndrome' and the root causes.

6 'Package of Measures for the Implementation of the Minsk agreements', 12 February 2015, note 1, <peacemaker.un.org/sites/peacemaker.un.org/files/UA_150212_MinskAgreement_en.pdf>, visited on 7 January 2018.

7 'Framework Agreement, Concluded at Ohrid, Macedonia', 13 August 2001, article 6.2, available on <ec.europa.eu/neighbourhood-enlargement/sites/near/files/pdf/the_former_yugoslav_republic_of_macedonia/framework_agreement_ohrid_130801_en.pdf>, visited on 7 January 2018.

8 M. Van der Stoel, 'Looking Back, Looking Forward: Reflections on Preventing Inter-Ethnic Conflict, Address to an International Conference on Facing Ethnic Conflicts, 14 November 2000', <www.osce.org/hcnm/42345>, visited on 7 January 2018.

9 J.D. Eller, *From Culture to Ethnicity to Conflict* (Michigan, 1999), p. 48.

10 P.H. Nelde, 'Language contact means language conflict', 8 *Journal of Multilingual and Multicultural Development* (1987), p. 35.

This gets to the heart of why language considerations are often at the heart of conflict prevention. The relative status of one language compared to another is closely linked to the relative status of a group, and can thus become what Horowitz, in his seminal 1985 book *Ethnic Groups in Conflict*, calls a 'symbol of domination':

> Language is so often an issue ... not because there is something special about linguistic difference or something mystical and therefore conflict-producing about the process of communication. The reason is more mundane: in a multilingual state, there has to be a language policy to decide trivial and important issues of linguistic choice .... Such issues find their way to the symbolic agenda wherever linguistic differences coincide with ethnic differences and so can be used as a measure of group status.[11]

In other words: groups often do not only argue over the language of street signs or of administrative forms used by municipal authorities because they want to avoid difficulties in communication; they argue over those symbols to assert their position relative to other groups. Some of these issues may appear trivial to outsiders, such as the protracted dispute over the spelling of Polish names in Lithuania, or the disagreement between citizens in Montenegro over whether they speak the Serbian or Montenegrin language, or in Moldova on the name of the State language. These arguments cannot be understood without a broader understanding of their complex history. Symbolic issues such as the spelling of personal names or toponyms are often at the heart of a power struggle that, if mismanaged or polarized, can significantly undermine inter-ethnic relations and social cohesion. Therefore, as we shall see later, the High Commissioner and the Council of Europe monitoring bodies have spent a great deal of time persuading states to pay close attention to them and, where applicable, to implement their obligations.

3 The Internationalisation of Linguistic Rights

The power struggle between different minority and majority groups is not new, and legal history reflects this. At the international level, some scholars contend that the question of majority-minority relations has tended to oscillate between an individual rights focus and a quasi-collective rights focus.[12]

11 D.L. Horowitz, *Ethnic Groups in Conflict* (2nd ed., Berkeley, 2000), pp. 219–224.

12 *See for example* D. Wippman, 'The Evolution and Implementation of Minority Rights', 66 Fordham L. Review 597 (1997), p. 598.

The Peace of Westphalia in 1648 already qualified the accepted principle of *cuius regio, eius religio* (literally translated, "whose realm, his religion") with certain rights for religious minorities, and we could reach back even further in time for examples. We start to recognise core features of the *modern* system following the Paris Peace Conference of 1919 and, over the course of the last century, states have tried to find ways to regulate tensions relating to language, both internally and internationally, including through experimenting with enforcement mechanisms.

After the collapse of the German, Ottoman, Russian and Austro-Hungarian Empires following the First World War, the prevailing consensus amongst the international decision makers acceded for the main part to the nationalistic proposition that the boundaries of the nation and the state should coincide. As John Packer has summarised:

> Unfortunately, despite the massive loss of life and property that was experienced in the Great War at the beginning of the twentieth century, there was a remarkable failure to recognise the essential cause. Rather than respond directly to the problem of nationalism, the victors (themselves, of course, nationalists) simply endeavoured to contain the problem by sorting out the nationalities with the hypothesis that monolithic nations coincident with states would allow peaceful relations between the states. This logic inspired the 'principle of nationalities' which was applied in the peace treaties ending the First World War.[13]

This saw the establishment of new nation states and, particularly in Eastern and Central Europe, the framers of the new European order and their cartographers tried to give certain nationalities their own state. Nevertheless, and regardless of the merits of attempting such an exercise, in no case could this be wholly successful. No matter how many times borders are drawn or redrawn, there will always be minorities.

The Paris Peace Conference rejected attempts to include in the Covenant of the League of Nations general provisions relating to the protection of minorities. Many diplomats of western European states considered minorities an 'eastern problem'[14] and instead established a regional system of protection

13 J. Packer, 'On the Definition of Minorities', in J. Packer and K. Myntti (eds.), *The Protection of Ethnic and Linguistic Minorities in Europe* (Turku/Abo: Institute for Human Rights, 1993) p. 35.

14 *See* for example C.A. Macartney, 'Minorities: a Problem of Eastern Europe', in *Foreign Affairs* (July 1931), <www.foreignaffairs.com> visited on 12 January 2018.

of minorities in the form of the *Minorities Treaties*, concluded between the Allied and Associated Powers on the one hand and the newly established or enlarged states on the other. As Francesco Capotorti has described in his seminal study on minorities for the United Nations Sub-Commission on Prevention of Discrimination and Protection of Minorities (1979), the legal foundation of this system of protection of minorities was contained in identical clauses in the Treaties of *Versailles, Saint-Germain, Neuilly* and *Trianon*, in which the newly established or enlarged states agreed "to embody in a Treaty [...] such provisions [...] to protect [...] the interests of the inhabitants who differ from the majority of the population in race, language or religion".[15] These treaties contained stipulations including: the acquisition of nationality; protection of life and liberty; the free exercise of religion or belief ("whose practices are not inconsistent with public order and public morals"); equality before the law; a prohibition on discrimination on admission to public employment or the exercise of a profession on the basis of race, language or religion; the possibility for minorities to establish ("at their own expense") charitable, religious or social institutions and schools, and to use their own language and religion therein.

For present purposes we are interested in language policies, and this is what was agreed in relation to the above:

> [...] States which have signed the Treaties have undertaken to place no restriction in the way of the free use by any national of the country of any language, in private intercourse, in commerce, in religion, in the press or in publications of any kind, or at public meetings. Those States have also agreed to grant adequate facilities to enable their nationals whose mother tongue is not the official language to use their own language, either orally or in writing, before the courts. They have further agreed, in towns and districts where a considerable proportion of nationals of the country whose mother tongue is not the official language of the country is resident, to make provision for adequate facilities for ensuring that, in the primary schools [...], instruction shall be given to the children of such nationals through the medium of their own language, it being understood that this provision does not prevent the teaching of the official language being made obligatory in those schools.[16]

15 F. Capotorti, *Study of the Rights of Persons Belonging to Ethnic, Religious and Linguistic Minorities*, Sub-Commission on Prevention of Discrimination and Protection of Minorities, U.N. ESCOR, 30th Session, pp. 17–18, U.N. Doc. E/CN.4/Sub. 2/384/REV. 1 (1979).

16 *Ibid.*, pp. 18–19, quoting where relevant from the treaties in question.

These treaties were negotiated outside of the League of Nations, however subsequent Resolutions of the Council of the League of Nations placed them under the "guarantee" of the League of Nations "so far as they affect persons belonging to racial, linguistic or religious minorities". The Council was to determine itself how this guarantee was to be effected, and it did so by establishing a right of petition, and by establishing a Minorities Committee within the Council, who would hear the petitions following an established procedure administered by the Secretariat.[17]

Another agreement of the time which remains relevant today, and which is still cited on a regular basis in diplomatic relations, is the *Treaty of Peace with Turkey Signed at Lausanne*, which officially settled the conflict between the Ottoman Empire and its adversaries.[18] *Lausanne* contained similar guarantees for the minorities within the new Turkish State similar to those in the League Minorities treaties, including, very prominently, the linguistic rights of minorities.[19]

Despite attempts by the various League Minorities Committees to negotiate with States Parties on the implementation of these measures however, they ultimately proved ineffective, for reasons that are echoed in some of the current problems facing minority rights protection mechanisms.[20] No doubt it

17 *Ibid.*, pp. 19–23.

18 *Treaty of Peace with Turkey Signed at Lausanne* (*'Lausanne'*), July 24, 1923, <treaties.fco.gov.uk/docs/pdf/1923/ts0016-1.pdf>, visited on 12 January 2018.

19 *Lausanne*, Chapter III, Article 39 provides that "No restrictions shall be imposed on the free use by any Turkish national of any language in private intercourse, in commerce, religion, in the press, or in publications of any kind or at public meetings. Notwithstanding the existence of the official language, adequate facilities shall be given to Turkish nationals of non-Turkish speech for the oral use of their own language before the Courts". Note that *Lausanne* only accords status to "non-Moslem" minorities thus, for example, excluding the Turkish Kurdish population from protection.

20 F. Capotorti., *supra* note 12, pp. 23–24, including quotes from a fascinating account by a former Director of the Minorities Section at the League of Nations ("In the vast majority of cases, the committees, whether in a sincere desire to complete their information, or as a means of negotiating concessions, brought to the notice of the government concerned on the points on which they considered its observations unsatisfactory, and asked for supplementary information. The minorities, and the governments which encouraged and supported them in their claims ... always displayed great animosity and distrust of this method of negotiation between communities and the 'accused' governments. And their attitude was shared by not a few men and women of standing [...]" *See also*, on the fate of the League minorities protection system, M. Shaw, *International Law* (Cambridge University Press, 4th ed., 1999), p. 218.

was because ethnic conflict was fresh in everyone's mind, that guarantees on minority rights, including language rights, were framed so progressively. Leaving aside the lack of efficacy in the guarantee system of the Minorities Treaties under the League of Nations system, the content is strikingly modern, and it remains profoundly relevant today.

In the interluding period, between the collapse of the League of Nations system, and the re-emergence of a focus on national minorities in the last 30 years, there has been more of a focus on human rights and individual rights. For many states, the International Covenant on Civil and Political Rights (ICCPR), in particular article 27 on the rights of persons belonging to minorities, remains the strongest instrument. In a later chapter, Rita Izsák-Ndiaye explores these issues in depth, bringing in a perspective based upon her extensive experience as the former UN Special Rapporteur on Minority Rights.[21] Looking both within and beyond the region covered by the Council of Europe and the OSCE, she demonstrates that linguistic communities face troubling times, with a rapidly contracting space for speakers of minority languages, and conflict between different language communities. She takes a critical look at how the UN approaches similar issues, at the work of the Human Rights Council and other bodies, and surveys the difficulties facing linguistic communities beyond Europe, including communities in Asia and Africa. She approaches the issue of linguistic minorities from a human rights perspective, considering issues of dignity, individual liberty, equality and non-discrimination and identity, before turning to specific linguistic rights. With one eye on the achievements of the OSCE system in this regard, Izsák-Ndiaye concludes with constructive suggestions on how the UN could better reform its institutional machinery to better fulfil its conflict prevention role, by strengthening its mechanisms dealing with minority rights protection.

Conflict prevention is a core aim of the OSCE, which operates as a regional arrangement under Chapter VIII of the Charter of the United Nations. OSCE commitments are meant not only to uphold values such as human rights, but to function as pillars of European security and stability, which has often been threatened by inter-ethnic conflict. It is therefore no coincidence that it is exactly within the OSCE that a specific mechanism was established to deal with national minorities from a conflict prevention perspective. We will therefore now turn to the OSCE and focus on how it deals with the issue of linguistic rights of national minorities.

---

21 R. Izsák-Ndiaye, *Protection of Linguistic Rights of Linguistic Minorities in the U.N. Context*, Chapter 12.

4 The High Commissioner and the Oslo Recommendations

The revival of interest in national minorities within the OSCE started in the early 1990s, for reasons not dissimilar to the interwar period: the turmoil following the collapse of large multi-ethnic states.[22] The rights of national minorities were already addressed at the political level in the 1990 Copenhagen Document.[23] Two years later, in the midst of violent conflicts that tore apart the former Yugoslavia and the former Soviet Union, OSCE participating States resolved to address the re-emergence of inter-ethnic conflict as part of the 'Challenges of Change'. They established the 'High Commissioner on National Minorities' to help them with this task.[24] The purpose of the HCNM is to reduce the risk of conflict, and its founding marked a rare long-term investment by the international community in a field where results are notoriously hard to demonstrate. The mandate-holder is tasked to provide 'early warning' and to take 'early action' to prevent tensions over national minority issues from escalating into conflict. Within defined parameters, when and how the High Commissioner does this is essentially left to his or her own judgement.

Seen against the current backdrop of renewed tensions within and between OSCE participating States, and the associated difficulties in obtaining consensus, the Institution's establishment now looks like one of the high-water marks of OSCE co-operation. Participating States entrusted the High Commissioner with both a wide margin of discretion and the ability to work in confidence. Accountability is nevertheless ensured by requiring the High Commissioner to consult with, and report directly to, the OSCE Chairman-in-Office, a position normally held by the Minister of Foreign Affairs of the Chairmanship of the OSCE.[25]

As an autonomous instrument of preventative diplomacy dealing with national minorities, the High Commissioner can engage in domestic matters of policy often deemed sensitive by sovereign states. Right from the start of the High Commissioner's work, the language policies of states, and the linguistic rights of persons belonging to national minorities came to the fore.

The first High Commissioner, Max van der Stoel, a former Dutch Foreign Minister, set the mould. He travelled frequently and extensively throughout

22 On terminology, *supra*, note 3.

23 Document of the Copenhagen Meeting of the Conference on the Human Dimension of the CSCE (1990), Chapter IV.

24 CSCE Helsinki Document 1992 'The Challenges of Change'; Decisions of the OSCE participating States are made by consensus. The Institution is often referred to as the 'HCNM'.

25 *Ibid.*, 'The Challenges of Change', paras 17–22.

the OSCE region, discreetly trying to contain tensions over identity issues that flared up in one country after another. While doing so he began to note recurring challenges that caused disputes between minorities and majorities in many OSCE participating States, and he often consulted experts for ideas on how he could assist in developing effective policies to accommodate divergent interests. The synthesis of knowledge which he developed and amassed, resulting from a partnership forged between the targeted diplomacy of the High Commissioner and his staff, and general expertise drawn from other practitioners and academic experts, was subsequently developed into thematic recommendations, and published.[26]

The first set of recommendations, known as 'The Hague Recommendations', dealt with educational rights. The second set of recommendations, on the linguistic rights of national minorities, became known as the 'Oslo Recommendations', after the city where they were published in 1998.[27] It is no coincidence that education and language were selected as the most pressing themes from a conflict prevention perspective, as they both touch upon issues crucial to the maintenance of ethno-linguistic identity and therefore frequently feature prominently in majority-minority relations as outlined above. Over the years subsequent High Commissioners have continued to build knowledge and expertise on minority issues and to synthesize this experience into further thematic recommendations, and a further six sets followed. The latest, the Graz Recommendations on Access to Justice and National Minorities, was launched by the current High Commissioner, Ambassador Lamberto Zannier, in November 2017.[28]

At the request of several participating States, Van der Stoel determined in 1996 to conduct a formal survey on the implementation of linguistic rights across the OSCE.[29] The Oslo Recommendations followed, and have, over the

26 In the early days of the HCNM, some of the thematic work was outsourced to an affiliated NGO, the 'Foundation on Inter-Ethnic Relations', which operated under the general supervision of, and out of the same premises, as the High Commissioner.

27 OSCE HCNM, *The Oslo Recommendations regarding the Linguistic Rights of National Minorities and Explanatory Note*, Oslo, 1 February 1998.

28 OSCE HCNM, The *Graz Recommendations on Access to Justice and National Minorities*, November 2017.

29 The High Commissioner wrote to the Foreign Ministers of all participating States (except the Holy See) requesting responses to a set of questions. Responses were received from the vast majority, with only two contacted participating States, Belgium and Albania, not responding. The final responses were received towards the end of 1997, informing the High Commissioners actions, however the report on practice was published

last two decades, set the stage for active HCNM engagement on language policy. The HCNM has assisted participating States to strike a balance between the legitimate aim of promoting the State or official languages, as well as respecting the rights of persons belonging to national minorities to maintain and develop their own identity, culture and language. Increasingly, the HCNM has contextualized this even-handed approach towards linguistic rights within a broader perspective of 'integration with respect for diversity', as outlined in the *Ljubljana Guidelines on the Integration of Diverse Societies* of 2012.[30] We maintain that, though difficult to quantify, the High Commissioner's methodical, balanced and long-term engagement that addresses both the symbolic and the structural causes of identity-based conflict has contributed to peace and stability within the OSCE.

5 From Paris to the Present: HCNM Advice on Language Issues

Recalling the guarantees given to certain minorities covered by the League Minorities Treaties following the Paris Conference, as described above, we can see that the guarantees of the interwar period remain relevant to accommodate the challenges of linguistic diversity. The use of language in commerce, in religion, in the press and publications, within the justice system, in public, in relation to the public administration and, crucially, within the education system, are all issues which the HCNM is regularly confronted with in practice, and upon which it provides advice and assistance to participating States.

Authors contributing to the Part 1 of this book, all current or former staff members of the HCNM, will elaborate numerous examples of solutions devised or supported by the High Commissioner to real problems facing participating States. A central feature of these solutions is their pragmatic and balanced approach.

For example, while the Minorities Treaties stipulated that instruction could be given to children in their own language, it was also clearly understood that this provision should not prevent the teaching of the official language being made obligatory in those schools. This dual approach was enshrined in the 1990 Copenhagen Document, which explicitly mentioned the "need to learn the official language or languages of the state". It was later taken up in the Oslo

subsequent to the Oslo Recommendations: *Report on the Linguistic Rights of Persons Belonging to National Minorities in the OSCE Area*, OSCE HCNM, March 1999, <www.osce.org/hcnm/42060> visited on 9 January 2018.

30 OSCE HCNM, *The Ljubljana Guidelines on Integration of Diverse Societies* (November 2012).

Recommendations, which argue that "integration is unlikely to take place without a sound knowledge of the official language(s) of the State".[31] In the following chapter, Laurenţiu Hadîrcă provides examples of how the HCNM has encouraged OSCE participating States to enhance their efforts at integration of diverse societies, both by providing minorities with the opportunities they need in their mother tongue, but also by supporting them in acquiring a reasonable command of the state language. The latter is recognized as not only a legitimate aim, but also as a measure to strengthen societal cohesion and empower minority representatives to take effective part in public affairs.[32]

As a result of this dual approach towards language acquisition, multilingual education is a keystone issue for the HCNM, and one in which much time and effort has been invested. Atanasia Stoianova and Michael Angermann will, in a subsequent chapter, work through a specific example of HCNM engagement, in the Central Asian states of Kazakhstan and Kyrgyzstan. Here, we can find a consistency in approach with HCNM advice given in other thematic areas. On the one hand, HCNM promotes the development of state language capacities, aiming at the better integration of society. On the other, it is recognised as important to preserve the mother tongue amongst national minority communities in order to preserve their identity. It is the balance between these two approaches that can vary from country to country, and indeed we find the same goal but different models in both Kazakhstan and Kyrgyzstan. Stoianova and Angermann outline in detail how HCNM project work has supported and encouraged policies of multi-lingual education in both countries, and that now, after 15 years of HCNM and international engagement, many parents and pupils no longer face the choice of one monolingual system or another.[33]

In the interwar treaties prominence was given to the use of language in commerce. The *Oslo Recommendations* noted that all persons, including persons belonging to national minorities, have the right to operate private enterprises in the language or languages of their choice.[34] In a later chapter, Jennifer Croft will look specifically at the area of the linguistic rights of national minorities in economic life. The HCNM has advised governments not to restrict the

31 OSCE HCNM, *The Oslo Recommendations regarding the Linguistic Rights of National Minorities & Explanatory Note* (February 1998), explanatory note, pp. 12–13.

32 *See* L. Hadîrcă, *The HCNM Approach to the Promotion of the State/Official Language in various OSCE Participating States*, Chapter 2.

33 *See* A. Stoianova and M. Angermann, *Education as a Key Tool for Minority Language Vitality and Social Integration of Diverse Societies: the cases of Kazakhstan and Kyrgyzstan*, Chapter 7.

34 *Oslo Recommendations*, *supra* note 31, recommendation 12.

choice of language in the operation of private enterprises, except in very limited circumstances. Where public and private spheres overlap, there can be a legitimate public interest within the grounds established by international law for limited restrictions. As Croft will show, HCNM has found cases where legislative provisions were insufficiently clear in drawing the line between public and private, and authorities were urged to ensure that language legislation makes a clear distinction between public and private entities. At the end of the day it is mutually beneficial for states, individuals and private enterprises when communities are active and engaged in the economic life of the state, aided by progressive language policies.[35]

Turning to the use by any national of any language in the press, or in publications, or at any kind of public meeting, this is a theme which is considerably elaborated upon by the High Commissioner in the Oslo Recommendations, as well as the subsequent Guidelines on the Use of Minority Languages in the Broadcast Media (2003). Sarah Stephan and Dmitry Nurumov will look at some of the examples in which HCNM has provided recommendations on the use of minority languages in the broadcast media.[36] They thoroughly analyse the various provisions of the Recommendations and Guidelines of the HCNM which are relevant to the issue of language use and media, and provide indicators of how the HCNM has provided country-specific recommendations based on these principles.

As noted above regarding the wars concluded by the Treaty of Westphalia, challenges to accommodate religious diversity far predate those regarding linguistic diversity. But sometimes disputes over the two markers of identity overlap. In a subsequent chapter, Asa Solway and Alessandro Rotta examine the legal and policy frameworks regulating the possibility to live one's religious life in one's own language. Somewhat reassuringly, the authors find few examples of contravention with Oslo Recommendation 4 on freedom of linguistic choice for practicing one's religion: the situation does appear to have improved during the last 100 years, and generally the principle of freedom of religion and the high levels of autonomy of religious organizations are respected. Naturally, in some cases there remain problems of both a religious and linguistic character, but there is not necessarily a connection. The authors also examine how

35 *See* J. Croft, *Mind Your Own Business: The Oslo Recommendations and the Linguistic Rights of National Minorities in Economic Life*, Chapter 4.

36 *See* S. Stephan and D. Nurumov, *HCNM Recommendations on the Use of Minority Languages in the Broadcast Media as a Baseline for Context-specific Advice to Participating States*, Chapter 6.

policy or legal frameworks might better effectively engage with the roles and rights of national minorities in this sensitive area.[37]

It is often in the interaction between individuals and official structures that attempts at linguistic dominance are asserted most visibly and where linguistic tensions come to the fore. Iryna Ulasiuk and Laurenţiu Hadîrcă together examine how the successive High Commissioners sought to use the Oslo Recommendations in their work and advised governments on the use of languages in relations with the public administration, as well as on the supervision and enforcement of linguistic requirements. They make the point that on one hand, there is no right of persons belonging to national minorities never to be expected to use the state language, and on the other, the state is expected to balance the promotion of the state language with the maintenance, promotion and protection of minority languages, including through allowing space for the use of minority languages in the public sphere. They attempt to trace a thread through the advice of the HCNM to participating States on the issue of thresholds for use of language, urging flexibility in application where thresholds are not met, and unconditionality in application where they are. Finally, there should also be guarantees for speakers of the state language, in areas where there are significant numbers of minority language speakers.[38] Then, there is the question of how linguistic requirements should be enforced. Most often this concerns the non-use of the state language, and the means which the state would use to enforce such a policy. Generally speaking, HCNM advises against the adoption of any kind of sanctions such as fines or other punitive measures, not only because they might be illegal *per se*, but rather because they are generally less effective than positive measures and may even result in increased tensions, which the HCNM through its mandate seeks to reduce.[39]

6 Developing, Promoting, and Monitoring the Implementation of Rights

Authors contributing to the Part 2 of this book, look further at language rights and evolving standards. Here we draw upon on the partnerships which exist

37 *See* A. Solway and A. Rotta, *The Intersection of Language and Religion in the Context of National Minorities*, Chapter 5.

38 I. Ulasiuk and L. Hadirca, *To Speak or not to Speak: Minority Languages and the Public Administration*, Chapter 3.

39 *Ibid.*

between the HCNM and its partner organisations, including the Council of Europe bodies dealing with national minorities and languages, the United Nations Special Rapporteur on Minority Issues, as well as some of the most prominent academic experts working closely with the HCNM in the field of language rights.

Fernand de Varennes and Elżbieta Kuzborska trace the post-Second World War development, through decades of dormancy, a concentration on individual rights (rights of 'persons belonging to national minorities'), and finally, a revival in the OSCE Copenhagen Document of 1990 and the adoption of standard setting multi-lateral treaties. They show how the Oslo Recommendations were issued in response to the need for more specific guidance and, twenty years after their launch, remain of relevance today.[40]

The OSCE institutions, including the HCNM, maintain working contact with the Council of Europe on a regular basis at all levels, and there are multiple synergies. The Council of Europe, as the leading human rights organisation within its geographical area, is the key organisation when it comes to legal standard setting, and monitoring for implementation compliance, in relation to the rights of persons belonging to national minorities.

The Framework Convention for the Protection of National Minorities (FCNM) is regarded as the most important instrument in the Council of Europe area specifically covering the rights of persons belonging to national minorities. There is strong geographic coverage; the vast majority of Member States of the Council of Europe are State Parties.[41] The 'Advisory Committee' is the independent expert committee responsible for evaluating the implementation of the Framework Convention in State Parties and advising the Council of Europe's Committee of Ministers. It carries out its monitoring function through a procedure involving the examination of State Reports, other sources of information, as well as conducting interviews during in-country visits.[42]

40 *See* F. de Varennes and E. Kuzborska, *Continued Relevance of an 'Oslo' Language Policy in a Changing World*, Chapter 8.

41 All Council of Europe Member States are States Parties, excepting Belgium, Greece, Iceland and Luxembourg (which have signed but not ratified the Convention) and Andorra, France, Monaco and Turkey (which have neither signed nor ratified the Convention). An up-to-date list is maintained on the website of the Council of Europe; see *State parties to the Framework Convention for the Protection of National Minorities*, <www.coe.int/en/web/minorities/etats-partie>, visited on 11 January 2018.

42 *See* website of the Advisory Committee on the Framework Convention for the Protection of National Minorities, <www.coe.int/en/web/minorities/advisory-committee>, visited on 11 January 2018.

On a practical level, there is co-operation between the Advisory Committee and the HCNM, with frequent exchanges between the two bodies.

Petra Roter and Brigitta Busch discuss the contribution of the Advisory Committee, as a body of 18 independent experts tasked to advise on how best to implement the FCNM, in the field of minority language rights, during its four monitoring cycles.[43] They further analyse the contemporary processes of 'exclusive nation-building', discussing how modern nationalism influences views towards languages and language policies, and describe the significance of a specific concept of nations, and national minorities, in policy-making on language use. They discuss language ideologies in practice, as observed by the Advisory Committee. Finally, Roter and Busch offer an alternative conceptual framework, within which the Advisory Committee has developed its approach to advising states on language rights. They conclude by highlighting the fundamental discrepancy between the prevailing policies of modern nationalism and primordial concepts of identity communities on the one hand, and on the other hand, the post-modern (linguistic) realities in contemporary societies.[44]

Aside from its specific monitoring function, and the issuance of country reports and recommendations, the Advisory Committee has also taken on an interpretative role, developing the expectations of its implementation. This work has been regarded as a form of standard setting. Francesco Palermo identifies a clear thread of development that departs from the Oslo Recommendations and is significantly developed in the Advisory Committee's Thematic Commentary on The Language Rights of Persons Belonging to National Minorities, and the HCNM Ljubljana Guidelines on Integration of Diverse Societies. He explains the evolution of the approach to minority rights and reflects on the future challenges for minority rights, especially language rights, in the contemporary context, where the political will for implementation could often considered to be lacking.[45]

The European Union is also continuously relevant as a partner for the HCNM, and has of course developed its own internal legal order, which many participating States of the OSCE are party to, and several others have applied to join. This legal order however rarely deals specifically with national minorities, with the notable exception of the Copenhagen Criteria for applicant countries.

43 *See* P. Roter and B. Busch, *Language Rights in the Work of the Advisory Committee*, Chapter 10.

44 *Ibid.*

45 See F. Palermo, *'The Borders of my Language Mean the Borders of my World': Language Rights and their Evolving Significance for Minority Rights and Integration of Societies*, Chapter 9.

Bruno de Witte demonstrates how within the European Union legal order, a set of specific language rights have been developed over the years, for the benefit of the citizens of the European Union. They come in addition to the language rights guaranteed in national law or by other European and international instruments however, these rights are of limited interest for the speakers of minority languages. The European Union does direct some of its resources specifically towards national minorities, but these activities do not amount to the formulation of genuine language rights.[46]

Jennifer Jackson-Preece 'takes Oslo online', where she shows the critical importance in many spheres of life for languages to have an online presence, and how the extension of linguistic rights into this sphere is essential both for the inclusion of people within society, and the long-term survival of their language.[47]

Touching upon a topic of great interest to many OSCE participating States, Joseph Marko and Roberta Medda-Windischer discuss both language rights and duties for 'new minorities' originating from recent migration flows, analysing the alleged dichotomy between 'old' and 'new' minorities. This distinction is an important one in practical terms for those working in this field, because most states view 'new minorities' as falling outside of the protection of some of the most important conventions which protect national minorities. Others, however, been more flexible and have taken a more progressive approach. The authors explore the normative framework pertaining to language rights and duties for new minorities and identify the areas where language policies have a particular relevance for new minorities, including education, the labour market and the law enforcement system.[48]

7 From Zero-sum Disputes to Pragmatic Solutions

As we have seen above, various attempts have been made to create an international legal framework for linguistic rights, but to a large extent these matters are left to the discretion of sovereign states and linguistic disputes are fought out in domestic politics. Virtually all OSCE participating States legislate the use of languages in one way or another. And here the nationalist ideal of a

46 See B. de Witte, *Language Rights and the Work of the European Union*, Chapter 13.

47 *See* J. Jackson-Preece, *'Taking Oslo Online': Minority Language Policy & the Internet*, Chapter 14.

48 *See* J. Marko and R. Medda-Windischer, *Language Rights and Duties for New Minorities: Integration through Diversity Governance*, Chapter 15.

mono-ethnic and monolingual nation-state clashes with the reality that virtually all states have ethnic and linguistic diversity within their borders; the very conundrum that the HCNM was designed to deal with.

Often the majority insists on the use of its language not only out of the legitimate need to build an integrated society in which all members can communicate with one another. A group in power can also do so to establish its pre-eminence over other linguistic groups, as a retribution for past historical grievances, or as reversal of previous policies of forced linguistic assimilation. These are profoundly political choices with significant legal and practical impact.

Sometimes more mundane considerations also play a role, for example to give members of the majority an advantage in the competition for public sector positions. And persons belonging to national minorities often insist on their right to use their mother tongue for exactly the same reasons: to assert their own place within society, to shield their distinct identity against what they perceive as a majority bent on assimilating them, or even to protect their share of representation within public institutions.

In the experience of the HCNM, both the political and the practical problems can be solved, even though the former are far more protracted than the latter. Since identity politics thrive on disputes over symbols as measures of relative group worth, these disputes are essentially perceived as zero-sum, with a 'victory' for one side seen as a 'defeat' for the other. This is ironic, since languages are not nearly as zero-sum as other potential markers of ethnic identity such as religion or shared historical memories; people can learn multiple languages, including those of other ethnic groups, without giving up their own. Identities and linguistic preferences are multi-layered and can change over time, requiring flexible policies that can accommodate these complexities. Communication barriers can be overcome through implementing inclusive and diversified language policies or, in some cases, pragmatic measures such as the involvement of interpreters.

In situations where the HCNM is actively engaged, politics have often trumped pragmatism, and the task is to try and bring the majority and the minorities back onto the middle ground. As well as the obvious task of securing certain guarantees for the minorities, this sometimes involves both lowering unrealistic demands made by minority representatives, and securing commitments on their engagement with the state.

Street signs or identity documents can contain multiple languages and modern means of digital communication can easily handle several scripts. Several countries in the OSCE area have populations that are functionally bilingual or even trilingual. In many countries where multiple official languages coexist, language disputes do emerge regularly, but they are usually resolved administratively and do not threaten political stability. In a later chapter, Vesna Crnić-Grotić surveys the practice of Advisory Committee on the Framework Convention and the Committee of Experts on the European Charter for Regional or Minority Languages in relation to their treatment of the practical implementation of the right to display place names in regional or minority languages, paying attention to the sensitivities of this issue in several Member States of the Council of Europe.[49]

8 Conclusion

In conflict prevention terms, there is often a deeper issue underlying a technical dispute about use of language. But the language issue must be solved to move forward. If the majority group unilaterally imposes its will on the other, for example by pushing through assertive policies to strengthen the state language at the expense of minority languages, then a minority group will feel excluded and threatened. This will generate a reaction, which if allowed to fester, may hold the potential for violence. It may also draw in other states, who might seek to protect what they see as the language of their ethnic 'kin' abroad. We have seen such disputes raise inter-state tensions, and we have seen such tensions morph into violence and conflict.

On the other hand, if a minority obtains linguistic privileges which are too far-reaching, there may be little or no incentive or interest to learn the state language, thus no way to communicate with the majority, and this can lead to the emergence of segregated, parallel societies that significantly undermine social cohesion and longer-term stability. This can unfortunately be observed today in several OSCE participating States. It only serves to generate detachment on the part of the minority, and resentment on the part of the majority, serving to further increase the social distance between groups.

This is why successive High Commissioners have argued that finding an appropriate balance, a sustainable compromise through which all sides feel valued and included, is crucial. A balanced language policy that administratively regulates and depoliticizes linguistic disputes can create the conditions and the confidence to resolve the other, underlying causes of tensions, including through an integration policy that fosters social cohesion within a

49 V. Crnić-Grotić, *The Right to Display Place Names in Regional or Minority Languages within the Council of Europe Legal Framework*, Chapter 11.

multi-ethnic society. Such a policy itself needs to be balanced between the acceptance of difference and efforts to foster a common sense of belonging.

Language policy, in all its aspects, as illustrated in the following chapters of this book, is a critical part of a successful integration strategy. This is why the Oslo Recommendations, twenty years after they were published, should be read in conjunction with later thematic work issued by the HCNM, most notably the *Ljubljana Guidelines on the Integration of Diverse Societies*. The challenges of accommodating diversity remain immense, and no solution is permanent as societies remain constantly in flux. But in the experience of the HCNM, and in the experience of the war-torn European continent in the last century, it is far preferable to pursue balanced policies that acknowledge, accommodate and value diversity than to try and impose one-sided solutions that sow the seeds for further conflict.

CHAPTER 2

The HCNM Approach to the Promotion of the State/Official Language in Various OSCE Participating States

Laurenţiu Hadîrcă

1 Introduction

The OSCE High Commissioner on National Minorities (OSCE HCNM) was set up in 1992 as a conflict-prevention institution mandated to act as "an instrument of conflict prevention at the earliest possible stage".[1] In essence, it is an office tasked to provide early warning and take appropriate early action to prevent ethnic tensions from developing into conflict. As the decades-long experience of the HCNM has repeatedly shown, the root causes of such ethnic tensions can be very diverse, encompassing – or rather exploiting – factors which bear on religion, ethnicity, language, history, culture and other identity proxies, often in contexts involving rising nationalism, irredentism, revisionism or aggressive kin-state policies. Of the various national identity attributes, language is commonly recognized as the cornerstone of national identity, often outranking other identity factors such as religion, native customs or birthplace.[2] Recognizing its critical importance and its crucial influence on inter-ethnic relations, the HCNM has over the years paid particular attention to issues and tensions involving national minorities that have revolved around the use of language(s).

This article analyzes how HCNM's unique mandate, as a political institution tasked to prevent inter-ethnic conflict chiefly through 'quiet diplomacy', has shaped its approach to matters pertaining to linguistic rights, and in particular its activities related to the promotion of the state/official language.[3]

* The views expressed in this article are those of the author alone and do not necessarily represent the official policy of the OSCE High Commissioner on National Minorities.

1 *See* Part II of the CSCE Helsinki Document 1992, available at <http://www.osce.org/mc/39530?download=true>.

2 For a recent comparative research on this topic, see the Pew Research Center's study on *Global Attitudes and Trends*, of 1 February 2017, titled 'What It Takes to Truly Be 'One of Us'', available at <http://www.pewglobal.org/2017/02/01/language-the-cornerstone-of-national-identity/>.

3 In this article, the terms 'state language' and 'official language' are used synonymously and inter-changeably, and refer to the national language or the language spoken by the majority

© KONINKLIJKE BRILL NV, LEIDEN, 2018 | DOI 10.1163/9789004357754_003

The overview contained herein is based upon an analysis of relevant HCNM thematic work, country-specific advice, official statements made by successive High Commissioners before the OSCE Permanent Council and other fora, as well as other projects and activities implemented by the HCNM in the course of the two-and-a-half decades of the institution's existence.

Before embarking upon this analysis, it bears recalling that the HCNM, in keeping with the rigors of its mandate, is a political institution established to help prevent conflicts, and not a human rights body as such (as is the OSCE ODIHR,[4] for instance), or an international 'minority ombudsman' of sorts. This is a crucial distinction, yet one which is often overlooked or forgotten – so much so that successive High Commissioners have frequently had to remind various interlocutors that they are High Commissioners 'on', and not necessarily 'for', national minorities.[5] As an institution established within OSCE's political-military dimension, the HCNM only becomes engaged in those minority-related issues that have security implications and a conflict potential. Also significantly, the HCNM is not mandated to receive and respond to individual claims alleging violations of human and minority rights.

This being said, the HCNM has recognized early on that the observance of human rights, including minority rights, is a necessary prerequisite for enduring social cohesion and lasting peace, both within and between OSCE participating States. This understanding reflects key OSCE commitments and principles, such as the ones enshrined in the 1990 OSCE Copenhagen Document, which recognized that the "respect for the rights of persons belonging to national minorities as part of universally recognized human rights is an essential factor for peace, justice, stability and democracy in the participating States",[6] and in the 1992 Helsinki Summit Declaration, which similarly reaffirmed that "[t]he protection and promotion of the human rights and fundamental freedoms

---

of the population, as in most domestic jurisdictions within the OSCE (and unlike, for instance, the case of the Kyrgyz Republic, which operates the dichotomy of recognizing a 'state language' (Kyrgyz) distinct from an 'official language' (Russian); see Article 10 of the Constitution of the Kyrgyz Republic).

4 The OSCE Office for Democratic Institutions and Human Rights is mandated to assist OSCE participating States to ensure full respect for human rights and fundamental freedoms; to abide by the rule of law; to promote principles of democracy; to build, strengthen and protect democratic institutions; and to promote tolerance throughout their societies. For more information on ODIHR's mandate, *see* <http://www.osce.org/odihr/109088>.

5 Here and elsewhere in the text of this article, the term 'minority' is used as a shorthand for "persons belonging to national minorities".

6 *See* paragraph 30 of the 1990 OSCE Copenhagen Document, available at <http://www.osce.org/odihr/elections/14304?download=true>.

and the strengthening of democratic institutions continue to be a vital basis for our comprehensive security". These OSCE commitments have enabled the HCNM to address, from its specific conflict-prevention perspective, particular human- and minority-rights issues that were threatening peace and security within and between states.

This HCNM's particular approach to human and minority rights is also evident in the institution's advice and assistance on matters pertaining to the protection and promotion of linguistic rights in various OSCE participating States. In this context, it must be acknowledged that the High Commissioners, whilst always emphasizing the need to reach an appropriate balance between the linguistic rights of the majority and those of the minority, have usually had to take the side of the latter, seeking to protect the right to use minority languages as they were coming under undue pressure. HCNM's work in this regard, i.e. in support of the right to use minority languages, is well documented, both in past works,[7] as well as in the subsequent pages of this book. What is less known however is that on occasion, the HCNM has also had to highlight, and defend, the need to promote the use of the state language – in some countries and in particular contexts – as a tool to reinforce social cohesion, enhance participation in social and public life, and ultimately as a prerequisite for the successful integration of diverse societies. Such efforts are premised, first and foremost, on "the need to learn the official language or languages of the State concerned", as recognized in the 1990 OSCE Copenhagen Document.[8] This article focuses precisely on this lesser known aspect of HCNM's activities. The analysis below reviews the relevant advice which the HCNM has put forward in this respect – throughout the years and across the OSCE space – in a variety of thematic recommendations, country-specific advice and other relevant engagements, and outlines the key tenets of HCNM's position on the promotion of the state language.

2 Relevant Thematic Recommendations

In discharging its conflict-prevention mandate, besides responding to immediate crises and emergencies, the HCNM has also sought to adopt a longer-term

7 *See*, for instance, J. Packer, 'The Protection of Minority Language Rights through the Work of OSCE Institutions', in S. Trifunovska (ed.) *Minority Rights in Europe – European Minorities and Languages* (Asser Press, The Hague, 2001), and W. Kemp, *Quiet Diplomacy in Action: The OSCE High Commissioner on National Minorities* (Martinus Nijhoff, 2001).

8 *See* paragraph 34 of the OSCE Copenhagen Document, available at <http://www.osce.org/odihr/elections/14304?download=true>.

perspective to conflict prevention, with a view to addressing the root causes of inter-ethnic conflict. To this aim, the institution has over the years drafted – jointly with internationally recognized experts – a series of so-called 'thematic recommendations', or general policy guidelines, on particular recurrent themes which the High Commissioners have identified as being relevant in more than one country or region. The thematic issues addressed in these guidelines have been very broad, encompassing the education rights of national minorities;[9] the linguistic rights of minorities;[10] the participation of minorities in public life;[11] media broadcasting in minority languages;[12] policing practices in multi-ethnic societies;[13] national minorities in inter-State relations;[14] the integration of diverse societies;[15] and, most recently, access to justice and national minorities.[16] On all these topics, the HNCM has sought to offer states strategic advice and practical solutions to various specific inter-ethnic problems.

Given the central role which language plays in the preservation and expression of one's identity, especially (though not exclusively) in its communicative and social dimension, but also in the very functioning of a state, it was inevitable that matters related to the use of language(s) would feature prominently in many of HCNM's thematic recommendations. This has indeed been the case, starting already from the very first recommendations. The HCNM has articulated its general rationale for addressing matters relating to the use of languages in the following manner:

> On the one hand, language is a personal matter closely connected with identity. On the other hand, language is an essential tool of social organisation which in many situations becomes a matter of public interest.

9 See *The Hague Recommendations Regarding the Education Rights of National Minorities*, available online at <http://www.osce.org/hcnm/32180>.

10 See the *Oslo Recommendations Regarding the Linguistic Rights of National Minorities*, available online at <http://www.osce.org/hcnm/67531>.

11 See the *Lund Recommendations on the Effective Participation of National Minorities in Public Life*, available online at <http://www.osce.org/hcnm/32240>.

12 See the *Guidelines on the Use of Minority Languages in the Broadcast Media*, available online at <http://www.osce.org/hcnm/32310>.

13 See the *Recommendations on Policing in Multi-Ethnic Societies*, available online at <http://www.osce.org/hcnm/32227>.

14 See the *Bolzano/Bozen Recommendations on National Minorities in Inter-State relations*, available online at <http://www.osce.org/hcnm/33633>.

15 See the *Ljubljana Guidelines on Integration of Diverse Societies*, available online at <http://www.osce.org/hcnm/96883>.

16 See the *Graz Recommendations on Access to Justice and National Minorities*, available online at <http://www.osce.org/hcnm/graz-recommendations>.

> Certainly, the use of language bears on numerous aspects of a State's functioning. In a democratic State committed to human rights, the accommodation of existing diversity thus becomes an important matter of policy and law. Failure to achieve the appropriate balance may be the source of inter-ethnic tensions.[17]

The promotion of the state language was addressed already in the first thematic set of recommendations issued by the HCNM, namely the 1996 *Hague Recommendations Regarding the Education Rights of National Minorities*. These Recommendations promote balanced and inclusive education systems for multi-lingual societies, with various combinations of tuition in the state and official language(s) and adequate opportunities for pupils to learn their minority language or receive instruction in that language. The *Recommendations* also provide, among others, that "[...] persons belonging to national minorities have a responsibility to integrate into the wider national society through the acquisition of a proper knowledge of the State language".[18] To ensure an efficient acquisition of the state language by minority representatives, the *Hague Recommendations* advise the *gradual* introduction of teaching of/in state language at successive stages of schooling, namely:

- In primary school: in parallel to teaching primarily in the minority language, "[t]he official State language should also be taught as a subject on a regular basis preferably by bilingual teachers who have a good understanding of the children's cultural and linguistic background. Towards the end of this period, a few practical or non-theoretical subjects should be taught through the medium of the State language.[19]
- In secondary school: while a substantial part of the curriculum should still be taught in minority language, "[t]he State language should also be taught as a subject on a regular basis, preferably by bilingual teachers who have a good understanding of the children's cultural and linguistic background. Throughout this period, the number of subjects taught in the State language, should gradually be increased. Research findings suggest that the more gradual the increase, the better for the child".[20]

17 *See* the *Oslo Recommendations Regarding the Linguistic Rights of National Minorities*, available online at <http://www.osce.org/hcnm/67531>, Introduction Section, p. 2.

18 *The Hague Recommendations Regarding the Education Rights of National Minorities*, para.1, p. 5.

19 *Ibid.*, para. 12, pp. 6–7.

20 *Ibid.*, para. 13, p. 7.

– In vocational schools: "The curriculum of vocational schools providing training in the mother -tongue should be devised in a way which ensures that, upon completion of these programmes, students are able to practice their occupation both in the minority and the State language".[21]

The *Hague Recommendations* thus recognize the legitimacy of the promotion of state language acquisition by all members of society, including national minorities, and they even ascertain a sort of correlative duty on the part of minority representatives in this respect. The Recommendations emphasize that "the right to maintain the collective identity through the minority language must be balanced by the responsibility to integrate and participate in the wider national society. Such integration requires the acquisition of a sound knowledge of both that society and the State language(s)".[22] In this respect, the *Hague Recommendations* echo the 1990 OSCE Copenhagen Document, which explicitly recognized "the need to learn the official language or languages of the State".[23]

The 1998 *Oslo Recommendations Regarding the Linguistic Rights of National Minorities*, which are the institution's main recommendations addressing linguistic rights, promote a similar balance between the right of persons belonging to national minorities to maintain and develop their own [identity, culture and] language and the necessity of ensuring that they are able to integrate into the wider society as full and equal members, including through learning the official language of the state. At the same time, the *Oslo Recommendations* stress that in particular situations, such as those pertaining to economic life, the obligation to use (also) the state language may only be imposed in very specific situations, when a strict necessity test is met:

> All persons, including persons belonging to national minorities, have the right to operate private enterprises in the language or languages of their choice. The State may require the additional use of the official language or languages of the State only where a legitimate public interest can be demonstrated, such as interests relating to the protection of workers or consumers, or in dealings between the enterprise and governmental authorities.[24]

21 *Ibid.*, para. 16, p. 7.

22 *Ibid*, Explanatory Note, p. 10.

23 *See* para. 34 of the OSCE Copenhagen Document, available at <http://www.osce.org/odihr/elections/14304?download=true>.

24 *See* the *Oslo Recommendations*, para. 12, p. 7.

In similar fashion, the *Oslo Recommendations* prescribe that when it comes to administrative and public services, "In regions and localities where persons belonging to a national minority are present in significant numbers and where the desire for it has been expressed, persons belonging to this national minority shall have the right to acquire civil documents and certificates both in the official language or languages of the State and in the language of the national minority in question from regional and/or local public institutions".[25] The Recommendations likewise provide that in the religious sphere, while all denominations may use whichever language they prefer, the state may legitimately require that the legal civil acts which religious communities are entitled to produce, be also recorded in the official language(s). As such, the main tenet of the *Oslo Recommendations* when it comes to balancing the state and minority languages is that "the State could never prohibit the use of a language, but it could, on the basis of a legitimate public interest, prescribe the additional use of the official language or languages of the State".[26] And the main validation for promoting the state language (besides and in parallel with minority language(s)), echoes that of the *Hague Recommendations*: "integration is unlikely to take place without a sound knowledge of the official language(s) of the State".[27]

The 2008 *Bolzano/Bozen Recommendations on National Minorities in Inter-State Relations* similarly reiterate the principle that persons belonging to national minorities, besides having the right to opportunities to develop their identity, also bear a "responsibility to participate in cultural, social and economic life and in public affairs, thus integrating into the wider national society. This includes, for instance, the need to learn the State language while at the same time enjoy adequate opportunities for learning of, and in, the minority language".[28]

Finally, the 2012 *Ljubljana Guidelines on Integration of Diverse Societies*, are the ones which most comprehensively articulate the institution's approach to various strategies for enhancing societal cohesion and integration, including through the use of the state language. In this regard, the *Guidelines* stress that the "right to use, preserve and promote minority languages has to be balanced with other rights and needs, including the designation of one or more

25 *Ibid.*, para. 13, p. 7.

26 *Ibid.*, Explanatory Report, p. 25.

27 *Ibid.*, Explanatory Note, p. 14.

28 *See* the *Bolzano/Bozen Recommendations on National Minorities in Inter-State Relations*, Explanatory Note, p. 15.

shared language(s) as a common basis for the functioning and integration of a society". More particularly, the *Ljubljana Guidelines* provide that:

> While States have an obligation to protect and promote minority languages and the right of persons belonging to minorities to learn and use them, minorities share with the majorities the responsibility to participate in the cultural, social and economic life and in the public affairs of their wider society. This participation implies, for instance, that persons belonging to minorities should acquire adequate knowledge of the State or official language(s).[29]

Furthermore, the *Guidelines* also stress, amongst others, that:

> Proficiency in the State language by all residents in that State is necessary for full and effective participation. In addition, language can be a powerful tool to enhance a shared sense of belonging. Therefore, it is legitimate to promote a State language through positive means and incentives, including accessible public programmes for learning that language.[30]

The latter point is particularly important. It underlines that while the promotion of the state language is a perfectly legitimate aim, the *means* through which this is done are equally essential. In particular, the promotion of the state or official language should be carried out through positive measures (such as providing various incentives for multilingualism, offering language classes (especially on-the-job, and workplace-related), and so on), rather than through punitive actions (such as fines and sanctions) which may actually prove counter-productive. As a side-note, it bears mentioning that the *Ljubljana Guidelines* also recognize that 'some knowledge' or 'an adequate knowledge of the State language' is a justified prerequisite for naturalization and the acquisition of citizenship.[31]

3 Country-specific Advice on the Promotion of the State Language

HCNM's advice on the promotion of the state language was also put forward through so-called country-specific recommendations, which successive High

29 *See* the *Ljubljana Guidelines on the Integration of Diverse Societies*, para. 42, p. 52.

30 *Ibid.*, p. 53.

31 *See* the *Ljubljana Guidelines on the Integration of Diverse Societies*, pp. 41 and 43.

Commissioners have presented to various OSCE participating States over the years. Such advice was presented both orally and in written form, most often through diplomatic correspondence in follow-up to official country visits undertaken by the High Commissioner.

Given that the mandate of the institution provides that the HCNM should provide its advice 'in confidence', and only subsequently report on it to the OSCE Chairmanship in Office,[32] the content of such country-specific advice cannot be disclosed. Having said this, the main elements of such advice were on occasion made public by High Commissioners, albeit in a more general fashion, through various public interventions and speeches, office publications, or in official statements before the OSCE Permanent Council.[33]

Thus, over the years successive High Commissioners have emphasized the need to [also] promote the knowledge of the state language among minority representatives in countries such as Latvia, Estonia, Georgia, the Republic of Moldova, and Ukraine. HCNM recognized that these countries, having regained independence following the collapse of the Soviet Union, sought to re-establish their national identity in various fields, including by reasserting their national languages and undoing the impact of the deliberate policy of Russification pursued under Soviet occupation.[34] In this context, HCNM stressed that promoting the state language can be a pre-requisite for strengthening the cohesion and integration of societies, and that acquiring some command of the official language was an important precondition for the participation of minorities in public life. In the Baltic States in particular, this was particularly important given that [some] knowledge of the state language was a precondition for the [re-]acquisition of nationality.

The HCNM thus encouraged these countries to enhance their efforts of reaching out to minority representatives and supporting them in acquiring a reasonable level of the state language. This could be done, for instance, through

32 The mandate of the HCNM provides that "the High Commissioner will work in confidence", and that "After a visit to a participating State, the High Commissioner will provide strictly confidential reports to the Chairman-in-Office on the findings and progress of the High Commissioner's involvement in a particular question". *See* the 1992 Helsinki Summit Document, available at <http://www.osce.org/mc/39530?download=true>.

33 The OSCE HCNM reports twice a year before the OSCE Permanent Council in Vienna, which is the main mechanism designed to ensure the institution's accountability before the OSCE as an organization and before the OSCE participating States themselves. The texts of all HCNM statements before the Permanent Council are available on the institution's website: <http://www.osce.org/hcnm/66055>.

34 As reflected in letters and speeches of successive High Commissioners. See also Zaagman 1999, *op cit.*; Kemp 2001, *op. cit.*

various ways and methods, including the media, education, as well as through specifically tailored programmes. At the same time, the HCNM also recognized that such policies "not only require an effort on the part of the government, but equally a contribution on the part of the [minority population]",[35] and emphasized repeatedly that minority representatives themselves should equally show commitment in this regard. Significantly, HCNM cautioned that such programmes and initiatives to promote the state language should be subject to particular limitations, namely they should not intrude into the private sphere; they should not be implemented through punitive measures; and they should not be pursued to the detriment of minority languages (see more on this below).

The HCNM has also provided specific legislative advice to assist various OSCE participating States in drafting legislation on the use of the state language. Such legislative assistance was provided, *inter alia*, to Latvia (throughout the 1990-s and in early 2000-s), Estonia (similar time-frame), Slovakia (late 1990-s and again in 2009), R. Moldova (early 2000, 2010), Georgia (2002, 2004, 2015), Ukraine (throughout the past two decades) and Kyrgyzstan (2006 and onwards). Such legislative assistance concerned a wide range of laws, including 'framework' laws on the use of languages, specific laws dedicated to the state language in particular, as well as laws on the rights of persons belonging to national minorities. In some cases, assistance was provided also as concerns the use of languages in particular spheres, such as in cinematography (for instance, in R. Moldova – where the HCNM recognized that there was a "pressing social need" to ensure that films shown in cinemas are also accessible in the state language).[36] HCNM also on occasion warned that some particularly assertive efforts to promote the state language could even lead to bilateral tensions among neighboring states, as happened, for instance, with the amendments to the State Language Law adopted by the Slovak Republic in June 2009, which was yet another situation where HCNM got involved (– "first, to ensure that the implementation of the amended State Language Law does not negatively affect persons belonging to national minorities; and second, to facilitate dialogue between Hungary and Slovakia in order to reduce tensions in their bilateral relations").[37]

In all instances, through its country-specific advice HCNM sought to ensure that the respective States achieve an appropriate balance between the rights of the majority, including the legitimate goal of the state to promote the use

35 Quote from HCNM official letter, dated 5 March 1993.

36 Quote from HCNM official letter, dated 24 February 2010.

37 *See* High Commissioner Knut Vollebaek's statement before the OSCE Permanent Council, 27 October 2009, available at <http://www.osce.org/hcnm/40116?download=true>.

of the state language, and the rights of minority representatives to retain and use their minority language(s). On occasion, the HCNM did not hesitate to caution that the balance should be re-adjusted in favor of the state language – for instance, as concerned the 2011 draft Law on Languages in Ukraine, which in the opinion of the HCNM was unbalanced in so far as it strongly protected the Russian language, without taking additional measures to simultaneously confirm and enforce the role of Ukrainian as the state language[38] – a factor which was deemed likely to exacerbate linguistic divisions in the country. Where necessary, the HCNM called for a review of legal provisions in the education, media, public administration and other spheres, to ensure that the state and minority languages are used in a complementary way so as to avoid areas or regions in which there are neither incentives nor opportunities to learn and use the State language.

The HCNM thus was always careful to consider linguistic rights within a wider context, and suggest measures which would avoid polarization and enhance social cohesion and integration, including through a gradual strengthening of the role of the state language, where appropriate. While more specific details about the exact nature of HCNM's country-specific advice cannot be disclosed due to the confidentiality clause enshrined in the institution's mandate, it bears emphasizing that overall, such country-specific advice has always been fully consistent with and reliant on the above-quoted thematic recommendations developed by the HNCM, first and foremost the *Oslo Recommendations on the Linguistic Rights of National Minorities*. Also significantly, HCNM's statements and recommendations in this regard have also been echoed by other international organizations, such as the Council of Europe's Commission for Democracy through Law ('Venice Commission'),[39] and the Advisory Committee of the Framework Convention for the Protection of National Minorities.[40]

38 As reflected in HCNM letter(s) to Ukrainian MP-s, concerning the then draft Law on Languages, dated 14 June 2011.

39 *See*, for instance, the Venice Commission *Opinion on the Draft Law on Principles of the State Language Policy of Ukraine* (Opinion no.651/2011, CDL-AD(2011)047, Strasbourg, 19 December 2011), which provides, in paragraph 66, that "the question remains whether, having regard to the specific situation in Ukraine, there are sufficient guarantees, in the current Draft Law, for the consolidation of the Ukrainian language as the sole State language, and of the role it has to play in the Ukrainian multilinguistic society" – effectively reiterating the position of the HCNM on the issue. The Venice Commission Opinion is available at <http://www.venice.coe.int/webforms/documents/default.aspx?pdffile=CDL-AD(2011)047-e>.

40 *See*, for instance, the ACFC *Third Opinion on Ukraine* (ACFC/OP/III(2012)002, Strasbourg, 28 March 2013), which in paragraph 100 mentions that "A well-balanced and comprehensive legislative framework promoting the state language as the main language of

4 Project Activities on the Promotion of the State Language

Over the years, successive High Commissioners have sought to assist various participating States through special country-tailored programmes, which were often also aimed at enhancing a state's language policies. Such activities took the form of various projects, through which HCNM sought to channel its expertise and capacity-building resources to countries and areas which were in a particularly acute need of such assistance. Generally speaking, HCNM project activities were always "designed to satisfy specific (and often basic) needs, to encourage people to work together, and to underline the importance of common interests and a common future".[41]

In Latvia, HCNM helped develop a practice manual for 'language inspectors', in follow-up to a project initially undertaken by the then OSCE Mission to Latvia. Thus, in 2002, HCNM commissioned two experts to elaborate guidelines for the implementation of the State Language Law in Latvia, with the aim of enhancing the capabilities of the implementing agency – the State Language Inspectorate – to apply and implement the law in a just and legitimate manner. HCNM helped rework the initial blueprint of the implementing manual, and during subsequent country visits, High Commissioner Rolf Ekéus reached preliminary understandings with the Head of the State Language Center on its intended application.[42] Through these engagements, as well as through separate workshops conducted with 'language inspectors', HCNM generally sought to assist the Latvian State Language Centre in amending their working methods to ensure conformity with applicable Latvian legislation and relevant international standards. HCNM also offered to assist the Latvian authorities with their education reforms, which aimed to enhance learning in and of the state language.[43] In general, in Latvia High Commissioner Rolf Ekéus often

communication while providing clear guarantees for the protection and use of all minority languages, including the numerically smaller ones, is urgently required to ensure full respect for the linguistic rights of persons belonging to national minorities". The Opinion is available at <https://rm.coe.int/168008c6c0>.

41 W. Kemp, *Quiet Diplomacy in Action: The OSCE High Commissioner on National Minorities* (Martinus Nijhoff, 2001) p. 75.

42 *See* High Commissioner Rolf Ekéus's statement before the OSCE Permanent Council, 7 March 2002, available at <http://www.osce.org/hcnm/15145?download=true>. *See* also the PC statement of 27 June 2002, available at <http://www.osce.org/hcnm/15148?download=true>.

43 High Commissioner Rolf Ekéus stated that "The introduction of a target for teaching 60% of the curriculum in the state languages in secondary schools is a reasonable measure, as part of the state integration programme", but cautioned that this should not undermine

restated his "long-standing support for the right, and indeed duty, of a State to promote national integration, in particular by supporting the acquisition of proficiency in the State language",[44] whilst seeking to simultaneously safeguard minority linguistic rights.

In Georgia, starting from 2002, HCNM implemented a project to support classes of the state language for civil servants as well as teachers and school graduates from the mainly ethnic Armenian minority in the Samtskhe-Javakheti region. With this project, HCNM sought to help integrate this relatively isolated region closer with the Georgian society.[45] Since 2005 and until present day, HCNM also supported the development of a multilingual education policy in Georgia, to introduce bilingual teaching of subjects and enable minority youth to learn both the mother tongue and the state language at school. HCNM's involvement coupled with the Government's efforts to introduce a national quota system for minority students, resulted in a significant increase in the number of ethnic minority students at the country's universities. HCNM also supported the training of teachers in language- and subject-integrated teaching methodology; the training of teachers of Georgian as a second language; and the preparation of supporting teaching materials. With HCNM's support, over 200 minority-language schools and school teachers were involved in different capacity-building activities. Throughout the years, HCNM generally supported the Georgian Governments' efforts to strengthen minorities' knowledge of the State language, which it recognized as a precondition for their full participation in Georgian society.

In R. Moldova, beginning in 2000, HCNM initiated and supported a multi-year project to improve the teaching of the State language to children from minority communities. This project, which has proven highly successful, included the publication of specialized textbooks and the training of some 1,500 teachers from across the country on the use of modern techniques for teaching non-native speakers the state language. Recognizing that "language is an

the quality of education in minority schools. *See* High Commissioner Rolf Ekéus's statement before the OSCE Permanent Council, 30 March 2004, <http://www.osce.org/hcnm/15143?download=true>.

44 *See* High Commissioner Rolf Ekéus's statement before the OSCE Permanent Council, 28 October 2004, available at <http://www.osce.org/hcnm/15146?download=true> as well as the statement of 23 November 2006, available at <http://www.osce.org/hcnm/23252?download=true>.

45 *See* High Commissioner Rolf Ekéus's statement before the OSCE Permanent Council, 31 October 2002, available at <http://www.osce.org/hcnm/15149?download=true>. *See* also the PC statement, 20 March 2003, available at <http://www.osce.org/hcnm/15144?download=true>.

important tool of social integration", HCNM encouraged the Moldovan Government to consider increasing language training for adults, and, more generally, to consider developing a general strategy for social integration (eventually adopted in 2016). These recommendations were put forward in response to HCNM's finding that in urban areas and in the South of R. Moldova a considerable part of the minority population still lacks a sufficient command of the state language. On a separate yet related note, the HCNM also supported, for over 10 years, courses promoting the acquisition of the state language for Gagauz civil servants, as part of its "overall efforts to strengthen the state language in Moldova and at the same time promote integration of the minority communities".[46]

Through similar project activities, which usually combined state-language promotion with multi-lingual education reform, over the years HCNM also supported the strengthening of the state language in other countries, such as Kyrgyzstan (by publishing school textbooks in Uzbek and Kyrgyz languages), Serbia (by *inter alia* assisting in the development of dictionaries to support state language acquisition), or the former Yugoslav Republic of Macedonia (through the establishment of a 'catch-up' transition year programme for ethnic Albanian students, to enable them to acquire sufficient knowledge of the state language to pursue higher education in it). Through such project activities, HCNM regularly stressed that efforts to promote the state language should be implemented gradually, and not at the expense of minority rights. In this context, HCNM commended the authorities of those countries which made clear that they intend to adopt a balanced and gradual approach to the strengthening of the role of the state language, with a special emphasis on education and a more intensive promotion of the official language and languages of national minorities (such as Kazakhstan).[47] HCNM conversely encouraged other countries (such as Estonia), to make their transition process to state language instruction in the minority education system more gradual and flexible.[48] To Kyrgyzstan, HCNM offered to assist "in developing a comprehensive and long-term policy which would lead to a gradual strengthening of the role of the State language, envisaging, *inter alia*, widespread language learning, based on modern methods, through public education and in the public

46 *See* High Commissioner Rolf Ekéus's statement before the OSCE Permanent Council, 29 June 2006 available at <http://www.osce.org/hcnm/15145?download=true>.

47 *See* High Commissioner Ekéus's statement before the OSCE Permanent Council, 4 November 2005, available at <http://www.osce.org/hcnm/16947?download=true>.

48 *See* High Commissioner Ekeus's statement before the OSCE Permanent Council, 27 June 2002, available at <http://www.osce.org/hcnm/15148?download=true>.

service, especially at local level in some regions", while simultaneously safeguarding "the position of the national minority languages so that the rights of individuals to use and develop their mother-tongue are not compromised".[49] For the five countries of Central Asia, beginning from 2012 HCNM has implemented a multi-year project promoting multi-lingual education, which seeks to advance both the learning of the state language by all persons, including minority representatives, and the parallel safeguarding of minority languages (for more information on this particular project, please refer to the article on *The HCNM Impact on Minority and State Language Promotion and on the Social Integration of Diverse Societies through Education: the cases of Kazakhstan and Kyrgyzstan*, in Chapter 7 below).

More generally, through all its project activities, HCNM has consistently sought to promote its overarching idea of integration with respect for diversity – an idea which requires respecting the right of minorities to maintain and develop their culture and to preserve the essential elements of their identity, such as their religion, language, traditions and cultural heritage, while at the same time entailing efforts towards a cohesive society where every person has the opportunity to participate in and influence the political, economic, social and cultural life of society as a whole (for which knowledge of the state language is often a prerequisite). As mentioned in the *Ljubljana Guidelines*, this approach "entails balancing the rights and interests of all groups, minorities and majorities alike. The appropriate balance is different in each society and can never be achieved once and for all because societies are inherently dynamic. It rather needs constant monitoring and rebalancing through adaptation to changing circumstances".[50]

5 Conclusion

As outlined above, HCNM's position on the promotion of the state language has followed a complex yet consistent approach, over the years. Successive High Commissioners have stressed that efforts to promote the state/official language are perfectly legitimate in and of themselves, in so far as it is generally accepted that all States have the sovereign right to choose a particular language – typically, that of the majority – for official purposes and to seek to strengthen the position of that language by prescribing it as the State language

49 *See* High Commissioner Ekeus's statement before the OSCE Permanent Council, 29 June 2006, available at <http://www.osce.org/hcnm/19968?download=true>.

50 *See* the *Ljubljana Guidelines on the Integration of Diverse Societies*, principle 10, p. 20.

for public administration and institutions, as well as in other domains (such as State education), on the basis of legitimate public interests. This general approach is reflected in both the thematic work of the HCNM (i.e., the guidelines and recommendations issued by the office), as well as in many [confidential] country-specific recommendations, and various project activities. HCNM has consistently emphasized the crucial role which the state language may play in facilitating the participation of persons belonging to national minorities in cultural, social and economic life and in public affairs, and more generally its key role for inclusion and integration. In this regard the position of the HCNM has been well aligned to that of other international instruments, such as the Council of Europe Framework Convention for the Protection of National Minorities,[51] or the European Charter for Regional or Minority Languages.[52]

This being said, HCNM has also been cautious to always remind OSCE participating States that the strengthening of the state language should not be achieved at the expense or to the detriment of minority languages, but rather that a delicate balance should be achieved between them. In other words, while it is legitimate to encourage minorities to learn the State language to facilitate their participation in public life and as a means to promote the integration of society, such programmes should not be seen as a zero-sum option implemented at the expense of the linguistic and education rights of national minorities. And as concerns the means through which States should promote the official language, HCNM has consistently encouraged the use of positive incentives (such as tax breaks, enhanced opportunities for learning the state language, efficient bilingual education, *etc.*), instead of punitive measures (such as sanctions or fines).[53] HCNM has also cautioned that in areas of language use, “States need to respect the scope of their regulatory authority. While they

51 *See*, for instance, the Explanatory Report to the Council of Europe's Framework Convention for the Protection of National Minorities, which recognizes that “The opportunities for being taught the minority language or for receiving instruction in this language are without prejudice to the learning of the official language or the teaching in this language. Indeed, knowledge of the official language is a factor of social cohesion and integration” (paragraph 78 of the Explanatory Report).

52 *See*, for instance, the Preamble of the European Charter for Regional or Minority Languages, which recognizes that “that the protection and encouragement of regional or minority languages should not be to the detriment of the official languages and the need to learn them”.

53 For more details on the HCNM position concerning linguistic sanctions, *see* the chapter “To Speak or Not to Speak: Minority Languages, the Public Administration, and the Enforcement of Linguistic Requirements”, by Iryna Ulasiuk and Laurenţiu Hadîrcă (originally published in the *International Journal on Minority and Group Rights* 23 (2016) 1–13 under

enjoy wide discretion in the public sphere, their authority remains restricted in the private domain".[54]

Overall, HCNM's advice on the promotion of the state language – with simultaneous due regard for minority linguistic rights – reflects the institution's overarching axiom that minority and majority interests are not mutually exclusive, and that it is perfectly possible to promote the integration and cohesion of society (including by strengthening the state language) without threatening or undermining the distinct identity (linguistic or otherwise) of persons belonging to national minorities.

---

the title of "OSCE HCNM Advice on the Use of Languages in Relations with the Public Administration, and on the Supervision and Enforcement of Linguistic Requirements").

54 *See* High Commissioner Knut Vollebaek's statement before the OSCE Permanent Council, 29 October 2009, available at <http://www.osce.org/hcnm/40116?download=true>.

CHAPTER 3

To Speak or Not to Speak: Minority Languages, the Public Administration and the Enforcement of Linguistic Requirements

Iryna Ulasiuk and Laurenţiu Hadîrcă

1 Introduction

Linguistic rights, and their implications for societal cohesion and state stability, have long been recognized as a core component in the conflict prevention work of the OSCE High Commissioner on National Minorities, despite not being explicitly mentioned in the institution's mandate as such.[1] Already the first High Commissioner, Max Van der Stoel, recognized that the linguistic rights of national minorities – *i.e.* the right of persons belonging to national minorities to use their language in the private and public spheres – represented a recurrent issue in a significant number of OSCE participating states. On the one hand, language is a highly personal matter, closely connected with identity, in both its individual and collective manifestations. On the other hand, language is an essential tool of social organization and cohesion, and it certainly bears directly on numerous aspects of a state's functioning. In a democratic state committed to human rights, the accommodation of the existing linguistic diversity, in keeping with international standards and relevant OSCE commitments,[2] thus becomes an important matter of policy and law.

* This contribution is the re-publication of the earlier article of the authors 'OSCE High Commissioner on National Minorities on the Use of Languages in Relations with the Public Administration, and on the Supervision and Enforcement of Linguistic Requirements', 23 *International Journal on Minority and Group Rights* (2016) pp. 237–249. The views expressed in this article are those of the authors alone, and do not necessarily represent the official policy of the OSCE HCNM.

1 The Office of the High Commissioner on National Minorities was established at the CSCE Helsinki Summit in 1992, as an institution tasked to provide early warning and take appropriate early action to prevent ethnic tensions from developing into conflict. Its mandate describes it as "an instrument of conflict prevention at the earliest possible stage".

2 *See* the 1990 OSCE Copenhagen Document, in particular paras. 32, 33, 35 and 40.2, <www.osce.org/odihr/elections/14304>, visited on 27 January 2016.

© KONINKLIJKE BRILL NV, LEIDEN, 2018 | DOI 10.1163/9789004357754_004

Recognizing that the failure to ensure an appropriate balance between a state (or official) language(s) and minority languages may become a serious source of inter-ethnic tensions, the HCNM developed the Oslo Recommendations Regarding the Linguistic Rights of National Minorities.[3] Launched in 1998, these were some of the first thematic recommendations developed by the institution. The Oslo Recommendations covered topics such as names, religion, community life and non-governmental organizations, the media, economic life, administrative authorities and public services, independent national institutions, the judicial authorities and deprivation of liberty. Their main goal was to provide guidance to OSCE participating states on how best to ensure the linguistic rights of national minorities within their borders.

Successive High Commissioners continued to pay close attention to the linguistic rights of national minorities, throughout their tenures, including through promotion of implementation of the Oslo Recommendations. Linguistic and associated rights proved a challenge in many OSCE participating states, including Slovakia, Georgia, Moldova, Latvia, Estonia, Kyrgyzstan, Kazakhstan, Ukraine and others, and the HCNM repeatedly advised the relevant authorities of these states on how to secure a fair balance between the promotion of the state language and the protection of linguistic minority rights. Linguistic rights also feature prominently in the latest set of thematic recommendations issued by the HNCM, the 2012 Ljubljana Guidelines on Integration of Diverse Societies, which reiterate the importance of language policies for strengthening societal integration and cohesiveness.

This article overviews the advice which the successive HCNMs have throughout the years put forward on two key areas touching upon the linguistic rights of national minorities – namely, the use of languages in relations with the public administration, and the supervision and enforcement of linguistic requirements – and analyses how this advice aligns with the recommendations put forward by other international actors and institutions working on minority rights and minority issues. Given that the High Commissioner is mandated to work 'in confidence', the article purposely omits to mention the individual countries concerned, and rather seeks to distil the general HCNM approach as it was conveyed through a variety of diplomatic correspondence, specific advice and expert submissions, in the course of over two decades.

3 The text of the OSCE HCNM Oslo Recommendations Regarding the Linguistic Rights of National Minorities is available, in various languages, <www.osce.org/hcnm/67531>, visited on 27 January 2016.

2 The Use of Languages in Relations with the Public Administration

Why is the use of minority languages in relations with public authorities important? There are situations when persons belonging to national minorities do not have a command of the state language and thus cannot resolve practical communication difficulty by resorting to it. In some cases, speakers of minority languages have a certain degree of knowledge of the official language. For them the use of the minority language is therefore not a practical necessity. It is more a voluntary exercise which can be explained by the satisfaction a person feels in speaking his/her language and the desire to make room for it in dealings with public bodies. A state which undertakes to provide for the use of minority languages in relations with public authorities recognizes the legitimacy of this wish and undertakes to respect it.[4]

By allowing the use of languages other than the state language before public authorities, the state ensures that minorities will be able to understand governmental policies, especially those that affect them and express their views to appropriate governmental bodies.[5] Moreover, the use of minority languages in relations with the administrative authorities is an important means of enhancing the visibility of minorities and enabling minorities to become actively involved in the civil life of the country and feel a sense of belonging to society without having to sacrifice their identity.[6]

The role of a minority language as a full-fledged means of communication between minorities and public authorities becomes even more important if the number of minority language speakers is significant and they reside compactly within a territory. In that case it is likely that many have a limited proficiency in the majority or official language because in most contexts of their daily lives these people are in contact with other members of their community and have relatively few occasions or little need to use another language.[7]

It is also important to note that the use of minority languages before public authorities contributes to the preservation of these languages. In the words of the drafters of the European Charter for Regional or Minority Languages (ECRML):

4 J.-M. Woehrling, *The European Charter for Regional or Minority Languages: A Critical Commentary* (Council of Europe Publishing, 2005) pp. 178–179.

5 OSCE, *Report on the Linguistic Rights of Persons Belonging to National Minorities in the OSCE Area*, p. 12, <www.osce.org/hcnm/42060>, visited on 27 January 2016.

6 Advisory Committee under the Framework Convention for the Protection of National Minorities (ACFC), *Second Opinion on Bosnia and Herzegovina*, para. 157.

7 F. De Varennes, *Language, Minorities and Human Rights* (Kluwer Law International, The Hague, 1996) p. 176.

> [I]f a language were to be completely barred from relations with the authorities, it would in fact be negated as such, for language is a means of public communication and cannot be reduced to the sphere of private relations alone. Furthermore, if a language is not given access to the political, legal or administrative sphere, it will gradually lose all its terminological potential in that field and become a 'handicapped' language, incapable of expressing every aspect of community life.[8]

3 International Standards Regarding the Use of Languages in Relations with Public Authorities: Main Challenges

The right of persons belonging to minorities to use their language in relations with public authorities is a right that is not widely enshrined in international legal instruments, and thus not generally the subject of international decisions to delimit its boundaries and content.

In addition to Article 10 of the Council of Europe Framework Convention for the Protection of National Minorities (FCNM), only Article 10 of the European Charter for Regional or Minority Languages sets forth a legal obligation to have minority languages used in dealings with public authorities. Other regional instruments of human rights protection, such as the European Convention for the Protection of Human Rights and Fundamental Freedoms, do not contain specific guarantees to safeguard the rights of linguistic minorities – an omission that was described as 'an unquestionable lacuna' by the Council of Europe's 'Venice Commission'.[9]

Notwithstanding this, in a number of cases, the public authorities have been obliged to use a minority language in dealings with minorities under traditional human rights standards in circumstances where the exclusive use of the state language has been deemed unreasonable or unjustified, and thus discriminatory towards minority language speakers. In *Diergaardt* v. *Namibia*[10] the UN Human Rights Committee confirmed that states cannot reject a

8 Explanatory Report to the ECRML, para. 101.

9 Council of Europe Venice Commission, *The Compilation of Venice Commission Opinions and Reports Concerning the Protection of National Minorities*, p. 27, <www.venice.coe.int/webforms/documents/default.aspx?pdffile=CDL(2011)018-e>, visited on 27 January 2016 and Council of Europe Venice Commission, *Opinion on the provisions of the European Charter for Regional or Minority Languages which should be accepted by all the contracting states*, p. 2, <www.venice.coe.int/webforms/documents/default.aspx?pdffile=CDL(1996)002-e>, visited on 27 January 2016.

10 *Diergaardt v. Namibia* (No.760/1997), UN Doc.CCPR/C/69/D/760/1997 (2000).

request for the provision of services and information in a minority language if it is not well justified. The European Court of Justice has also acknowledged language as a 'service' or 'benefit' for citizens of the EU which cannot be denied in a discriminatory manner.[11]

Moreover, even the existing provisions dealing with language rights of national minorities in the public field have in common clauses that make their exercise dependent upon preconditions and/or impose certain limitations on them. These encompass, in particular, numerical thresholds, 'traditional settlement' and the 'possibility' and 'necessity' criteria.

What the above suggests is that the right of minority speakers to have their language used in the public domain is far from being a general, well-established legal guarantee in international law. [12]

4 The Approach of the HCNM to the Question of the Use of Minority Languages in Relations with Public Authorities

In addressing the question of the right of persons belonging to national minorities to use their language in relations with public authorities, the HCNM has consistently followed an important distinction that was made back in 1993 by the UN Human Rights Committee in the *Ballantyne, Davidson and McIntyre* case.[13] The HCNM clearly distinguishes between the use of language in public and private affairs, and recognizes that while a state may not exclude, outside the spheres of public life, the freedom to express oneself in a language of one's choice, the state may choose one or more official languages to be used in the public field. The HCNM has on various occasions indicated that all members of society, including persons belonging to national minorities, may be expected to use the State language in certain communicative situations in the public domain, as specified by law. To put it differently, the HCNM has made it clear that there is no right of persons belonging to national minorities never to be expected to use the state language.

11 Case 137/84 *Ministère public* v. *Mutsch* [1985] ECR 2681 and Case C-275/96 *Bickel and Franz* v. *Italy* [1998] ECR I-7637.

12 For a detailed overview of international standards on the use of languages in relations with public authorities, *see* I. Ulasiuk, 'Language Rights in Relations with Public Administration: European Perspectives', 18 *International Journal on Minority and Group Rights* (2011) pp. 93–113.

13 The case dealt with the use of languages in commercial signs in Canada.

On the other hand, the HCNM, in line with the FCNM (Article 10) and the ECRML (Article 10) and the HCNM Oslo Recommendations (Recs 13–15), considers the use of minority languages in contacts with public authorities as an essential element of dealing with persons belonging to national minorities in an inclusive and equitable manner and, ultimately, a pre-requisite for their effective participation in various fields of life.

Thus, the HCNM has encouraged the states to balance the promotion of the state language with the maintenance, re-production and protection of minority languages, including through allowing space for the use of minority languages in the public sphere.

An important step in recognising this right, in the HCNM's opinion, is the adoption of a legal framework on the basis of clearly defined criteria on which national minorities must first be consulted, and which should take due account of the demands voiced by persons belonging to minorities and allow the public authorities to apply the facilitated use of minority languages, taking into consideration the local circumstances.

As none of the international or European instruments contains a specific threshold (percentage or number) at which public authorities are obligated to use a minority language in their relations with minority speakers, the HCNM has primarily relied on the 'soft law' jurisprudence of the Advisory Committee on the Framework Convention for the Protection of National Minorities (ACFC). In their opinions on Austria, Romania and the Slovak Republic, the Advisory Committee found a 10 per cent threshold (in Austria), and a 20 per cent threshold (in Romania and the Slovak Republic) to be "an important step in the implementation of the Framework Convention".[14] At the same time, the majority threshold adopted in Bosnia and Herzegovina, Croatia and Moldova was found to be so "high that it might constitute an obstacle with respect to certain minority languages in areas inhabited by persons belonging to national minorities either traditionally or in substantial numbers, particularly at the level of local communities".[15] Similar comments were made by the Venice Commission with regard to Ukraine.[16] While sharing the rationale for accepting/criticizing the above mentioned thresholds, the HCNM has also argued, in keeping with its conflict-prevention mandate, that providing clarity on the obligations of public authorities to implement the corresponding right in a

14 *See* the ACFC Opinion on Austria, para. 45; on Romania, para. 49; and on Croatia, para. 43.

15 *See* the ACFC Opinion on Moldova, paras. 61–62; Second Opinion on the Slovak Republic, paras. 86–87; and Second Opinion on Bosnia and Herzegovina, paras. 159–160.

16 CDL-AD(2004)022, paras. 12, 14, *supra* note 10.

meaningful manner would also substantially contribute to decreasing tensions around the issue of language use.

The HCNM has noted in different opinions that:

(1) States should be aware that undertaking obligations to ensure the use of minority languages in relations with public authorities requires a corresponding commitment of human and financial resources from the state. Thus, the costs of measures needed to implement the legislative provisions should be given serious consideration and it is important that unrealistic expectations are not created.
(2) Where thresholds are set, they should be applied flexibly and cautiously, and reviewed as and when appropriate.
(3) The HCNM has also encouraged the states to ensure that the introduction of low thresholds (10 per cent in Ukraine, or the reduction of the threshold from 20 to 10 per cent in the Slovak Republic, for example) should not lead to reducing incentives to use the state language in the public domain as an effective tool in ensuring social cohesion.
(4) In areas where the threshold is met, the HCNM has encouraged the authorities to make the entitlement to use a minority language clear and unconditional upon the consent of a civil servant.
(5) Finally, in areas where the use of a minority language is dominant and where local authorities are also dominated by the minority, the HCNM recommended specific guarantees for speakers of the state language.

Concerning what exactly the obligations of public authorities to effectively fulfil the right to use a minority language in public entail, the HCNM considered that these may comprise entitlements to the recruitment and training of relevant staff, as well as the translation of specific documents. As to whether public officials should be obliged or not obliged to speak minority languages, the HCNM looked upon the knowledge of a minority language as a merit, rather than obligation, in accessing civil service. In some contexts, however, especially in areas densely populated by persons belonging to minorities, the HCNM has regretted the lack of an obligation for public officials to have the knowledge of minority languages. In all fairness it should be said that other international bodies dealing with similar issues have not been particularly clear as to whether the knowledge of a minority language should be made an obligation for public servants where the specific entitling threshold has been met. Overall such requirement depends on the case concerned. If such obligation is directly or indirectly provided in legislation, the Advisory Committee under the FCNM has supported that. If not, the FCNM has encouraged to do so or at least to give preference in hiring to those who have command of the minority language. In their thematic commentary on language rights, the experts have mentioned that "proficiency in the minority language should always be considered an asset and, in areas of traditional settlement, even a requirement in recruitment proceedings for the civil service".[17] Reference has been made to both people belonging to national minorities as well as the majority.

With regard to the requirement for minority language employees of public institutions to know and use the state language, the HCNM has clearly indicated that while such a requirement is permissible under international law, it should only be used to the extent necessary for the performance of the professional and employment duties of persons belonging to national minorities. Moreover, the HCNM has drawn the attention of the states to the fact that different levels of language proficiency should be required for different levels of professional functions in the public service. Furthermore, the HCNM has stressed the importance of allowing sufficient time for civil servants to acquire the necessary proficiency in the state language. In case language legislation foresees such a requirement for the first time, the HCNM urged the states to provide a transitional period for the entering into force of the law. In the countries where new official languages are introduced, the HCNM stressed the importance of making it attractive for persons belonging to national minorities to learn the new official language, for instance, by offering career opportunities for persons who speak official and minority languages. The HCNM strongly discouraged institutionalizing a punitive system for the lack of knowledge of the state language (see next section for further details).

More generally, the HCNM has consistently encouraged states to support in-service and other language training and education programmes aimed at ensuring the availability of personnel with adequate minority language skills. The provisions for language training, also for civil servants who do not belong to a national minority, as well as measures for hiring the staff with the relevant linguistic knowledge have been deemed necessary measures to satisfy the demands of the linguistic communities in their relations with public authorities.

Finally, and more generally, while recognising that it is the free choice of persons belonging to national minorities to make use or not of the legal possibilities open to them, the HCNM has advocated a pro-active, open, flexible and pragmatic approach of the authorities with regard to the use of minority languages in dealings with public administration.

---

17 ACFC Thematic Commentary no. 3, *The Language Rights of Persons Belonging to National Minorities under the Framework Convention*, para. 89.

5 The Supervision and Enforcement of Linguistic Requirements

Throughout the years, the HCNM has also provided numerous recommendations on the issue of supervision over, and enforcement of, specific language requirements. This has usually concerned the (non-)use of the state language, and the various means employed by states to enforce such a policy, for instance inspections, sanctions or fines. This section overviews the HCNM recommendations on these matters and analyses how they compare to the advice put forward by other international organizations dealing with human and minority rights.

To begin with, the HCNM recognizes the legitimacy of efforts to promote the state language, which are considered instrumental to strengthening social cohesion and facilitating integration. That said, the *means* that states choose to employ in the pursuit of the legitimate goal of promoting the state language, in the opinion of the HCNM, should involve positive incentives (such as tax breaks, enhanced opportunities for learning the state language, efficient bilingual education, *etc.*), rather than punitive measures (such as sanctions or fines). This overarching principle is expressed in many HCNM letters and opinions, and is also enshrined in the OSCE HCNM Ljubljana Guidelines on the Integration of Diverse Societies, albeit in qualified fashion ("When possible, ... In many cases, ...").[18]

Generally speaking, the HCNM advises against the adoption of any kind of sanctions, fines or other 'punitive measures' to enforce language laws. The rationale behind this approach is somewhat elaborate: while recognizing that such sanctions would not be *per se* 'illegal' (unless applied in the private sphere), the argument is that they are likely to be ineffective, potentially counter-productive, and possibly conducive to tensions within society – that is, a good-governance rationale, imbued with conflict-prevention considerations, dictated by HCNM's specific mandate. It is therefore advised that fines and sanctions should either be removed altogether from the text of the law – this would be a general principle or recommendation – or otherwise be applied only in the public sphere, and even there with great caution and only 'exceptionally', when required by a pressing and overriding interest (see below).

A fundamental distinction is thus operated between linguistic sanctions and fines which intrude into the private sphere, and those that are constrained

18 *See* the OSCE HCNM, *Ljubljana Guidelines on the Integration of Diverse Societies*, in particular Recommendation no. 11, p. 21, <www.osce.org/hcnm/96883?download=true>, visited on 27 January 2016.

to the public domain. Recognizing that the distinction between the private and public spheres is not always easy to draw, the HCNM has indicated that:

> *The public sphere* ... pertains to the functions of State authorities, including public administration. On the other hand, *the private sphere* pertains not only to all that is purely personal and is not limited to 'activities behind closed doors with family and friends', but pertains also to activities which can be observed by the public or engage the public, such as performances in a club or theatre; such public observation and engagement does not render the matter 'public' in the sense of the international instruments.[19]

Based on this distinction, the HCNM has advised that in the private sphere, any kind of sanction or fine is entirely unacceptable and would represent a manifest breach of international standards on freedom of expression. On this point the HCNM often makes reference to opinions of the Advisory Committee of the FCNM, which held that:

> the mere legal possibility of imposing fines ... for using minority language languages in the private sphere is not compatible with the Framework Convention. Equally incompatible with the Framework Convention is the imposition of language inspection systems in the private sector, as they may disproportionately intrude in the private sphere of the individual.[20]

There is thus a general position, also within the HCNM, that there should be no linguistic sanctions or fines or inspections in the private sphere.

Even as concerns the public sphere, the HCNM has recommended that sanctions and fines are best avoided, as a matter of principle. However, the HCNM seems prepared to accept, in exceptional and narrowly tailored circumstances, the appropriateness of certain linguistic fines and sanctions in the public sphere – if they are proportionate and correspond to a clearly demonstrated, legitimate and overriding public interest, such as protecting national security, public order, public health and morals or the rights and reputation of others. Although each such situation is highly particular and context-specific, there may occasionally appear to be some ambiguity or even a slight contradiction between the principled approach (that there should be no fines in the public

19 As noted with reference to the 2002 Draft Law of Georgia on the State Language (emphasis added).

20 ACFC Thematic Commentary no. 3, *supra* note 18, para. 54.

sphere as well) and the fall-back provision (eventually admitting that fines can be introduced to the public sphere, if necessary and proportionate).

Since sanctions and fines imposed on the basis of lack of state language knowledge or use interfere with freedom of expression, the HCNM has also looked into the 'quality of the law' prescribing such measures, and the mechanism for their implementation. The HCNM has stated that the law prescribing such sanctions must be clear and foreseeable, and should frame with reasonable clarity the scope and manner of exercise of the relevant discretion conferred onto the implementing public authorities. This reflects the reasoning of other international bodies on the issue of 'quality of the law', first and foremost that of the European Court of Human Rights (although the Court itself has found that the European Convention of Human Rights does not guarantee linguistic freedom as such).[21]

As regards the particular category of fines issued for lack of language knowledge or use, HCNM's assessment does not elaborate on the various possible degrees or levels thereof – *i.e.*, what is their pecuniary amount, or how appreciably detrimental they are for the individual concerned – nor does it analyse whether a particular fine is in effect deterrent, or merely dissuasive and preventive. Rather, any and all fines imposed for the non-observance of language requirements are presumed to be 'punitive', and thus most likely disproportionate and inappropriate.

6 Conclusion

Given the highly context-specific nature of states' language policies, assessing the overall consistency of HCNM's advice and recommendations in this field is not a straightforward task. The authors nevertheless have attempted to provide an accessible comparative overview of the advice provided by the HCNM on two specific linguistic issues over time, as well as to compare this advice with the position of other international bodies.

Overall, the HCNM advice on the use of languages in the public domain and with regard to the supervision and enforcement of linguistic rights reflects the opinions and jurisprudence of specialized international bodies dealing with human and minority rights, especially the opinions of the Advisory Committee on the FCNM. In its advice and recommendations the HCNM often relies on,

21 *See* the decisions of the European Commission of Human Rights on the cases of *Inhabitants of Leeuw – St. Pierre* v. *Belgium* (1965), and *Fryske Nasjonale Partij* v. *The Netherlands* (1986).

and directly references, the relevant positions developed by those institutions. At the same time, the HCNM supports such positions not only with minority-rights legal arguments, but also with a different rationale, inspired by the institution's conflict-prevention mandate. That rationale is premised on the conviction that reaching a fair balance between promoting the state language and protecting minorities' linguistic rights is in fact a prerequisite for consolidating national unity and avoiding tensions that may arise out of ill-conceived linguistic policies. Depending on the specific context, such arguments may occasionally prove particularly persuasive, given that they appeal directly to states' self-interest and societal concerns. The HCNM position on the use of languages in relations with the public administration, and on the supervision and enforcement of linguistic requirements, is thus not only consistent with but in fact also further reinforces the message of other international bodies dealing with the use of minority languages.

CHAPTER 4

Mind Your Own Business: The Oslo Recommendations and the Linguistic Rights of National Minorities in Economic Life

Jennifer Croft

1 Introduction

In September 1997, the first OSCE High Commissioner on National Minorities, Max van der Stoel, and the Council of Europe sent the Latvian authorities a joint opinion on the draft State Language Law. The draft law sought to increase the protection of the State language in private enterprises, including through State language proficiency requirements for private-sector employees and requirements that private enterprises should only accept documents in the State language or with a notarized translation. The HCNM followed up the strongly critical joint opinion with a visit to Latvia in October to meet with the head of the relevant parliamentary committee and, in November, he raised his concerns about the law with the Latvian President. The second reading of the draft, which had been scheduled for March 1998, was delayed and a revised text was sent to the High Commissioner for comments.[1]

Considering what was taking up the High Commissioner's attention in the months preceding the publication of the Oslo Recommendations in February 1998, it was especially timely that the Recommendations included a specific provision on 'Economic Life'. Recommendation number 12 states that:

> All persons, including persons belonging to national minorities, have the right to operate private enterprises in the language or languages of their choice. The State may require the additional use of the official language

* The views expressed in this chapter are those of the authors, and do not necessarily represent those of the High Commissioner on National Minorities.

1 J. Dorodnova, 'Challenging Ethnic Democracy: Implementation of the Recommendations of the OSCE High Commissioner on National Minorities to Latvia, 1993–2001 (Working Paper 10)', in W. Zellner *et al.* (eds.), *Comparative Case Studies on the Effectiveness of the OSCE HCNM*, (Institute for Peace Research and Security Policy at the University of Hamburg, 2003), pp. 100–101.

© KONINKLIJKE BRILL NV, LEIDEN, 2018 | DOI 10.1163/9789004357754_005

> or languages of the State only where a legitimate public interest can be demonstrated, such as interests related to the protection of workers or consumers, or in dealings between the enterprise and governmental authorities.

It is worth noting that the Oslo Recommendations took a stance on an issue that had not been explicitly addressed in other international minority rights instruments. As pointed out in the Explanatory Note, "International instruments make little reference to the rights of persons belonging to national minorities in the field of economic activity". For example, the Council of Europe Framework Convention for the Protection of National Minorities does not contain specific provisions on economic activity, but refers to economic life alongside other areas of life – social, cultural, and political– in which Parties to the FCNM should ensure effective participation and full and effective equality of persons belonging to national minorities. The UN Declaration on the Rights of Persons Belonging to National or Ethnic, Religious and Linguistic Minorities contains similar references to economic life and encourages States to take measures so that minorities may participate fully in the economic progress and development in their country. Meanwhile, the commentary to the UN Declaration contains no specific references to the use of minority languages in economic life.[2]

As the HCNM was already observing in his work, however, limitations on the choice of language used by private enterprises could affect the ability of minorities to fully participate in economic life, which in turn could increase potential for conflict. Early on the HCNM noted the importance of economic issues in this regard: "One cannot say that it is economic factors in themselves which have caused the tensions in the CSCE states in which I am involved. These factors do, however, make up an important element of the context in which minority tensions arise and evolve, often exacerbating matters".[3]

Clearly the experts tasked by HCNM to develop the Oslo Recommendations determined that this was an area where States could benefit from guidance on how to achieve an appropriate balance in protecting the public interest while

2 UN Sub-Commission on the Promotion and Protection of Human Rights, *Commentary Of The Working Group On Minorities To The United Nations Declaration On The Rights Of Persons Belonging To National Or Ethnic, Religious And Linguistic Minorities*, 4 April 2005, E/CN.4/Sub.2/AC.5/2005/2, available at: <http://www.refworld.org/docid/43f30ac80.html>, visited on 5 January 2018.

3 M. Van der Stoel, 'Political Order, Human Rights, and Development, Introduction by Max van der Stoel, CSCE High Commissioner on National Minorities to the Seminar on Conflict and Development: Causes, Effects, and Remedies', 24 March 1994, <http://www.osce.org/hcnm/37920?download=true>, visited on 5 January 2018.

also protecting the linguistic rights of minorities, so as to avoid possible tensions over this issue.

1.1 *Public versus Private and Legitimate Public Interest*

While entering new territory to some extent, the Oslo Recommendation concerning economic life was also well grounded in international standards. According to the Explanatory Note to the Oslo Recommendations, the right of minorities to run their businesses in the language of their choice can be implied from the right to use minority languages in public and in private as well as the right to freedom of expression, including with respect to language as a medium of communication, coupled with the right to equality and non-discrimination. The Note also cites provisions of the Framework Convention concerning the right to display minority-language signs, inscriptions or other information of a private nature visible to the public, noting that "of a private nature" refers to any non-official information and concluding that States may not restrict the choice of language in the administration of private business enterprises.

The Oslo Recommendations emphasize that private enterprises fall squarely in the private sphere. However, it is not difficult to imagine cases when public and private might overlap in the area of business activity. What about companies which produce or sell food or medicines? How can authorities responsible for taxation or health and sanitation check important records which are in a language they do not understand? Acknowledging such situations, the Explanatory Note points out that in sectors of economic activity which affect the enjoyment of the rights of others or require exchange and communication with public bodies, the State may require the accommodation of the official or State languages. The Note gives examples where this might apply, such as workplace health and safety, consumer protection, and taxation. In addition, the Note explains that the State may require use of the State or official languages in addition to another language in business activities such as signage and labelling, if a legitimate public interest is involved.

Reference is made to the permissible restrictions on freedom of expression which are specified in Article 19(3) of the ICCPR and Article 10(2) of the ECHR.[4] However the Explanatory Note maintains that limited permissible restrictions

4 In the case of ICCPR, these grounds are respect of the rights or reputations of others; protection of national security, public order, public health or morals; in the case of ECHR, national security, territorial integrity or public safety, for the prevention of disorder or crime, for the protection of health or morals, for the protection of the reputation or rights of others, for preventing the disclosure of information received in confidence, or for maintaining the authority and impartiality of the judiciary.

can only justify restrictions on content, not on the use of a language as a medium of communication.

The Explanatory Note further clarifies that the logic of 'legitimate public interest' implies that any State-prescribed language requirement must be proportional to the public interest served, and that this proportionality is determined by the extent to which such a requirement is necessary. For example, a justified requirement might specify that taxation-related administrative forms be submitted in the official or State languages, with the private enterprise bearing the burden of possible translation in case additional records are needed in the event of an audit.

In practice, of course, determining what falls within the legitimate public interest, and assessing the proportionality and necessity of measures designed to serve that interest, is far from clear-cut. What about when States outsource public service provision to private companies? It seems obvious that workers in a private hospital have an impact on public health and safety, but does the work of a beautician, a hotel cleaner, a taxi driver, a postal worker or an entertainer fall within the scope of legitimate public interest? What States may deem to be justifiable restrictions, persons belonging to national minorities may perceive as unfair attempts to shut them out of certain labour market sectors or out of the economy as a whole.

2 Oslo Recommendation #12 in Practice

In the two decades since the Oslo Recommendations were published, successive High Commissioners have addressed these difficult questions and have provided OSCE participating States with advice on laws and policies affecting the linguistic rights of minorities in economic life. The HCNM has on numerous occasions advised governments not to restrict the choice of language in the operation of private enterprises except in very limited circumstances. This advice has encompassed issues such as attempts to restrict the language used in business meetings or public meetings, in documentation maintained by private enterprises, and in signage and advertising. It has also addressed efforts to regulate the knowledge and use of the State language by private-sector employees, business owners and self-employed individuals, and to enforce such requirements through the use of inspections and the imposition of sanctions including fines. Language-related regulations affecting private media and cinema have also drawn the attention of the HCNM.

Due to the fact that the HCNM works in confidence and country-specific recommendations are provided only to the participating State concerned, references to HCNM advice in this article will not name specific countries unless some public communication was made in this regard. In Estonia and Latvia, the first HCNM was deeply engaged on language legislation among other issues. The fact that correspondence between HCNM and the Latvian and Estonian authorities was at one time made public make these especially informative case studies. Below, the main areas of HCNM advice to participating States related to the issue of linguistic rights in economic life will be considered in turn.

2.1 *Language Regulation in the Private Sphere*

In a number of countries, the HCNM has intervened when States sought to regulate the use of language in the private sphere and to impose use of the State language in the operations and activities of private enterprises. While maintaining that the State may not regulate the use of language in the private sphere, the HCNM has acknowledged that the public and private spheres may sometimes overlap, but only when a legitimate public interest exists may language use be regulated. In cases where HCNM has found legislative provisions to be insufficiently clear in drawing the line between public and private, authorities have been urged to ensure that language legislation clearly distinguishes between public and private entities. The practical burdens that regulation of language use in the private sphere may impose, and the difficulties in enforcing such provisions, have been additional arguments raised by HCNM.

In the case of Latvia, the HCNM considered that the draft State Language Law of 1997–1998 failed to distinguish between permissible regulation of use of language in the public sphere and impermissible interference in the private sphere. In addition to noting that regulation of language use in the private sphere was problematic in terms of freedom of association and freedom of expression, the HCNM also invoked practical arguments, warning that interference in the private sphere would be difficult to implement and could undermine investment and business development, also in terms of EU accession and requirements related to the functioning of the single market.[5]

When the Latvian State Language Law was initially passed in 1997, the HCNM recommended that it should be harmonized with international standards, noting that it required the State language to be used in the private sphere of commercial activities and that it required all public information, including with regard to private activities, to be in the Latvian language. The Latvian authorities were encouraged to achieve their aim of strengthening the Latvian language by adopting a general State language law that mainly prescribed the

5 Dorodnova, *supra* note 1, p. 104.

use of the State language in the public sphere, while prescribing permissible interferences in the private sphere in specific legislation.[6]

The HCNM acknowledged that Latvia could prescribe language use in the private sphere in cases of a legitimate public interest within the limited grounds established by international law. Pressure brought to bear by HCNM and other international organizations resulted in the introduction of a reference to legitimate public interest in the final version of the State Language Law and in a narrower list of legitimate public interests being included in the law. However, the list remained broader than the criteria cited in the Explanatory Note to the Oslo Recommendations.[7]

On other issues related to language regulation in the private sphere in Latvia, some HCNM recommendations were taken on board to some extent. A provision to impose the use of Latvian language in all record-keeping by private enterprises was scaled back to require that only documents submitted to State institutions be in Latvian. A requirement that only Latvian be used in all formal meetings was softened to require translation into Latvian at formal work meetings only if requested by at least one participant. The HCNM argued against a proposal to require private entities to have only Latvian-language names. While such a requirement was not explicitly stated in the final version of the law, the relevant regulation requires that private entities' names should use only Latvian or Latin-alphabet letters.[8]

2.2 *Language Proficiency Requirements in Private Enterprises*

The extension of State language proficiency requirements to private-sector workers has been an issue taken up by HCNM in several countries. HCNM has maintained that blanket requirements that employees use the State language at work and when performing official duties are excessive, and that – notwithstanding the obligation of all members of society to learn the State language – such requirements should only apply in limited circumstances, such as in official contacts with the State authorities and when involving a legitimate public interest. Generally, HCNM has maintained, private companies should decide for themselves in which language services are provided to customers, while providing conditions for employees to acquire and improve knowledge of the State language in those situations when it is needed for their duties, as justified by a legitimate public interest. In some cases HCNM has

6 W. Kemp, *Quiet Diplomacy in Action: The OSCE High Commissioner on National Minorities*, (Martinus Nijhoff Publishers, The Hague, 2001), pp. 122, 150.

7 Dorodnova, *supra* note 1, pp. 111–113.

8 Dorodnova, *supra* note 1, p. 124.

disagreed with the application of 'legitimate public interest' to certain occupations, including private transport and telecommunications service employees.

The HCNM was engaged on this issue in Estonia in the late 1990s. In 1999 the HCNM expressed reservations about amendments to the Law on Languages which in his view intruded into the private sphere and were not consistent with international standards. Among other provisions, the amendments introduced an obligatory level of Estonian language for private businesspeople and employees of commercial organizations. The HCNM also criticized a controversial provision requiring the use of Estonian when offering goods and services. The European Commission reinforced the HCNM arguments, adding a warning that the amended language law could conflict with the obligations of Estonia under the Europe Agreement. The law was changed to stipulate that Estonian language proficiency requirements should be in proportion to the aim sought and should not distort the nature of the rights which are restricted.[9] Estonian language legislation specifies that "the use of language of legal persons in private law and natural persons is regulated if it is justified for protection of fundamental rights or in the public interest". However, as in Latvia the list of public interests is somewhat broader than the ICCPR or ECHR definitions cited in the Oslo Recommendations, and was not revised when the Estonian Language Act was amended in February 2011.[10] After the High Commissioner visited Estonia in June that year, he noted concern about excessive regulation of language use in the private sector.[11]

After HCNM cooperated with the Latvian Government on the elaboration of implementing regulations under the State Language Law following its adoption, he expressed his expectations concerning a list that would specify language proficiency requirements in the private sector: "I trust that the prospective list will, in accordance with international standards, be precise, justified, proportionate to the legitimate aim sought, and limited".[12] However HCNM returned to this issue later as subsequent Cabinet of Ministers

9 M. Sarv, 'Integration by Reframing Legislation: Implementation of the Recommendations of the OSCE HCNM to Estonia, 1993–2001, Working Paper 7', in W. Zellner *et al.* (eds.), *Comparative Case Studies on the Effectiveness of the OSCE HCNM*, (Institute for Peace Research and Security Policy at the University of Hamburg, 2002), pp. 94–95.

10 Language Act, <www.riigiteataja.ee/en/eli/506112013016/>, visited on 5 January 2018.

11 'Statement by Knut Vollebaek, OSCE High Commissioner on National Minorities, to the 868th Plenary Meeting of the OSCE Permanent Council', 16 June 2011, <www.osce.org/hcnm/78915?download=true>, visited on 5 January 2018.

12 M. Van der Stoel, 'Statement regarding the adoption of regulations implementing the Latvian State Language Law', 31 August 2000, <http://www.osce.org/hcnm/52843>, visited on 5 January 2018.

regulations gradually expanded the list of private-sector professions to which State language requirements applied. During a 2011 visit to Latvia, the HCNM questioned whether a State language requirement was justified for a profession such as hairdressers, inspiring a newspaper cartoonist to depict him with an extreme haircut and the hairdresser apologizing: "I didn't understand you!"[13] In his statement to the Permanent Council following his visit, the High Commissioner noted that the gradual expansion of language requirements to more than 1,000 private-sector professions, and fines imposed for not meeting such requirements, fuelled unnecessary resentment.[14]

2.3 *Inspections, Sanctions and Fines*

Related to the issue of language proficiency requirements in the private sphere is the question of how such requirements are enforced. The HCNM has also provided recommendations concerning language inspection systems and sanctions, such as imposition of fines, arguing that such an approach to enforcement of language legislation not only violates international standards of freedom of expression but can be counterproductive in terms of fostering a positive attitude toward the State language among minorities.[15] The Advisory Committee on the Framework Convention for the Protection of National Minorities has taken a strong stance concerning the incompatibility with the Convention of language inspection systems in the private sector and the imposition of fines for the use of minority languages in the private sphere.[16] In a number of countries the HCNM has discouraged the introduction and application of punitive measures to enforce language policy, especially in the private sphere, and has instead encouraged positive incentives to promote State language knowledge and use, such as tax breaks. In Latvia, for example, the HCNM

13 *Latvijas Avize* newspaper, 16 February 2011, p. 3, <http://www.la.lv/izdevumi/la/2011/02/16/3>, visited on 5 January 2018.

14 'Statement by Knut Vollebaek, OSCE High Commissioner on National Minorities to the 868th Plenary Meeting of the OSCE Permanent Council', 16 June 2011, <http://www.osce.org/hcnm/78915?download=true>, visited on 5 January 2018.

15 For a more detailed discussion of the topic of supervision and enforcement of language requirements, *see* I. Ulasiuk and L. Hadirca, 'OSCE High Commissioner on National Minorities on the Use of Languages in Relations with the Public Administration, and on the Supervision and Enforcement of Linguistic Requirements', 23 International Journal on Minority and Group Rights (2016), pp. 237–249.

16 'Thematic Commentary No.3, The Language Rights of Persons Belonging to National Minorities under the Framework Convention', Advisory Committee on the Framework Convention for the Protection of National Minorities (ACFC/44DOC(2012)001 rev), para. 54.

advocated against proposed legal provisions to require employers to terminate the contracts of employees who did not meet legally stipulated language requirements and to penalize employers whose employees did not have acceptable proof of their language proficiency levels.[17]

2.4 *Advertising and Signage*

Another issue related to the use of minority languages in the economic sphere is advertising, signage and other forms of communicating public information – obviously an important issue for entrepreneurs seeking to advertise their goods or services. In a number of countries the HCNM has advised against restrictions on the language used in signs or advertisements by private persons or commercial entities, unless specifically justified, for example if the subject matter of the advertisement concerns a matter of legitimate public interest. Even when the provision of information in the State language can be justified, it should be alongside, not instead of, other languages, according to the HCNM. In 1999, for example, the HCNM criticized a draft amendment to the Law on Advertising in Moldova which effectively imposed mandatory use of the State language in private advertising. HCNM wrote to the Moldovan authorities that this constituted a measure to regulate language use in the private sphere and argued that it contradicted freedom of expression. The Moldovan Foreign Minister was not receptive to the HCNM arguments, however, pointing to the country's specific linguistic situation.[18] In a speech in Chisinau in May 2000 the HCNM publicly registered concern about the proposed amendments, noting, "Efforts to increase the knowledge and use of the Moldovan language – which I fully support – should not come at the expense of minority rights or the effective development of the free market".[19]

In Latvia, the HCNM objected to a provision in the draft State Language Law which would have required all signs, billboards, posters, and other kinds of public notices in places accessible to the public to be in the State language. In accordance with HCNM advice, the final law adopted in December 1999 required private entities to provide public information in the State language only in cases of legitimate public interest or in the performance of certain public

17 Kemp, *supra* note 6, p. 150.

18 J. Packer and S. Holt, 'OSCE Developments and Linguistic Minorities', in *International Journal on Multicultural Societies* (UNESCO, Vol. 3, No.2, 2001) "The Human Rights of Linguistic Minorities and Language Policies", pp. 99–126.

19 Keynote speech by M. Van der Stoel, 'The Linguistic and Education Rights of National Minorities and their Application in Moldova' (Chisinau, 18 May 2000), <www.osce.org/hcnm/42353?download=true>, visited on 5 January 2018.

functions. Subsequent regulations were also revised following HCNM correspondence with the Minister of Justice. However a requirement to use correct Latvian language in public information was retained despite the warning of the HCNM that it 'excessively broadens the area of state interference'.[20]

In recommendations to other countries, HCNM has maintained that restrictions related to the language of advertising could cause unnecessary market interference and that consumer protection does not imply a right to be informed via advertising in one's own language. The HCNM has also drawn a distinction between advertising and labelling, noting that consumer protection requires a vendor to provide relevant information about a product once a consumer has entered into a transaction with the vendor. Requirements to have descriptions of goods or price tags on products in the State language should not exclude having such information in other languages, the HCNM has argued. Concerning printed information provided to the public, for example at cultural events organized by private entities, the HCNM has considered excessive the imposition of requirements to translate such information, suggesting that this decision should be left to the event organizers.

2.5 *Media and Cinema*

While not explicitly mentioned under Oslo Recommendation 12, language-related restrictions placed on private media and cinema enterprises – such as requirements to provide State-language content, or to provide dubbing or translation – should also be considered in the context of economic life. The Oslo Recommendations on media mention rather generally the regulation of private media. The Explanatory Note focuses on the right of persons belonging to national minorities to establish and maintain private media and the need for regulatory restrictions (e.g. licensing requirements) to be justified and necessary. The question of restrictions on content is addressed with reference to the limited permissible grounds for restricting freedom of expression. However the issue of restrictions on the language of broadcasting in private media is not explicitly touched upon.

In 2003, the HCNM Guidelines on the Use of Minority Languages in the Broadcast Media addressed this issue, noting in the Introduction that a number of States had sought to impose restrictions on media in minority languages, including through the imposition of broadcasting quotas. The Guidelines advise that measures to promote certain languages should not restrict others, and discourages undue requirements for translation and subtitling. In addition, States are encouraged to assist the establishment of private broadcasting by national

20 Dorodnova, *supra* note 1, pp. 122–123.

minorities, also through licensing. The 2012 Ljubljana Guidelines on Integration of Diverse Societies contain targeted language concerning language regulation in private broadcasting, warning that State-language quotas, while not illegitimate per se, may unduly limit private initiative and the very existence of minority-language media.[21]

The HCNM has advised against unjustified regulation of private media in minority languages in a number of countries, pointing out that restrictions on language are not only problematic in terms of freedom of expression but can put a disproportionate burden on small private broadcasters. Indirect language quotas affecting digital broadcasting, including for the private media, make it increasingly difficult for minority voices to be heard in the mainstream media environment, HCNM has warned.[22] In fact, HCNM has suggested that promoting private broadcasting, alongside public broadcasting, in minority languages is in a State's interest, because it can foster loyalty to the State and reduce the chances that minorities will turn to transfrontier broadcasts for their news.[23] If regulation of language in the private media is pursued, according to HCNM, exceptions should be provided for private broadcasters at the regional level. In some cases HCNM has recommended States to clearly distinguish in legislation between public and private broadcasting, when provisions concerning the language of broadcasting are unclear in this regard.

While language regulations concerning cinema are scarcely mentioned in HCNM thematic recommendations, this topic has emerged several times in OSCE participating States and has drawn the attention of the HCNM. The HCNM has maintained that promoting the State language can in principle be among the legitimate aims justifying the regulation of language in cinemas and in cinema distribution. However such regulation should be proportionate to the desired aim; cinema producers and operators should have a choice of which method to use to meet language requirements (e.g. subtitling, dubbing); and exceptions should be available, such as for films produced or distributed

21 *The Ljubljana Guidelines on Integration of Diverse Societies*, guideline no. 49, p. 61.

22 'Address by Astrid Thors, OSCE High Commissioner on National Minorities to the 1102nd Plenary Meeting of the OSCE Permanent Council', 2 June 2016, <www.osce.org/hcnm/244281?download=true>, visited on 5 January 2018.

23 *See* for example 'Address by Knut Vollebaek, OSCE High Commissioner on National Minorities to the Seventh Winter Meeting of the OSCE Parliamentary Assembly, General Committee on Political Affairs and Security', 21 February 2008, <www.osce.org/hcnm/30872?download=true> visited on 5 January 2018; 'Address by Rolf Ekéus, OSCE High Commissioner on National Minorities, to the Sixth Winter Meeting of the OSCE Parliamentary Assembly', 22 February 2007, <www.osce.org/hcnm/24200?download=true>, visited on 5 January 2018.

in the languages of small minority communities, as unconditional translation requirements can place a burden on producers of minority-language programmes and films. While acknowledging compulsory dubbing of children's films into the State language as a widespread practice in many States, the HCNM has registered concerns regarding the availability of programmes and films for children in their own languages.

3 Other HCNM Tools to Promote Oslo Recommendation #12

In some cases the HCNM has provided not only critical feedback but also assistance with practical guidelines to ensure a balanced approach to the implementation of language legislation, including as concerns language regulation in the private sphere. In 2006 the HCNM published a guide for Latvian State language inspectors to assist in interpreting and applying language law provisions in accordance with international standards.[24] HCNM provided assistance to Tajikistan in the development of implementing guidelines for the State Language Law which came into force in 2009. The law, which addressed *inter alia* the use of languages in entrepreneurial activities, contained provisions which the HCNM felt were ambiguous and open to possible misinterpretation.[25] In 2010, the Slovakia authorities took up the HCNM recommendation to develop a detailed set of guidelines for the implementation of the amended Slovak State Language Law, the adoption of which had caused controversy within Slovakia and in its relations with Hungary.[26]

Balancing the advice to States not to encroach unnecessarily in the private sphere, the HCNM has consistently supported efforts to promote the State language and its acquisition by national minorities and has reminded minorities of their interest and responsibility to learn and use the State language. Such support has taken the shape of HCNM projects to promote teaching of the State language in State education systems and through adult training opportunities, in countries including Moldova, Georgia, Kyrgyzstan and Kazakhstan.

24 Press release, 'Guide for the State language inspectors presented in Riga with OSCE support', 15 November 2006, <http://www.osce.org/hcnm/47898>, visited on 5 January 2018.

25 'Statement by Knut Vollebaek, OSCE High Commissioner on National Minorities, to the 888th Plenary Meeting of the OSCE Permanent Council', 17 November 2011, <www.osce.org/hcnm/85212?download=true>, visited on 5 January 2018.

26 'Statement by Knut Vollebaek, OSCE High Commissioner on National Minorities, to the 813th Plenary Meeting of the OSCE Permanent Council', 17 June 2010, <www.osce.org/hcnm/68988?download=true>, visited on 5 January 2018.

One HCNM-supported initiative directly addressing the issue of languages in economic life is the Bujanovac Department of the Subotica Faculty of Economics of the University of Novi Sad. Since 2015, the Department has offered ethnic Serb and ethnic Albanian students the opportunity to study together and to obtain economics degrees through a multilingual curriculum. Thus if one were to describe the HCNM vision of Oslo Recommendation #12, it would not involve minority-owned private enterprises operating in a linguistic bubble; rather, it would involve participation in economic life facilitating interaction, communication and equal opportunities across a multilingual society.

4 Conclusion

Over the years, the HCNM has taken a consistent approach of discouraging regulation of language in private enterprises, except in very limited circumstances. Advice in this vein was provided to various OSCE participating States since the Oslo Recommendations were published, with particularly intense HCNM involvement on language legislation in Estonia and Latvia in the late 1990s and early 2000s. The first HCNM identified this issue as a potential source of tensions in those countries at the time and he was able to use the unique leverage provided by the EU accession process to advocate his position. However not all of the HCNM recommendations were taken on board, and the issue has not faded away in subsequent years. The Labour Law in Latvia has since been amended to require that employment contracts are drawn up in the Latvian language and to forbid employers from including foreign proficiency requirements in employment contracts or job advertisements unless it is reasonably necessary for performance of job duties.[27] In 2016, lobbying by transport companies and protests by taxi drivers led the Estonian parliament to amend legislation that would have required taxi drivers to show language proficiency certificates at B1 level to obtain transport operator licenses. However the language requirement remains in place and will continue to be enforced by language inspectors.[28] Such developments reflect not only the particular context in these countries, but also the continued relevance of HCNM recommendations in this area.

27 T. Sulmanis, 'Employment Law Review 2015: Latvia', 25 February 2015, <www.globalhrlaw.com/resources/employment-law-review-2015-latvia> visited on 5 January 2018.

28 Press release, 'Riigikogu removed requirement of language proficiency level for taxi drivers from Public Transport Act', 17 March 2016, <www.riigikogu.ee/en/sitting-reviews/riigikogu-removed-requirement-language-proficiency-level-taxi-drivers-public-transport-act/>, visited on 5 January 2018.

On balance, however, HCNM advice on language issues across the OSCE region has tended to focus more on the public sphere – for example, on issues related to the use of minority languages in public administration and to the linguistic balance in education. This may be an indicator that even when States may have been interested to take a more active approach to regulating and enforcing the use of language in the private sphere, they may have found doing so to be impractical or ultimately unnecessary. In some cases official or unofficial bilingualism eases the practical burden for private-sector actors and reduces the potential for tensions in this area. In addition, private companies and entrepreneurs are likely to be pragmatic and to conduct business in whatever languages will yield the most profits and the least bureaucratic hassles. As the saying goes, money talks – sometimes without any language at all. Globalization is also making multilingualism not a choice but a necessity for many companies, and today's technology may make it easier for businesses to accommodate different languages than was the case when the Oslo Recommendations were drafted.

From an integration perspective, as pointed out in the HCNM Ljubljana Guidelines, ensuring equal opportunities for all to participate in and contribute to the economy requires States to take proactive measures and to consider the potential impact of language and other requirements on such opportunities. The Ljubljana Guidelines also note that actors in the private sector, including employers, trade unions and private media, can play a key role in contributing to integration policies. In addition to continuing to provide relevant advice to OSCE participating States, in future the HCNM could increase contacts with private-sector actors to hear their concerns and to encourage their engagement in integration efforts, such as through valuing multilingualism in the labour market and providing opportunities to learn and use the State language and minority languages at the workplace. As the HCNM stated in 2008 while discussing how to engage the private sector in conflict prevention, "Good inter-ethnic relations, especially respect for the rights of minorities, within a country is simply good business policy".[29]

29 'Bringing Communities Together', Speech by Knut Vollebaek, OSCE High Commissioner on National Minorities, to the Fredskorpset (FK) North-South Forum 2008 'Dialogue and Development', Oslo, 4 September 2008, <www.osce.org/hcnm/33314?download=true>, visited on 5 January 2018.

CHAPTER 5

The Intersection of Language and Religion in the Context of National Minorities

Asa Solway and Alessandro Rotta

1 Introduction

Language and religion are often central to the formation and identity of individuals and communities. The right to maintain and develop an identity, including through the use of language and the practice of religion, is also recognized in international law as a fundamental pillar of protection for national minorities.[1] These elements can also come to define the differences between majority and minority communities which may speak different languages or practice different religions. As noted by the Organization for Security and Co-operation in Europe ('OSCE') High Commissioner on National Minorities ('HCNM'), language, as much or more than religion, "serves as a means of unity of the group and source of self-identification of the individual".[2] Promoting and protecting this identity, as recognized by the United Nations, can "prevent forced assimilation and the loss of cultures, religions and languages – the basis of the richness of the world and therefore part of its heritage".[3] This article outlines the legal and policy framework governing language and religion with a focus on the intersection of the two in the context of national minorities. It does not purport to provide a comprehensive summary of every instance in which language or religion are important to the lives of national minorities, but considers, through an analysis of relevant international standards, empirical examples and the work of the HCNM and other actors, the intersection of language and religion as an issue of concern in the context of national minorities.

---

* The views expressed in this chapter are those of the authors, and do not necessarily represent those of the High Commissioner on National Minorities.

1 OSCE HCNM, *Report on the Linguistic Rights of Persons Belonging to National Minorities in the OSCE Area* (March 1999), p. 8.

2 *Ibid.*, p. 3.

3 UN OHCHR, *Minority Rights: International Standards and Guidance for Implementation* (2010) p. 8.

© KONINKLIJKE BRILL NV, LEIDEN, 2018 | DOI 10.1163/9789004357754_006

The article finds that the intersection of language and religion has warranted the attention of international actors in relatively few circumstances and where such attention has been paid it involves the use of language in religious services. International institutions or bodies, including the HCNM, the United Nations, and the Advisory Committee of the Framework Convention on National Minorities ('FCNM'), have addressed this issue to a limited extent and also focused, to a degree, on the issue of religious services. While there is a more significant body of scholarship on the relationship between religion and language outlined in other disciplines, a review of policy, legal and rights-based frameworks addressing national minorities, including the HCNM *Oslo Recommendations regarding the Linguistic Rights of National Minorities* ('Oslo Recommendations'), devote relatively little attention to the interplay between the two issues. Despite this lack of attention, it is clear that these two dimensions elicit strong conceptions of national or ethnic identity and are fundamental to the process of self-identification for national minorities. It is necessary, however, to separate situations in which language and religion are both features of a conflict without directly impacting on each other and where there is a genuine relationship between the two which merits specific attention. This article studies the latter circumstance with the intent to better understand how policy or legal frameworks can effectively engage with the roles and rights of national minorities including with respect to the use of language in religious services.

As a final note, the primary focus of this article is to consider the applicability of international law and practice and, accordingly, it does not carry out an extensive survey of domestic legislation. Nor does the article deal with the issue of education, which is often considered as a separate topic of discussion, although the issue of teaching of a specific language in religious schools is relevant to the subject matter.

2 Legal and Policy Framework

The importance of language and religion to the identity of national minorities is outlined in the international framework setting out the rights of national minorities and their interaction with state authorities.[4] Where international law addresses the two issues as inter-related, it often focuses on the use of language

4 This article sets out to consider the relation between language and religion in the context of the larger field of minority rights, which is primarily outlined in international law and policy. Accordingly, it is not within the scope of this analysis to set out or consider approaches by individual States towards language and religion.

in religious services or ceremonies and also tends to reflect the importance of both religion and language as central to the identity and existence of national minorities.

The guiding human rights principles of the OSCE consider the interrelation between language and religion in the context of national minorities including the right to express, preserve and develop a 'linguistic or religious identity' and to conduct religious educational activities in another tongue.[5] Protections afforded by international human rights law similarly place language and religion in the same context and afford similar protections.[6] The UN Human Rights Committee has established that under customary international law minorities have the right to enjoy their own culture, profess their own religion, or use their own language.[7] In general, international law requires that States should not impose any restrictions on the use of language or manifestation of religion in private or public life and, where such restrictions are imposed in the public sphere they should be necessary and proportionate.[8]

Language and religion are also addressed in the legal framework of the Council of Europe, including the FCNM, which, taking a proactive approach, recommends that States should "where appropriate, take measures in the

---

5 OSCE, *Document of the Copenhagen Meeting of the Conference on the Human Dimension of the CSCE* ('Copenhagen Document') (29 June 1990), paras. 32, 32.1, 32.2 and 32.3. *See also* Copenhagen Document, para 25.4, on non-discrimination.

6 *See* for example: General Assembly, *International Covenant on Civil and Political Rights*, G.A. res. 2200A (XXI) of 19 December 1966, 21 U.N. GAOR Supp. (No. 16) ('ICCPR'), Article 27; General Assembly, *International Covenant on Economic, Social and Cultural Rights*, 16 December 1966, United Nations, Treaty Series, vol. 993, p. 3, Article 2(2); General Assembly, *Declaration on the Rights of Persons Belonging to National or Ethnic, Religious and Linguistic Minorities*, 3 February 1992, A/RES/47/135 ('UN Declaration on Minorities'), Article 2(1). International treaties and instruments outline additional provisions on the protection of language and religion and this should not be viewed as an exhaustive list.

7 UN Human Rights Committee, *General Comment No. 24: Issues relating to reservations made upon ratification or accession to the Covenant or the Optional Protocols thereto, or in relation to declarations under article 41 of the Covenant*, 4 November 1994, para. 8 in Report of the Human Rights Committee, UN GAOR, 50th Sess., Supp. No 40, Annex V, at 124, UN Doc. A/50/40 (1995).

8 *See* HCNM, *Oslo Recommendations regarding the Linguistic Rights of National Minorities* (1998) ('Oslo Recommendations') p. 16; ICCPR, Articles 18(1) and 27; UN Declaration on Minorities, Articles 2, 3(1); Council of Europe, *European Convention for the Protection of Human Rights and Fundamental Freedoms*, as amended by Protocols Nos. 11 and 14, 4 November 1950, ETS 5 ('ECHR'), Article 9(2); Council of Europe, *Framework Convention for the Protection of National Minorities*, 1 February 1995, ETS 157 ('FCNM'), Articles 8, 10(1), 19; OSCE ODIHR, *Guidelines on the Legal Personality of Religious or Belief Communities* (2014), p. 10.

fields of education and research to foster knowledge of the [...] language and religion of their national minorities and of the majority".[9] The European Court of Human Rights ('ECtHR') has also affirmed, to a more limited degree, the right of minorities to preserve and promote their own culture including through language and religion. While the European Convention for Human Rights ('ECHR') contains limited references to national minorities, relating to general prohibitions against discrimination,[10] the ECtHR has considered issues related to language and religion through protections afforded on the basis of freedom of religion and freedom of expression.[11] With respect to religious ceremonies the Court has found that "the right of a religious community to an autonomous existence is at the very heart of the guarantees in Article 9 of the [European Convention]".[12] While the jurisprudence of the ECtHR does not *per se* guarantee the right to use a particular language in relations with public authorities, it has found a violation has occurred where an undue restriction was imposed by a state on the use of language.[13] The UN Human Rights Committee has also found that the "observance and practice of religion or belief may include not only ceremonial acts but also ... the use of a particular language customarily spoken by a group".[14]

The recommendations and guidelines of the HCNM also outline relevant international law and policy in spelling out the relationship, and importance, of language and religion to national minorities. This includes the clearly defined right for individuals and communities to manifest their religion and speak their language in both public and private life[15] and that each person, in practicing his or religion, "shall be entitled to use the language(s) of his or her

9 FCNM, Article 12.

10 ECHR, Article 14.

11 ECHR, Articles 9, 10.

12 *Izzetin Doğan and Others* v. *Turkey*, no. 62649/10, § 93, European Court of Human Rights ('ECtHR') 2016.

13 *See* Council of Europe Research Division, *Cultural Rights in the case-law of the European Court of Human Rights* (January 2017) p. 23.

14 UN Human Rights Committee, *CCPR General Comment No. 22: Article 18 (Freedom of Thought, Conscience or Religion)*, 30 July 1993, CCPR/C/21/Rev.1/Add.4 ("General Comment No. 22") para. 4.

15 OSCE HCNM, *The Ljubljana Guidelines on Integration of Diverse Societies* (2012) ('Ljubljana Guidelines'), pp. 51–52. The ECtHR has also found that "the believer's right to freedom of religion encompasses the expectation that the community will be allowed to function peacefully, free from arbitrary State intervention. Indeed, the autonomous existence of religious communities is indispensable for pluralism in a democratic society and is thus an issue at the very heart of the protection, which Article 9 affords". *Hasan and Chaush v. Bulgaria*, no. 30985/96, ECtHR 2000.

choice".[16] The Ljubljana Guidelines conclude that States are "obliged to promote the rights of persons belonging to minorities to effectively participate in public affairs and to maintain their identities by providing adequate opportunities to develop their culture, to use their language and to practise their religion".[17] The Oslo Recommendations, in considering applicable rights and protections, expand on the fundamental relationship between language and religion and their importance in the formation of minority (as well as majority) identity and culture. Noting that "the practice of religion is often especially closely related to the preservation of cultural and linguistic identity", the Oslo Recommendations assert that the "right to use a minority language in public worship is as inherent as the right to establish religious institutions and the right to public worship itself".[18]

3 Case Studies

The above summary of international law and standards suggests that the use of language and the practice of religion are interrelated and an area of concern in the protection of minority rights. A survey of the work of the HCNM, and of international organizations more broadly, however, suggests that the direct interaction of the two issues is limited to specific and relatively defined circumstances. The Ljubljana Guidelines, for example, observe that activities carried out by States which may lead to violations of religious and linguistic rights could include "disproportionate limitations on the public display of cultural or religious symbols and clothing" and "undue restrictions on what language(s) can be used during cultural or religious events".[19] Accordingly, a review of examples suggests that access to church services in the language of a national minority appears as the most persistent area in which the rights of national minorities may be violated. These rights are enumerated within the previously discussed international legal framework on national minorities and, in particular, in the context of freedom of religion and the protection of worship, observance, practice and teaching.[20] This reality may be reflected in

16 Oslo Recommendations, p. 5.

17 Ljubljana Guidelines, p. 12 citing *inter alia* ICCPR, Article 27; UN Declaration on Minorities, Articles 1, 2(2) and 2(3); Copenhagen Document, paras 33, 35; FCNM, Articles 5(1), 8 and 10–15.

18 Oslo Recommendations, p. 16.

19 Ljubljana Guidelines, p. 51.

20 *See* P. Taylor, *Freedom of Religion: UN and European Human Rights Law and Practice* (Cambridge University Press, 2005) p. 278; General Assembly, *Declaration on the Elimination*

the conclusion that "one of *the most important linguistic human rights* would be that of having the chance to attend public religious service in one's own mother tongue and to live one's religious life in the very same language".[21] The findings below reflect this reality and suggest that violations of rights, as a possible source of tensions, are most likely to occur where distinct (although possibly related) churches operate in the same jurisdiction but utilize different languages.

The use of the Romanian language in church services in eastern Serbia has served as an emblematic example of possible tensions associated with the use of language in the context of religious services. The Advisory Committee of the FCNM, in its Second Opinion on Serbia, reported concerns over interruptions in Romanian language services in Romanian Orthodox Churches in eastern Serbia including instances of harassment of priests belonging to the Vlach-Romanian minorities which raised issues related to Article 8 of FCNM.[22] These concerns were reiterated in the Third Opinion on Serbia, with the Advisory Committee noting that "due to issues relating to the (absence of a) right of the Romanian Orthodox church to operate in certain parts of Serbian territory, persons belonging to the Vlach/Romanian minority/minorities do not always have access to worship in the language of their choice" while also observing that "members of the Bulgarian national minority have also requested access to worship in their mother tongue".[23] The HCNM has also considered this issue in a statement to the Permanent Council of the OSCE, noting that "access to church services in the Romanian language – the situation remains difficult … I therefore continue to encourage the two Churches to establish a constructive dialogue on issues of interest to them and the communities affected. Independently of this dialogue and its outcome, however, the State should provide the appropriate framework based on its obligations".[24]

---

of All Forms of Intolerance and of Discrimination on Religion or Belief, A/RES/36/55 (25 November 1981), Article 6(h); ICCPR, Article 18.

21 S. Szilágyi, "Linguistic rights and language use in church – the question of Hungarian masses in Moldavia" in L. Peti and V. Támczps (eds.), *Language Use, Attitudes, Strategies. Linguistic Identity and Ethnicity in the Moldavian Csángós Villages* (Cluj-Napoca: The Romanian Institute for Research on National Minorities, 2012) p. 197 (emphasis in original quotation).

22 Council of Europe Advisory Committee on the Framework Convention for the Protection of National Minorities ('Advisory Committee'), *Second Opinion on Serbia*, 2 February 2016, para. 144.

23 Advisory Committee, *Third Opinion on Serbia*, 23 June 2014 ('Third Opinion'), para. 120.

24 Report by K. Vollebaek, OSCE HCNM, *960th Meeting of the OSCE Permanent Council*, Vienna (11 July 2013).

The dispute over languages in eastern Serbia is multifaceted and involves a number of overlapping issues. In general, there "is an understanding between orthodox churches that orthodox churches may operate on canonical territory of another orthodox church solely upon its approval".[25] The Serbian *Law on Churches and Religious Communities* recognizes five traditional churches and two traditional religious communities[26] while preventing the registration and operation of other churches with a name similar to traditional churches unless otherwise approved by a pre-existing or recognised church.[27] Lack of registration prevents acquisition of legal personality, tax exemptions and the right to construct religious buildings.[28] In addition to the seven groups mentioned above, Serbia "grants traditional status, solely in Vojvodina Province, to the Diocese of Dacia Felix of the Romanian Orthodox Church, with its seat in Romania and administrative seat in Vršac in Vojvodina but not in eastern Serbia".[29] The Advisory Committee of the FNCM recommended, in order to solve the dispute, that there should be "finding of pragmatic solutions in all cases where these could help resolve difficulties in access of persons belonging to national minorities to worship in their mother tongue".[30] According to recent reports the Romanian Orthodox Church "which the government recognized as a traditional group solely in Vojvodina Province, [was able to] hold services in the Romanian language in eastern Serbia".[31] Language, however, serves as a small portion of a larger, more challenging set of issues between the Serbian Orthodox Church and Romanian Orthodox Church, as questions of

25 International and Security Affairs Centre, *Serbian-Romanian Relations and the Status of the Vlach Minority in Serbia* (Belgrade 2015) p. 63.

26 The five traditional churches are: the Serbian Orthodox Church, the Roman Catholic Church, the Slovak Evangelical Church, the Christian Reformed Church and the Evangelical Christian Church; the traditional religious communities are the Islamic Religious Community and the Jewish Religious Community; Official Gazette of the Republic of Serbia, no. 36/06, *Act on Churches and Religious Communities*, Article 10.

27 See International and Security Affairs Centre, *supra* note 26, p. 61; *Act on Churches and Religious Communities*, *supra* note 27, Article 19.

28 R. Hofmann, D. Jilek and F. Palermo, *Expert Report on the Situation of Minority Rights in the Republic of Serbia* (14 September 2012) p. 14.

29 United States Department of State, Bureau of Democracy, Human Rights and Labor, *International Religious Freedom Report for 2016: Serbia*; Act on Churches and Religious Communities, *supra* note 27, Article 10.

30 Third Opinion, *supra* note 24, para. 123.

31 United States Department of State, Bureau of Democracy, Human Rights and Labor, *International Religious Freedom Report for 2015*, Serbia, p. 4.

property, construction of new churches, national identity, church jurisdiction, naming and other issues remain unresolved.[32]

In addition to the situation in Serbia, the Vlach community in the former Yugoslav Republic of Macedonia have faced challenges in registering their religious community resulting in the inability to hold religious services in the Vlach language.[33] Additional examples of such restrictions include "Orthodox priests [being allegedly] subject to pressure by the authorities to conduct their liturgy in Albanian rather than in Greek [in Albania]".[34] These various examples illustrate a recurrent theme which may lead to disputes, namely where there is a claim of exclusive, or semi-exclusive, canonical jurisdiction, for example by Serbian, Russian or other orthodox churches, and an implied prerogative to use a specific language, such as Old Church Slavonic. Newly independent states, or changing circumstances within a state which may impact national minorities, may be particularly likely to promote the use of an official or state language in various spheres including religious life.

Tensions can also occur directly between a national minority and a religious institution with respect to the use of language in church services. In Moldova, for example, the "Roman Catholic Episcopate of Jászvásár (Iaşi) even after 1989 continuously refused the Csángós' [a group of Roman Catholic faith] demands regarding the Hungarian mass in their villages all divine services being held in a compulsory fashion in the Romanian language".[35] In this circumstance, the author points to the Oslo Recommendations and international law to establish that the decision to hold religious services in a specific language is left to the discretion of the church in which the service is held, and that the State should not intervene in such decisions.[36] In such an instance, the question becomes an internal source of potential tension, one in which a national minority desires the use of a certain language disallowed by the church to which the minority belongs. The origins of this dispute, moreover, are deep rooted and originated where language was used as a tool for religious conversion in the 17th Century when "the Vatican ordered Polish and Italian priests ... who did

32 *See* R. Hofmann, D. Jilek and F. Palermo, *supra* note 29, pp. 15–16; International and Security Affairs Centre *supra* note 26, pp. 60–66.

33 *See* International Helsinki Federation for Human Rights (IHF), *Human Rights in the OSCE Region Report* (2001), p. 218; IHF, *Human Rights in the OSCE Region Report* (2002) p. 223.

34 Economic and Social Council Commission on Human Rights, *Implementation of the Declaration on the Elimination of All Forms of Intolerance and of Discrimination Based on Religion or Belief*, UN Doc. E/CN.4/1995/91 (22 December 1994) p. 9.

35 S. Szilágyi, *supra* note 22, pp. 197–198.

36 *Ibid.*, p. 198.

not speak Hungarian, and who gradually made the Csángós get accustomed to the lack of the Hungarian language in the religious service".[37]

Disputes between churches within a country (or countries) often include language, but the previous examples suggest that restrictions on language occur within the context of State restrictions on the use and practice of specific religions. Additional disagreements, accordingly, may arise in the context of a religious dispute with respect to property, jurisdiction, national legislation or a range of other issues. Restrictions on language, in such circumstances, may be implemented to impact the practice of religion. An inverse situation could also arise in which language restrictions intentionally or inadvertently lead to violations of religious rights. For example, in Ukraine, ongoing disputes are present between the Moscow Patriarchate and Kyiv Patriarchate relating, in particular, to property disputes[38] and not necessarily with respect to language.[39] A change in circumstances could arise if restrictions on the use of the Russian language, or obligations to use the Ukrainian language, were implemented and led to restrictions on the use of such language in the Moscow Patriarchate. A survey of empirical examples, however, suggests the latter situation is less prevalent.

Where language becomes a source of dispute in the context of church services, a specific legal question may initially be examined – namely, can one

37 J. Kiss, *On the Hungarian Language use of the Moldavian Csángós*, in L. Peti and V. Támczps, *supra* note 22, p. 115.

38 *See* OSCE Special Monitoring Mission to Ukraine, *Thematic Report: The Impact of the Crisis in Ukraine on its Western Regions* (30 March 2015), p. 5: "[I]n the Ivano-Frankivsk region, the SMM witnessed two disputes in Kosiv and Kolomyya between local authorities and the Ukrainian Orthodox Church – Moscow Patriarchate. Both cases revolved around property disputes, which originate from Ukraine's independence but their revival is viewed by some interlocutors as linked to the ongoing conflict. In the Chernivtsi region, several church communities in villages transferred from the Ukrainian Orthodox Church – Moscow Patriarchate to the Ukrainian Orthodox Church – Kyiv Patriarchate as well. Finally, from amongst the minority communities, the Jewish community organized a performance held in Lviv city against what they said was the Russian Federation's attempt to divide the Ukrainian people".

39 *See* for example A. Markovich, "As more Ukrainians choose Kyiv Patriarchate, push intensifies for unified national Orthodox church", *Kyiv Post*, 23 June 2016 stating "[t]he Kyiv Patriarchate mostly holds their services in modern Ukrainian, while the Moscow Patriarchate – in Church Slavonic or modern Russian. When asked if the divide between the patriarchates was language-based, Dmytriev and Zoria explained that language was not the deciding factor. Like the political divide, language is only [an] element of Ukrainian nationalism, but Russian speakers are not necessarily shamed … some Kyiv Patriarchate churches hold services in Russian if that is the language their congregation speaks".

infer the creation of additional language rights on the basis of freedom of religion and rights associated with autonomy over religious proceedings. The inverse situation, in which religious rights might be guaranteed on the basis of freedom of the right to use a language, lacks empirical examples and appears to be less likely to occur in the context of national minorities. While the right to use a language in religious proceedings may be protected by freedom of religion, the international human rights regime, as previously discussed, also prevents unnecessary state interference into the use of language and guarantees the right to use language in the private sphere. This lessens the necessity for language rights to be incorporated into protections for freedom of religion.

The extent to which freedom of religion may create additional space for the use of languages, however, is articulated most clearly by the Human Rights Committee's pronouncement that "freedom to manifest religion or belief in worship, observance, practice and teaching encompasses a broad range of acts" including "the use of a particular language customarily spoken by a group".[40] While the protection for the use of language in a religious space may be duplicative, these protections reinforce empirical findings that the most likely source of tensions, including inter-ethnic, or rights violations in the context of language and religion, emanates from the use of languages in religious services. This is further reflected in international policy and law, including in the findings of the HCNM, which focus on the use of language in religious ceremonies as a protected right.

4 Widening the Perspective

The intersection of language and religion in the context of national minorities, from a legal and policy perspective, suggests that where tensions or concerns may arise they will usually involve disagreements over the use of language in religious services. The legal framework protecting the rights of national minorities adequately accounts for this scenario by not only protecting each right separately, but also explicitly providing for the right to use language in religious services. But the question arises whether this is the extent to which these two issues intersect, or whether further consideration would illuminate other important connections and interrelations. In this regard, sociological, anthropological and political science studies may indicate future avenues of

40 General Comment No. 22, *supra* note 15, para. 4.

research and contribute to an understanding of the development and dynamics of national minority communities.

Research in the field of sociology and politics will often, by design, focus on different questions related to the impact of language on religion, and vice versa, attempting to answer potentially fundamental questions about identity while considering a broader set of issues outside of minority rights and protections.[41] While one of the earliest, and most well regarded, definitions of national minorities incorporates concepts of sociology to outline which groups should be protected, sociology often frames and analyzes the relationship between language and religion in a different context.[42] Sociologists, for example, may begin with a very different starting point, in attempting to compare the meaning and function of language versus religion to human beings. This may lead, for example, to findings that "language is a pervasive, inescapable medium of social interaction, religion is not" and that "public life can be a-religious, but not a-linguistic".[43] The author of these findings, interestingly, concludes that "religious pluralism tends to be more intergenerationally robust and more deeply institutionalized than linguistic pluralism in contemporary societies, [...] entails deeper and more divisive forms of diversity [and] tended to displace language as the cutting edge of contestation over the political accommodation of cultural difference – a striking reversal of the longer-term historical process through which language had previously displaced religion as the primary focus of contention".[44] Different eras have also seen different relations between language and religion, with aspirations for statehood in the 19th century often conceived of "in terms of ethnic nationalism based on language; and linguistic claims were often based on a legitimating connection with religion" which led to the Bulgarian, Macedonian and Serbian languages

41 *See*, for example, J. Darquennes and W. Vandenbussche (eds.), 25 *Sociolinguistica* (January 2011); R. Brubaker, "Language, Religion, and the Politics of Difference", *19 Nations and Nationalism* (2013).

42 The international community, in general, agrees that there is no single definition of a national minority. Fracesco Caporti's attempt to define national minorities stands as one of the nearest attempts, defining national minorities as "[a] group numerically inferior to the rest of the population of a State, in a non-dominant position, whose members, being nationals of the state, possess ethnic, religious or linguistic characteristics differing from those of the rest of the population and show, if only implicitly, a sense of solidarity, directed towards preserving their culture, traditions, religion, or language", F. Capotorti, *Study on the Rights of Persons belonging to Ethnic, Religious and Linguistic Minorities*, U.N. Doc. E/CN/.4/Sub.2/384/Rev.1 (1979).

43 Brubaker, *supra* note 42, p. 9.

44 *Ibid.*

all advancing "mutually excluding claims to the unbroken continuity of their national language with Old Church Slavonic".[45]

Sociological and social sciences' studies as those mentioned above may therefore provide additional context and understanding for how and why language and religion are important, and connected, to national minorities. They offer a different, possibly richer, frame of understanding than international legal frameworks, which equate religion and language as traits of national minority communities situated as similar rights to be protected. Moving forward, lawyers and policy makers may wish to incorporate such ideas into their work in order to better understand the relation between language and religion and to identify other relevant features for national minorities in the interplay between the two. For example, and as noted above, this article has identified that disputes over language in the context of church or religious ceremonies appears to be the primary area of focus when considering the relationship between language and religion for international actors focused on national minorities. Sociological studies of language and religion may in fact reinforce this finding and some authors have explicitly considered that the combination of language and religion could be referred to as 'religious language' which "is mainly meant to allow the learner, the writer or the scholar to participate in religious custom".[46] This finding can be compared to the protections afforded to the use of language in religious ceremonies in international law and policy.[47]

Additional avenues of investigation may also be warranted, including findings by sociologists relating to "religious discourse [which could] include the political exploitation of religious language and the nature of religious meaning expressed linguistically".[48] This may apply in the case of Ukraine, as previously discussed, where political considerations related to the use of the Russian language may be exploited in order to impact the Moscow Patriarchate, or vice versa. Sociology may also assist in developing a framework to consider racial or ethnic discrimination against national minorities on the basis *inter alia* of language such that while "biological racist discourses have declined, racism derived from perceptions of cultural and religious superiority has emerged as a

45 W. Safran, 'Language, ethnicity and religion: a complex and persistent linkage', *Nations and Nationalism* 14 (2008) p. 10 *citing* T. Kamuela, 'On the Similarity Between the Concepts of Nation and Language', 31*Canadian Review of Studies in Nationalism* (2004) pp. 107–112.

46 J. Darquennes and W. Vandenbussche, *supra* note 42, p. 6 *citing* Colin Baker, *A Parents' and Teachers' Guide to Bilingualism*, 2nd Edition (2000), pp. 178–179.

47 See for example Oslo Recommendations, p. 16; General Comment No. 22, *supra* note 14, para. 4.

48 J. Darquennes and W. Vandenbussche, *supra* note 42, p. 7 *citing* Paul Chilton, *Analysing Political Discourse: Theory and practice*, (Routledge, 2004).

dominant form of racism worldwide" and this racism does "not even mention the word 'race' [and] draws links between physical characteristics and perceived social customs, manners and behavior, religious and moral beliefs, as well as [...] language".[49] In this manner, language may be used to infer the presence of a specific religion leading to discrimination, for example, the "willingness to communicate publicly in a language (Arabic) associated with Islam, as well as 'looking Muslim', is correlated with being 'religiously Muslim'".[50] While empirical examples and the work of international organizations do not appear to strongly engage with this possibility, it is an area worthy of future consideration which may need to be addressed through relevant legal and policy frameworks.

5 Glancing Ahead

This article finds that the international framework governing the overlap and intersection of language and religion rights of national minorities is relatively robust. Despite this, the actual number of situations in which the linguistic and religious rights of national minorities, exercised in tandem, are directly infringed appears to be limited and relates, primarily, to issues of language in religious services. This specific issue is directly addressed in numerous international instruments and commentaries, as outlined in this article. The intersection of language and religion, however, remains understudied and lawyers, policy makers, human rights advocates and others should continue to expand on international law and policy, including the conclusions contained in the Oslo Recommendations, with respect to the relationship between language and religion in the context of national minorities. This should be supplemented by sociological and socio-political perspectives which may broaden the manner in which language and religion may impact national minorities.

49 C. Considine, "The Racialization of Islam in the United States: Islamophobia, Hate Crimes, and Flying while Brown", 8 *Religions* (2017) p. 8.

50 *Ibid.*, p. 13.

CHAPTER 6

HCNM Recommendations on the Use of Minority Languages in the Broadcast Media as a Baseline for Context-specific Advice to Participating States

Sarah Stephan and Dmitry Nurumov

1 Introduction

Being an instrument of conflict prevention at the earliest possible stage, the HCNM offers advice and assistance to the OSCE's participating States, through means of quiet diplomacy but also by synthesizing the institution's experiences into thematic Recommendations and Guidelines. The HCNM's thematic Recommendations and Guidelines provide policymakers and States' representatives with guiding principles and practical advice for developing policies which alleviate inter-ethnic tensions and contribute to building resilient multiethnic societies. Many of the policy areas addressed by the HCNM's thematic Recommendations and Guidelines intersect. It seems fair to argue, however, that language plays a central role across the board. High Commissioner Knut Vollebaek illustrated this very practically in one of his addresses to the OSCE's Permanent Council:

> [b]ilingual or multilingual education equips children with an adequate knowledge of both their mother tongue and the State language. Subtitling, rather than the dubbing of news bulletins, movies, talk shows and other broadcasts, meets multiple linguistic needs. Ballot papers and election materials distributed in both the State and minority languages increase turnout and, ultimately, election legitimacy. Public services in minority languages, particularly at the local level, enhance the sense of belonging amongst minorities. A simple greeting in a minority language by a police officer can make friends and improve community safety.[1]

* The views expressed in this article are those of the authors alone and do not necessarily represent the official view of the OSCE HCNM.

1 Statement by Knut Vollebaek, OSCE High Commissioner on National Minorities, to the 778th Plenary Meeting of the OSCE Permanent Council, Vienna, 29 October 2009, p. 1.

© KONINKLIJKE BRILL NV, LEIDEN, 2018 | DOI 10.1163/9789004357754_007

Because language is a personal matter closely connected with identity on the one hand, and an essential tool of social organization which bears on numerous aspects of a State's functioning on the other hand, failure to achieve the appropriate balance may be a source of inter-ethnic tension.[2] The 1998 Oslo Recommendations on the Linguistic Rights of National Minorities, to which 20th anniversary the current volume is dedicated, thus touch upon the use of languages in many areas of public and private life. Of course, the linguistic rights of persons belonging to national minorities emanate from international human rights law. Language is inherently linked to the exercise of numerous fundamental rights, such as the rights to effective participation, education, access to justice and not least to the freedom of expression as enshrined in International Human Rights Law.[3] The freedom of expression entails that persons belonging to minorities have the right to receive and impart information also in their own languages and shall not be discriminated in this respect in their access to media.[4] It is this issue, the use of minority languages in the media, broadcast media more specifically, which this article seeks to address. It is one of many intersections where language rights meet a densely regulated policy area that can play a crucial role in conflict prevention.

To begin with, it should be mentioned that language is not the only issue related to media that can cause or contribute to interethnic tension – the treatment of minority and interethnic issues in the media[5] as well as the participation of persons belonging to national minorities in decision-making processes concerning the media[6] are likewise of concern from the perspective of conflict prevention. What is equally important is the positive role that media can play in shaping perceptions, combating discrimination and promoting the

2 *The Oslo Recommendation regarding the Linguistic Rights of National Minorities and Explanatory Note*, p. 2.

3 *Cf. i.a.* Article 19 Universal Declaration of Human Rights, Article 19 International Covenant on Civil and Political Rights, Article 10 European Convention for the Protection of Human Rights and Fundamental Freedoms and Article 11 Charter of Fundamental Rights of the European Union.

4 Article 9 (1) of the Framework Convention for the Protection of National Minorities (FCNM) spells out the intersection between the freedom of expression, language and access to media: "[…] the freedom of expression of every person belonging to a national minority includes freedom to hold opinions and to receive and impart information and ideas in the minority language, without interference by public authorities and regardless of frontiers. The Parties shall ensure, within the framework of their legal systems, that persons belonging to a national minority are not discriminated against in their access to the media".

5 *The Ljubljana Guidelines on the Integration of Diverse Societies*, guideline 48.

6 *The Oslo Recommendations regarding the Linguistic Rights of National Minorities*, recommendation 10.

integration of diverse societies.[7] Furthermore, issues relating to content or language use do not only concern broadcast media but arise with regard to the press and other types of media. HCNM has held that no limitations solely on language choice are permitted for print and internet-based media.[8] While internet-based media is increasingly blurring many lines, including between print and audio-visual content, traditional minority-language print media faces their own set of challenges. These may not be adequately addressed by the negative obligation not to restrict the creation and use of print media but requires facilitative measures.[9]

That said, the use of minority languages in broadcast media was singled out early on by the HCNM to warrant particular attention being "an important industry with substantial investment costs, both the market dimensions of the broadcast media ... and its substantial regulation pose challenges for speakers of minority languages, especially numerically small or geographically dispersed groups".[10] And indeed the HCNM observed and continues to observe that disputes arise where regulation effectively limits, and sometimes practically excludes, the use of minority languages in radio and television broadcasting, typically through licensing requirements and quotas aimed at promoting the official/State language. Tarlach McGonagle, a principle expert involved in the elaboration of the Guidelines on the use of Minority Languages in the Broadcast Media, which shall be scrutinized further below, summarized that "[t]he key concern here is determining – in light of all relevant circumstances – the cut-off point at which a prescription favouring the use of one language becomes a restriction on the use of others".[11] While it may be a difficult balance it is hardly a zero-sum game and the HCNM has advocated for diversity also with regard to the use of languages in the broadcast media.

2 Thematic Recommendations

The Oslo Recommendations were published in 1998 and are formulated in the language of rights and respective obligations of the State. It is worth noting

7 *The Ljubljana Guidelines on the Integration of Diverse Societies*, guideline 49.

8 *Ibid.*, guideline 61.

9 FCNM Art. 9(3); Advisory Committee on the Framework Convention, *Thematic Commentary No. 3 on the Language Rights of Persons Belonging to National Minorities under the Framework Convention*, para. 47.

10 J. Packer and S. Holt, 'Editorial', 8 *Mercator Media Forum* (2005), p. 2.

11 T. McGonagle, "Introduction to and Summary of the Survey of State Practice: Minority-Language Related Broadcasting and Legislation in the OSCE", 8 *Mercator Media Forum* (2005), p. 93.

that at the time of drafting, there were no legally binding instruments addressing the linguistic rights of national minorities. The Framework Convention for the Protection of National Minorities and the European Charter for Regional or Minority Languages were open for ratification but had not yet entered into force at the time. In fact, they did so more or less simultaneously with the publication of the Oslo Recommendations, in February and March 1998 respectively. It has been observed about the time that followed that

> [...] the practical application of the Framework Convention remained largely undetermined for most of the first decade of the HCNM's mandate. This diffuse normative context meant that there was little practical guidance that the HCNM could call upon as he began his work to diffuse minority/majority tensions. Existing normative frameworks did not provide sufficient answers to concrete policy dilemmas much beyond the general requirement to "respect the rights of persons belonging to minorities". Yet it was precisely this sort of specific policy guidance that OSCE [participating] States required from the HCNM ... This declared goal suggests that [first High Commissioner] Max van der Stoel understood himself to be engaged in norm entrepreneurship and regarded this activity as a necessary and legitimate part of his mandate.[12]

With the exception of linguistic rights in education, which the drafters felt were sufficiently covered by the 1996 Hague Recommendations Regarding the Education Rights of National Minorities, the Oslo Recommendations constitute a comprehensive but not exhaustive catalogue of the linguistic rights of persons belonging to national minorities. The Oslo Recommendations address those media-related linguistic rights which, in the experience of the HCNM at the time of drafting, had proven to be at the highest risk of arbitrary curtailment or restriction by the State and thus are prone to generate tensions.

Access to minority language broadcast media is rarely restricted with the outright justification of limiting the use of one or more minority languages but based on a range of pretexts, such as a scarcity of broadcasting frequencies, national security consideration, the need to ensure formal equality, the need to promote the official or State language or a lack of funds. While these as such may be legitimate aims, policies which in effect restrict the use of minority languages in broadcast media are often not proportionate to these aims.

The Oslo Recommendations advise that

12 J. Jackson-Preece, "The High Commissioner on National Minorities as a Normative Actor", 12:3 *Journal on Ethnopolitics and Minority Issues in Europe* (2013), p. 78 *et seq.*

> (8) [p]ersons belonging to national minorities have the right to establish and maintain their own minority language media. State regulation of the broadcast media shall be based on objective and non-discriminatory criteria and shall not be used to restrict enjoyment of minority rights.
> (9) Persons belonging to national minorities should have access to broadcast time in their own language on publicly funded media. At national, regional and local levels the amount and quality of time allocated to broadcasting in the language of a given minority should be commensurate with the numerical size and concentration of the national minority and appropriate to its situation and needs.
> (10) The independent nature of the programming of public and private media in the language(s) of national minorities shall be safeguarded. Public media editorial boards overseeing the content and orientation of programming should be independent and should include persons belonging to national minorities serving in their independent capacity.
> (11) Access to media originating from abroad shall not be unduly restricted. Such access should not justify a diminution of broadcast time allocated to the minority in the publicly funded media of the State of residence of the minorities concerned.

The Oslo Recommendations have remained relevant to the work of the HCNM. They constitute a baseline for context-specific advice provided to participating States and have informed the development of subsequent HCNM thematic recommendations. They have also had an impact on how the Council of Europe's Advisory Committee to the Framework Convention interprets the relevant provisions of the Framework Convention.[13]

As mentioned above, the HCNM observed and continues to observe that inter-ethnic relations in a number of OSCE participating States are particularly affected by policies promoting the use of the official/State language in the broadcast media. In effect such policies often restrict the use of minority languages. Having discussed this recurring pattern, the HCNM decided to further detail its recommendations on the use of languages in the broadcast media. A strong interest in issues concerning media and minorities had also been expressed by a number of OSCE participating States at the March 2001 OSCE Supplementary Human Dimension Meeting on Freedom of Expression. Some participating States subsequently requested in the OSCE Permanent Council that the HCNM and the Representative of the Freedom of the Media address this issue in more detail. In response, and in coordination with RFOM,

13 *Thematic Commentary No. 3*, *supra* note 9, para. 10.

the HCNM undertook to survey State practice[14] and legislation across the OSCE region and in a separate but closely related process engaged a group of experts drawn from various fields in developing the Guidelines on the use of Minority Languages in the Broadcast Media. The Representative of the Freedom of the Media undertook a parallel project investigating the practical working environments and conditions for the free and responsible operation of media in multilingual societies.[15] Both institutions cooperated in organizing an international conference in Baden/Austria in 2003 where the Guidelines on the use of Minority Languages in the Broadcast Media were launched.[16]

State practice was surveyed with regard to (1) whether there are any stipulated quotas on the use of language as a vehicle of broadcasting, both for publicly- and privately-owned and run broadcasters, and (2) whether there is any accommodation, such as specifically allotted time, bands, financial support, for minority-language broadcasting.[17] The survey brought to light a number of factors affecting, and the mechanisms used to regulate, the use of languages in broadcasting, whether restrictive or facilitative. The results of the survey were compiled in a comprehensive report, which highlights the patterns and trends that have influenced the media landscape in the OSCE region in the early 2000's and which are well worth recalling as they are mirrored to some extent in contemporary developments, both technological and political. By 2003 privately-licensed radio and television stations had become more abundant, resulting in more linguistic diversity in some OSCE contexts.[18] At the same time, the arrival of new technologies, including satellite and multi-channel cable systems but also the internet, upset the balance of language uses that often had been carefully implemented in times dominated by radio and television.[19] The proliferation of foreign channels did not only make broadcasts in minority languages more easily available but also provided a platform for kin-states, thus adding a sensitive geo-political dimension to the phenomenon. The use of languages in

14 The HCNM commissioned the Programme in Comparative Media Law and Policy at the Centre for Socio-Legal Studies at the Wolfson College at Oxford University and the Institute for Information Law at the University of Amsterdam to conduct the survey.

15 OSCE representative on the Freedom of the Media, *Media in Multilingual Societies. Freedom and Responsibility*, Vienna, 2003.

16 The conference proceedings have been published in 8 *Mercator Media Forum* (2005).

17 T. McGonagle, B. Davis Noll, M. Price (eds), *Minority-Language related Broadcasting and Legislation in the OSCE*, Programme in Comparative Media Law and Policy, Centre for Socio-Legal Studies, Wolfson College at Oxford University and the Institute for Information Law (Universiteit van Amsterdam, 2003) p. 1.

18 *Ibid.*, p. 8.

19 *Ibid.*

broadcast media carried political connotations specifically in the post-Soviet sphere, where newly independent states sought to privilege official/State languages and to counter the dominance of Russian language broadcasting as part of their nation building efforts.[20] But also in countries with increasing federalist tendencies, such as the United Kingdom and Spain, public broadcasting and licensing regimes were altered to reflect new political needs and language sensitivities.[21] The survey counts a diverse array of measures devised to regulate the use of the official/State language(s). On the one hand, this includes mandatory use, quotas and translation requirements. On the other hand, it includes measures aimed at the accommodation and promotion of minority languages, such as exceptions from the aforementioned regulations, mandatory use or quotas for minority languages or measures encouraging the use of minority languages on a voluntary basis.[22] It also found that in a number of States, the role of protecting and promoting the official/State language or minority languages was assigned specifically to public service broadcasting.[23]

The result of the survey of State practice informed the 2003 Guidelines on the use of Minority Languages in the Broadcast Media, which in their first chapter list the relevant general principles based on international standards, in their second and third chapters provide states with guidance regarding policy and regulation respectively and in Chapter 4 suggest facilitative measures that can be taken by States to counter inequality and discrimination – altogether 17 guidelines.

At the core of a State's obligations with regard to the use of minority language in the broadcast media stand the freedom of expression,[24] cultural and linguistic diversity,[25] the protection of identity[26] as well as equality and non-discrimination.[27] With these as a baseline, the Guidelines recommend States to develop policy to address the use of minority language(s) in the broadcast media, based on an ascertainment of the needs of persons belonging to national minorities to maintain and develop their identities and be designed and applied based on the effective participation of persons belonging to national minorities.[28] The Guidelines further recommend that State policy should

20 *Ibid.*

21 *Ibid.*

22 *Ibid.*, pp. 10 *et seq.*

23 *Ibid.*, p. 18.

24 *The Guidelines on the Use of Minority Languages in the Broadcast* Media, guideline 1.

25 *Ibid.*, guideline 2.

26 *Ibid.*, guideline 3.

27 *Ibid.*, guideline 4.

28 *Ibid.*, guidelines 5 & 6.

support public service broadcasting which provides a wide and balanced range of informational, educational, cultural and entertainment programming of high quality in order, *inter alia*, to meet the needs of persons belonging to national minorities.[29] To illustrate the point, Tarlach McGonagle remarked "[t]raditional singing and traditional dancing in traditional costumes at the *un*-traditional hour of 4.00 a.m. falls far short of meeting the needs and interests of minority groups".[30] While States may regulate the broadcast media, it is further recommended that such regulation, including licensing, must be prescribed by law, based on objective and non-discriminatory criteria and shall not aim to restrict or have the effect of restricting broadcasting in minority languages.[31] Any regulation, whether prescriptive or proscriptive, must pursue a legitimate aim and be proportionate to that aim. When assessing the proportionality of any regulation, specific factors concerning the nature of the media and wider social environment should be considered, such as the nature and objective of the measure; the existing political, social and religious context; the number, variety, geographical reach, character, function and languages of available broadcasting services; and the rights, needs, expressed desires and nature of the audience(s).[32] The Guidelines also address regulation regarding translation and transfrontier broadcasting. Minority language broadcasting should not be subject to the imposition of undue or disproportionate requirements for translation, dubbing, post-synchronization or subtitling.[33] The free reception of transfrontier broadcasts, whether direct or by means of retransmission or rebroadcasting, shall not be prohibited on the basis of language. The availability of foreign broadcasting in a minority language does not negate the State's obligation to facilitate domestically produced broadcasting in that language nor does it justify a reduction of the broadcast time in that language.[34]

The Guidelines recommend States to support broadcasting in minority languages through, *inter alia*, provision of access to broadcasting, subsidies and capacity building for minority language broadcasting.[35] Access to broadcasting can be achieved, *inter alia*, through the allocation of frequencies, the establishment and support of broadcasters and program scheduling.[36] Public

29 *Ibid.*, guideline 7.

30 McGonagle, *supra* note 12, p. 93.

31 *The Guidelines on the Use of Minority Languages in the Broadcast* Media, guideline 9.

32 *Ibid.*, guideline 11.

33 *Ibid.*, guideline 12.

34 *Ibid.*, guideline 13.

35 *Ibid.*, guideline 14.

36 *Ibid.*, guideline 15.

funding may be achieved through direct grants, favourable financing/tax regimes, and exemption from certain fees payable on award or alteration of a license. To ensure effective equality, minority language broadcasters in numerically smaller communities may require funds or facilities disproportionate to their size as a percentage of available resources.[37] Capacity building may be done through technical support to distribute minority language productions both domestically and abroad and to facilitate transfrontier broadcasting in minority languages. In addition, States should consider supporting the education and training of personnel for minority language broadcasting.[38]

The Guidelines became an important reference tool in advising participating States on how to develop the policies on use of languages in the broadcast media, taking into account the rights of persons belonging to minorities. By means of 'quiet diplomacy' the HCNM often addressed the issue of restrictions on the provision of meaningful access of minorities to the media. These issues continue to be raised in HCNM official country visits, diplomatic correspondence with participating States and legal opinions on draft legislation related to the regulation of broadcast media.

Devoting a set of guidelines specifically to the broadcast media was a timely decision – the broadcast media remains a popular and important media platform, albeit the radical technological transformation of last ten years, which has led to the proliferation and convergence of various media platforms. Policies and legislation affecting the use of languages in broadcast media have become more complex and detailed over the years, in many cases further restricting minorities' access to the broadcast media. In some countries of the OSCE region, not only mandatory quotas for broadcasting without distinction between public and private broadcasters were retained, but new requirements were added to provide programming in certain languages at specific intervals and for certain types of programming. Other requirements prescribe onerous rules for translation, dubbing and sub-titling. In recent years, many countries also introduced more stringent regulation on retransmission of foreign TV broadcasts through cable channels. Moreover, the digital switchover saw a slate of new regulations affecting broadcasters that cater to the needs and interests of persons belonging to national minorities. The effect of these changes may not always be beneficial to minorities. Also, some countries have introduced quotas for radio playlists in official/State language. Other governments moved to privatize or consolidate public broadcasters at the local level – reforms that often lead to decrease in minority language broadcasting.

37 *Ibid.*, guideline 16.

38 *Ibid.*, guideline 17.

In 2012, the HCNM published the Ljubljana Guidelines on the Integration of Diverse Societies. The Ljubljana Guidelines provide policy makers with guidance and practical advice on how to elaborate and implement policies facilitating the integration of diverse societies. The underlying understanding is that integration is a dynamic, multi-actor process of mutual engagement that facilitates effective participation by all members of a diverse society in economic, political, social and cultural life, and fosters a shared and inclusive sense of belonging at the national and local levels.[39] The Ljubljana Guidelines keep it with a rather straightforward recommendation regarding the use of minority languages in the broadcast media: measures to promote the State or official language(s) in the media should not disproportionately curtail the right to use a minority language.[40] The explanatory note further elaborates specific practical advice:

- Quotas for public broadcasting in the State language may be legitimate, but should be complemented by special provisions to ensure that the linguistic rights of persons belonging to national minorities are guaranteed; for instance, through the flexible implementation of such quotas and/or through exemptions for regions where minority communities live in substantial numbers. Furthermore, imposing language quotas must never imply regulation of content and must fully respect the freedom of the media. The imposition of rigid quotas on private broadcasters may conflict with freedom of expression. Therefore, promotion of the State language in private broadcasting, where justified by a legitimate aim, may be better achieved through using various economic incentives, including distribution of State grants and support for content production;
- If subtitling, quotas and/or rebroadcasting requirements are introduced to promote integration, the State should provide adequate financial and technical support to ensure it does not disproportionately affect minority-language use. In some contexts, subtitling can be an effective tool for improving cross-community communication and outreach. For example, multilingual programmes are sometimes created and subtitled in both majority and minority languages to encourage interaction among groups and overcome language barriers;
- With regard to private media, States should consider creating incentives for private and community media providers; for instance, through funding and allocating frequencies, and by increasing, especially numerically

39 *The Ljubljana Guidelines on the Integration of Diverse Societies & Explanatory Note*, p. 3.

40 *Ibid.*, guideline 49.

smaller, minorities' access to the media, including media in their languages. Although it may not be illegitimate, per se, to require that private media meet some clearly justified, context-specific State-language quotas, this is particularly problematic, as it has the potential to unduly limit private initiative and the very existence of minority-language media.

In 2016, the HCNM embarked on the project of developing a new set of Guidelines that would take note of the technical advances and could complement the preceding sets of Recommendations and Guidelines in this respect. High Commissioner Astrid Thors commented on this endeavour:

> [w]e have seen extensive and momentous changes in our social, political, economic and personal communications, with the line between the traditional media and other communications platforms becoming less clear-cut. These changes directly affect communication between majorities and minorities in our diverse societies. [...] From the conflict prevention perspective, it remains essential to ensure that the new communications landscape will not lead to marginalization of minority voices – whether politically or commercially – but instead provides a means to develop their culture ... This work will further develop respective elements of The Ljubljana Guidelines on Integration of Diverse Societies and other relevant HCNM Recommendations.[41]

This new set of Guidelines is expected to be published in 2018.

3 Practice

The HCNM has engaged with a number of participating States in order to provide advice on how the appropriate linguistic balance, also regarding the media, can be attained in specific contexts. As has been mentioned elsewhere in the current book, this is most often done in confidence through diplomatic correspondence in follow-up to official country visits undertaken by the High Commissioner. Any review of the institution's experiences will thus be limited by virtue of the confidential nature of the HCNM's mandate. The advice summarized below, which has been made public by the HCNM, should thus neither

41 Statement address by Astrid Thors, OSCE High Commissioner on National Minorities, to the 1102nd Plenary Meeting of the OSCE Permanent Council, Vienna, 2 June 2016, p. 14.

be understood to be exhaustive nor meant to single out individual participating States.

Over the years the HCNM has encouraged the subtitling of news broadcasts into minority languages, and worked particularly close on this issue with the government of Kazakhstan so as to ensure that minority communities will have access to news about their country in their native languages.[42] The HCNM has advised Ukraine that in the area of media regulation voluntary methods based on incentives are more effective than rigid language requirements enforced upon broadcasters with fines and other penalties. At the same time the HCNM reminded that policies promoting the State language should not be pursued in isolation of policies to preserve and strengthen minority rights.[43] On numerous occasions the HCNM commented on draft language and draft media legislation, such as in Latvia and Kazakhstan regarding quotas on broadcasting in the official language and access to broadcasting for smaller minorities.[44] In 2013, High Commissioner Vollebaek provided the institution's good offices for bilateral consultations between Serbia and Romania regarding among others access to minority language media, by the end of which locally produced content in the Romanian language has been made available in some areas of eastern Serbia and Romanian-language programmes produced in Vojvodina were rebroadcast in eastern Serbia.[45]

The HCNM has used statements to the OSCE Permanent Council to make known when the institution had been alerted by reports of the closure of minority language broadcasting outlets, such as in 2010 when two Uzbek TV

42 Statement by Knut Vollebaek, OSCE High Commissioner on National Minorities, to the 687th Plenary Meeting of the OSCE Permanent Council, Vienna, 8 November 2007, p. 5; Statement by Knut Vollebaek, OSCE High Commissioner on National Minorities, to the 718th Plenary Meeting of the OSCE Permanent Council Vienna, 26 June 2008, p. 6; Statement by Knut Vollebaek, OSCE High Commissioner on National Minorities, to the 742nd Plenary Meeting of the OSCE Permanent Council, Vienna, 27 November 2008, p. 6.

43 Statement by Knut Vollebaek, OSCE High Commissioner on National Minorities, to the 742nd Plenary Meeting of the OSCE Permanent Council, Vienna, 27 November 2008, p. 4.

44 Statement by Knut Vollebaek, OSCE High Commissioner on National Minorities, to the 888th Plenary Meeting of the OSCE Permanent Council, Vienna, 17 November 2011, p. 10; Statement by Knut Vollebaek, OSCE High Commissioner on National Minorities, to the 837th Plenary Meeting of the OSCE Permanent Council Vienna, 18 November 2010, p. 8; Statement by Astrid Thors, OSCE High Commissioner on National Minorities, to the 977th Plenary Meeting of the OSCE Permanent Council, Vienna, 12 December 2013, p. 5.

45 Statement by Knut Vollebaek, OSCE High Commissioner on National Minorities, to the 932nd Plenary Meeting of the OSCE Permanent Council, Vienna, 22 November 2012, p. 9; Statement by Knut Vollebaek, OSCE High Commissioner on National Minorities, to the 960th meeting of the OSCE Permanent Council, Vienna, 11 July 2013, p. 7.

stations in Kyrgyzstan closed.[46] In 2015 High Commissioner Thors voiced concern that "effectively forcing community-run media outlets, such as ATR [Crimean Tatar TV channel], to close by denying their registration does not only restrict media freedom and access to information, but also deprives the Crimean Tatar community of a vital instrument to maintain its identity".[47] Likewise, the HCNM has used PC statements to publicly recognize positive steps with regard to access to broadcasting in minority languages, for instance in Latvia where Russian-language programming by the public broadcaster was understood to constitute a positive step in reaching out to minority communities with locally produced content.[48]

HCNM initiated and supported projects may constitute the more visible part of the institution's practice. In general terms projects start where guidelines and advice left off and pilot their implementation. HCNM projects are often presented as tools to operationalize the HCNM's advice and provide governments with instruments they can implement to follow up on their commitments. While the more general theme of media diversity has been addressed within the framework of numerous projects, in Georgia the HCNM has actively supported the promotion of the use of minority languages in the broadcast media. From 2003 to 2008 the HCNM implemented a broad conflict prevention and integration programme in the Samtskhe-Javakheti and Kvemo Kartli regions of Georgia, which among other objectives aimed to increase access to national television by rebroadcasting Georgian-language news programmes in Armenian and Azeri as 20 minute programmes aired during weekdays. The broadcasts have since been sustained locally.

4 Conclusion

The HCNM has adopted an open ended approach to address the issues at the core of its mandate, including through a continuous review of the institutional experiences that are synthesized into Thematic Recommendations and Guidelines. Media has an important function, sometimes referred to as the fourth

46 Statement by Knut Vollebaek, OSCE High Commissioner on National Minorities, to the 837th Plenary Meeting of the OSCE Permanent Council, Vienna, 18 November 2010, p. 3.

47 Statement by Astrid Thors, OSCE High Commissioner on National Minorities, to the 1062nd Plenary Meeting of the OSCE Permanent Council, Vienna, 16 July 2015, p. 4.

48 Statement address by Astrid Thors, OSCE High Commissioner on National Minorities, to the 1026th Plenary Meeting of the OSCE Permanent Council, Vienna, 20 November 2014, p. 6.

estate in addition to the legislative, executive and judiciary. Access to media without interference is crucial to exercise the fundamental right of freedom of expression and it is a State responsibility to create an environment, in which all, including persons belonging to national minorities, can enjoy the freedom of expression by receiving, seeking and imparting information and ideas in a language and media of their choice.

How this can be achieved has been addressed by the HCNM in the Oslo Recommendations, the Guidelines on the use of Minority Languages in the Broadcast Media and the Ljubljana Guidelines, which have served as the baseline for context-specific advise provided to participating States on policies and law and for good practices piloted within specific projects.

The HCNM's work on the use of minority languages in the media has contributed to a clearer understanding of both the obstacles to the use of minority languages in broadcast media as well as good practices. Media, including broadcast media, is a dynamic field and as such requires HCNM to regularly revisit and reassess how the pertinent developments impact minority-majority relations in different contexts. A new set of Guidelines on the role of the media in the digital age is in the drafting and will yet make its contribution by helping States to design inclusive polices to build cohesive and resilient societies and thus prevent conflict.

CHAPTER 7

The HCNM Impact on Minority and State Language Promotion and on the Social Integration of Diverse Societies Through Education: The Cases of Kazakhstan and Kyrgyzstan

Atanasia Stoianova and Michael Angermann

1 Introduction

The role of languages in education is a key issue in many societies and due to its importance has been extensively covered by the first ever Recommendations of the OSCE High Commissioner on National Minorities (HCNM) published in 1996 – The Hague Recommendations regarding the Education Rights of National Minorities.[1] Two years later when the Oslo Recommendations regarding the Linguistic Rights of National Minorities were published, they acknowledge that the use of minority languages 'in public and in private' by persons belonging to national minorities cannot be considered without making reference to education but then clearly refer on this topic to The Hague Recommendations themselves.[2]

Since the end of the 1990-s, the HCNM has been engaged in providing policy advice and conducting project work with education authorities and practitioners in various OSCE participating States to promote a balanced approach towards the use of minority, state and official languages in general education. Looking at the role of languages in education, the HCNM's recommendation has been to promote on the one hand the development of State language capacities among the population of a country for a better integration of the society. On the other hand, it is equally important to preserve the mother tongue among the national minority communities in order to preserve their

* The views expressed in this article are those of the authors alone and do not necessarily represent the official policy of the OSCE High Commissioner on National Minorities

1 OSCE HCNM, *The Hague Recommendations Regarding the Education Rights of National Minorities* (The Hague, 1996), <http://www.osce.org/hcnm/32180>, visited on 4 January 2018.

2 OSCE HCNM, *The Oslo Recommendations regarding the Linguistic Rights of National Minorities* (The Hague, 1998) p. 13. <http://www.osce.org/hcnm/67531>, visited on 4 January 2018.

© KONINKLIJKE BRILL NV, LEIDEN, 2018 | DOI 10.1163/9789004357754_008

identity and to safeguard their linguistic rights.[3] The balance between these two facets of language promotion is contextual, varying from country to country. Promoting of mother tongue-based multilingual education (MLE)[4] as advocated by HCNM can contribute to social integration in linguistically diverse societies.

The first part of this article will start with addressing the country background of Kazakhstan and Kyrgyzstan regarding the status of minority, state and official languages and their role in education. The second part will focus on the manner in which HCNM has promoted over the past 15 years balanced approaches in education in Central Asia and particular in Kazakhstan and Kyrgyzstan, which have similar aims but different solutions due to the country background and specific minority demands. The article will focus on the process and outcomes of the "Inter-state Dialogue on Social Integration and National Minority Education" and the "Central Asia Education Programme" facilitated and implemented by the HCNM in co-operation with the education authorities and target groups in Central Asia and specifically in Kazakhstan and Kyrgyzstan. The two country cases and the impact of the HCNM involvement are then compared on the basis of their 'best practices' and 'challenges'. A number of conclusions and recommendations are formulated on the basis of this analysis, all of which can assist improving the education for national minority communities living in these countries.

2 Background Information

2.1 *Minority Education in Kazakhstan and Kyrgyzstan*

The population of the Central Asian States is multi-ethnic, while in each of the states the titular ethnic group constitutes an absolute majority. Minorities in

3 Recommendation 1: "The right of persons belonging to national minorities to maintain their identity can only be fully realized if they acquire proper knowledge of their mother tongue during the educational process. At the same time, persons belonging to national minorities have a responsibility to integrate into the wider national society through the acquisition of a proper knowledge of the State language". *See* OSCE HCNM, *The Hague Recommendations Regarding the Education Rights of National Minorities* (The Hague, 1996) p. 5.

4 "Bilingual and multilingual education refers to the use of two or more languages as mediums of instruction ... the use of at least three languages, the mother tongue, a regional or national language and an international language in education" *See* UNESCO 30 C/Resolution 12: *Implementation of a Language Policy for the World Based on Multilingualism* (Paris, 1999); UNESCO *Education Position Paper: Education in a multilingual world* (Paris, 2003) pp. 17–18, <http://unesdoc.unesco.org/images/0012/001297/129728e.pdf>, visited on 4 January 2018.

these countries are primarily comprised of ethnicities autochthonous to the region; however, Kyrgyzstan and Kazakhstan also have sizable, albeit gradually shrinking, Russian and other Slavic communities. Since independence, the languages of titular nations were adopted as State languages: Kazakh language in Kazakhstan, and Kyrgyz language in Kyrgyzstan. Russian is still widely spoken and has an official status in Kyrgyzstan while in Kazakhstan it "shall be officially used on equal grounds along with the Kazakh language".[5]

Kazakhstan and Kyrgyzstan inherited an education system from the Soviet Union that was oriented towards providing monolingual education in the mother tongue for different ethnic groups on a segregated basis. Furthermore, minority language schools effectively belonged to the educational system of the neighbouring Socialist republics – 'home republic' of the minority: the textbooks, curriculum modules, and teacher training, were provided by these republics. It should be also mentioned that Russian was a predominant language of instruction at schools and universities. It was also taught as a subject from grade five with two-three hours per week in all the schools with mother tongues as a language of instruction. At the same time, though Kazakh and Kyrgyz had the status of official languages in their republics, they were studied symbolically and inefficiently in schools with Russian and minority languages of instruction: Kazakh was taught one hour per week, while Kyrgyz language was not taught at all in these types of schools. The languages of the most numerous minority groups: Uzbek, Tajik and Uighur were not considered in the school curriculum for Russian, Kazakh and Kyrgyz language schools.

The existing data evidences the disparity of languages promotion through education: according to the 1999 national census the absolute majority of population in Kyrgyzstan spoke Russian as a second language – 75.5 per cent, while only 11.5 per cent of population used Kyrgyz as a second language.[6] In Kazakhstan – 30 per cent of urban ethnic Kazakh population did not speak their mother tongue at all.[7]

After the breakdown of the Soviet Union these newly independent states had to cope with this legacy of having a multi-ethnic population and a segregated monolingual educational system, as well as a very low status and standard of acquisition of the State language. Following independence both

5 *The Constitution of the Republic of Kazakhstan* (August 30, 1995), Section 1, Article 7, <http://www.parlam.kz/en/constitution>, visited on 4 January 2018.

6 'Demograficheskie tendencii, formirovanie nacii i mezhetnicheskie otnosheniya v Kirgizii', *Demoscope Weekly*, 4–17 April 2005, <www.demoscope.ru/weekly/2005/0197/analit04.php>, visited on 3 January 2018.

7 *Rossiya i sovremennyi mir*, No. 1 (INION RAN, 1999) p. 133.

countries maintained schools with minority languages of instruction (Uzbek, Tajik in both countries, plus also Uighur in Kazakhstan) alongside the schools with State or Russian languages of instruction.

In the last two decades, Kazakhstan and Kyrgyzstan have faced considerable challenges in their efforts to maintain and modernize their education systems. They put an emphasis on the development of the State language schools and enhancing the State language teaching. In the aftermath of the dissolution of the USSR, the collapse of the established textbook supply chains between the Central Asian countries, and, in part, insufficient attention to minority schools' needs, led to serious shortages of textbooks and qualified teachers, as well as insufficient methodological support to and poor monitoring of these schools, all of which in turn negatively influenced the quality of education and the competitiveness of their school leavers. Expert studies in the field within the last decade, as well as national and international assessment (PISA) data, have revealed a decrease in the quality of education and compatibility of minority school students, low access to higher education, and a decrease in the number of minority language schools. It became also evident, that the traditional minority education approach does not ensure the level of State language proficiency required for efficient inter-ethnic communication. The need for changes in the education of national minorities was also due to the strengthening of the role of the State language as a tool for social integration of society, the need to ensure equal access to secondary and higher vocational education, and creating conditions for the effective participation of persons belonging to national minorities in all spheres of social, economic and cultural life.

2.2 *Challenges and Approaches to Improving Minority Education*

In *Kyrgyzstan*, despite considerable efforts to improve State language acquisition at Russian language and minority language schools, non-Kyrgyz speakers comprising about 27 per cent of the population, continue to have a low level of competence in the State language. According to existing data around 30 per cent of the population speaks Russian as a second language, while only 4 per cent of the population uses Kyrgyz as a second language.[8] Furthermore, in the aftermath of the 2010 inter-ethnic clashes in Osh, the number of schools with Uzbek as language of instruction has been reduced by more than three times: from 133 schools in 2010 to 43 schools in 2017, while the number of students in Uzbek language schools has diminished four times: from 67,060 to 16,128 (*See* Table 7.1).

8 Aminov K., Jansen V., Juraev S., Overland I., 'Language Use and Language Policy in Central Asia', 2:1 *Central Asia Regional Data Review* (Spring 2010), p. 3.

TABLE 7.1 *Kyrgyzstan: Schools and schools students by language of instruction*[a].

School years	2009/ 2010	2010/ 2011	2011/ 2012	2012/ 2013	2013/ 2014	2014/ 2015	2015/ 2016	2016/ 2017
Schools with one language of instruction, including:	1742	1735	1721	1718	1714	1698	1692	1685
Kyrgyz	1406	1410	1424	1437	1443	1434	1439	1423
Russian	200	201	203	202	203	203	198	216
Uzbek	133	121	91	76	65	58	52	43
Tajik	3	3	3	3	3	3	3	3
Number of students, including	681190	664955	649166	639517	641472	629406	643662	680399
Kyrgyz language of instruction	491529	485867	480878	476660	479776	472847	485205	509069
Russian language of instruction	120648	119201	125519	126953	133784	132643	138471	152964
Uzbek language of instruction	67060	57960	40833	33940	25951	21965	17926	16128
Tajik language of instruction	1953	1927	1936	1964	1961	1951	2060	2238

a National Statistical Committee of the Kyrgyz Republic, 2017.

Most of the minority language schools were transformed into schools with two or more parallel classes teaching either in Kyrgyz, Russian and Uzbek, while in the classes teaching in Kyrgyz or Russian languages, Uzbek and Tajik students do not have a possibility to learn their mother tongue even as a subject. In this context, it is worth mentioning that the choice of the language of instruction is a complex issue, which depends not only on the state policy but also on the position of parents and the individual preferences of the child.

The 2014 decision to abolish the Uzbek language version of the university entrance exam in Kyrgyzstan created additional obstacles for graduates of Uzbek language schools wishing to access higher education. In addition to poor provision with quality textbooks, insufficient acquisition of Kyrgyz and Russian languages, as well as lower quality of education in these schools, the limited prospects after graduation negatively affected parental choices for minority mother tongue as a language of schooling.

It became quite evident that school education exclusively in minority language:

- does not provide the necessary level of mastering the State language and other languages that are in demand in the region and beyond;
- makes it difficult for graduates of these schools to access higher education;
- limits the possibilities of their social interaction and career growth;
- has a negative impact resulting in the segregation of the diverse society of Kyrgyzstan and may create prerequisites for discrimination and social tension in the country.

Consequently, some local education departments took far-reaching measures, by imposing full immersion Kyrgyz language teaching to Uzbek schools depriving the children from studying their mother tongue even as a subject, as well as without any consideration of parents' position and existing human resources in the schools. Being not satisfied with the textbooks' supply in minority languages, as well as the low standard of Kyrgyz and Russian language acquisition, parents more often started to choose schools with other languages of instruction for their children, most often Russian language schools. In their search for possible alternatives, the authorities, teachers and parents came to a mutual agreement that bilingual/multilingual education can be a better solution.

Thus, with the support of the HCNM, in 2011 the piloting of mother tongue-based MLE programmes started in these types of schools. In 2013, MLE piloting was expanded to Kyrgyz and Russian language schools and today it covers all levels of education, from kindergarten to university, as well as all types of language schools. The Ministry of Education and Science of Kyrgyzstan is taking a strong position on this and has made practical steps to promote integrative education models for minorities. Nevertheless the steps undertaken to introduce MLE are not accompanied by sufficient reassurances that teaching in minority languages will be maintained, which could elicit a negative reaction among minority communities, as they may perceive MLE as a tool for assimilation.

Currently, efforts are being put to extend pilot MLE models to the entire education system. However, Kyrgyzstan does not yet have the capacity required to address such a complex challenge adequately: more efforts are needed to introduce new educational standards, ensure that quality textbooks are available, improve teacher pre-service and in-service training, as well as the capacity of teaching staff throughout the sector.

In *Kazakhstan*, the legal and normative basis regarding minority rights and education are based on principles of non-discrimination and equal treatment.

At the same time, some implementation practices might benefit from a better adjustment to those principles, since one can see equality deficits in the education policy implementation process. For example, the current State Programme of Education Development does not tackle any specific issues related to minority education. Further support is needed to mother tongue education in kindergartens, which becomes especially important in conditions of multilingual education. Pre-school groups need to be provided with relevant materials in their language of education. Further efforts and measures of encouragement are needed for improving teacher training opportunities for minority schools, as the need for qualified teachers, including teachers of minority languages, in these schools becomes ever more relevant. Along with this, insufficient proficiency of minority school leavers in the State language and other languages functioning in the region complicates their access to higher education and, consequently, reduces their professional career perspectives. These considerations led to a questioning of the effectiveness of minority school education exclusively in their mother tongue.

While acknowledging that language is an essential component of individual and collective identity, and that education in one's the mother tongue is an inalienable right of any person, including those belonging to national minorities; it is also evident that an adequate command of other languages functioning in society, and above all the State language, is an instrument of inclusion and increased opportunities in terms of access to further education, career development and social activity. That is the reason why the demand for the study of several languages is very high among minority communities. This is evidenced by the results of our study conducted in 2014–2015 in two regions of Kazakhstan – Almaty Region and South Kazakhstan Region: 74% and 69% of the students surveyed were interested in studying at a school where subjects are taught in several languages.

These high numbers can be, at least partially, attributed to the successful piloting of bilingual and multilingual education programmes, which have been supported by the HCNM. Multilingual education is being perceived by minority communities in Kazakhstan as an effective way of preserving their native languages in education, along with qualitative mastering of the state and official languages. This approach, on the one hand, allows satisfying the basic human and minority rights, and on the other hand, reduces the risks of discrimination due to insufficient knowledge of the State language.

The recent adoption of the Trilingual Education Policy, focusing on introducing Kazakh, Russian and English languages throughout the school system, aims at integrating the diverse society of the country through the promotion of a balanced language policy in education. Among the positive factors of the latest reforms one can mention the requirement of mother tongue instruction at primary school level; the provision of new textbooks and educational materials for primary school students in all languages of instruction, including Uzbek, Uighur and Tajik; separation of final school exams and the university entrance exams, which allows taking the final school exams in the first language of instruction including in Uzbek, Uighur and Tajik; and the introduction of trilingual education in all types of schools, including minority schools.

The introduction of trilingual education in all types of schools, including minority schools, provides for the de-segregation of minority schools and assures a general education standard for all types of schools. However, as a result of this policy, maintaining instruction in minority languages such as Uzbek, Uighur and Tajik in the school system becomes an increasingly challenging task, as it requires the implementation of quadri-lingual education in these schools which leaves less space for minority languages within the new curriculum.

3 HCNM Involvement in the Educational Sphere of Kazakhstan and Kyrgyzstan

3.1 *The Role of the HCNM in Promoting Balanced Integrative Education*

The institution of the HCNM was created to help prevent conflicts involving national minority issues at the earliest stage.[9] Therefore the HCNM seeks to address also the underlying causes of tensions between minorities and majorities. One way to achieve this is by investing in education policies and practices designed to meet the special needs and concerns of all communities. A key consideration in education-related matters in almost all societies is the issue of language, which is usually one of the defining elements of an ethnic group and is central to the right of national minorities to maintain and develop their identity. Ethnic mobilization and the politicization of identity have brought the language issue to the fore of political debates, including in the Central Asian republics of Kazakhstan and Kyrgyzstan.

Accommodating minority and majority needs, interests and desires in terms of education in the mother tongue is not mutually exclusive but rather mutually enriching. It is essential to integrate diversity through education within culturally diverse States. The Hague Recommendations Regarding the

9 *See* Part II of the CSCE Helsinki Document 1992, <http://www.osce.org/mc/39530?download=true>, visited on 3 January 2018.

Education Rights of National Minorities set out two parameters in this regard: on the one hand, the preservation of identity through education in the mother tongue and, on the other hand, the integration of society.[10] Research into educational approaches and international practices suggests the option of bi- or multi-lingual instruction in minority schools as a mean to achieve this aim. Multilingual programming is considered necessary to maintain the linguistic, cultural and ethnic identity of minority communities. At the same time, young people belonging to national minorities should be prepared to enter higher education institutions as equal citizens with the same opportunities as members of majority communities, so as to be able to effectively participate in the cultural, social and economic life and in the public affairs of their wider society.

3.2 *Regional Dialogue on Integration and Minority Education*

The HCNM has been engaged in the support of MLE projects in Central Asia since 2003. In this regard, the HCNM facilitated a regional "Inter-state Dialogue Process on Social Integration and National Minority Education", which was initiated at the meeting of the Central Asian Ministers of Education in Tashkent in 2006. It aimed at developing practical measures to strengthen the process of educational modernization in the states of Central Asia and also at fostering the types of co-operation across the region that would further promote social integration in Central Asia's multi-ethnic nations. The dialogue focused on promoting practical co-operation in teacher training, the development of curricula and textbooks, mutual recognition of qualifications and the exchange of experience over the introduction of modern methods, including distance learning, interactive methods of language teaching and MLE.

In the Tashkent Meeting Declaration,[11] the Central Asian states undertook to "promote social integration with respect for diversity" and "recognize the value of inter-state cooperation in matters of national minority education and social integration". The process was formalized by establishing four working groups gathering experts from the Ministries of Education of the countries of the region. The working groups discussed issues of 'Teacher Training and In-service Training' (Astana, Kazakhstan; February 2007), 'Language Teaching' (Bishkek, Kyrgyzstan; June 2007), 'Textbooks and Curriculum Development' (Tashkent, Uzbekistan; November 2007) and 'Distance Learning and Information

10 *See* OSCE HCNM, *The Hague Recommendations Regarding the Education Rights of National Minorities* (The Hague, 1996) p. 5.

11 Tashkent Meeting Declaration '*The Objectives of Education Reform in the Context of Multinational Central Asia*' (Tashkent, 28 November 2006).

Technology' (Ashgabat, Turkmenistan; April 2008). Concluding recommendations to their Governments were adopted at each round of consultations at the expert level of the education authorities of the Central Asian states. The recommendations were aimed at assisting the process of education reform as well as promoting the respect for the educational rights of persons belonging to national minorities and contributing to good neighbourly relations and inter-state co-operation.

The Review Conference of the Dialogue held in Samarkand, Uzbekistan, on 3 April 2009 recommended "setting up a Project Resource Centre of the Inter-State Dialogue under the auspices of the OSCE High Commissioner on National Minorities". The HCNM then further elaborated on the idea of regional co-operation, as outlined below.

3.3 *The Central Asia Education Programme*

Following the Samarkand recommendations, the HCNM launched the Central Asia Education Programme (CAEP) in October 2012. The CAEP aimed to renew regional dialogue on integration and minority education and foster the development and promotion of multilingual education in the region.

As part of this Programme, HCNM deployed a Regional Education Liaison Officer to the region and tasked her to build on previous experiences, provide further practical support for the introduction of multilingual and multicultural education in Central Asia, and to facilitate the co-ordination of different approaches followed in the region. The Officer provided expert assistance to the education ministries and relevant partner organizations, and also established and maintained contacts with other international organizations, attracting their assistance for projects and initiatives related to minority education.

Kazakhstan, Kyrgyzstan and Tajikistan nominated representatives of their education ministries as national focal points and members of the CAEP Board. The CAEP action plan and priority areas for bilateral projects and inter-State cooperation were discussed and co-ordinated within joint meetings with country focal points and the Programme's implementing partners.

The CAEP contributed to the development of integrative education policies, the acquisition, circulation and application of international standards of minority education in participating countries, and the strengthening of regional co-operation in the field of multilingual and multicultural education. The Programme also organized a number of concrete joint activities aimed at exchanging experiences and strengthening institutional capacities for minority education.

The first phase of the CAEP (2012–2014) revealed that country-specific approaches and expert advice as well as practical assistance are crucial for the development of comprehensive integrative education policies as well as their successful implementation. Furthermore, regional dialogue helped to enhance the capacity of education practitioners and facilitated practical co-operation and experience sharing between the countries involved.

Within the second phase of CAEP (2014–2017), these approaches were further fine-tuned and developed. As the recent external evaluation report of CAEP II stated, the CAEP had demonstrated that HCNM interventions in the education sector have a distinct added value if they are targeted to support country-level initiatives and strategies, alongside with the promotion of international standards and best practices as well as the sharing of expertise and experience in the field.[12] It is to be noted, that the Programme activities had a clear impact on the visibility and appreciation of the HCNM education project in the region in general. They contributed to improving the experts and teachers capacity in MLE and enhancing regional co-operation in the field of MLE in and across Central Asia.

In particular, the Programme beneficiaries considered the following activities and initiatives as being the most efficient and highly relevant:

- *Baseline studies*: the evaluation of the situation of minority education at all levels and the drafting of recommendations aimed at improving education policies and practices in Kazakhstan, Kyrgyzstan and Tajikistan.
- *Activities on raising awareness*: the organization of round tables and meetings with education authorities and relevant stakeholders on thematic issues aimed at facilitating discussions among the stakeholders on developments in the field of MLE policies in Kazakhstan, Kyrgyzstan and Tajikistan.
- *Promotion of MLE in minority language schools*: the provision of expert assistance to build capacities of pilot school managers and teachers, education authorities, pre-service and in-service teacher training institutions and other related stakeholders in the introduction and effective implementation of MLE programmes within Kazakhstan, Kyrgyzstan and Tajikistan.
- *Focal Point Meetings*: the organization of regular meetings for Focal Points within the Central Asian countries and other relevant education representatives to exchange information on developments of minority education policies and strengthen regional co-operation.
- *Regional Schools*: the organization of annual Regional Schools to facilitate a regional network of ministries of education, other related education institutions, experts and practitioners and strengthening their capacities in MLE.

12 L. Nicolaescu-Onofrei, *Evaluation Report of the Central Asia Education Programme Phase II (CAEP II)* (January 2017).

- *Study visits*: organization of study visits for school managers, teachers and representatives of educational institutions within each of the countries as well as across the countries of the region; study visits are intended to encourage co-operation and exchanges of best practice and challenges between MLE pilot schools.
- *Central Asian Multilingual Students' Olympiad:* aimed at preserving and developing linguistic and cultural diversity of the region, the Olympiad attracted more than 100 (pedagogical) students from 25 universities in Kazakhstan, Kyrgyzstan and Tajikistan, who collectively spoke a total of 18 languages during the various stages of the Olympiad.
- *Resources and tools promoting MLE targeted for practitioners and experts in MLE, as well as students and their parents*:
  a) the elaboration of a handbook on MLE planning and management, which is available in three languages (Russian, Kyrgyz and Uzbek);
  b) the creation and on-going support for the functioning of one of the first Russian language web-sites dedicated to MLE (http://www.edu-resource.net/) with updated news, as well as relevant guidelines and materials on MLE;
  c) the regular publishing of the Newsletter DIALOG on regional and international developments in the field of MLE (http://edu-resource.net/vestnik/) in seven languages (Kazakh, Kyrgyz, Russian, Uighur, Uzbek, Tajik and Turkmen).

The overview of the CAEP activities, based on reflections of participants in the evaluation process and CAEP documents, proves that there was a high level of relevance and responsiveness to beneficiaries' needs, and that they had a positive impact on the policy development and on decision-makers, practitioners, teachers, students, parents and minority communities as a whole. This has been achieved due to the following key elements of the Programme:

- A complex approach to the various activities, targeted and flexible assistance to education authorities and practitioners in their efforts to promote integrative multilingual education policy for national minorities, thereby creating conditions for its sustainable development and implementation;
- The efficient facilitation of partnership and co-operation development, starting with building school teams, enhancing the interaction between educational institutions; encouraging and facilitating partnerships between authorities and civil society, as well as minority communities; impact on the better interaction between different public institutions in promoting multilingual and multicultural education policies;

- The facilitation of the study and promotion of international standards and exchanges of advanced experience on multilingual and multicultural education;
- The support for expanding co-operation with European countries and institutions, having relevant expertise in the field;
- The professional input to improving the expert potential, and the multilingual and multicultural teaching competences of national teacher-trainers and school teachers;
- Last but not least, the building of partnerships with international development partners and co-ordinating relevant activities and initiatives related to minority education, and promoting linguistic and cultural diversity, in and across the Central Asian countries.

3.4 *Bilateral Projects and Initiatives*

In *Kazakhstan*, the HCNM involvement in bi-lateral projects was mandated by the annulment in 2003 of minority languages' usage for the newly introduced Unified National Test (UNT), which served both as a high school graduation exam and also as the university entrance competition. Minority school leavers were not allowed to pass the UNT, they had school graduation exams provided in the language of school teaching and a Complex Admission Test for University (CAT) conducted only in Kazakh and Russian. Limiting the language of university access testing to Kazakh and Russian languages had an immediate negative effect on minority language school leavers' access to higher education and caused serious disturbances and anxiety among national minority representatives.

To avoid further intensification of such tensions, the HCNM supported in-country projects targeting policy level improvements, which focused at facilitating the dialogue between authorities and minority communities on the issue, as well as at providing practical solutions for improving minority school leavers' access to higher education through a better acquisition of the State language. Within the first phase of the project (2003–2005), the HCNM supported the delivery of optional classes in Kazakh and Russian language for the senior grades' students from two Uzbek language schools aimed at improving their chances for succeeding at entrance examinations for universities. Alongside, teacher trainings were delivered for subject teachers from Uzbek and Tajik language schools on methods of teaching terminology and preparing the school leavers for the entrance exams. The project supported developing of terminological vocabularies on different subjects as well as sharing the experience between teachers through organizing seminars and workshops. Much effort has been invested in awareness raising among communities, parents and teachers about different approaches to national minority education for social integration. Study visits, involving community leaders, school directors and teachers have been organized to Kyrgyzstan, where bilingual teaching was piloted at several kindergartens and primary schools, as well as to Latvia and the Netherlands.

Within the second phase of cooperation (2005–2007), the project activities focused on the capacity building of minority school teachers. Trainings in communicative second language teaching methodology and bilingual teaching were delivered by experienced trainers from Latvia and Moldova. A range of seminars and round table discussions aiming at raising the awareness of authorities, communities and teachers about the advantages of MLE, were organized with the participation of representatives of every minority school and community. Some schools started applying bilingual mother tongue-Kazakh language teaching within regular classes. On the demand of community leaders and school directors, in 2008 minority school leavers were permitted to pass the UNT voluntarily. The first volunteers showed favourable results. Due to this, as well as a better awareness of stakeholders about the essence and advantages of MLE, more schools got motivated and applied for MLE piloting.

While within the first two phases the implementing partner of the HCNM project involvement in South Kazakhstan Region was a local NGO, at the next stage of cooperation (2008–2011) the HCNM project was administrated by a consortium including the Uzbek Cultural Centre, the regional Teacher In-service Training Institute and the Saremi pilot school #107. This helped streamline inter-institutional co-operation and helped to improve the local education authorities' involvement in the project activities, as well as enhanced their ownership over the multilingual education piloting in schools. It also had a positive impact in terms of confidence building and improving co-operation among the stakeholders.

By 2011, the HCNM was supporting multilingual teaching in 19 minority language schools in Kazakhstan, aimed at maintaining instruction in minority languages while strengthening the acquisition of the State language among minority pupils, thereby enhancing conditions for interaction between communities and helping to improve access of minority youth to higher education and employment opportunities. According to official data, there were 7,175 school leavers at schools with national minority languages of instruction in 2010, of whom 7.5% participated in the UNT and 17.8% took the CAT. As one can see from the data provided below (*See* Graphs 7.3 and 7.4), the pilot school graduates demonstrate much better results at university admission exams, which is one of the arguments in favour of MLE further development in minority language schools.

HCNM staff and experts contributed through consultancy and monitoring, additional trainings in MLE management and methodology, by providing assistance in project management, mediation between the implementing partners, as well as encouraging education authorities to assume ownership of the process. The Ministry of Education and Science supported the project and encouraged the South Kazakhstan Region Department of Education to provide the necessary assistance for the delivery of the project activities.

As a result of the HCNM-supported education projects:

- The number of students in all pilot schools increased over the past years (e.g.):

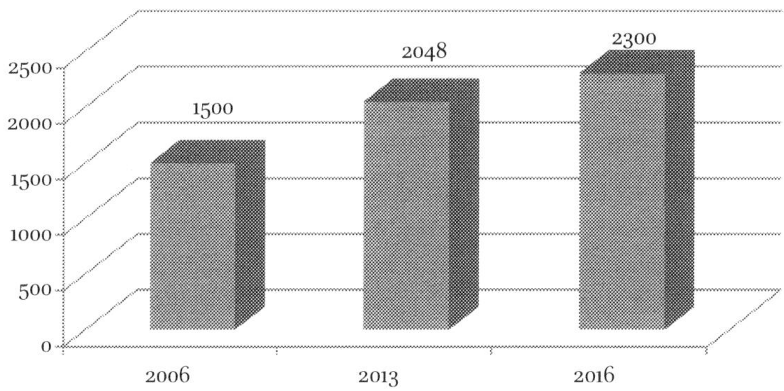

GRAPH 7.1 *Number of students per year, School 107, Shymkent (Uzbek Language).*

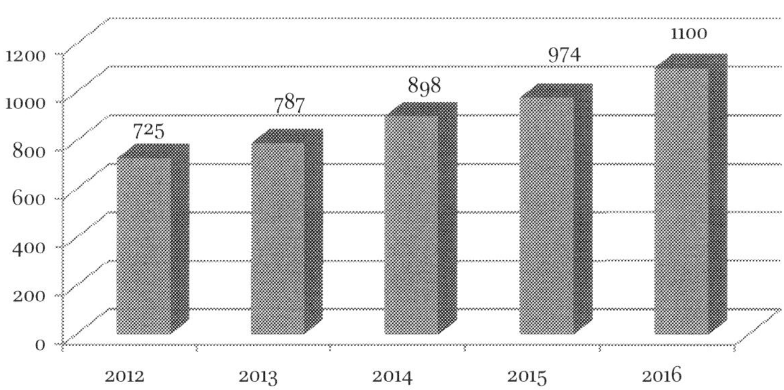

GRAPH 7.2 *Number of students per year, School 101, Almaty (Uighur Language).*

- Uzbek and Uighur language school leavers were allowed on a voluntary basis to pass the UNT. The number of test takers and examination scores in the UNT in all pilot schools improved, as did university admission rates (e.g.):

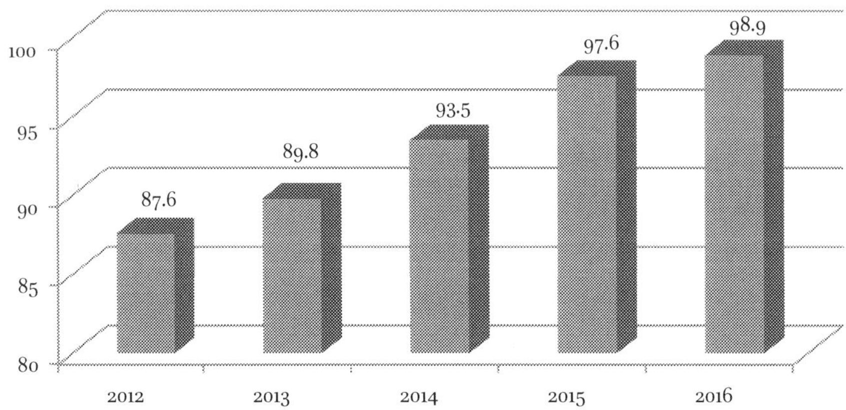

GRAPH 7.3 *Grade Point Average (national testing exams), School named after Kashkori, Kentau (Uzbek Language).*

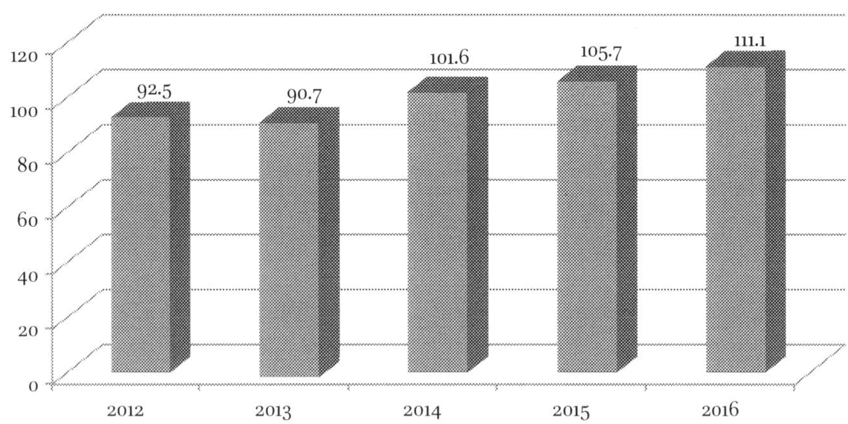

GRAPH 7.4 *Grade Point Average (national testing exams), School 153 Almaty (Uighur Language).*

- Participants in the project activities assessed positively the Programme's impact on students' ability to acquire the State language as well as to obtain instruction in their mother tongue. They supported the multilingual approach as a "remedy for minority schools' and languages' survival", for developing multilingual competences of students and for ensuring their better integration in modern Kazakhstani society.
- Participants expressed their motivation to further promote MLE and recommended that education authorities undertake full ownership of the process by improving the legal and normative basis with regard to multilingual and multicultural education, introducing the necessary changes in teacher preservice and in-service training curriculum, and developing relevant teaching and learning materials for bilingual / multilingual teaching.
- The South Kazakhstan Teachers In-Service Training Institute incorporated a four-hour module on bilingual teaching methodology into the programmes of all training courses provided for primary school teachers and Uzbek language teachers.
- Nine pilot schools became 'base units' of the In-Service Teacher Training Institute for further training seminars and awareness raising activities regarding MLE.
- A network of minority schools was established in the South Kazakhstan Region, which contributed to teachers' capacity improvement and further awareness raising about MLE and its advantages.
- Close partnership relations were established between the Saremi pilot school #107 and Uighur language School #153 in Almaty, which also contributed to the introduction of MLE piloting in this school and to awareness raising about MLE in Uighur minority schools in the Almaty Region.
- The experience of pilot schools has also been shared through the publishing of seven sets of materials on MLE management and methodology.
- The Ministry of Education and Science appreciated the impact of the HCNM involvement and recommended the experience of the Saremi School #107 and School #153 in multilingual teaching to other minority schools as a model to be followed.

It has to be said however that while Kazakhstani authorities have been positive about HCNM's support for introducing and expanding MLE in minority language schools, they refrained from taking full ownership of the process. Due to HCNM's encouragement, an Action Plan on the Introduction of Multilingual Education in Schools with Minority Language of Instruction was adopted by the Ministry of Education and Science in November 2013. It became a step forward towards undertaking ownership of the process and promoting integrative MLE policy considering minority languages.

Establishing partnerships with the Division on Content and Methodology of Education at the Department of Pre-school and Primary Education of the Ministry of Education and Science, the National Academy of Education, and the National Centre for Professional Development 'ORLEU', contributed to the institutionalization of MLE management with better consideration of minority schools' needs and acknowledging the specificity of multilingual programmes in these schools. A new window of opportunity for engagement has been opened now that the nationwide introduction of trilingual education is envisaged in Kazakhstan. In particular, in accordance with the Road Map on Trilingual Education Development in Kazakhstan, in 2016 the Ministry of Education and Science started the first phase of expanding the trilingual education model of Kazakh, Russian and English to schools throughout the country. In the wake of this recent development, the office of the HCNM is advocating for a balanced approach towards minority schools, building on the positive experience of previous HCNM projects in Uzbek language schools in Southern Kazakhstan.

In *Kyrgyzstan*, the long-term interventions of the HCNM have been constructed as a multidimensional support to the country's educational authorities. They played a significant role in developing balanced integrative education polices, as well as promoting them in educational practice. In terms of content, second language methodology, content and language integrated teaching (CLIL),[13] multicultural education, and the teaching of mother tongues were targeted, considering all educational levels: pre-school, general school and tertiary education, as well as the teacher in-service education. Improving the coordination and management mechanisms, strengthening the institutional capacity and expert potential in multilingual and multicultural education were also addressed within the HCNM projects. Such a diligent approach contributed to the gradual development of a sense of ownership by the authorities.

Initially, the HCNM (in 2004–2006) encouraged the authorities to review their language policy in the field of education and to define a strategy for minority education in conditions of the country's independence. In this regard, the HCNM supported the setting up of a *Working Group on Integration through Education*. The recommendations of the *Working Group*, suggesting the promotion of multicultural and multilingual education as a means of minority integration in Kyrgyzstan, were supported by the national Coordination Forum "Multilingual and Multicultural education development in Kyrgyzstan: from piecemeal actions – to programmatic management and development". It bears

13 Within CLIL the target language is used as a tool in the learning of a non-language subject.

mentioning that all the following studies and surveys showed sustainable interest and support for mother tongue-based MLE on behalf of national minorities.[14]

In line with the working group's recommendations, the HCNM provided assistance in improving the human and institutional capacity for further development and implementation of integrative education policies. In this regard, an Educational Liaison Officer was deployed to Kyrgyzstan in 2006, entitled to offer expert assistance and facilitate the process. The Ministry of Education and Sciences was encouraged to establish a Sector for Multicultural Education as a co-ordination and resource centre for the development of multilingual and multicultural education. In parallel, support was provided for the creation of a Centre for Uzbek language textbooks development and publishing, in Osh, Southern Kyrgyzstan. HCNM provided the necessary technical equipment for both centres, along with expert assistance to support their activity.

At the first stage, many efforts were directed towards developing professional capacities among the staff. In 2006–2008, efforts were made to improve teachers' competencies in multicultural education and second language teaching methodology, as well as sharing international practices of minority education. Opportunities were provided for study visits to countries practicing MLE. A pool of teacher trainers have become multipliers of the new teaching approaches. They also contributed to raising awareness among the teachers, students and their parents on the relevance and advantages of multicultural and multilingual education. With HCNM's expert assistance, in April 2008 a Concept Paper and a Programme for Multicultural and Multilingual Education Development in the Kyrgyz Republic were elaborated and adopted by the Ministry of Education and Science. These documents place multicultural and multilingual approaches among the priorities of the educational policy of Kyrgyzstan, setting up guidelines and practical measures to foster the transformation "from a multilingual country – to a multilingual citizen".[15]

Due to the HCNM's direct or implicit assistance, multicultural and multilingual education has also become enshrined in the main legal documents concerning the education sector.[16]

---

14 M. Tagaev 'Feasibility of MLE Development in Kyrgyzstan', (Bishkek, 2009); E.S. Ahn 'Evaluation of the Multilingual Education Component of the Unity in Diversity Project in Kyrgyzstan', UNICEF (Bishkek, 2016); CSIP 'Assessment Report on MLE Piloting in Kyrgyzstan' (Bishkek, 2017).

15 Concept of Multicultural and Multilingual Education Development in the Kyrgyz Republic <http://edu-resource.net/old/images/docs/NPA/Conc_ML_EDU.pdf>, visited on 3 January 2018.

16 The main legal documents mentioning MLE include the following: the Concept Paper for Multicultural and Multilingual Education and the Programme for Development of

On the institutional level, the entities that promote the further sustainable development and implementation of MLE in Kyrgyzstan include the following:

- The *Resource Centre on Multilingual and Multicultural Education*, created by the Ministry of Education and Science in 2006. It is administered by an implementing partner, jointly identified by the Ministry and the HCNM in 2008, namely the local NGO Center for Social Integration Policy. The Governmental authorities consider the co-operation with the organization as an important factor of achieving success due to its expert potential and management capacity.
- The *Co-ordination Council on Multicultural and Multilingual Education*, chaired by the Minister of Education, which since 2012 oversees the co-ordination of MLE development and implementation nationwide through the representation of stakeholders and donor organizations involved in multilingual and multicultural education promotion in the Kyrgyzstan.
- The *Centre of Innovative Technologies for Language Teachers In-Service Training*, within the National Teachers In-Service Training Institute, initiated by the Ministry of Education and Science in 2017, and tasked to provide in-service training courses on language teaching methodology and CLIL, organize certification of teachers for multilingual programmes, as well as facilitate the mentoring of teachers involved in multilingual programmes' implementation.
- The *Teachers In-Service Training Institute by the Osh State University*, which provides Kyrgyz and Russian language courses for school teachers and school leavers in the Southern part of the country; delivers trainings in language teaching methodologies and CLIL; offers on-site consultancy and assistance to school managers and teachers involved in the implementation of multilingual programmes.

Multicultural and Multilingual Education in the Kyrgyz Republic, which state the measures to foster the transformation "from a multilingual country – to a multilingual citizen" (approved in April 2008); the Concept for the Development of Education by the year 2020 and the Strategy for the Development of Education for the period of 2012–2020, accompanied by the subsequent Action Plans (approved in March 2012); the Concept for Strengthening of the Unity of the Nation and of the Inter-Ethnic Relations in the Kyrgyz Republic (approved in April 2013); the National Strategy for Sustainable Development of the Kyrgyz Republic for the period of 2013–2017 (approved in January 2013) and the subsequent Action Plans; the National Programme for Development of the State Language and Improvement of Language Policy in the Kyrgyz Republic for the period of 2014–2020 (approved in June 2014).

In 2011, multilingual programmes' piloting was launched in ten schools and then further expanded to seven more schools in 2012. The HCNM also encouraged UNICEF to engage in MLE promotion in Kyrgyzstan. With the support of the UN Peace Building Fund, UNICEF expanded MLE piloting in Kyrgyzstan to 30 additional schools, five kindergartens and two pilot universities (2013–2015). While closely cooperating with the UNICEF project, the HCNM put more efforts in the capacity building of teacher trainers, national consultants and experts in multilingual programmes planning and management, second language teaching methodology, as well as content and language integrated learning. In addition, input was provided to strengthening the regulatory framework and implementation mechanisms, monitoring and evaluation tools for multilingual programmes' piloting.

The HCNM supported the evaluation and certification of multilingual programmes applied in pilot schools, as well as the certification of teachers. Additional efforts were made to enhance in-school methodological assistance for teachers, including the teachers of minority languages, supporting the activity of the best pilot schools as MLE resource centres; investing in the capacity development of university lecturers in second language teaching methodology and CLIL, as well as introducing improvements in teacher training and in-service training programmes. Expert assistance was provided to adjust and apply various monitoring and evaluation tools, which help to timely update MLE practice at different levels.

Being inspired by the achievements of MLE pilot school students in the acquisition of the State language, the Parliament and the Government of Kyrgyzstan remain interested and insist on the rapid expansion of MLE to the entire education system. Unfortunately, the Kyrgyzstani education system at present does not have the relevant capacity to address such a complex challenge adequately; rather, it should be implemented with a step-by-step approach. The Government is considering investing in this field, as well as further attracting donor support for this commitment. The Ministry of Education and Science is tasked to develop a State Programme for MLE Development in Kyrgyzstan, which will be examined and discussed by the Parliament. Most importantly, MLE is supported by minority parents and students, and an increasing number of universities, schools and kindergartens are interested in starting MLE piloting, requesting relevant assistance in this regard.

This being said, the monitoring and evaluation results evidence that keeping a balance between minority mother tongue and state/official languages within MLE programmes remains a serious challenge that needs to be further monitored and safeguarded through normative acts, recommendations and collaboration with all stakeholders. The support of the HCNM remains crucial in this regard, in order to assist the process of updating and implementing the policies and to strengthen the current investment for supporting the social integration and active participation of citizens belonging to national minorities.

Thus, along with the impact of the Regional Dialogue project, the CAEP and the HCNM supported in-country education projects have played a decisive role in promoting MLE as a tool for greater social integration in Kyrgyzstan and Kazakhstan. These efforts contributed to an enhanced dialogue between authorities and minority communities with regard to minority education issues and demonstrated that multilingual mother tongue-based teaching models may play a crucial integrative role.

4 'Best Practices' and 'Challenges'

According to international norms and advanced practice, the integration of diverse societies through education is a complex task which involves the following aspects:

- Creation of a common educational space that provides equal opportunities for realizing the potential of everyone recognizing and appreciating diversity, as well as promoting a culture of peace, tolerance and respect for the 'other';[17]
- Combination of teaching in the state and official languages with the appropriate opportunities for students to learn their native language, or to receive education in this language;[18]
- Promotion of MLE for both minority and majority students;[19]
- Inclusion in the content of education courses of history, culture, religion; the reflection in the educational programmes of the traditions and contributions of both the majority and minority representatives residing within

17 OSCE HCNM, *The Ljubljana Guidelines on Integration of Diverse Societies* (The Hague, 2012) p. 55, <http://www.osce.org/hcnm/96883>, visited on 3 January 2018.

18 Council of Europe, *Framework Convention for the Protection of National Minorities* (Strasbourg, 1995) article 14, <https://rm.coe.int/16800c10cf>, visited on 3 January 2018; OSCE HCNM, *The Hague Recommendations Regarding the Education Rights of National Minorities* (The Hague, 1996).

19 OSCE HCNM, *The Ljubljana Guidelines on Integration of Diverse Societies* (The Hague, 2012) p. 55.

the state, as well as a respectful reflection of diversity and pluralism in all the subject areas covered by the curriculum;[20]

- Involvement and participation of all stakeholders in the development of a friendly and balanced content of education, consultation and monitoring of the educational process, evaluation of its effectiveness, which ensures their ownership and sharing of responsibility with public authority for the success of education.[21]

The promotion of multilingual approaches that ensure a high quality of education and enhance inter-ethnic harmony, equality of opportunities for all graduates, cohesion and social integration, are among the main objectives of educational reforms in Kazakhstan and Kyrgyzstan. In this regard, both countries have undertaken several important measures that may be considered by other states. Along with reviewing the content of education, the ongoing education reforms in Kazakhstan and Kyrgyzstan provide for the transition to MLE in schools with instruction in the State and Russian languages, as well as schools where instruction is provided in the languages of national minorities. This approach allows taking into account the needs of different language groups in access to native, state, regional and international languages, and also promotes a positive perception of MLE programmes and the strengthening of a common educational space in the country.

The provisions and objectives for the formation of a multilingual citizen, regardless of ethnic or linguistic affiliation, form part of relevant national strategies and the educational legal framework. |In parallel, the two countries are putting efforts in developing programmatic documents and improving the institutional capacity for the coordination and management of MLE implementation.

Mother-tongue based bilingual and multilingual programmes, applied in minority pilot schools in Kazakhstan and Kyrgyzstan, have been supported by community representatives, parents and teachers, who play an active role in this process. They questioned the models of 'full' or 'absolute immersion',

20 UN OHCHR, *Convention on the Rights of the Child* (New York 1990), article 7, <http://www.ohchr.org/Documents/ProfessionalInterest/crc.pdf>, visited on 3 January 2018; OSCE HCNM, *The Ljubljana Guidelines on Integration of Diverse Societies* (The Hague, 2012) pp. 55–56.

21 Council of Europe, *Framework Convention for the Protection of National Minorities and Explanatory report* (Strasbourg, 1995) article 15 p. 6, p. 22; OSCE HCNM, *The Ljubljana Guidelines on Integration of Diverse Societies* (The Hague, 2012) p. 25, p. 56.

believing that they are just a transition to teaching in another language and do not adequately consider and account for mother tongue and minority culture.

Additive (enrichment) bilingual and multilingual language education programmes, in which the state and native languages are used as languages of instruction, have proved to be the most preferable since they allow for the acquisition of the State language at the level necessary for the socialization of the individual within the given country; retain the teaching of minority language as well as using it as the language of instruction throughout the course of schooling, which contributes to the preservation of the cultural identity of minority students; and create opportunities for mastering foreign languages, thus increasing access to information, opportunities for professional development and the self-realization of minority schools' graduates.

Another factor for success that has been respected in both countries is a voluntary choice for MLE application, agreed between the main stakeholders: parents, school, community, educational authorities, etc. In the pilot phase, it may also imply an expert conclusion and recommendations regarding the relevance of conditions and the level of preparedness for application of such a programme. The authorities are advised to safeguard and consider applying the requirement for a 'voluntary choice' at the next stages of MLE expansion.

While respecting the requirements of state educational standards, the schools should also have a choice for selecting between partial immersion models: early, middle, late, or two-way immersion, as well as for choosing the subjects to be taught in the target language(s).[22]

Most schools introduced target languages for studying subjects from grade two-three. They purposefully use two languages within the lesson. The proportion of time-sharing between languages within a subject depends on the stage of instruction and the extent to which students know the target language. The proportion of using the target language within the lesson increases gradually (native/target language in a ratio of 80/20, 70/30, 60/40, 50/50 percent). Also, the number of subjects taught bilingually is gradually increasing. By grade nine, all basic subjects included in the final national testing are taught on a bilingual basis, and the ratio of languages is changing in favour of the target language(s).

The monitoring and evaluation of multilingual programmes undertaken by these schools and independent experts proved the improvement of communication skills of students in target languages, including the skills of intercultural communication and tolerance. Teachers and students have become more and more part of a common educational space: the number of students

22 The target language is a language other than one's native language that is being learned.

and teachers participating in various contests, and projects implemented in the State language is gradually growing. Representatives of these schools demonstrate good results and often turn out to be among the winners of various school contests, which proves their growing competitiveness. The number of graduates of pilot schools that successfully continue their studies in higher education institutions is much higher than in monolingual schools with instruction in the languages of national minorities.

Despite difficulties with textbooks' supply and shortages of methodological materials, reference books and fiction in minority languages, teachers nonetheless note the increased opportunities for using available materials, including electronic ones, in various languages, which contributes to raising the motivation of students and the effectiveness of the teaching. Schools also encourage teachers to create their own teaching materials: worksheets, terminology dictionaries, didactic projects. The expanding cooperation of pilot schools within the country and in the region is also contributing to the replenishment of the teaching and methodological resources used by teachers.

School managers and teachers of schools, methodologists and parents note the increased professional level of teachers involved in the implementation of multilingual programmes, their role in promoting new methodological approaches, and sharing practical experience both at school and within the network of schools.

At the same time, schools face certain challenges that make it difficult to further expand the coverage of MLE programmes. The quality and sustainability of MLE with any set of languages is closely related to the use and study of the mother tongue at pre-school and school level, the quality of subject standards and teaching methodology, availability of teaching materials and, above all, qualified teachers. The certification of teachers involved in the implementation of MLE programmes, as well as the certification of the school programmes themselves, is an important factor in the successful implementation and sustainability of these programmes. The monitoring data indicates the need to take measures for improving the level of language proficiency of teachers in the target languages (Kazakh, Kyrgyz, Russian) and their qualification in CLIL and other multilingual teaching methodologies. This task can be fulfilled by making changes in the programmes for training and professional development of teachers. The comprehensive programme for improving the skills of school teams for the implementation of MLE would include courses on the methodology of teaching the native language, the methodology of teaching the second language, the CLIL methodology, as well as multicultural education. It is also necessary to improve the methodological service and the system of professional development within schools: enhancing the activity of school teams, development of mentoring and inter-schools networking, and the provision of on-the-spot methodological assistance to teachers and education managers.

5 Conclusions and Recommendations

Both Kazakhstan and Kyrgyzstan have traditionally diverse societies in which the individual identities of persons belonging to minorities are often multiple and multi-layered. It is clear that managing such a diversity is a complex and challenging task. It needs to be valued and promoted as an important asset and heritage of the country.

In both Kazakhstan and Kyrgyzstan, there is a clearly articulated demand at the local level, as well as a clear trend at the policy level to promote MLE. This is a favourable context for enhancing the support to education authorities and practitioners in their efforts to promote integrative multilingual and multicultural education policies for national minorities.

Despite the continuing concern for the future of the mother tongue in education, the society in both countries recognizes the benefits of MLE. Parents no longer face the dilemma of choosing only one language of instruction, which used to be often different from the family language, since multilingual programmes allow mastering both: the student's mother tongue, as well as other target languages: the State language, Russian, and a foreign language. This approach, on the one hand, allows satisfying the basic rights of citizens to preserve their identity, and on the other hand, creates the opportunity for the formation of a multiple identity of the individual. The better acquisition of the State language and access to regional and world languages in the programmes of MLE contributes to the expansion of the boundaries of personal identification, social mobility, reduction of risks of discrimination and integration of society.

Applying mother tongue-based MLE programmes, as well as giving a choice in adhering to and developing of MLE school programmes, taking into account the views of parents and the linguistic situation of the regions, strengthens the trust of ethnic groups and shapes their positive perception of the language education reform.

The recent adoption of the Road Map on Trilingual Education Development in Kazakhstan for 2015–2020, focusing on the Kazakh, Russian and English languages throughout the school system is the next step in strengthening the unified educational space in Kazakhstan. However, the implementation of this programme in schools with instruction in languages that are not among the target languages of the trilingual programme requires consideration of minority pilot schools' experience in the field. Underestimation of the specifics of schools with instruction in the languages of national minorities can lead to a decline in the quality of education in these schools, the formation of asymmetric or subtractive bilingualism among students, and the narrowing of the use of minority languages in the education system, up to their expulsion from the education system.

For the further successful extension of the pilot schools' experience and to safeguard the sustainability of MLE, both countries are encouraged to *safeguard minority mother tongues education and teaching through relevant regulations, provision of adequate conditions and on-going collaboration with stakeholders.*

The HCNM experience in other countries shows that if steps are taken to introduce multilingual education without reassurance that the teaching of subjects in minority languages will be maintained, and without the mechanisms that ensure that such instruction will be of a high standard, this could lead to a negative reaction by minority communities that may perceive that MLE is being introduced with the ultimate goal of assimilation. In addition, as foreseen by the HCNM Hague Recommendations, there are strong pedagogical reasons for ensuring an appropriate balance in languages of instruction at different levels of schooling.

The countries are advised *to apply a complex approach to MLE, in terms of targeted levels of intervention: pre-school, general school and higher education.* In this regard, it should be clear that disregarding some key methodological requirements in education practice, namely that "the medium of teaching at pre-school and kindergarten levels should ideally be the child's language",[23] may preclude the achievement of positive results through MLE. Consequently, countries need to create adequate conditions for minority mother tongue teaching at pre-school and kindergarten levels.

At university level the education authorities should refrain from focusing almost exclusively at English language promotion, but also consider teaching and certification of students' proficiency in minority mother tongues and other target languages as well as providing relevant attention to the methodological component of MLE and developing of multicultural competencies of future teachers.

The promotion of improvements in teacher training and in-service training through changing the training curriculum, capacity building of the staff and

23 OSCE HCNM, *The Hague Recommendations Regarding the Education Rights of National Minorities* (The Hague, 1996) p. 6.

strengthening the networking and cooperation between the institutions and teacher training needs to go along with enhancing the assistance for capacity building of local education authorities, developing the expert potential of the best pilot schools and transforming them in local resource centres in order to ensure adequate methodological guidance and assistance at the local level.

Experience has shown that the introduction of significant changes to the education system requires an appropriate financing, as well as a transition period to enable education authorities and other stakeholders to sufficiently prepare for the new measures and to gradually introduce them. Proper monitoring and evaluation mechanisms and analyses will allow making timely adjustments.

Public discussions with key stakeholders are very useful in order to generate support for planned policy changes and to clarify and address the potential concerns among those who will be affected. In this regard, it is important to take measures not only to inform parents about multilingual education, but to engage them in a dialogue at the school level about planned activities and to respect their right to make informed choices about their children's education. Minority representatives should also be involved in working groups or councils that are tasked with formulating and implementing multilingual education policies at the national and local levels.

Cooperation between the neighbouring Central Asian states, aimed at promoting mother tongue-based multilingual education, proved to be mutually beneficial. Further strengthening the dialogue and inter-state collaboration through study visits, new common initiatives and regional activities, developing professional networks and partnership, common studies and exchange of experiences, etc., would certainly have a positive impact on promoting integrative education policies in these countries.

Finally, respect for the HCNM Oslo Recommendations and their adequate consideration in the process of designing and implementing states' policies and practices would enable a balanced linguistic diversity management. This in turn would represent a strong instrument of motivation for the development of mother tongue-based multilingual education, as well as for confidence building and for the integration of diverse societies.

PART 2

Language Rights and Evolving Standards and Practice

CHAPTER 8

Continued Relevance of an 'Oslo' Language Policy in a Changing World

Fernand de Varennes and Elżbieta Kuzborska

1 Introduction

The issue of whether minorities are particularly vulnerable, and whether therefore there should be legal measures for their protection beyond general human rights standards applicable to all, has been an ongoing matter of some dispute predating the Second World War. A number of 'Minorities Treaties' operated under the United Nations' predecessor, the League of Nations, but this series of bilateral and unilateral instruments were neither comprehensive nor were, as described at times, exclusively preoccupied with collective rights. They did however seek to recognise in many of their terms the rights of well-established minorities, even if they also at the same time contained more general human rights provisions, and were premised on the view that the recognition and protection of their rights would alleviate the kind of ethnic tensions which contributed to the eruption of the world's first world war, starting with the assassination of Archduke Franz Ferdinand of Austria, heir presumptive to the Austro-Hungarian throne, and his wife Sophie, by a Southern Slav separatist group.

The orthodox view however is that the minority rights system was instrumentalised in the 1930s by Nazi Germany, and under the guise of the need to protect the Sudeten German minority because of alleged discrimination and oppression suffered by the ethnic German population living there, led to the German annexation of Czechoslovakia's northern and western border regions, and was one of the precipitating factors in the collapse of that state and the beginning of World War II. This view explains the reluctance to refer to any kind of minority rights in both the Charter of the United Nations and the UN's Universal Declaration of Human Rights in 1948. Only with the adoption of the 1966 International Covenant on Civil and Political Rights did the concept of a minority right enter again into the realm of international human rights instruments, and clearly only from an individualistic point of view to surmount the almost instinctive dislike for any kind of collective right. This is true of European human rights instruments during much of the same period.

© KONINKLIJKE BRILL NV, LEIDEN, 2018 | DOI 10.1163/9789004357754_009

There is for example no reference to minorities in the 1950 European Convention on Human Rights (ECHR).

But minority issues never went away, and particularly in Europe there was a continuing concern that ignoring or refusing to acknowledge and address grievances around claims of discrimination, exclusion and injustice would not be conducive to much needed peace and stability in Europe, and that a general human rights approach was not sufficiently clear to address many of these grievances. The 1950s and 1960s were still perturbed by new and disturbing ethnic tensions and violence in regions such as the Basque Country, Northern Ireland, and South Tyrol, among others, which made certain that the need to protect minorities in order to ensure stability was never too far off the radar, at least in Western Europe.

In light of the general hesitancy of some States to make any kind of commitment in relation to legal minority protection, early political and diplomatic initiatives came from the Conference for Security and Cooperation in Europe (CSCE), particularly during the Cold War and against the backdrop of escalating ethnic tensions in the successor states of the former Soviet bloc, and of course following the breakup of Yugoslavia. Among the most important of these initial steps is the 1990 Copenhagen Document, which linked minority protection to democratic values and the need for a concept of security that combines peace and security directly with democracy and the human rights of minorities.[1] From there it was but a few more short steps to the recognition that it is crucial to accommodate the legitimate linguistic and cultural aspirations of minorities in order to prevent ethnic conflicts.

The mandate of the High Commissioner on National Minorities (HCNM) was established in 1993 in line with these historical developments, to prevent inter-ethnic tensions and conflicts from eruption. It focuses on situations involving 'national minorities', undefined because of a lack of consensus and governmental authorities in order to prevent possible unrests. The High Commissioner has issued so far a series of eight recommendations and guidelines on how governmental policies can take into account and address the human rights of minorities in order to maintain harmonious and inclusive societies conducive to maintaining peace and stability.[2] One of these is of course HCNM's

1 *See* J. Packer, G. Siemienski, 'The Language of Equity: The Origin and Development of the Oslo Recommendations regarding the Linguistic Rights of National Minorities', 6 *International Journal on Minority & Group Rights* (1999) pp. 329–330.

2 OSCE High Commissioner on National Minorities, *The Hague Recommendations Regarding the Education Rights of National Minorities* (OSCE/HCNM, 1996); *The Oslo Recommendations regarding the Linguistic Rights of National Minorities* (OSCE/HCNM, 1998); *The Lund Recommendations on the Effective Participation of National Minorities in Public Life,*

Oslo Recommendations on the linguistic rights of national minorities published in February 1988. Based on the experience of the OSCE High Commissioner and the advice of internationally recognized experts,[3] they seek to provide guidance to OSCE participating States on how best to ensure the linguistic rights of national minorities within their borders, keeping in mind the role of the HCNM as a conflict preventive mechanism and the urgency to identify and apply effective tools for the prevention of ethnic conflicts. They therefore identify certain recurrent issues and themes which have become the subject of attention of the High Commissioner in a number of OSCE States. These recommendations cover names, religion, community life and non-governmental organizations, the media, economic life, administrative authorities and public services, independent national institutions, and judicial authorities.

It may be useful to underline that the Oslo Recommendations provide guidance as to how human rights can impact on, and even assist in, the accommodation of European linguistic diversity in both the private as well as the public context of the use of language. They place a special emphasis on the need to achieve the appropriate balance in this regard in order to avoid the inter-ethnic tensions. The Oslo Recommendations thus provide concrete guidelines and useful references for the development of State policies and legislation on language-related issues, consonant with human rights obligations, which arise in practice. They are divided into sub-headings which respond to a particular linguistic issue and are accompanied by the more detailed Explanatory Note.

(OSCE/HCNM, 1999); *Guidelines on the Use of Minority Languages in the Broadcast Media* (OSCE/HCNM, 2003); *Recommendations on Policing in Multi-Ethnic Societies* (OSCE/HCNM, 2006); *The Bolzano/Bozen Recommendations on National Minorities in Inter-State Relations* (OSCE/HCNM, 2008); *The Ljubljana Guidelines on Integration of Diverse Societies* (OSCE/HCNM, 2012); and *the Graz Recommendations on Access to Justice and National Minorities* (OSCE/HCNM, 2017).

3 Specifically, the experts involved in drafting the recommendations were: Professor Gudmundur Alfredsson, Co-Director, Raoul Wallenberg Institute (Sweden); Professor Asbjørn Eide, Senior Fellow, Norwegian Institute of Human Rights (Norway); Ms. Angelita Kamenska, Senior Researcher, Latvian Centre for Human Rights and Ethnic Studies (Latvia); Mr. Dónall Ó Riagáin, Secretary General, European Bureau of Lesser Used Languages (Ireland); Ms. Beate Slydal, Advisor, Norwegian Forum for the Freedom of Expression (Norway); Dr. Miquel Strubell, Director, Institute of Catalan Sociolinguistics, Government of Catalonia (Spain); Professor György Szepe, Department of Language Sciences at Janus Panonius University (Hungary); Professor Patrick Thornberry, Department of Law, Keele University (United Kingdom); Dr. Fernand de Varennes, Director of the Asia-Pacific Centre for Human Rights and the Prevention of Ethnic Conflict (Australia); Professor Bruno de Witte, Faculty of Law, University of Maastricht (the Netherlands); Jean-Marie Woehrling, Institut de droit local alsacien-mosellan (France).

The Oslo Recommendations at their most basic therefore reflect and seek to reach at the very essence of human rights – the full, free and respectful development of the individual human personality, in all the richness of what makes us human and unique in our identities, in conditions of equality.[4]

2 Continued Relevance in a Changing World

> The importance of language rights is straightforward: in addition to the obligation to respect human rights, there are important implications of language use that go to the core of inclusion and participation in a society with minorities.[5]

2.1 *The Main Characteristics of the Oslo Recommendations*

As the historical background highlights, the Oslo Recommendations were drafted by a group of internationally recognised experts commissioned by the OSCE High Commissioner on National Minorities (HCNM).[6] Support for these, and the other recommendations commissioned by the HCNM, as a valuable reference, has been continuously expressed within the Organization for Security and Co-operation in Europe.

That contextualisation is still necessary to emphasise the continued – and perhaps even increasingly important – relevance of the Oslo Recommendations twenty years later, as these are part of the HCNM toolkit for the prevention of ethnic conflicts.

While the OSCE High Commissioner's mandate is in a strict sense to monitor the situation of minorities and to act as an institutionalised mediation

4 OSCE High Commissioner on National Minorities, *The Oslo Recommendations regarding the Linguistic Rights of National Minorities & Explanatory Note* (OSCE/HCNM, 1998) p. 3, <http://www.osce.org/hcnm/oslo-recommendations?download=true>.

5 United Nations Special Rapporteur on Minority Issues, *Language Rights of Linguistic Minorities: A Practical Guide for Implementation* (UN, 2017) p. 7, <http://www.ohchr.org/Documents/Issues/Minorities/SR/LanguageRightsLinguisticMinorities_EN.pdf>.

6 Minority standards also figure in the activities of the Office for Democratic Institutions and Human Rights, although not to the same obvious extent as with the High Commissioner on National Minorities. Because this Office is one of the OSCE's main institutions working in monitoring the implementation of human dimension commitments which deals with human rights in general, this will also cover minority issues. The Office for Democratic Institutions and Human Rights therefore has responsibility for determining how well States are complying with the human dimensions commitments affecting minorities and that are contained, for the most part, in the 1990 Document of the Copenhagen Meeting of the Conference on the Human Dimension.

mechanism to intervene when things escalate between the relevant States and minorities, the preventive aspect of which the Oslo Recommendations is a part that has frequently in practice been utilised and useful, if not always recognised outside of OSCE or diplomatic circles.

Thus the Oslo Recommendations were – and continue to be – intended as an instrument of conflict prevention to guide government policies which might fuel minority-related conflicts were they not to respect international human rights standards in sensitive areas, such as language policies. This points to one of the fundamental premises of the Oslo Recommendations, and their continued relevance: language policies remain recurrent issues in terms of their potential for conflict within States. There are therefore at a very basic level two essential dimensions to the *raison d'être* of the Oslo Recommendations: (1) they serve as reference points to guide state policy-makers and lawmakers on their human rights obligations in relation to language issues affecting minorities, and (2) policies and legislation which disregard or fail to respect these human rights standards may contribute to tensions and potential violent conflicts. As the wording of the first set of recommendations, the 1996 Hague Recommendations Regarding the Education Rights, acknowledges, "[the OSCE High Commissioner] employs the international standards to which each State has agreed as his principal framework of analysis and the foundation of his specific recommendations".[7] Indeed, these dimensions have always constituted the very essence and framework of all HCNM recommendations so that Max van der Stoel, the first OSCE High Commissioner, frequently asserted over the years that States should not believe that in satisfying their commitments vis-à-vis minorities they are either granting something or giving something away. It is not for States to 'give' rights to minorities since these are human rights, a point acknowledged in paragraph 31 of the CSCE Copenhagen Document:

> ...persons belonging to national minorities have the right freely to express, preserve and develop their ethnic, cultural, linguistic or religious identity and to maintain and develop their culture in all its aspects, free of any attempts at assimilation against their will.

Other parts of this book deal with the substantive dimensions of the Oslo Recommendations, but it may still be useful to briefly point out that the Oslo

7 OSCE High Commissioner on National Minorities, 'The Hague Recommendations Regarding the Education Rights of National Minorities', reprinted in 2 *International Journal on Minority and Group Rights* (1997) pp. 199–213, p. 199.

Recommendations are based on OSCE commitments contained in the Copenhagen Document, as well as the human rights obligations contained in treaties such as the International Covenant on Civil and Political Rights and the Council of Europe's Framework Convention on the Protection of National Minorities. To give just two examples of the direct and intimate connection between the language rights contained in the Oslo Recommendations and specific international human rights standards, Recommendation 1 of the Oslo Recommendations indicates that persons belonging to minorities "have the right to use their personal names in their own language according to their own traditions and linguistic systems. These shall be given official recognition and be used by the public authorities". Such a right is also recognised through the international human rights standard of the right to private life.[8] Similarly, Recommendation 14 provides for:

> ...adequate possibilities to use their language in communications with administrative authorities especially in regions and localities where they have expressed a desire for it and where they are present in significant numbers. Similarly, administrative authorities shall, wherever possible, ensure that public services are provided also in the language of the national minority. To this end, they shall adopt appropriate recruitment and/or training policies and programmes.

When the number of speakers of a minority language is 'significant', a State must according to this Oslo Recommendation ensure that public services are provided in the language of the national minority and adopt appropriate recruitment and/or training policies and programmes. International jurisprudence appears to consider the absence of such an approach in relation to language preferences and policies as potentially discriminatory where not reasonably justified. In other words, not to provide an appropriate degree of public services in a minority's language could be discrimination as to language unless there is a reasonable and permitted justification for not using the minority language.[9]

8 *See* especially *Raihman* v. *Latvia*, Communication No. 1621/2007, U.N. Doc. CCPR/C/100/D/1621/2007 (2010).

9 *See in particular Kevin Mgwanga Gunme et al.* v. *Cameroon*, African Commission on Human and Peoples Rights, Communication 266/2003, 27 May 2009, and *J.G.A. Diergaardt et al.* v. *Namibia*, CCPR/C/69/D/760/1997, 25 July 2000. In practical terms, this can also be linked to the proportionality principle in the application of the right to equality without discrimination, described in United Nations Special Rapporteur on Minority Issues, *Language Rights of Linguistic Minorities: A Practical Guide for Implementation* (2017) p. 13.

2.2 *Continued Relevance*

> When minority rights are enshrined in constitutions, and implemented through electoral, justice and education systems before a conflict has the chance to fester, there is a chance that conflict might not occur at all.[10]

The world in the second decade of the 21st Century may appear, at least for some, to be light years away from the realities and 'mood' in the 1990s, but does this affect – and in what way – the continued relevance of the Oslo Recommendations? Any response to such a question must reflect on two core issues: the international standards relating to the human rights of minorities in areas where language issues may come into play, and the use of these standards in helping to avoid tensions potentially leading to ethnic conflicts. Put differently, is there any reason today, some 20 years after the Oslo Recommendations were published, to disregard international human rights standards in relation to minorities, or is there no need for guidelines on how to prevent ethnic conflicts?

It would seem problematic to suggest that somehow minorities are today no longer deserving of the full protection of international human rights. Indeed, many would arguably feel that the first half of the 21st Century has become rather less tolerant of minorities in many parts of the world, with xenophobia, hate speech and racism targeting particularly vulnerable minorities apparently becoming more widespread and an even greater challenge to address. Even the OSCE's first High Commissioner on National Minorities seemed almost prescient when he signaled even in 2001 growing intolerance, xenophobia and racism throughout Europe and the danger of such a drift:

> The failure to integrate usually leads to disintegration. Wars in the former Yugoslavia give clear warnings about the cancer of intolerance in multi-ethnic societies. Such conflicts feature grave violations of human rights, the systematic exclusion and suppression of one or several groups by another. In some cases marginalization spawns frustration. In others, difference is perceived as threat, and the threat is confronted by violence. These phenomena are not limited to the Balkans. Xenophobia, racism, anti-Semitism and extreme nationalism are alive and well throughout Europe.[11]

---

10 C. Baldwin, C. Chapman and Z. Gray, *Minority Rights: The Key to Conflict Prevention* (Minority Rights International, London, 2007) p. 2.

11 M. van der Stoel, OSCE High Commissioner on National Minorities, *Easing the Sisyphus Task: Preventing the Conflicts of the Future, Speech at the Verleihung des Hessichen*

If anything, one should assume that the universal recognition of and respect for the rights of minorities become even more urgent and pressing rather than no longer relevant. In any event, the lessons of the Second World War and the almost inconceivable horrors of the Holocaust and racist policies which targeted mainly Jews, Roma, and other minorities – and directly contributed to the building of the whole postwar international human rights edifice – are that human rights are universal, indivisible, and just as relevant today as they were some 70 years ago.[12] Until such time as the international community abandons completely the international human rights system which protects some of the world's most vulnerable, the relevance of the Oslo Recommendations and others of their ilk does not seem to have faded in any way.

Is the prevention of ethnic conflict no longer a relevant consideration, or has the threat of ethnic conflicts involving minorities receded so much that concerns over language issues have become redundant or insignificant? Once again, it would seem as difficult to arrive at such conclusions today as it would have been in the 1990s. One of the foundational premises of the Oslo Recommendations is that ethnic conflicts tend to erupt when the human rights of minorities are disregarded or discarded with the result that they are excluded, discriminated or feel that their existence is threatened. Those conditions continue to this day in a number of countries, without any indication that such grievances are becoming less prevalent. Although relating more to issues of statelessness and religious minorities, it is clear that the massive and systematic violations of the human rights of the Rohingya minority fueled the eventual use of violence by Rohingya insurgents (the Arakan Rohingya Salvation Army) in 2016, and the ensuing brutal repression and even ethnic cleansing, descent towards conflict, and humanitarian crises.[13]

It may be useful to reflect in greater detail as to what is involved precisely in relation to language issues and the Oslo Recommendations.

Friedenspreises, Wiesbaden Germany, 20 June 2001, <http://www.osce.org/hcnm/42334?download=true>.

12 As a historical and legal footnote, the first human rights treaty is arguably the 1948 Convention on the Prevention and Punishment of the Crime of Genocide. Though not specifically limiting genocide to the destruction of minorities, its genesis was very much connected to the genocidal crimes committed against Jews, a minority, during the Second World War, and the groups identified in the treaty's definition "a national, ethnical, racial or religious" mainly envisaged the particular vulnerability of minorities.

13 *See* UN News Centre, *UN human rights chief points to 'textbook example of ethnic cleansing' in Myanmar*, 11 September, 2017, <http://www.un.org/apps/news/story.asp?NewsID=57490#.WhryVjdrw2w>.

2.3 *The Growing Relevance of the Oslo Recommendations (and Conflicts)*

> A human rights-based approach to language can be framed as a 'recognize-implement-improve' method for ensuring that state authorities effectively comply with their obligations. Laws, policies and processes must recognize language rights within a human rights framework i.e., authorities must integrate these into their conduct and activities, and mechanisms must be put in place to effectively address problem areas where they exist and improve compliance.[14]

The 1998 Oslo Recommendations regarding the Linguistic Rights of National Minorities was a response to the many conflicts with a linguistic dimension that followed the collapse of the Eastern bloc.[15] Preventing minority communities from using their own language, or excluding or disadvantaging them because or through their language, raises human rights matters in relation to international standards such as Article 27 of the International Covenant on Civil and Political Rights, as well as freedom of expression, non-discrimination, and other human rights standards. Moreover, as the object of human rights instruments as well as all of the thematic instruments developed through the OSCE High Commissioner on National Minorities is to provide useful and targeted signposts on how States should address the presence, role and inclusion of minorities within their borders to avoid or to seek early resolution of ethnic tensions and conflicts,[16] their relevance would naturally seem to be predicated

---

14 United Nations Special Rapporteur on Minority Issues, *Language Rights of Linguistic Minorities: A Practical Guide for Implementation* (2017) p. 11.

15 J. Packer and G. Siemienski, 'The Language of Equity: The Origin and Development of the Oslo Recommendations Regarding the Linguistic Rights of National Minorities', 3 *International Journal on Minority and Group Rights* (1999) pp. 329–350, pp. 329–330.

16 These are in chronological order the OSCE High Commissioner on National Minorities, *The Hague Recommendations Regarding the Education Rights of National Minorities* (1996); *the Oslo Recommendations regarding the Linguistic Rights of National Minorities* (1998); *the Lund Recommendations on the Effective Participation of National Minorities in Public Life* (1999); *the Guidelines on the Use of Minority Languages in the Broadcast Media* (2003); *the Recommendations on Policing in Multi-Ethnic Societies* (2006); *the Bolzano/Bozen Recommendations on National Minorities in Inter-State Relations* (2008); *the Ljubljana Guidelines on Integration of Diverse Societies* (2012); and the *Graz Recommendations on Access to Justice and National Minorities* (2017). All of these are available, in a number of European languages, at the OSCE High Commissioner on National Minorities official website, <http://www.osce.org/hcnm/thematic-recommendations

on whether such tensions and conflicts still blight relations between states. Unfortunately, they still do.

Without passing judgement on the instrumentalisation or validity of minority grievances around language issues, claims of discrimination or exclusion linked to state language policies and preferences continue to pepper the world. One of the most recent of these is in Cameroon, where some members of the English-speaking minority, representing roughly 20% of the country's population and inhabiting the Northwest and Southwest regions of the country, claim they have been marginalized by a predominately French-speaking government despite English being also an official language alongside French. More specifically, their grievances centre around perceived discrimination, especially in education and the judicial system, where English is not used to the extent their relative demographic weight, concentration and status would seem to warrant. As a result, tensions have escalated to the point of violence, with reports of demonstrators shot dead by soldiers in 2016, 2017 and 2018 during protests connected to these grievances.[17] Nor have more recent tensions over language grievances escaped the European landscape in light of situations in Spain, Ukraine, Russia and the Baltic States.

What these and other recent examples signal is that far from lacking any further relevance 20 years after their development, the Oslo Recommendations and their 'relatives' are still as relevant today, and perhaps even more so, as there is still an evident need for the OSCE High Commissioner on National Minorities to function as initially conceived, namely "to identify and seek early resolution of ethnic tensions that might endanger peace, stability or friendly relations between the participating States of the OSCE".[18] The emergence of new tensions and conflicts involving language issues in Europe and elsewhere would seem to suggest that the relevance of the Oslo Recommendations, and other efforts of the HCNM directed towards ensuring that persons belonging to minorities have the right to exercise fully and effectively their human rights and fundamental freedoms without any discrimination and in full equality before the law because, as one of the effective ways of ensuring peace, justice and stability is just as strong today as it was two decades ago, if not more. It would

-and-guidelines>. It should also be pointed out that the OSCE ODIHR also produced some other sets of similar recommendations or guidelines, premised once again on human rights standards, such as *Guidelines to Assist National Minority Participation in the Electoral Process* (2001), <http://www.osce.org/odihr/elections/17569>.

17 *See* United Nations, 'UN chief to meet Biya over anglophone crisis', *Journal du Cameroun*, 27 October 2017, <https://www.journalducameroun.com/en/un-chief-meet-biya-anglophone-crisis/>.

18 OSCE High Commissioner on National Minorities, *Who we are*, <http://www.osce.org/hcnm/107876>.

seem that the accommodation of linguistic diversity through the recognition of the language rights of minorities remains an important matter of policy and law, and that the failure to address and achieve the appropriate balance in accommodating this diversity still can be a major source of inter-ethnic tensions.

3 Conclusion

> It is hoped that these Recommendations will provide a useful reference for the development of State policies and laws which will contribute to an effective implementation of the language rights of persons belonging to national minorities, especially in the public sphere.[19]

In recent decades, it seems that intolerance, "discrimination and violence on the grounds of ethnicity, nationality and religion were on the rise in all parts of the world".[20] This suggests an even greater relevance for the international human rights approach found in the Oslo Recommendations and related efforts of the High Commissioner on National Minorities with the objective of developing stable and harmonious inter-ethnic relations through the creation of frameworks for protecting minorities. They provide guidelines to help achieve a balance between the maintenance of the territorial integrity of States and the claims of minorities that they are not treated properly as full citizens by their government. The Oslo Recommendations are an attempt to address these issues at an early stage before positions become polarized and questions of identity and rights give way, if left unresolved, to tensions and potential conflicts.

The fundamental assumption behind these objectives, one which evidence tends to support, is that "the forceful imposition of the will of one group of people onto another and the failure to respect international standards[...] is a breach of human rights and, moreover, can lead to internal instability and even regional insecurity".[21] This view is also shared by other European institutions, including the Council of Europe's Parliamentary Assembly, which stated in a

19 OSCE High Commissioner on National Minorities, *The Oslo Recommendations regarding the Linguistic Rights of National Minorities & Explanatory Note* (1998) p. 4, <http://www.osce.org/hcnm/oslo-recommendations?download=true>.

20 Human Rights Council holds a general debate on racism, racial discrimination, xenophobia and related forms of intolerance, 20 March 2017, <http://www.ohchr.org/EN/NewsEvents/Pages/DisplayNews.aspx?NewsID=21414&LangID=E>.

21 Speech by OSCE High Commissioner on National Minorities Max van der Stoel at the OSCE Review Conference, Vienna, 20 September 1999, <http://www.osce.org/hcnm/32077?download=true>.

recommendation and reflected in a subsequent decision of the Committee of Ministers, that the effective protection of the human rights of minorities is of great importance for "stability, democratic security and peace in Europe".[22]

While the world today may be different from two decades ago, the situation since has not changed in such a way as to dilute the relevance of the Oslo Recommendations. On the contrary, as tensions continue to exist and even grow around language issues, so does the need to prevent them from degenerating into conflicts. As Max van der Stoel, the first OSCE High Commissioner on National Minorities, emphasised when he received the Hessische Peace Prize in 2001, "I am under no illusions that all inter-ethnic conflicts can be solved. However, I do not believe inter-ethnic conflict is inevitable. We now have a better understanding of why conflicts erupt and how they can be prevented. Standards are in place to protect minority rights and there is a growing 'toolbox' of techniques to prevent conflict".[23]

Perhaps one of the most significant techniques in the HCNM toolbox remains the Oslo Recommendations given the continuing, even increasing, situations where language issues continue to arise as sources of tensions in Europe and other parts of the world.

22 Parliamentary Assembly of the Council of Europe, Recommendation 1492 (2001), *Rights of national minorities*, <http://assembly.coe.int/nw/xml/XRef/Xref-XML2HTML-EN.asp?fileid=16861&lang=en>.

23 M. van der Stoel, OSCE High Commissioner on National Minorities, *Easing the Sisyphus Task: Preventing the Conflicts of the Future, Speech at the Verleihung des Hessichen Friedenspreises, Wiesbaden Germany*, 20 June 2001, <http://www.osce.org/hcnm/42334?download=true>.

CHAPTER 9

"The Borders of My Language Mean the Borders of My World". Language Rights and Their Evolving Significance for Minority Rights and Integration of Societies

Francesco Palermo

1 Introduction

Wittgenstein's famous sentence echoed in the title of this chapter underlines the essential importance of language in understanding, explaining and ultimately framing the world. "All I know" – the quote continues – "is what I have words for".[1] The same goes, more modestly, for language rights and their role in the overall system of minority rights: through the position of and the attitude towards language, the attitude of society vis-à-vis diversity is unveiled.

This chapter reflects on the evolution of language rights (something that goes beyond linguistic rights as it covers the regulation of language more broadly and not only the right to use minority languages)[2] in Europe. The European continent is much less linguistically diverse than other regions of the world,[3] but at the same time it has the highest density of norms in this field, both at international (hard and soft) and at domestic level and is thus a laboratory and an incubator for minority rights.

Especially in European history, language is not a 'simple' right. In the nation-State culture which still permeates Europe, language is the essential component of (national) identity.[4] Language rights are at the same time the most

1 L. Wittgenstein, *Tractatus logico-philosophicus*, German-English ed. (Routledge, London, 1981), pp. 5–6.

2 *See* United Nations Special Rapporteur on minority issues, *Language Rights of Linguistic Minorities. A Practical Guide for Implementation* (Geneva, 2017), p. 5.

3 According to P. Juaristi, T. Reagan and H. Tonkin, 'Language diversity in the European Union. An overview', in X. Arzoz (ed.), *Respecting Linguistic Diversity in the European Union* (John Benjamins, Amsterdam-Philadelphia, 2008), pp. 47–72, the EU has 7% of the world's total population but it includes only 1% of the world's linguistic diversity.

4 One may think of the German romantics – *see* D. Martyn, 'Borrowed Fatherland: Nationalism and Language Purism in Fichte's Addresses to the German Nation', 72:4 *Germanic Review* (1997), pp. 303–315.

© KONINKLIJKE BRILL NV, LEIDEN, 2018 | DOI 10.1163/9789004357754_010

basic and the most articulated rights of persons belonging to national minorities. They are basic, because the use of language is one of the first and most essential claims of persons belonging to minorities, which to a large extent identify along linguistic lines. But they are also complex, because their implementation poses extraordinary practical and theoretical difficulties – just to mention one: language rights are individual rights (groups do not speak) but with an obvious and dominant group dimension, thus going at the heart of one of the most debated theoretical controversies on the very nature of minority rights.[5]

This chapter tries to identify the link between such rights and the approach to diversity management at least in the approach followed by the international community, notably by the two specialized institutions in the field: the Advisory Committee on the Framework Convention for the Protection of National Minorities of the Council of Europe (ACFC) and the OSCE High Commissioner on National Minorities (HCNM). There is in fact a clear and consistent guiding thread that departs from the HCNM Oslo Recommendations Regarding the Linguistic Rights of National Minorities (1998), developed mostly in the Thematic Commentary of the ACFC on The Language Rights of Persons Belonging to National Minorities under the Framework Convention (2012), and deeply influences the further trajectory inaugurated by the HCNM Ljubljana Guidelines on Integration of Diverse Societies (2012) and by the fourth ACFC Thematic Commentary on The Framework Convention: a key tool to managing diversity through minority rights (2016).

Against this background, the evolution of the approach to minority rights will be illustrated (Part 2). Subsequently, the context and the contents of the turning-point document – the Commentary on Linguistic Rights – will be closely examined (Part 3). The further developments logically following from there and enshrined in the two most recent documents (Ljubljana Guidelines and Fourth Thematic Commentary) will be dealt with in Part 4. Finally, the chapter concludes by reflecting on the future challenges for minority rights, including especially language rights, in the nuanced and sophisticated contemporary context (Part 5).

5 *See* R. Hofmann, 'Minority Rights: Individual or Group Rights? A Comparative View on European Legal Systems', 40 *German Yearbook of International Law* (1998), pp. 356–382; A. Spiliopoulou Åkermark, *Justification of Minority Protection in International Law* (Kluwer, London, The Hague, Boston, 1996), A. Rosas and M. Scheinin, 'Categories and beneficiaries of human rights', in R. Hanski, M. Suksi (eds.), *An Introduction to the International Protection of Human Rights: A Textbook* (Åbo Academy, Åbo/Turku, 1999), pp. 49–61.

2 The Quick Development of Minority (Linguistic) Rights, between Risk of Obsolescence, New Challenges and Responses

2.1 *The Ups and Downs of International Minority Rights' Influence*

Looking at how minority rights instruments have developed over the past two decades, and taking into account their implementation and practical impact, a clear trajectory can be identified. From the early 1990s onwards, international minority rights law rapidly evolved from a marginal domain into an extremely powerful conditionality tool in the course of just a few years. Then, it has gradually stabilized, working towards deepening the standards and making them more effective. Finally, in more recent times, an overall fatigue seems to be emerging, and something like a step backwards can be noticed, linked to the difficulties in implementation of some of the standards, and to the emergence of more pressing issues on the international scene. The most recent responses by the international community open-up new ground for a more balanced, holistic and effective approach to the current challenges.

As to language rights more specifically, all major international human rights instruments address them.[6] In order to offer guidance in managing the multifaceted aspects and implications of language rights, and partly to give consistency to the language-related provisions in the (legally or politically) binding texts, relevant international standard-setting bodies have extensively dealt with language rights of persons belonging to minorities.[7] However, until very recently, the approach to language issues has been essentially 'piecemeal and reactive',[8] and quite paradoxically the most comprehensive and detailed international document in this regard (the European Charter for Regional or Minority Languages) is not a human/minority rights instrument.[9] For this

6 For a systematic overview *see* F. de Varennes, *Language, Minorities and Human Rights* (Martinus Nijhoff, Leiden, 1996).

7 At UN level, the Declaration on the Rights of Persons belonging to National or Ethnic, Religious and Linguistic Minorities (1992), as well as the Commentary of the Working Group on Minorities to the Declaration (2005), the Declaration on the Rights of Indigenous Peoples (2007) and relevant recommendations from the UN Minority Forum, in particular related to education and participation are of particular importance.

8 R. Dunbar, 'European Traditional Linguistic Diversity and Human Rights: A Critical Assessment of International Instruments', in E.J. Ruiz Vieytez and R. Dunbar (eds.), *Human Rights and Diversity: New Challenges for Plural Societies* (University of Deusto, Bilbao, 2007), pp. 85–110, p. 88.

9 Although it is in practice very close to one such. Not by chance a recent and important commentary on the Charter, published by the Council of Europe itself, has the very telling title 'Shaping language rights'. *See* A. Nogueira López, E.J. Ruiz Vieytez, I. Urrutia Libarona (eds.),

reason, in the most recent phase, new responses are being developed in order to tackle the current challenges in a more holistic way, parallel to and influencing the developments concerning minority issues more broadly.

2.2 *The 1990s: The Establishment of Minority (Linguistic) Rights and the Oslo Recommendations*

The eruption of ethnic conflicts throughout the former Communist bloc and elsewhere after 1989 took the international community by surprise. The almost exclusive attention to individual rights paid since the end of the Second World War in the international arena, which proved successful under the cold war regime, failed in addressing the ethnic turmoil that followed the end of that regime, asking for the recognition of a broader (including collective) dimension of minority rights. The mass violations of human and minority rights and even more so the immediate threats for State security and integrity associated with the post-1989 revolutions pushed the international community to work quickly towards new and more effective instruments aimed at balancing the individual human rights dimension with rights of minorities and groups bearing therefore an (albeit indirect) collective dimension.

International law quickly acknowledged that minority rights are an issue of international concern and do not fall exclusively in the domain of the States.[10] Against this background, a tremendous amount of law was produced, both soft and hard, aimed at directly or indirectly protecting minority rights, and by this means preserving States' security.[11]

These developments produced a phenomenon which can be defined as the 'internationalization of constitutional law and constitutionalization of international law', especially with regard to minority issues.[12] In fact, on the one hand, international law has developed a body of law which, while not entirely

---

Shaping Language Rights. Commentary on the European Charter for Regional or Minority Languages in light of the Committee of Expert's evaluation (Council of Europe Publishing, Strasbourg, 2012).

10 CSCE Copenhagen Document (1990), Part IV and Article 1 FCNM.

11 On the link between minority issues and security *see*, with critical accents, P. Roe, 'Securitization and Minority Rights: Conditions of Desecuritization', in 35:3 *Security Dialogue* (2004), pp. 279–294 and W. Kymlicka, *Multicultural Odysseys: Navigating the New International Politics of Diversity* (Oxford Univ. Press, Oxford, 2007).

12 F. Palermo, 'The Protection of Minorities in International Law. Recent Developments and Trends', in *Les minorités: un défi pour les États. Actes du colloque international (22 et 23 mai 2011)* (Académie Royale de Belgique, Bruxelles, 2012), pp. 165–185.

prescriptive and very rarely justiciable,[13] has become specific, legally or politically binding and is monitored by several bodies including some quasi-judicial ones such as the Advisory Committee of the FCNM and the Committees of Experts under the ECRML, which developed a 'soft jurisprudence'.[14] On the other hand, the increasingly prescriptive nature of international law has had an enormous influence on constitutional transitions and constitutional developments in various countries, deeply conditioning the constitutional choices with regard to the protection of minority rights. Such interplay between internationalization of constitutions and constitutionalization of international norms, combined with the link between minority protection and security, the political and financial assistance for minority protection and the unique political climate in the 1990s, proved very effective in overcoming the emergency phase and in quickly developing an impressive body of international and domestic law on the protection of minority rights.

It is in this context that the Oslo Recommendations Regarding the Linguistic Rights of National Minorities (the 'Recommendations') were adopted in 1998. They originate from the experience of the first years of activity of the HCNM, in which the establishment and securement of linguistic rights of minority groups, especially in conflict and post-conflict societies, was of the utmost importance.[15] The Recommendations were concerned with the guarantee for minorities to be able to use their languages in the public sphere and with the entrenchment of such rights, providing a secured space for minorities in societies, making them visible and accepted and, by so doing, decisively contributing to peace and security within and among societies.[16]

13 Important achievements have been reached however by some international courts in developing a consistent body of jurisprudence on relevant minority issues. This goes above all for the European Court of Human Rights. *See inter alia* G. Gilbert, 'The Burgeoning Minority Rights Jurisprudence of the European Court of Human Rights', 24:3 *Human Rights Quarterly* (2002), pp. 736–780 and R. Medda-Windischer, 'The European court of Human Rights and Minority Rights', 25:3 *Journal of European Integration* (2003), pp. 249–271.

14 For the term 'soft jurisprudence' *see* J. Packer, 'Situating the Framework Convention in a Wider Context: Achievements and Challenges', in Council of Europe, *Filling the Frame. Five years of monitoring the Framework Convention for the Protection of National Minorities* (Council of Europe Publishing, Strasbourg, 2004), p. 45.

15 J. Packer and G. Siemienski, 'The Language of Equity: The Origin and Development of The Oslo Recommendations Regarding the Linguistic Rights of National Minorities', 6 *International Journal on Minority and Group Rights* (1999), pp. 329–350.

16 A. Eide, 'The Oslo Recommendations Regarding the Linguistic Rights of National Minorities: An Overview', 6 *International Journal on Minority and Group Rights* (1999), pp. 319–328.

They therefore deal with the main and in some way more 'basic' linguistic rights of persons belonging to national minorities, such as the right to use their names in their own languages and according to their own tradition (Recs. 1–3), to use minority languages in religious ceremonies (4–5), in community life including NGOs (6–7), in the media (8–11), in economic life (12), with administrative authorities and public services (13–15), with judicial authorities (17–19) and in prisons (20–21). A clear 'defensive' approach is to be noted, aimed at making sure that such basic and vital guarantees for existence and development of languages of minorities are given and secured. In fact, this is the first and necessary step, as the absence of such guarantees threatens the very existence of national minorities, and is quite typical of the 1990s, when the absence of such guarantees had to be addressed as a matter of urgency. The same approach is to be noted in the first monitoring cycle on the implementation of the FCNM in the very same years.

2.3 *Consolidation in the Years 2000*

The success of the measures taken during the 1990s by the international community brought (overall) peace throughout the wider European continent. However, in some way, in the subsequent era of consolidation, the international instruments became victims of their own success: after proving effective in order to stop violence and to improve the international and domestic legal guarantees for minority rights to an extraordinary degree, they showed less effectiveness in coping with the subtler challenges of effective implementation of minority rights.[17]

This was primarily due to changed external circumstances. One should consider, in particular, the overall and quick re-emergence of the role of the States on the international and European scene, linked to factors such as the terrorist threat after the attacks of September 11th, 2001, the subsequent bombings in Europe and elsewhere, the global financial crisis, the new terrorist attacks more recently and the ongoing migration crisis. Security concerns re-empowered the States and, more generally, the overall environment for minority groups became much less favourable as they were increasingly seen as potentially disloyal groups, and thus as a permanent potential threat on national security. Moreover, overall attention shifted from autochthonous national minorities to the new security priorities, including the 'new' minorities with immigration background and religious diversity. States became much-less inclined to leave

17 R. Hofmann, 'The Future of Minority Issues in the Council of Europe and the Organization for Security and Cooperation in Europe', in M. Weller, D. Blacklock and K. Nobbs (eds.), *The Protection of Minorities in the Wider Europe* (Palgrave Macmillan, London, New York, 2008), pp. 171–205.

a broad leverage to international organizations in dealing with minority issues. Moreover, the recent financial crisis shifted a considerable amount of power back in the hands of the States, which in several countries adopted emergency economic measures, of which minorities were often the first victims.

The combined outcome of these phenomena between 2000 and 2010 was the emergence of a new 'statism', which considerably reduced the role of the international community in this field, pushed minority issues back into the domestic arena, limited the impact of conditionality and, in overall terms, put the minority question much lower on the priority scale of both States and international community as compared to the previous decade. In the last decade no new country ratified the Framework Convention,[18] very few the European Charter for Regional or Minority Languages[19] and it seems unlikely that new ratifications will come in the near future. As a consequence, the monitoring bodies under both the Charter and the Framework Convention find themselves in the difficult situation of highlighting deficits and shortcomings in the implementation of the respective treaty for the fourth time in a row,[20] without having at their disposal instruments to enforce effective measures to address the most problematic situations.

2.4 *Current Challenges and (Limited) Responses*

Since the 1990s, the effective implementation of minority rights has proved more complex and difficult than drafting valuable legislation. Some structural problems have not been resolved, states do not put the necessary effort in implementing minority rights, funds are cut and full and effective implementation of minority rights becomes more difficult rather than easier. The rather obsolete approach of international instruments tailored to the situation of the 1990s calls for a contextual, dynamic and progressive interpretation in order to make the standards living instruments.[21]

18 The last ratification of the Framework Convention so far was the one by Montenegro in 2007 after independence, although one should consider the last 'substantial' ratification that of Georgia in 2005.

19 Bosnia and Herzegovina ratified the Charter in 2010, due to strong international pressure. Poland ratified it in 2009 after completing a rather uncontroversial but yet technically complex process (signature was done in 2003). Many countries never signed the Charter and so far only 25 have ratified it. Even more interestingly, 8 countries have signed it between 1992 and 2001 but not yet ratified it.

20 Both the Framework Convention and the Charter are currently undergoing their fourth monitoring cycle.

21 R. Hofmann, 'Implementation of the FCNM: Substantive Challenges', in A. Verstichel, A. Alen, B. de Witte and P. Lemmens (eds.), *The Framework Convention for the Protection of*

A revision of existing instruments is politically impossible and probably not even desirable: it is close to impossible due to the unfavorable international context, which is much less ready than in the 1990s to put minority issues on the top of the agenda; as to desirability, the same international context does not seem to be overly open and 'generous' vis-à-vis minorities and it is therefore most likely that any amendment to existing instruments would result in a restriction of the rights of persons belonging to minorities and of the role of international actors in this field. Therefore, the natural response by international actors in order to keep the instruments up-to-date with the contemporary challenges could not but be to adopt a modern interpretation, which is not only allowed but imposed by the broad and living nature of the instruments themselves. The best suited tools to do this are commentaries (in the terminology adopted by the ACFC) or recommendations and guidelines (as provided by the HCNM). The HCNM's recommendations and guidelines take stock of the results of the institution's work, presenting it in a systematic and comparative way: this helps avoid inconsistencies or even accusations of applying double standards in addressing issues in different countries and different contexts. Secondly, they offer both theoretical and practical guidance to all actors involved in the protection of minority rights, such as national, regional and local administrations, NGOs, minority organizations and academia. Third, they help the FCNM and the HCNM to address contemporary challenges. While they do not aim to create new law or doctrine, the commentaries and recommendations are more than just a mere compilation of the work of the respective institution on one particular subject. Especially in the case of the FCNM, State Parties bind themselves to its principles, and these include the acceptance of the (non-binding) opinions of the Advisory Committee; moreover, the opinions of the Advisory Committee establish an *acquis* that becomes *de facto* binding to new States Parties, because they ratify the Convention aware of the interpretation given to it by the monitoring body. Not least, it must be noted that, in a few cases, the non-binding interpretations given by the Advisory Committee become normative because of their inclusion in decisions by national or international courts.[22]

National Minorities: a Useful Pan-European Instrument? (Intersentia, Antwerpen, 2008), pp. 159–185.

22 *See on this* F. Palermo, 'Domestic Enforcement and Direct Effect of the Framework Convention for the Protection of National Minorities. On the Judicial Implementation of the (Soft?) Law of Integration', in A. Verstichel, A. Alen, B. de Witte, P. Lemmens (eds.), *The Framework Convention for the Protection of National Minorities, cit.*, pp. 187–214.

Against this background, Commentaries and Recommendations, like other soft law mechanisms, "give substance to the provisions in international law and facilitate at the national level the practical implementation of the international commitments, so making it possible to find the appropriate balance between the legitimate concerns of the State and the majority on the one hand and the concerns and requirements of the minority on the other".[23] In pursuing these functions, Commentaries and Recommendations are fundamental tools for the 'maintenance' of the underlying institutions: a medicine against aging – if not obsolescence – of minority-relevant institutions in times of quick and challenging changes.

3 The Commentary on Language as a Turning Point

3.1 *Updating the Identity Paradigm*

In this context, in the new phase of minority protection, the attitude towards and the interpretation of language rights also needed an update after the 'first generation' approach of the Oslo Recommendations. In particular, it was necessary to put the language rights in the broader context that defines the relationship of societies with their diversities, instead of just securing the basic linguistic rights of minorities. This opportunity was seized by the ACFC when adopting the Commentary on language rights of persons belonging to national minorities under the Framework Convention in 2012.[24]

Over time, subsequent opinions of the Advisory Committee[25] reflected the evolving situation in most States parties: from an initial (and in many countries post-conflict) phase when the pressing priority was the adoption of legal safeguards for persons belonging to minorities in the enjoyment of their rights, to the more recent challenges. In more peaceful environments, where minority rights are largely established at least on paper, many States have turned their attention to issues such as societal integration and social cohesion. But in doing so, they often (deliberately or involuntarily) have reduced the factual scope of minority rights by, for example, increasingly demanding 'loyalty' from minorities, placing additional requirements on the knowledge of State

23 A. Eide, 'The Oslo Recommendations Regarding the Linguistic Rights of National Minorities: An Overview', 6:3 *IJMGR* (1999), pp. 319–328, p. 325.

24 ACFC/44DOC(2012)001 rev.

25 At the time of the adoption of the Commentary on Language some 75 opinions had been adopted by the Advisory Committee.

languages, promoting a national 'leading' culture, putting emphasis on avoiding the development of parallel societies and segregation, and the like.

The problem also lies, to a large extent, in an incorrect perception of the nature of minority rights. In fact, in the practice of States there is still a predominant perception of minority issues as something involving homogeneous groups that sometimes clash with other homogeneous groups, trying to look for solutions on how to accommodate groups' demands by granting rights to individuals. Based on this assumption, also international minority law often aims at accommodating majority and minority *homogeneous* groups. To belong to a minority, in the prevailing perspective, is a sort of all-encompassing issue, and the divide between belonging or not belonging to a minority is supposed to be always clear for each and every person.

However, such homogeneity, if it ever existed, is far from mirroring the present reality, and minorities of whatever kind are now much less homogeneous than ever in the past: diversities are increasingly present within each group and the factors for differentiation potentially countless. Migrants, people belonging to more than one culture, multilingualism, shifting identities, mobility, less compactness in social structures: all these issues are not or at least not sufficiently dealt with by national nor by international minority law, thus creating some confusion when implementing minority rights and allowing for political misuse (and sometimes abuse) of the legitimate aim to establish an integrated society, which often turns into a subtle limitation of minority rights.

In its monitoring work, the Advisory Committee has come to the conclusion that the right balance between the protection of linguistic rights of persons belonging to minorities and the development of an integrated society can hardly be achieved if identities (both majority and minority identity) are portrayed (in law and in society) as something set in stone.

This also goes for supposedly objective criteria such as language. Linguistic identity might well be clearly defined for some, but for others, especially for persons belonging to minorities, such identity might be shifting, complex, plural and nevertheless be one of the main factors of their identity and identification.[26] Language, like identity, is not static but evolves throughout a person's life. Linguistic identities are often multiple, and their relations change depending on a number of factors, including societal ones such as hierarchy or different prestige among languages or just their different instrumental position

26 For a philosophical reading of (individual and collective) linguistic diversity *see* P. van Parijs, 'Linguistic Diversity as Curse and as By-Product', in X. Arzoz (ed.), *Respecting Linguistic Diversity in the European Union* (John Benjamins, Amsterdam/Philadelphia, 2008), pp. 17–46.

in different contexts. The full and effective guarantee of the right to use one's (minority) language(s) implies that instruments must allow free identification of persons through language, and abstain from constraining personal identities into rigid (and often hierarchical) language categories.

Following the 'multicultural' approach underpinned by the Framework Convention, the Commentary spells out the issue of multiple and contextual identities and even of hierarchical structures in societies in a way that allows to focus on the current challenges much more effectively as if identities were seen as something permanent, immutable and static.

Examples can be found in several paragraphs of the Commentary. Para. 18 directly addresses the issue of multiple affiliation,[27] para. 8 suggests that different hierarchical relations among languages should be taken into account in drafting and implementing language-related provisions,[28] para. 13 makes explicit the consequences of multiple affiliations with regard to the scope of application of the Framework Convention,[29] and more generally the

---

27 Para. 18 Commentary: "a person might wish to identify herself or himself with several groups. The phenomenon of multiple affiliation is in fact quite common, due to mixed marriages, for instance, or cases of state succession. A person may also identify himself or herself in different ways for different purposes, depending on the relevance of identification for him or for her in a particular situation. The Advisory Committee considers that the principle of self-identification, as contained in Article 3 of the Framework Convention, also guarantees the possibility of multiple affiliation. This implies that, in principle, a person may claim linguistic rights with regard to several minority languages, as long as the relevant conditions, such as demand and/or traditional residence, contained in the respective articles of the Framework Convention are fulfilled".

28 Para. 8 states: "While states continue to play an essential role in defining the legal regime governing the use of languages, other entities are gaining momentum, such as local, regional or transnational bodies in which the functionality and prestige of languages are influenced by different actors. Unequal power relations between different groups of speakers may lead to social hierarchies that can also be reflected in language practices and political discourse on languages. This influences the way in which speakers of certain languages are perceived by others and, to some extent, perceive themselves. Language policies aiming at valuing linguistic resources at the individual and social level therefore also have to address the question of hierarchy in language and society, and the issue of unequal access to full participation in society".

29 Para. 13 reads: "Language is an essential component of individual and collective identity. For many persons belonging to national minorities, language is one of the main factors of their minority identity and identification. However, language, like identity, is not static but evolves throughout a person's life. The full and effective guarantee of the right to use one's (minority) language(s) implies that authorities allow free identification of persons through language, and abstain from constraining personal identities into rigid language categories. The choice of each person belonging to a national minority to choose freely

substantial provisions of the Commentary are inspired by a reading of language identities and rights that takes into account the developments these issues have faced in the course of the last two decades since the adoption of the Oslo Recommendations.

3.2 *Old and New Challenges for Language Rights*

While some attention to new challenges is to be found in previous documents, such as a more balanced approach to not only rights but also duties of minorities,[30] or the overall balance of society as a whole,[31] such contextualization of language rights within overall societal challenges is the main tenet of the Commentary. This document is structured in six main parts, reflecting the main interlinks between language rights and other rights provided for by the Convention: 'Language Rights and Identities' (reflecting essentially articles 3 and 5 of the FCNM), 'Language Rights and Equality' (articles 4 and 6 of the FCNM), 'Language Rights and Media' (article 9 of the FCNM), 'Public and Private Use of Minority Languages' (articles 10–11 of the FCNM), 'Language Rights and Education' (articles 12–14 of the FCNM) and 'Language Rights and Participation' (articles 15 and 16 of the FCNM).

In each section, both the traditional and the most recent challenges facing the effective enjoyment of language rights by persons belonging to minorities are dealt with, and the consolidated interpretation of the Advisory Committee, including practical guidance, is given. Inspiration for both the monitoring

---

to be treated or not to be treated as such, must be respected in line with Article 3.1 of the Framework Convention".

30 While in principle international law clearly provides for rights for minorities and respective duties for States, the protection and safeguard of other fundamental principles such as social cohesion, good neighbourly relations, effective integration and participation in societies require that minority protection be a two-way process, in which both minorities and majorities have rights and duties. *See further* G. Poggeschi, *Language Rights and Duties in the Evolution of Public Law* (Baden Baden, Nomos, 2013).

31 *See in particular* the Second Thematic Commentary to the FCNM on Participation (2008), on which F. Palermo, 'The Dual Meaning of Participation: The Advisory Committee's Commentary to Article 15 of the FCNM', in 7 *European Yearbook of Minority Issues* (2008), (Brill, Leiden/Boston, 2009), pp. 409–424 and J. Marko, 'The Council of Europe Framework Convention on the Protection of National Minorities and the Advisory Committee's Thematic Commentary on Effective Participation', in M. Weller (ed.), *Political Participation of Minorities* (Oxford University Press, Oxford, 2010), pp. 222–255. *See also* the UN Recommendations on 'Minorities and the Right to Effective Political Participation' (2009) as well as on 'Minorities and the Right to Education' (2008), I. Klímová-Alexander, 'Effective Participation of Minorities. United Nations standards and practice', in M. Weller (ed.), *Political Participation of Minorities, cit.*, pp. 286–307.

and the thematic work of the Committee is drawn from other international documents on language rights. These include, in particular, the case law of the European Court of Human Rights, the European Social Charter, the OSCE High Commissioner on National Minorities' Recommendations, the UN documents, and the European Charter for Regional or Minority Languages.[32]

More 'traditional' language-related issues are those that recur from the very beginning in the monitoring of the Framework Convention in a wide number of countries. One may think, among many others, of questions regarding the scope of application of language rights,[33] census and collection of data on linguistic affiliation,[34] language quotas in the media[35] (both public and private) and in film industry,[36] training and recruitment of journalists able to work in minority languages,[37] access to education in and of minority languages,[38] linguistic requirements for the enjoyment of language rights such as thresholds,[39] territorial and cultural autonomy arrangements,[40] language requirements in electoral provisions,[41] in judicial proceedings,[42] etc.

Among the more recent issues, the Commentary tackles complex and even more subtle, nuanced questions mostly arising after the legislation on minority rights has largely been established. These issues include, *inter alia*, how to combine multiple identities with participation in cultural, social and economic life and in public affairs,[43] the balance between freedom of the media and promotion of minority rights in the media,[44] the rights of 'minorities in the minority' but also of 'majorities in the minorities',[45] the linguistic duties of persons belonging to majorities, especially in areas inhabited by minorities in large numbers,[46] the difficult and not always straightforward distinction

32 *See* paras. 10 and 11 Commentary.
33 *See* paras. 14–17 Commentary.
34 *See* paras. 14–21 Commentary.
35 *See* para. 43 Commentary.
36 Para. 50 Commentary.
37 *See* para. 41 Commentary.
38 Paras. 68–69 Commentary.
39 *See* paras. 56, 57 Commentary.
40 Paras. 90–91 Commentary.
41 *See* paras. 92–93 Commentary.
42 Para. 59 Commentary.
43 *See inter alia* paras. 84, 85, 86, 87, 92, 93 Commentary.
44 *See e.g.,* paras. 42, 45, 47 of the Commentary.
45 *See* para. 91 Commentary.
46 *See e.g.,* para. 79 Commentary.

between public and private use of languages,[47] the balance between promotion of the State language(s) and protection of minority languages in different fields,[48] the balance between the right to separate education for persons belonging to minorities and the interest of the society to avoid parallel development of its communities,[49] including by promoting linguistic diversity and intercultural education,[50] etc.

In all these and other issues the Commentary tries to give both the systematic interpretation of the relevant provision in the Framework Convention and some practical guidance as to how possibly resolve problems, based on recommendations that have been elaborated in the course of the monitoring.

While the selection of the issues dealt with by the Commentary naturally emerges from the systematic reading of the opinions, the refinement of the interpretation, the exemplification of problems, the logical order followed in presenting the relevant issues are also the product of the open and participatory process that has guided the elaboration of the document.[51]

4 From Language Rights to Society as a Whole: Ljubljana Guidelines and Fourth Thematic Commentary on the Framework Convention

The approach inaugurated by the thematic commentary on language rights can be called holistic or, more precisely, societal, as it broadens the view from specific minority rights in the strict sense to their impact on (and importance for) society as a whole. Minorities are not separated from the societies they live in, but rather are their integral part. To protect their basic linguistic rights is of course a *sine qua non*, but is by far not sufficient if the goal is to establish

47 For instance, information visible to the public on private grounds or buildings, possible limitations to the use of minority languages for consumers' protection, language regulation in new media, etc. *See* paras. 64–67 Commentary.

48 *See* paras. 52–54 Commentary.

49 *See* paras. 70–75 Commentary.

50 *See* paras. 82–83 Commentary.

51 Following the practice inaugurated with the second thematic Commentary on effective participation (2008), also the Commentary on Language has been drafted in consultation with both all relevant Council of Europe and other international bodies dealing with minority issues, and key stakeholders such as in particular civil society and minority representatives. A pre-final text was thoroughly discussed in a consultation conference where minority representatives, national and local authorities, NGOs, international bodies and individual experts made their comments and practical suggestions on how to possibly improve the document.

balanced, peaceful and integrated societies that are aware of and celebrate their diversity. Minority issues are not affecting the minority only and targets of minority policies must be majorities as well, since integration is a two-way process that involves all segments of societies and not only one (smaller) part that, depending on the perspective, has to be 'normalized' (i.e. absorbed) by the other (and bigger) one or has to fight against it in order to preserve its distinctiveness.

Such essential achievement, which with the passing of time became more and more evident in the work of relevant international bodies such as the HCNM and the ACFC, could not but be taken up and further developed with regard to general minority issues. It is therefore not surprising that the subsequent soft law documents of both institutions dealt with the integration of diverse societies through minority rights.

The first, and breakthrough, move was the adoption of the HCNM Ljubljana Guidelines on Integration of Diverse Societies, launched just a few months after the ACFC Commentary on Language Rights. It demonstrated, on one hand, the necessary coordination between the involved institutions and, on the other, that they both face the same problems in their work and come to the same conclusions.

The Ljubljana Guidelines move precisely from the acknowledgement that "simply recognizing and accommodating minority culture, identity and political interests, and promoting the participation of all may not be sufficient to build sustainable and lasting peace". In addition, "measures and (…) policies aimed at promoting the integration and cohesion of diverse, multi-ethnic societies" are needed.[52] By integration, the HCNM means "a dynamic, multi-actor process of mutual engagement that facilitates effective participation by all members of a diverse society in the economic, political, social and cultural life, and fosters a shared and inclusive sense of belonging at national and local levels".[53] Even more importantly, this "process can lead to changes in majority and minority cultures".[54] This is the key point emerging from the experience of successive High Commissioners – and confirmed by the work of the ACFC[55] – and it is what, in a way, tends to scare the most traditional segments of both majority and minority groups. The assumption of homogeneity of groups and the little openness towards changes originating from contact with diversity

52 Ljubljana Guidelines, Introduction, p. 4.

53 *Ibid.*

54 *Ibid.*

55 The text of para. 25 of the Commentary on Language Rights is almost identical: integration "may often lead to changes within both the majority and the minority cultures".

is very frequent in group relations, and it inevitably leads to conflicts when groups compete for whatever reason (resources, territory, prestige). To accept the idea and the consequences of diversity is equally difficult but equally necessary for majorities and minorities alike. At the same time, progress can hardly be made if the assumption – rigidity of identities – does not reflect reality, which shows growing fluidity of positions in society.

The Guidelines make clear that certain structural principles are needed, such as good and democratic governance, non-discrimination and effective equality, as well as respect for and protection of human including minority rights (Part I). When such principles are guaranteed, further ones allow more specifically for integration in and of societies: recognition of diversity and multiple identities, the primacy of voluntary self-identification, a non-isolationist approach to minority issues, the establishment of shared public institutions, a sense of belonging and mutual accommodation, inclusion and effective participation, the awareness of rights and duties of both majorities and minorities, the establishment of inter-community relations and the design of policies targeting both majorities and minorities (Part II). How such principles can be concretely implemented is specified in the guidelines and in the explanatory text to each of them. Finally, the basic elements of integration policies (Part III) as well as the key policy areas where integration can take place (Part IV) are dealt with in a way that is far more detailed as compared to previous HCNM recommendations.

The main achievements of the Ljubljana Guidelines are further developed and contextualized in the fourth, and (so far) latest, thematic Commentary to the FCNM, entitled "The Framework Convention: A Key Tool to Manage Diversity through Minority Rights" and dealing with the tricky and long debated issue of the scope of application of the FCNM. Adopted in May 2016, the commentary represents the more mature and systematic elaboration of the 'societal approach' so far and gives the most complete account of the wisdom of the ACFC on how to properly address minority issues but also on how dealing with minority issues can help societies as a whole. The very title makes it clear, that minority rights have also a societal function, as they are an indispensable tool to manage diversity, which is the overall challenge for contemporary societies. Since its inception, "the Framework Convention has been and continues to be a key tool for states to accommodate increasing pluralism through minority protection in a way that carefully balances broader societal concerns with individual rights".[56] The FCNM is not a goal in itself, but

56 Fourth Thematic Commentary, Executive Summary.

rather a tool, a support for states to manage diversity "by creating appropriate societal conditions that allow for the expression and acknowledgement *of* difference, for equal access to rights and resources *despite* difference and for social interaction and inclusion *across* difference"[57] (emphasis added). As its main purpose is "to prevent interethnic tensions and to promote dialogue in open and inclusive societies (…) the Framework Convention addresses society as a whole, not individuals or specific groups only. Rather than asking 'who' should be protected, it asks 'what' is required to manage diversity most effectively through the protection of minority rights".[58] As a consequence, the point of departure is the principle of free self-identification, as codified in article 3 FCNM (Part II of the Commentary). The rights provided for in the Convention all aim at supporting societies to develop a positive approach to diversity. While some such rights apply to all persons living on the territory of the country (irrespective of their belonging to a national minority or not), such as non-discrimination (Part V of the Commentary), others demand a broad scope of application: equality, culture, freedom of association and religion, access to the media, use of language, education and participation should be available to groups irrespective of their being recognized as national minorities if certain conditions are met at least, as the ACFC often puts it, on an article-by-article basis. Further rights have a specific scope of application, i.e. they apply only to certain groups and under given circumstances. This goes for the right to use a minority language in relations with local administrative authorities, the right to have topographical indications and signposts displayed also in the minority language, and the right to learn minority languages or receive instruction in minority languages may be limited to certain areas, where persons belonging to national minorities reside traditionally, and/or in substantial numbers.[59]

The conclusions of the Commentary make the societal approach even clearer. When the FCNM – and even more the mandate of the HCNM – was drafted, «the concept of minority rights was mainly associated with the preservation of minority identities and with their protection from assimilation during partially violent state-formation and nation-building processes. Since then, the increased global and regional mobility of populations has transformed the demographic profile of European societies, and attention has shifted to the challenge of forming integrated and inclusive societies where diversity is

57 *Ibid.*

58 *Ibid.*

59 *Ibid.*, para. 79.

acknowledged and welcomed as their integral feature. The present-day European context is further marked by migratory movements of an unprecedented scale which, coupled with the effects of recurrent economic crises and with growing security concerns, are destabilising societies and altering the manner in which minority rights are perceived in society and by policy makers. The FCNM is based on the understanding that minority identities are not exclusive. Persons belonging to national minorities must be allowed both, preserve their identities, and effectively participate in public life as an integral part of society. The Framework Convention therefore lays out a catalogue of rights that are of particular importance in order to maintain and encourage diversity whilst also promoting integration and social interaction.»[60] Only the full understanding of such principles and their committed implementation can allow European societies to effectively and positively cope with diversity.

5 Twenty Years of the Oslo Recommendations, Twenty Years of the Framework Convention: What's Next?

In the course of just twenty years, societies have radically changed and so have the challenges they are facing when dealing with diversity. Since the entry into force of the FCNM and the adoption of the Oslo Recommendations, legislation pertaining to (language) rights of persons belonging to national minorities has been adopted in most European countries. Its implementation, however, has been faced with several obstacles that in most countries obstructed the development of a positive culture of diversity.[61] In such context, the rights of minorities are generally still seen as competing with those of majorities: in some cases, legislation aimed at strengthening state languages has directly or indirectly limited the right to use minority languages.[62] The prevailing diagnosis identifies the reason for such difficulties in a very generic lack of political will. This seems to be, however, the consequence rather than the reason. Political

60 *Ibid*, paras. 84–85.

61 F. de Varennes, 'The Human Rights Dimension and Challenges of Linguistic Rights', in E. Kuzborska (ed.), *Integration and Exclusion. Linguistic Rights of National Minorities in Europe* (Vilnius, 2015), pp. 39–55.

62 *See* J-M. Arraiza, *Making Home Rules for Mother Tongues. The Legal Implications of Linguistic Diversity in the Design of Autonomy Regimes* (Åbo Akademi University Press, Åbo, 2015) and J-M. Arraiza, 'Minority Language Rights: Ideas and Norms', *SSRN Electronic Journal*, (2014). *See also* L. Hannikainen, 'How Serious Are the Violations of Minorities' Linguistic Rights in Contemporary European States?' in E. Kuzborska (ed.), *Integration and Exclusion*, *cit.*, pp. 57–76.

will is certainly lacking when it comes to properly addressing the challenges of diversity, but is itself the consequence of the prevailing and deeply rooted attitude in societies (including in minority groups of course) that see diversity as a cake, as a limited resource whose beneficiaries are limited. This remains the main obstacle to a proper integration of society as a whole, and without addressing such attitude, progress is doomed to remain limited.

If this analysis is true, it is easy to predict that the most difficult time for bodies such as the ACFC and the HCNM is ahead, not behind. Their role will increasingly be to convince of the key importance of prevention through rights, looking to minorities as a vehicle to improve the diversity-fitness of societies and not as competitors for resources. Such a difficult endeavor requires the specialized international actors such as the HCNM and the ACFC to stress the importance of and devote more attention to their thematic work. The systematic summary of hard and soft law on specific aspects of minority issues, in form of commentaries, recommendations or guidelines, is the most effective tool to make the HCNM and the FCNM living instruments. It could be said that while the county work (in form of quiet diplomacy for the HCNM[63] and of opinions for the FCNM) is 'filling the frame',[64] the thematic work could be thought of as a pair of 3-D glasses allowing us to see and comprehensively understand the picture within that filled frame.

Minority issues will increasingly become a question of nuances rather than either-or, and of changing rather than clear-cut identities. Moving from a black-and-white approach to multiple identity factors, from homogeneity to multiculturalism, from protection to integration, from a dogmatic to a functional approach to identity issues would help not only the international community regain its role, but also, and more importantly, minority issues to be properly addressed. This goes even for language, which is the most complex and powerful, and in many ways also the most clear-cut aspect of identity: the focus of the societal approach must evolve from mere protection of linguistic rights of individual minorities to the more complex enhancement of linguistic diversity within societies.

To sum up in a sentence: while the historic achievement of the Copenhagen Document was that minority rights are not a merely domestic issue but an international concern, the current and future challenge is to acknowledge

63 W. Kemp, *Quiet Diplomacy in Action: The OSCE High Commissioner on National Minorities* (Brill/Nijhoff, The Hague, 2001).

64 Council of Europe, *Filling the Frame. Five years of monitoring the Framework Convention for the Protection of National Minorities, cit.* (Council of Europe Publishing, Strasbourg, 2004), p. 45.

that they are also a societal concern. As this chapter opens with a quote from Ludwig Wittgenstein, it is appropriate to close with another one of the same Austrian philosopher: "Language is a part of our organism and no less complicated than it".[65] This goes not only for individuals, but also – and probably even more so – for societies.

65 Quoted from R. Monk, *Wittgenstein: The Duty of Genius* (London, Penguin, 1990), p. 48.

CHAPTER 10

Language Rights in the Work of the Advisory Committee

Petra Roter and Brigitta Busch

1 Introduction

The goal of the Framework Convention for the Protection of National Minorities (FCNM)[1] is to protect 'the existence of national minorities' as an essential precondition for stability, democratic security and peace.[2] To this effect, the FCNM – as a human rights instrument of the Council of Europe (CoE) – establishes a normative framework on minority rights. Its state parties "undertake to promote the conditions necessary for persons belonging to national minorities to maintain and develop their culture, and to preserve the essential elements of their identity, namely their religion, language, traditions and cultural heritage".[3] Not only does this require respect of diversity (i.e. ethnic, cultural, linguistic identities of persons belonging to national minorities), but also the creation of "appropriate conditions enabling them to express, preserve and develop" these identities.[4]

As a human rights instrument, the FCNM thus provides a normative framework for the protection of individual rights of persons belonging to national minorities, including language rights. Whereas minority rights in the FCNM are not framed as collective rights, they certainly have a collective (societal) dimension: they can be exercised individually or in community with others, which is particularly relevant also for language rights. Instead of protecting certain languages (as part of linguistic diversity and cultural heritage in Europe), the FCNM takes a speaker-centred approach that focuses on the language needs, aspirations and practices of persons belonging to national minorities. Such an approach corresponds with the understanding of the language that led to the Oslo Recommendations Regarding the Linguistic Rights

1 Adopted on 10 November 1994 by the Committee of Ministers, open for signature on 1 February 1995, in force since 1 February 1998, ETS No. 157.

2 FCNM, Preamble.

3 *Ibid.*, Article 5(1).

4 *Ibid.*, Preamble.

© KONINKLIJKE BRILL NV, LEIDEN, 2018 | DOI 10.1163/9789004357754_011

of National Minorities (1998): "linguistic rights of national minorities, i.e. the right of persons belonging to national minorities to use their language in the private and public spheres", has been identified as a recurrent issue by the High Commissioner on National Minorities (HCNM), given that a failure to address adequately the existing diversity and the issue of language being "a personal matter closely connected with identity" and as "an essential tool of social organisation", "may be the source of inter-ethnic tensions".[5]

In this paper we seek to analyse the contribution of the Advisory Committee, as a body of 18 independent experts tasked to advise on how best to implement the FCNM, in the field of minority language rights, during its four monitoring cycles. The Advisory Committee has observed many difficulties faced by persons belonging to national minorities when exercising their language rights in different fields. Indeed, the on-going and in some cases strengthened or long-term processes of exclusive nation-building are often centred around the issues of language, language use and the scope of minority language rights. In such contexts language questions often serve as a pretext to mask struggles for power that can result in violent intra- or inter-state conflicts. Pressure and conflict can lead to forced linguistic assimilation and language loss. For, according to May: "Language loss is not only, perhaps not even primarily, a linguistic issue – it has much more to do with power, prejudice, (unequal) competition and, in many cases, overt discrimination and subordination".[6]

In addition to the introduction and the conclusion, the chapter is composed of three parts. In the following Section 2, we analyse the role of the language in the context of nationalising nation-states whereby we analyse the contemporary processes of exclusive nation-building. In particular, we discuss how modern nationalism influences views towards languages and language policies (Section 2.1). We also analyse the significance of a specific (primordial) concept of nations (and national minorities) in policy-making on language use (Section 2.2). In section three, we then focus on language ideologies in practice, as observed by the Advisory Committee, and present scholarly responses to language policies. Finally, Section 4 offers an alternative conceptual framework, within which the Advisory Committee has developed its approach to advising states on language rights. This framework is based on the understanding of language as a transversal matter with three dimensions – identity, instrumental and interactional. The chapter concludes (Section 5) with highlighting

5 The Oslo Recommendations Regarding the Linguistic Rights of National Minorities & Explanatory Note, February 1998, Introduction, p. 2.

6 St. May, *Language and Minority Rights. Ethnicity, Nationalism and the Politics of Language*. Second edition (New York and London, Routledge, 2012) p. 4.

the fundamental discrepancy between the prevailing policies of modern nationalism and primordial concepts of identity communities on the one hand, and on the other hand, the post-modern (linguistic) realities in contemporary societies. It is this discrepancy and the ability of states to adjust their policies, including on language use, to the contemporary realities and accompanying needs of persons affiliating with different communities, that will be the key in determining the pace and success rate of societal integration, and consequently also peace, stability and security.

2 The Role of Language and Language Policies in the Context of Nationalising Nation-States

Policies on the role of language and language rights unfold in the context of nation-states, often nationalising states,[7] which tend to find it problematic to strike a balance in accommodating and managing ethno-national, including linguistic, diversity. This is linked to at least two problematic assumptions that have accompanied and permeated the twin-processes of (European) state-formation and nation-building in the contemporary international community. The first one stems from the ideology of nationalism and expects congruence of nations and states, and the second one is a specific (primordial) concept of nations (and by implication national minorities) as communities with a given (i.e. inherited, in-born) identity.

2.1 *The Role of Languages in the Context of Nationalism*

Nationalism, according to Gellner, is "a theory of political legitimacy which requires that ethnic boundaries should not cut across political ones".[8] This notion of nations and states coinciding is at the core of the modern form of the nation-state, which, in its nationalising fervour, seeks to become as homogenous as possible – a one-nation-state. The French model of nation-building that is based on the notion of the people as *demos* as well as models based on the idea of the people as *ethnos*, a community of descent and fate, attribute to language a central identity-establishing role. In both cases, policies of homogenisation within the imagined language community go hand in hand with policies of delineation towards a (linguistic) 'outside'. Diversity is

7 R. Brubaker, *Nationalism Reframed: Nationhood and the National Question in the New Europe* (Cambridge, Cambridge Univeristy Press, 1996).

8 E. Gellner, *Nations and Nationalism: New Perspectives on the Past* (Oxford, Basil Blackwell, 1983) p. 1.

perceived as an unnecessary cost that potentially threatens stability of states and their security, whereas national minorities are seen as 'a problem'.[9] This refers to a perception that is not, however, confined to the boundaries of individual states, but it is very much an international phenomenon: although the nationalistic congruence myth cannot be materialised in practice, nation-states still aspire to act as guardians of their particular (ethnic) nation, even regardless of (at least normatively) where persons identifying or identified with this community live. In Brubaker's words: this can be captured by the coexistence of several nationalisms, which "are interlocking and interactive, bound together in a single relational nexus", forming "a triad linking national minorities, the newly nationalizing states in which they live, and the external national"homelands"to which they belong, or can be construed as belonging, by ethnocultural affinity /…/".[10]

In this nationalist landscape, policies, including those on language use, that stem from these 'nationalising nationalisms' are characterised by "claims made in the name of a"core nation"or nationality, defined in ethnocultural terms, and sharply distinguished from the citizenry as a whole. The core nation is understood as the legitimate"owner"of the state, which is conceived as the state *of* and *for* the core nation", and the later is, importantly, "conceived as being in a weak cultural, economic, or demographic position within the state".[11] Consequently, ongoing policies to 'defend' the core nation are not just needed, but are also justified by the perceived weakness of the 'core nation'. Such nation-building policies seek to address this seemingly fundamental and omnipresent fear of dominant nations being under threat in the ethno-national/cultural sense, by other ethno-cultural groups such as national minorities, as well as by neighbouring nations and thus also nation-states.[12]

In such a context, the question about how well founded, if at all, these fears and perceptions are, is irrelevant as the nationalising political elites very much take them for granted, they instrumentalise them in their political discourses and use them to justify the adoption of (exclusive) nation-building policies, also known as Russification, Macedonisation or Ukrainisation – to name but a few.[13] The more the core nation is perceived as being under threat, the more

9 P. Roter, 'Locating the "Minority Problem" in Europe: a Historical Perspective', 4:3 *Journal of International Relations and Development* (2001) pp. 221–249.

10 Brubaker, *supra* note 7, p. 4.

11 *Ibid.*, at p. 5.

12 *See* Roter, *supra* note 9.

13 A recent example of a combination of such internal and external threats affecting domestic policies on identity markers of the dominant (core) nation, such as language, is

exclusive these policies are. For their core idea is not to strengthen the nation as a civic community, but to defend the nation as an ethnic (linguistic, cultural) community, typically from the threats (perceived as being) posed by other ethno-cultural communities, whereby 'others' can exist within state frontiers and/or externally.[14]

What is worrying in this context is that if Brubaker wrote about the phenomenon of 'nationalising nationalisms' in the context of post-Cold War state-formation processes in Central and Eastern Europe, the phenomenon has since then spread across the continent, partly in the context of the enlargement of the European Union and subsequent effects of the freedom of movement,[15] partly due to migratory flows (or just fears of such flows),[16] and partly due to

---

Ukraine's Law 'On Education', adopted by Verkhovna Rada on 5 September 2017. When signing the controversial law on 25 September, Ukraine's President Poroshenko stated that the law "raises the role of the official Ukrainian language in the learning process", but it also emphasises the "importance of steadfast observance during education of the humanitarian rights of national minorities who live on the territory of Ukraine". However, as pointed out by Yegor Stadnyi, an analyst for the Kyiv-based NGO migration and urban development center CEDOS, this "law, in general, promotes the consolidation of the Ukrainian nation" as it enables integration of minorities into the Ukrainian society through providing them with opportunities to learn Ukrainian (he thus referred to a one-way adjustment process as expected from persons belonging to communities other than the Ukrainian nation). He defended the law as it 'is about integration', whereas it "still allows minority-language speakers to continue studying their native tongues", it also gives minorities 'more access to Ukrainian', which is needed as otherwise "they won't go into other spheres after graduating [high] school, they won't enter a university [where instruction is exclusively in Ukrainian], they won't enter public administration". Nevertheless, he added, "the law doesn't prevent additional schooling in minority languages on a private level, whether the initiative is parental, funded by foreign governments or through non-profit groups". In: M. Raczkiewycz, 'Neighbors Balk at New Education Law that Reinforces Ukraine's State Language', *The Ukrainian Weekly*, 6 October 2017, <http://www.ukrweekly.com/uwwp/neighbors-balk-at-new-education-law-that-reinforces-ukraines-state-language/>, visited on 31 October 2017.

14 Roter, *supra* note 9.

15 K. Burrell (ed.), *Polish Migration to the UK in the 'New' European Union* (London and New York, 2009); R. Black, G. Engbersen, M. Okólski and Ch. Panţîru (eds.), *A Continent Moving West?: EU Enlargement and Labour Migration from Central and Eastern Europe* (Amsterdam, Amsterdam University Press, 2010); C.E. Griffiths, 'Group Conflict and 'Confined' and 'Collaborative' Collective Efficacy: The Importance of a Normative Core between Immigrants and Natives in an English Town', 185:1 *Polish Sociological Review* (2014) pp. 91–112.

16 *See*, among many others, L. Fulton, 'Europe's Immigrant Problem: Integrating Minority Populations', 31:3 *Harvard International Review* (2009) pp. 28–33; C. Diehl and M. Blohm,

renewed autonomy requests (typically following years of lacking consultations on how to address open concerns and possibly opposing interests).[17] It is therefore safe to argue that most nation-states still aspire to this mythical congruence and homogenising model, which profoundly affects persons belonging to national minorities, including possibilities for preserving, developing or simply using freely their minority languages at different occasions, in private and public spheres. Access to rights of persons belonging to national minorities thus continues to face the threat of, or obstacles posed by, the nation-state. The threat is inherent in the very political entity that defines minority languages as such and has the power and competences to regulate their use and presence in the public sphere. Language policies therefore need to be understood in the broader context of nation-building tendencies of contemporary states. Another effect of such nationalising nationalism is that those who do not 'fit' the homogenising, monolingual ideology tend to conceive or construct themselves following the same model as homogeneous, clearly defined entities. Language can then can play the role of an identity marker, a *shibboleth* that regiments inclusion and exclusion.[18]

When analysing the language aspect of nationalism in the early 1940s, Deutsch made it clear that the national language was a matter of choice, that it was not uniform but rather composed of different dialects and idioms; however, in the nineteenth and particularly in the twentieth century, a tendency could be observed "to increase deliberately the difference between kindred, and particularly between neighbouring, languages".[19] Some nations and nationalists (like Scottish or Irish, Zionist Jewish or Norwegian) went as far as accepting new languages, typically spoken by their ancestors but not by themselves, only to be able to distinguish themselves from the neighbouring nations.[20] According to Deutsch, "all these are examples of a new trend to

---

'Rights or Identity? Naturalization Processes among 'Labor Migrants' in Germany', 37:1 *The International Migration Review* (2003) pp. 133–162.

17 Th. J. Miley, 'The Discourse of Language and Nation in Catalonia', 46 *Berkeley Journal of Sociology* (2002) pp. 46–78; C. Colino, 'Constitutional Change without Constitutional Reform: Spanish Federalism and the Revision of Catalonia's Statute of Autonomy', 39:2 *Publius* (2009) pp. 262–288; X. Vilà Carrera, 'The Domain of Spain: How Likely Is Catalan Independence?' 176:5 *World Affairs* (2014) pp. 77–83.

18 P. Bourdieu, *Language and Symbolic Power* (Oxford, Polity Press, 1991); B. Busch, 'New National Languages in Eastern Europe', in N. Coupland (ed.), *Language and Globalization* (Malden and Oxford, Blackwell, 2010) pp. 182–200.

19 K.W. Deutsch, 'The trend of European Nationalism – the Language Aspect', 36:3 *American Political Science Review* (1942) p. 538.

20 *Ibid.*, pp. 538–539.

increase consciously, indeed even to create, new linguistic differences by an act of the political will. It can be done; the languages of whole communities, in time of whole nations, can be changed to suit the desire for nationalistic separation".[21] Simultaneously, as "new ways of speech are formed through the changing and splitting up of old languages into new accents and idioms under the influence of time and geographic separation", such a possibility of changing alignments and combinations led Deutsch conclude that "the national languages of today appear not only as a cause, but also as a result, of national differentiation".[22] Although this study of the linguistic aspect of European nationalism was devoted to the role of the dominant language, these findings clearly have implications for other languages and speakers of non-dominant or minority languages in nation-states.

Within contemporary nation-states, substance of language policies is closely related to power relations between and within identity groups. As argued by Grillo, the prevalent approach to language policies (language use) in European polities has been the one of linguistic stratification as "an ideology of contempt: subordinate languages are despised languages".[23] Dorian further argues that this "has been true both where regional dialects are concerned and where the languages of subordinate ethnicities are concerned".[24] Histories of many European languages are therefore, writes Dorian,

> histories of a growing monopoly on legitimacy and prestige by a single dominant speech form, all others being relegated to inferior status. The standard language is typically considered a rich, precise, rationally organized and rationally organizing instrument; dialects and ethnic-minority languages, by contrast, are considered impoverished and crude, most likely inadequate to organize the subordinate world itself and certainly inadequate to organize other worlds.[25]

2.2 *Primordialism in Conceptualising Nations and National Minorities*

In addition to nationalism and its implications on the role of language and language policies, the second assumption that no discussion about language

21 *Ibid.*, p. 539.

22 *Ibid.*

23 R.D. Grillo, *Dominant Languages: Language and Hierarchy in Britain and France* (Cambridge, Cambridge University Press, 1989) pp. 173–174.

24 N.C. Dorian, 'Western Language Ideologies and Small-Language Prospects', in L.A. Grenoble and L.J. Whaley (eds.), *Endangered Languages: Language Loss and Community Response* (Cambridge, Cambridge University Press, 1998) p. 7.

25 *Ibid.*, p. 8.

rights can overlook is a specific (primordial) concept of nations (and by implication national minorities) as communities with a given (i.e. inherited, inborn) identity of which language is an important marker. National minorities are thus perceived as communities with a given (inherited) identity, including a linguistic identity. By implication, identities tend to be perceived as coherent, 'pure' and internally homogenous. Not only is intra-group diversity ignored, which has implications for language policies and language use (in the form of linguistic heterogeneity), but identity groups are separated along these seemingly clearly defined boundaries that define 'us' and 'them' and simultaneously separate 'us' from 'them'.[26]

Such a view is problematic in at least three respects: firstly, it ignores the fact that individuals do not originate from one or the other nation or ethnolinguistic group, but they (more or less freely) affiliate themselves with such a group. Secondly, they can affiliate with none or more than one group simultaneously, which means that they define their identities as multiple or situational, rather than unitary/uniform. Thirdly, they can change their affiliation over time, thereby reflecting their changing personal circumstances, for example. All these three dimensions are captured by one of the core principles of minority rights: the principle of free self-identification,[27] which – as explained by the Advisory Committee – "also extends to multiple affiliations".[28]

Whereas empirical evidence leaves no doubt that multiple affiliations are indeed very much present in our societies, their recording (e.g. in terms of data collection at census) still seems to be very problematic in many states. Interlocutors of the Advisory Committee from national offices of statistics are often overwhelmingly surprised by questions on multiple affiliations, and by implication, on data collection allowing individuals to record more than one 'mother tongue'. The principle of free self-identification further implies that data on ethnicity and language use need to be provided and recorded separately, for a choice of one language does not necessarily imply ethnic affiliation with the national community speaking that language. To allow for a free choice of individuals as the criterion for data collection on language use, as opposed to promote a primordial view of being born into a language community,

26 Grillo, *supra* note 23, p. 2.

27 *See* Article 3 of the FCNM, and Section 4.1 below.

28 Advisory Committee's Thematic Commentary No. 4, *The Framework Convention: a key tool to managing diversity through minority rights The Scope of Application of the Framework Convention for the Protection of National Minorities*, adopted on 27 May 2016, <https://rm.coe.int/16806a4811>, visited on 23 September 2017, para. 13. *See* further Section 4.1 below.

the Advisory Committee has increasingly used the terminology of the 'first language(s)',[29] rather than 'mother tongue(s)'.

Although many national censuses, if they are conducted in the traditional sense with questionnaires as opposed to a collection of already existing data, are carried out according to the European statisticians' guidelines on censuses, which recommend that "/r/espondents should be free to indicate more than one ethnic affiliation or a combination of ethnic affiliations if they wish to do so",[30] this is still very much a contested issue across Europe. The Advisory Committee has recorded disproval from state authorities as well as, in some cases, of persons belonging to national minorities. In general, minority representatives are supportive of a prospect to record more than one ethnic affiliation and more than one 'first language', particularly if this paves the way for a new category (or simply another empty line) of minority identity to be added to the list of possible affiliations. They also support such a recording if a significant number of individuals either identify in multiple terms, or if persons belonging to national minorities fear to identify as such because this could be perceived as disloyalty to the state. By contract, some numerically and politically strong national minorities that adhere to the nation-state ideology typically oppose such multiple affiliations just like state authorities. This should come as no surprise given the mutually inter-linked triad of different nationalisms.[31]

This practice may thus not entirely confirm Dorian's assessment of the existing 'multiple allegiances' – namely, that they "might be seen as an extension into the sphere of political organization of the sociologist's status sets, the totality of all the statuses one occupies (not always entirely congruently) in one's social life. In the political sphere this suggestion is to some extent"postnationalist"and to that degree perhaps an escape hatch from the demands of mutually exclusive nationalisms".[32] Still, she points out that "the fact that recognition of multiple allegiances is being recommended as a solution for otherwise irresolvable nationalist conflicts precisely in Europe could be especially helpful, since it is the concept of the nation-state coupled with its official standard language, developed in modern Europe and extended to the

29 *Ibid.*, paras. 74 and 83.

30 United National Economic Commission for Europe, Conference of European Statisticians. *Recommendations for the 2020 Censuses of Population and Housing* (New York and Geneva, 2015) <https://www.unece.org/fileadmin/DAM/stats/publications/2015/ECECES41_EN.pdf>, visited on 5 October 2017, para. 708.

31 Brubaker. *supra* note 7.

32 Dorian, *supra* note, p. 18.

many once-colonial territories of European states, that has in modern times posed the keenest threat to both the identities and the languages of small communities".[33]

This (non-existing) congruence of the state and the nation, the latter being as homogenous as possible, resonates in language policies that should not only help the dominant language survive, but by implication, also the dominant national group as well as the nation-state.[34] As states are faced with the existing heterogenous reality (ethnic, national, linguistic, religious and/or cultural diversity that manifests itself in different identity groups but also in differences within them), they frequently pursue nation-building policies, aimed at making this congruence myth a reality. Such exclusive nation-building (nationalisation) is frequently centred on the role of language, whereby the language of the dominant group seeks to become the accepted norm, and all other languages dependent on the more or less limited opportunities for their use and presence in the public domain within the nation-state. In such a context, language-related policies are typically interpreted according to the level of perceived threat to the dominant nation and the state, be it by internal identity groups (minorities) or by neighbouring nations.[35]

In extreme cases, the use and presence of non-dominant (minority) languages is therefore perceived as endangering the coherence and hence stability of states. In such a context, language becomes a political tool and its use and presence dependent on access to power of those who speak it or who purport to represent the dominant nation and hence the nation-state. Speakers of minority or minoritised languages are left to defend their language and language rights, often relying on external support, by their so-called 'kin-states' where these minority languages enjoy the status of dominant ones. All these power relations[36] thus make language and language rights become a highly contested political issue and the identity marker that can lead to intra- as well as inter-state conflicts, as frequently pointed out by the High Commissioner on National Minorities who sought to address the matter systematically already

33 *Ibid.*

34 Roter, *supra* note 9.

35 On the changing language policies, as a result of the perception of 'Slovenian smallness' *vis-à-vis* other (neighbouring) states and nations, see P. Roter, 'Language Issues in the Context of 'Slovenian Smallness'', in F. Daftary and F. Grin (eds.), *Nation-Building, Ethnicity and Language Politics in Transition Countries* (Budapest, Local Government and Public Service Reform Initiative, Open Society Institute, 2003) pp. 211–241.

36 It is not surprising, therefore, that Grillo, in his study of dominant languages in the context of France and Britain, leaves no doubt that central to such a project are "/l/inguistic inequality, and the connection between language and power". *See* Grillo, *supra* note 23, p. 2.

two decades ago – in the Oslo Recommendations Regarding the Linguistic Rights of National Minorities.

3 Language Ideologies in Practice and (Scholarly) Responses to Language Policies

As for practice observed by the Advisory Committee in the past two decades, there are numerous examples that would seem to confirm this. The so-called nationalising policies clearly manifest in, if not centre on, the use of languages in the public sphere. Such policies aim at, on the one hand, promoting the use of the 'national language' as the sole official language, which is reduced to its identity function. Language then tends to be interpreted as a means of exclusion and a tool to prove one's (dis)loyalty to the state. In such a context, all other non-dominant languages are downgraded to the status of minority languages whose use is not only limited, as determined by the dominant nation based on its perceptions of threats of those non-dominant languages to the coherence of the dominant nation and the state, but it is also perceived as a threat to the coherence and stability of the state itself.

Such a scenario is at present unfolding in Ukraine, where – in the context of its lack of effective control in Crimea (following the illegal annexation of Crimea by the Russian Federation in 2014) and self-proclaimed entities in the East – the exclusive nation-building (the so-called Ukrainisation) is very clearly aimed at promoting the Ukrainian language as the sole legitimate language in the public domain, at the expense of other languages, particularly Russian, but also other minority languages. Their use may have been affected as a 'collateral damage' of the process of Ukrainisation as anti-Russian policies, but it is not less painful for the speakers of those languages. This has been demonstrated in Ukraine's new 2017 Law 'On Education' (Article 7),[37] which abandons the current possibility to study all 11 years in a minority language, with Ukrainian being present only for studying separate subjects such as Ukrainian language, literature and history.[38]

37 The English translation of the Law 'On Education' is available in *CDL-REF(2017)047-eUkraine – The Law on Education adopted by the Verkhovna Rada on 5 September 2017 (for issue of language, see Article 7 and Concluding Remarks and Transitional Provision N° 18)*, <http://www.venice.coe.int/webforms/documents/?pdf=CDL-REF(2017)047-e>, visited on 25 November 2017.

38 This option is used by approximately 10 per cent or 400,000 students. 'Ukraine's New Education Law Unleashes International Storm over Minority Language Status', *Euromaidan Press*, 19 September 2017<http://euromaidanpress.com/2017/09/19/ukraines-new

Similarly, the Baltic states have for a number of years defended their exclusive language policies by referring to their status as small nations under threat of large Russian populations that at the time of their independence in early 1990s largely spoke only Russian. The nation-building in the Baltic states was very much centred on the role of language with language tests as a precondition for obtaining citizenship, with a reduction of teaching hours in non-dominant language, with language tests for certain professions or posts such as school directors, and with language inspectorates empowered to impose fines on those not complying with the legal framework on language use.[39] Whereas such measures were perceived and defended, and continue to be supported, by the national(ist) political elites as necessary and legitimate in the context of new nation-states that needed to secure their citizens' loyalty to the state,[40] in reality, they have alienated at least a proportion of the non-dominant (typically Russian-speaking) population of their states. Integration of society is thus unlikely to occur through the implementation of a strict state language policy.[41]

In the context of Yugoslavia's break-up, the simultaneous processes of state-formation and nation-building went hand in hand and were centred on purposeful efforts to distinguish one nation from another by emphasising differences, rather than similarities, in what was commonly known as Serbo-Croatian language in the former Yugoslavia. Croatia, for example, established a committee that underwent the process of looking for 'old Croatian words' and thus creating what is today known as *novorijek* (new expressions).[42] Similarly, Bosnia and Herzegovina ended up with three official languages (as defined in the constitutions of both entities – the Federation and Republika Srpska): Bosnian (or the language of the Bosniak nation), Serbian (the language of the

-education-law-causes-international-storm-over-minority-language-status/#arvlbdata>, visited on 25 November 2017.

39 *See* Opinion of the Advisory Committee on Latvia and Estonia, <https://www.coe.int/en/web/minorities/country-specific-monitoring>, visited on 10 October 2017.

40 C. Schmid, B. Zepa and A. Snipe, 'Language Policy and Ethnic Tensions in Quebec and Latvia', 45:3–4 *International Journal of Comparative Sociology* (2004) pp. 231–252; G. Hogan-Brun, 'At the Interface of Language Ideology and Practice: The Public Discourse Surrounding the 2004 Education Reform in Latvia', 5:3 *Language Policy* (2006) pp. 315–335; C. Schmid, 'Ethnicity and Language Tensions in Latvia', 7:1 *Language Policy* (2008) pp. 3–19.

41 See The Fourth Opinion on Estonia (19 March 2015), paras 43–48.

42 R.D. Greenberg, '*Language and Identity in the Balkans. Serbo-Croatian and its Disintegration*' (Oxford, Oxford university Press, 2004), *see* Chapter 5, particularly 5.2 on 'The new Croatian'.

Serbian nation) and Croatian (the language of the Croatian nation).[43] In general, emphasis has been on differences, rather than commonalities, and any initiative or a suggestion to overcome those in the post-Yugoslav space has been met by concerted resistance.[44]

Whereas the reality of exclusive nation-building, including or above all in the field of language policies, is certainly not surprising, it is the conceptual views of how minority languages should be dealt with that warrants more attention. If political scientists addressed these issues predominantly in the context of power relations and processes of nationalism and nation-building, then sociolinguistics focused on the presence of languages. Supporters of the so-called language ecology movement have emphasised the worldwide loss of linguistic diversity due to linguistic imperialism.[45] Their answer to this problem lies in the need to protect languages and prevent language loss. But, as argued by May, the danger in this line of argument "is an obvious tendency to present a 'preservationist' and 'romanticist' account of minority languages and their loss – amounting, in effect, to an overly utopian view of language and language change".[46] Moreover, "the language ecology paradigm actually reinforces, albeit unwittingly, the inevitability of the evolutionary change that it is protesting about", and it thus fails to highlight sufficiently "the wider political power relations that underlie language loss".[47]

As opposed to language ecology proponents, other academics have instead focused on disadvantages experienced by speakers of minoritised languages,

43 See Amendment XXIX to the Constitution of the Federation of Bosnia and Herzegovina, and Amendment LXXI to the Constitution of the Republika Srpska.

44 *See*, among others, reactions to the 2010 book titled *Jezik i Nacioonalizam* (*Language and Nationalism*) by a linguist form Osijek, Croatia, who argued that there was one Serbo-Croat language with different variations ('Lingvistica Kordić: Hrvati, Srbi I Bošnjaci govore jedan jezik', *Večernji list*, 15 August 2010,<https://www.vecernji.hr/vijesti/lingvistica-kordic-hrvati-srbi-i-bosnjaci-govore-istim-jezikom-179058>, visited on 20 October 2017). The 2017 Declaration on a Common Language signed by hundreds of intellectuals, writers and public figures from the former Yugoslavia was – not surprisingly – described by the President of the Croatian Academy of Arts and Sciences as "pointless, absurd and in vain" ('HAZU: Deklaracija o zajedničkom jeziku je besmislena, apsurdna i uzaludna inicijativa!', *Jutarnji list*, 30 March 2017,<https://www.jutarnji.hr/kultura/knjizevnost/hazu-deklaracija-o-zajednickom-jeziku-je-besmislena-apsurdna-i-uzaludna-inicijativa/5836063/>, visited on 20 October 2017).

45 T. Skutnabb-Kangas, *Linguistic Genocide in Education – or Worldwide Diversity and Human Rights?*' (Mahwah, NJ: Lawrence Erlbaum Associates, 2000).

46 May, *supra* note 6, p. 3.

47 *Ibid.*, pp. 3–4.

such as those faced by children being educated in an imposed language.[48] Sociolinguistists have also analysed the concept of linguistic human rights, which has been the central focus also of many lawyers. But the linguistic human rights approach has been criticised for a number of (not always compatible) reasons. Scepticism has been formulated concerning tendencies to essentialise identity constructions and to reify the link between language and identity, not taking into account the necessity to cater for expressions of multiple identities, and neglecting the situatedness of acts of identification. Linguistic human rights concepts have also been questioned because they might result in policies that confine speakers to languages, which restrict their access to equal participation in society.[49]

The prevalent understanding in this body of literature is problematic, argues May, because "the way the argument is formulated assumes that the linguistic community in question is easily definable in the first place – or, rather that all members of this group are (or will want to be) principally identified and identifiable by their language".[50] May thus calls for "a more *contingent* understanding of linguistic identity – an acknowledgement that the languages we speak are not ineluctably linked to our (ethnic) identity".[51] This is closely linked to a constuctivist view of identity, perhaps best known in Anderson's argument of nations being 'imagined communities'.[52] From a social constructivist point of view, conceptions of ethnicity are characterised by notions of hybridity, fluidity and malleability of identity construction.[53] This is in stark contrast to the prevailing political discourse arguments on contests to language rights based on the assumption that linguistic diversity might undermine national unity and social cohesion. This has been reflected in the approach by the Advisory Committee in its monitoring work in the field of language rights of persons belonging to national minorities, as reflected in more details also in its thematic commentaries.

48 J. Freeland and D. Patrick, 'Language Rights and Language Survival', in J. Freeland and D. Patrick (eds.), *Language Rights and Language Survival* (Manchester and Northampton: St. Jerome, 2004) pp. 1–34, at p. 1.

49 For an overview of different positions *see* St. May, 'Rethinking Linguistic Human Rights. Answering Questions of Identity, Essentialism and Mobility', in J. Freeland and D. Patrick, *supra* note 48, pp. 35–55.

50 May, *supra* note 6, p. 8.

51 *Ibid.*, p. 9.

52 B. Anderson, *Imagined Communities: Reflections on the Origin and Spread of Nationalism*. Revised edition (London and New York, Verso, 1996).

53 May, *supra* note 6, Chapter 1.

4 Language Rights in the Framework Convention: Language as a Transversal Matter

The Advisory Committee has addressed the challenges posed by nationalising states and exclusive nation-building policies by challenging the very notions of language that are associated with such nationalist ideologies and discourses. The FCNM has been drafted in a manner that it has allowed the Advisory Committee to move away from the traditional notion of language protection, which assumes, as its point of departure, the view of languages as bounded and clear cut categories. This understanding was challenged by Bakhtin as early as in the 1920s. He argued that unified languages are not naturally given but imposed and opposed to the heteroglossic character of language practices in society.[54] For Bakhtin, "at any given moment of its historical existence language is heteroglot from top to bottom".[55] Heteroglossia as a multi-voicedness encompasses, according to Bakhtin,[56] three dimensions: the diversity of discourses, the diversity of languages and codes, and the diversity of individual voices. As explained in Section 2 above, the codification of standard languages is historically linked to the political and economic process of nation-state building in which a common, unified, national language is seen as a crucial factor for achieving and preserving national unity. In practice, this is more an ideological and political question than a linguistic one; or, as Joseph puts it: "languages too are 'imagined communities' whose very existence and maintenance depend on the belief of the nation".[57]

As language is an essential element in how people identify themselves or are identified by others, in how they are enabled or disabled in their access to, among others, education, employment, media and justice, and in how they find themselves represented in the public space, it is not surprising that language questions are at the core of various fields covered by the FCNM. Consequently, language matters or language rights are not treated in the FCNM in one specific article, but topics related to language use and linguistic practices are spread over a range of different articles, which focus on language in various contexts,

54 Busch, *supra* note 18, New national Languages in Eastern Europe.

55 Quoted in J.E. Joseph and T.J. Taylor, 'Introduction: Ideology, Science and Language', in J.E. Joseph and T.J. Taylor (eds.), *Ideologies of Language* (London and New York: Routledge, 1990) pp. 1–6, at p. 3.

56 M. Bakhtin, '*The Dialogical Principle*', edited by Tzvetan Todorov (Manchester: Manchester University Press, 1984), p. 56.

57 J.E. Joseph, 'Language and Politics', in A. Davies and C. Elder (eds.), *The Handbook of Applied Linguistics* (Malden, Oxford and Carlton, Blackwell, 2004) pp. 345–366, at p. 359.

such as education (Article 12(1), Article 14), media (Article 9(1)), administration (Article 10(2)), the judiciary (Article 10(3)), personal names (Article 11(1)), signs and display of information (Article 11(2)) or toponomastic signs (Article 11(3)).[58] This variety of norms in the FCNM on language use and linguistic practices suggests that language rights must be considered as a transversal matter of central importance to the individual, to groups and to society as a whole. Additionally, as language performs different functions, language rights have to follow suit. Language rights need to cater for expressions of multiple identities and affiliations, and to take into account the fact that acts of identification are situational, rather than primordially given.

That language does not perform just one function (that of identity marker), but three, was suggested by Bühler in his seminal analysis of semiotics, communication and language published in 1934. Bühler distinguishes three main functions of language: *Darstellung* (representation of an object or a state of affairs), *Ausdruck* (expression of the sender's feelings) and *Appell* (appeal to the receiver).[59] These functions are thus related to the message as well as to both partners in an interaction, the addresser and the addressee. As Jakobson explains, these functions correspond to the three grammatical persons – the first person of the addresser, the second person of the addressee and a 'third person', someone or something spoken of.[60] In every interaction, speakers simultaneously refer to themselves and, through the exchange of content related messages, constitute and modify social relations with others. Consequently, language practices can be analysed in a perspective taking into account the multilayered nature of language in its dimensions of identity, instrumentality and interaction. Translated into a human rights terminology, the identity dimension corresponds to the right of self-identification and the right of being recognised. The instrumental dimension refers to the right to access information, education, services and resources in the same terms as other members of society. Finally, the interaction dimension points to a need to communicate across differences and to participate actively in society. These three dimensions have been explained by the Advisory Committee in its third thematic commentary.[61]

58 For the scope of application of these provisions, and the conditions attached to these rights, *see* the Advisory Committee's Thematic Commentary No. 4.

59 K. Bühler, *Theory of Language: the Representational Function of Language*, translated by Donald Fraser Goodwin (Amsterdam and Philadelphia, John Benjamins Publishing Company, 1990 [1934]) p. 35.

60 R. Jakobson, 'Linguisitics and Poetics', in Th. A. Sebeok (ed.), *Style in Language* (New York, Wiley, 1960) pp. 350–377.

61 Advisory Committee's Thematic Commentary No. 3, *The Language Rights of Persons Belonging to National Minorities under the Framework Convention*, adopted on 24 May 2012,

4.1 *The Identity Dimension: Heteroglossic and Situated Linguistic Repertoires*

The link between language and identity becomes apparent in several articles of the FCNM, but it is a core concern of Articles 3, 5 and 11. Article 5 obliges state parties "to promote the conditions necessary for persons belonging to national minorities to maintain and to develop their culture, and to preserve the essential elements of their identity" whereby language is explicitly stated as one of these essential elements. Article 11 stipulates the right of persons belonging to a national minority to use their surname and first names in the minority language, to display language signs, inscriptions and other information of a private nature visible to the public in the minority language; and calls upon state parties to display traditional toponyms intended for the public also in the minority language. Article 3 stipulates that "every person belonging to a national minority shall have the right freely to choose to be treated or not to be treated as such and no disadvantage shall result from this choice or from the exercise of the rights which are connected to that choice". Article 3 does not explicitly mention language, but in practice, (declaration on) language use can be considered as an expression of identity and of belonging to a particular group. Such declarations on linguistic affiliation can be required for population census, school enrolment, inscription into electoral registers, military conscription, job applications in public service, police and judiciary investigations.

The Advisory Committee has in its monitoring process taken an open approach, discarding a simple equation between language and identity. Compulsory declarations of linguistic affiliation are contrary to the freedom of choice,[62] especially when those declarations are not anonymous, when individuals cannot change them for a longer period and when individuals' refusal to declare their linguistic affiliation leads to their exclusion from certain political or civic rights.[63] Also, any classification of persons without their knowledge and consent is not in line with the FCNM.[64] The Advisory Committee has consistently emphasised that multiple and situational affiliations should be guaranteed within the principle of self-identification.[65]

---

available at <https://rm.coe.int/16800c108d> , visited on 23 September 2017; *see* also the Advisory Committee's Thematic Commentary No. 4.

62 Advisory Committee's Thematic Commentary No. 4, para. 11.

63 *E.g.*, First Opinion on Italy, Third Opinion on Cyprus. (All opinions of the Advisory Committee are available at <https://www.coe.int/en/web/minorities/country-specific-monitoring>, visited on 15 October 2017.

64 *E.g.*, First Opinion on Germany, First Opinion on the Slovak Republic.

65 Advisory Committee's Thematic Commentary No. 4, paras. 11 and 13.

In a sociolinguistic perspective, situations in which minority languages are present are by definition linguistically diverse settings in which power relations come into play. This complex relationship between language practices and acts of identification can be usefully grasped with the concept of linguistic repertoire.[66] The latter refers to a totality of linguistic and communicative possibilities, which are available to speakers in specific situational contexts. These include register specific, stylistic and dialectal varieties as well as pragmatic knowledge to apply these linguistic possibilities adequately in specific situations. Importantly, instead of deriving from the understanding of languages as bounded entities, the concept of linguistic repertoire is based on a speaker-centred perspective, which highlights experiences and desires linked to language. It is linked to personal life trajectories: it "reflects a *life*, not just birth, a life that is lived in a real sociocultural, historical, and political space".[67] The linguistic repertoire develops through interaction and is thus constantly changing, whether due to a change of living circumstances such as mobility, or as a result of political change.[68] The state-formation process after the end of the Cold War, for example, also changed linguistic hierarchies: former minority languages became majority languages and *vice versa*, and this has had a profound effect on language rights of speakers of these languages.[69]

In social interaction, speakers draw on the complex structure of linguistic resources and potentialities of their repertoire to position themselves through distinction from and identification with others. This implies the construction of a collective – and exclusive – 'we' within which inequalities and power relations seem, at least for a moment, to be erased. The relevance of language in identity constructions and in discourses about identity points to the crucial role that particular language practices – as dialects, accents, registers – can play in terms of being identified (or misidentified) by others and, subsequently, in practices of self-identification and distinction from others. Linguistic practices can thus become a tool for individuals' identifying as belonging or not belonging to a particular group. Fear of discrimination can urge persons to

66 B. Busch., 'The Linguistic Repertoire Revisited', 33:5 *Applied Linguistics* (2012) pp. 503–523; B. Busch, 'Expanding the Notion of the Linguistic Repertoire: On the Concept of the Lived Experience of Language', 38:3 *Applied Linguistics* (2017), pp. 340–358.

67 J. Blommaert, 'Language, Asylum, and the National Order', 50:4 *Current Anthropology* (2009) pp. 415–441, at p. 424.

68 B. Busch., 'Die Macht präbabylonischer Phantasien. Ressourcenorientiertes sprachbiographisches Arbeiten', 40 *Zeitschrift für Literaturwissenschaft und Linguistik LiLi* (2011), 58–82, at p. 58 ff.

69 Nation-building policies thus typically centre on the role of language and language use (language rights), as discussed in Section 2 above.

hide or deny parts of their repertoire. The desire to identify with a specific language can become powerful especially when linked to experiences of oppression, non-recognition or misrecognition – e.g. by imposed forms of patronyms or toponyms conforming to the majority language. Linguistic affiliation can also be used to legitimise conflicts concerning the distribution of economic resources, social status and political power.[70]

In its opinions concerning the implementation of Article 3 of the FCNM, the Advisory Committee has focused on questions related to census, as these frequently are moments when declarations of linguistic or ethnic affiliations are asked. Data are interpreted as information on the numerical size of particular groups, also determining access to rights conditional by a "substantial number" of persons belonging to a national minority (FCNM, Articles 10(2) on the use of minority languages in relations with administrative authorities, 11(3) on topographical indications and 14(2) on teaching in an of minority languages). Following the assumption that for every person, one language is dominant, all persons indicating more than one language in the census form are still today in most countries treated as monolingual when the census data are processed and published in statistical charts. Given the heteroglossic nature of individual linguistic repertoires, such a simple assumption is highly problematic.

The Advisory Committee has thus encouraged states to collect data in strict conformity with the principle of free self-identification, allowing respondents to indicate more than one language (multiple linguistic affiliations, which are particularly relevant for children born to parents with different affiliations). Such flexibility, including in terms of optional questions and an open list of alternative answers, is essential for the census results to reflect each individual's actual choices.[71] Mandatory questions on ethnic or linguistic affiliation are not considered compatible with the principle of freedom of choice laid down in Article 3(2) of the Framework Convention.[72] The Advisory Committee has also encouraged authorities to take specific initiatives to include persons affiliating with minorities, and persons speaking a minority language among the census officials and to translate the census questionnaires into minority languages.[73] During the preparatory phase of the census, the authorities should consult the

70 St. May, 'Rethinking Linguistic Human Rights', in J. Freeland and D. Patrick (eds), *Language Rights and Language Survival* (Manchester, St Jerome, 2004) pp. 35–54, at p. 44.

71 *E.g.*, Third Opinion on Cyprus, Third Opinion on the Slovak Republic, Fourth Opinion on Estonia.

72 *E.g.*, First Opinion on Estonia.

73 *E.g.*, Third Opinion on Croatia, Third Opinion on Cyprus, Third Opinion on Poland.

representatives of minorities, and sufficient information has to be available for persons making an informed decision at census.[74]

Furthermore, data processing has to respect the free expression of ethnic and linguistic identities, including multiple affiliations.[75] When interpreting the data, authorities must be aware that past experience and fear of discrimination can prompt persons to hide their linguistic affiliations and identities.[76] Census and other quantitative data cannot be regarded as a sole means of obtaining reliable information for language policies but have to be supplemented with sociological studies. This is particularly important in case of decreasing numbers or when statistical data differ considerably from estimates by minority representatives.[77] Demographic changes can be a result of intra-state migrations, e.g. to urban centres, which can lead to different language needs and thereby also language policies outside areas traditionally inhabited by persons belonging to national minorities.[78]

4.2 *The Instrumental Dimension: Language as a Means for Accessing Resources and Basic Rights*

In communication models, which highlight the multi-functionality of language, the instrumental dimension of language, also known as the representational function, points to the objects and state of affairs in reality, to the contents and contexts of the messages exchanged between interaction partners.[79] In terms of language rights, this means that the right to express oneself in one's own language is only of symbolic value if full access to social, economic, political and cultural life is possible only by using another language (that of the dominant majority community). Given the role of language as a means to the enjoyment of human rights such as the right to education, access to the media, health care or justice, the use of minority languages in these domains has to be guaranteed and regulated.

To raise the question of the instrumental or functional value of minority languages is to address the hierarchical relation between different languages, their unequal legal status and a disparity between what Bourdieu[80] has

74 *E.g.*, Third Opinion on Croatia.

75 *E.g.*, Third Opinion on Cyprus, Third Opinion on Hungary.

76 *E.g.*, Second Opinion on Croatia.

77 *E.g.*, Third Opinion on the Slovak Republic.

78 *E.g.*, Second Opinion on Austria, Fourth Opinion on Finland.

79 *See* Bühler, *supra* note 59.

80 P. Bourdieu, *Ce que parler veut dire. L'économie des échanges linguistiques* (Paris, Fayard 1982).

identified as the social and symbolic value of languages or linguistic practices in a given language market. This is, however, not just a language matter, but it also concerns power relations between different groups of speakers. Language can in this context become an argument in struggles for access to and redistribution of resources. But it can also function as a barrier to access to resources and rights. If a minority language is perceived among its speakers as functional only in certain mainly private domains, it can be experienced as a limiting factor, which tends to confine the speakers to given social and geographical boundaries. This can urge speakers to move away from their language, to decide not to pass it on to the next generation and to choose to educate their children in the majority language.[81]

Traditionally, the issues of language maintenance and language loss have been addressed in the context of the nation-state and/or its particular territories populated by language communities. But more recent approaches take in account mobility processes, the increasing transnational and multidirectional character of communication flows or the commodification of local 'authenticity'; all these have led to co-presence of different, sometimes contradictory frames of reference to which persons are exposed to as speaking subjects.[82] A single nationwide linguistic market has been transformed to a multiplicity of overlapping spaces and places, on local as well as on translocal scales, in which speakers participate in their everyday life and in which different language regimes (i.e. habituated practices, rules, language ideologies and hierarchies) are present. All these changes require a shift in language use from the latter being tied to certain geographically and/or socially demarcated entities to a more deterritorialised conception of communication spaces.[83] Local language regimes regulating language use within such spaces can differ considerably from linguistic hierarchies at the national level. In some contexts, the use of a minority language is still considered in terms of deficiency in relation to the normative power of a single standard language;[84] but in other contexts, multilingualism and the facility to communicate in a minority language can be perceived as an added value, particularly where the competence in a minority language is

81 A. Portes and L. Hao, 'The Price of Uniformity: Language, Family and Personality Adjustment in the Immigrant Second Generation, 25:6 *Ethnic and Racial Studies* (2002) pp. 889–912; Busch 2017, *supra* note 66.

82 J. Blommaert, J. Collins and St. Slembrouck, 'Polycentricity and Interactional Regimes in 'Global Neighborhoods', 6:2 *Ethnography* (2005) pp. 205–235.

83 *Ibid.*; J. Blommaert, J. Collins and St. Slembrouck, 'Spaces of Multilingualism', 25:3 *Language and Communication* (2005) pp. 197–216.

84 *E.g.,* Third Opinion on the Russian Federation and Third Opinion on Azerbaijan, particularly in urban centres in both states.

seen as a symbolic or economic asset or when it facilitates access to networks, spaces and markets beyond the national level.[85]

The FCNM addresses questions related to language as a means of access to other rights in a number of its articles. Article 4 obliges the state parties to adopt "adequate measures in order to promote, in all areas of economic, social, political and cultural life, full and effective equality between persons belonging to a national minority and those belonging to the majority". Article 9 contains a range of measures in the field of media policy and access to media that are included in order to recognise "the freedom to hold opinions and to receive and impart information and ideas in the minority language". Article 10 calls upon state parties to recognise the right to use minority languages in public freely and without interference and to endeavour to ensure favourable conditions for the use of these languages within the administration and judiciary. Article 14 refers to access to education including efforts to ensure "opportunities for being taught the minority language or for receiving instruction in the minority language".

When assessing the implementation of the FCNM, the Advisory Committee has demonstrated its awareness of the need for language policies in fields such as education to take into account the multi-functionality of language. An over-emphasis on the identity dimension which can translate in the field of education to policies promoting exclusively the use of the minority language would likely result in confining speakers to an imposed locality and in limiting their social mobility.[86] On the other hand, an over-emphasis on the instrumental dimension of language can result in an educational system that overrules the minority language by favouring the majority language, as well as a policy that disregards the communicative value of minority languages and instead favours assimilative practices. The Advisory Committee has thus made it clear that the rights enshrined in the FCNM should be translated into language policies in such a way that individuals belonging to national minorities, in order to be able to enjoy their rights and to participate in society on an equal basis, are empowered to move freely between different spaces in which differing language regimes are present.

In the field of education, the Advisory Committee has stressed that the learning of the minority language or the state language(s) should not be a mutually exclusive choice[87] and that authorities should consider encouraging

85 B. Busch, 'Slovene in Carinthian – Language beyond Ethnic Categories', in W. Wintersteiner, G. Gombos and D. Gronold (eds.), *Border Dis/solutions. Multilingualism, Transculturality and Education*, (Klagenfurt, Wieser, 2010) pp. 144–157.

86 *E.g.*, Third Opinion on Ukraine.

87 *E.g.*, First Opinion on Serbia and Montenegro, First Opinion on Norway.

multilingual and dual medium education models, which would attract children from both majority and minority backgrounds[88] and cater for children who grow up bilingually in 'mixed' families. It has invited authorities to take into account demographic changes as there can be trends of increased migration from areas traditionally inhabited by persons belonging to national minorities to near and distant urban centres outside these areas.[89] Local school networks in such areas should nevertheless be secured in a sustainable way,[90] and persons living outside of these areas should also have access to teaching in and of their language.[91] The Advisory Committee has also encouraged a more proactive approach to minority language education with regard to immigrant populations, particularly in areas where they live in substantial numbers.[92]

4.3 *The Interactional Dimension: Intercultural Dialogue and Co-operation*

Traditional approaches to language rights concentrate on identity and instrumental aspects, which are sometimes presented as contradictory or even mutually exclusive. It is one of the qualities of the FCNM that it not only takes into account these two dimensions of language rights, but it introduces a third dimension that is expressed in the terms 'intercultural dialogue' and 'effective participation'. Peter Leuprecht, Deputy Secretary-General of the Council of Europe from 1993 to 1997, was one of the prominent protagonists of this innovative approach before the FCNM was adopted; he called for overcoming conventional ways of thinking in majority/minority categories and called for a different approach:

> What we should aim at, is neither assimilation or oppression of the minority by the majority, nor segregation, apartheid, ghettoisation or conservation of a minority in a reservation as a curiosity and attraction for tourists ... The point is not to retreat anxiously, not to close oneself off, not to demarcate or exclude, but to dare opening up and approaching one another.[93]

---

88 *E.g.,* Third Opinion on Croatia, Fourth Opinion on Moldova.

89 *E.g.,* Third Opinion on the Slovak Republic, Fourth Opinion on Austria, Fourth Opinion on Croatia.

90 *E.g.,* Third Opinion on Germany.

91 *E.g.,* Second Opinion on Austria.

92 *E.g.,* First Opinion on the United Kingdom, Third Opinion on Azerbaijan.

93 P. Leuprecht, 'Eröffnung des Seminars – Begründung des Seminarthemas', in V. Wakounig and B. Busch (eds.), *Interkulturelle Erziehung und Menschenrechte*, (Klagenfurt/Celovec, Drava, 1992) pp. 23–30, at p. 27.

This vision relates precisely to the interactional dimension of language. The term 'interaction' implies the presence of 'the other', the execution of an action directed towards 'the other', and the reciprocity of the process. The importance of this third, appellative function of language is visible in several articles of the FCNM. When Article 3(2) stipulates that the rights and freedoms flowing from the principles of the FCNM may be exercised individually or in community with others, the Explanatory Report (para. 37) gives an important specification: "The term 'others' shall be understood in the widest possible sense and shall include persons belonging to the same national minority, to another national minority, or to the majority". Article 6 in a programmatic sense stipulates that the parties are to take effective measures "to promote mutual respect and understanding and co-operation among all persons living on their territory, irrespective of those persons' ethnic, cultural, linguistic or religious identity". Article 6 thus has the broadest scope of application as it addresses society as a whole, to *all* persons living in a state,[94] calling for policies which reflect and promote diversity, eliminate barriers and encourage contact and co-operation between persons belonging to different communities on the basis of mutuality as a leading principle. Education, culture and media are identified as particularly relevant for intercultural action, thereby recognising a potential danger for societal integration and cohesion stemming from parallel school or media systems, separated from each other by language or ethnicity.[95] Article 12(1) specifies how these goals are to be applied in the fields of education, including by taking measures "to foster knowledge of the culture, history, language and religion of their national minorities and the majority". Finally, Article 15 calls for the creation of "the conditions necessary for the effective participation of persons belonging to national minorities in cultural, social and economic life and in public affairs, in particular those affecting them".

In terms of language policies, the Advisory Committee has interpreted the provisions of Article 6 in such a manner that the languages present in society must be represented – made visible and audible – in the public domain so that all persons can gain awareness of the multilingual character of society and can see themselves as being an integral part of the society. Language policies should therefore encourage the creation of spaces, where different linguistic practices can meet and be negotiated in a spirit of mutual respect. In this sense not only speakers of minority languages should be encouraged to learn

94 Advisory Committee's Thematic Commentary No. 4, Part V.

95 *E.g.*, the Fourth Opinion on the Former Yugoslav Republic of Macedonia, the Third Opinion on Bosnia and Herzegovina.

majority languages but also *vice versa*.[96] Inclusive language policies must cater to all, including individuals belonging to national minorities living outside areas where they traditionally settle, and persons belonging to non-traditional (migrant) communities and others. The Advisory Committee has been particularly critical of cases where language is used for gate-keeping purposes or is used to justify policies of segregation (e.g. Roma or immigrant children), when linguistic divisions are used for political purposes and presented as a root cause for societal cleavages and when intolerance based on linguistic affiliations is stirred up in political discourse.[97]

Special attention is also required when laws and policies exclusively emphasise the use of the state language(s) at the expense of minority languages, which is particularly notable in the context of the adoption of state language laws.[98] With regard to the latter, the Advisory Committee has highlighted that a successfully integrated society involves both the majority and minorities, all perceived as integral part of the society, and requires support for all persons to preserve and maintain their identities and cultures, including multilingual repertoires and multiple (linguistic) affiliations.[99]

5 Conclusion

Minority rights, including language rights, as enshrined in the FCNM and developed further through the monitoring work of the Advisory Committee require inclusive language policies which rely on three pillars: the right to express difference and the recognition of difference; the facilitation of equal access to resources and rights despite difference; and, in Fraser's words,[100] the need for 'social interaction across difference'.[101] As she explains, policies of self-affirmation which concentrate only on the recognition of difference tend to fix and reify identity ascriptions and can result in exerting moral pressure on individuals to conform to a given group culture: "Ironically, then, the identity model

96 On such mutual obligations in the so-called ethnically mixed areas in Slovenia, *see* the First Opinion on Slovenia.

97 *E.g.*, Third Opinion on Moldova, Third Opinion on Ukraine, First Opinion on Latvia, Second Opinion on Latvia, First Opinion on Estonia, Third Opinion on the Former Yugoslav Republic of Macedonia.

98 *E.g.*, Third Opinion on Ukraine, First Opinion on Latvia, Second Opinion on Latvia.

99 *E.g.*, Third Opinion on Liechtenstein.

100 N. Fraser, 'Rethinking Recognition', 3 *New Left Review* (May-June 2000), pp. 107–120, at p. 113.

101 *See* also Advisory Committee's Thematic Commentary No. 4.

serves as a vehicle for misrecognition".[102] Fraser pleads for an alternative approach to recognition, which takes into account questions of social status and social subordination – insofar as one is prevented from participating as a peer in social life. In this sense, misrecognition means being denied the status of a full partner in social interaction. Only when one is enabled to act as a full partner and to interact with others on an equal footing, does it become possible to expose oneself to interaction across difference.[103]

But to engage in a process of intercultural dialogic interaction, one needs to deconstruct the pre-established identity categories and primordially given and omnipresent dichotomies (of 'us' and 'them'). By making visible traces of the excluded, non-dominant, minority 'other', strategies of deconstruction aim at transforming the way in which categories are conceived as homogeneous and hierarchical by breaking them up and acknowledging heterogeneity within what was conceived as one, the same and non-changing identity community. Using his own language experiences, Derrida has demonstrated the alienating power of a dominant language in a colonial context both through processes of assimilation and of exclusion.[104] Deconstructing languages as 'given' categories thus becomes a means to reverse practices of linguistic de-propriation towards practices of appropriation while avoiding the trap of nationalist phantasms.

A language is appropriated not just by learning and using it, but by transforming and adapting it to new contexts and needs. Interaction across difference thus assumes accepting that 'minority' and 'majority' languages are exposed to permanent transformation and the latter comes in different directions simultaneously. Although some practices (e.g. code mixing) undermine language ideologies of monolingualism and hierarchical orders of languages, there is a need for language policies that promote affirmative recognition and facilitate access to resources and rights in minority languages to counterbalance the hegemonic position of majority languages. Language use and language policies are still overwhelmingly dominated by nationalism, nation-building and nationalisation, all based on language identities (and origins) assumed as given and internally coherent (thereby denying any intra-group diversity, including linguistic one) and presented in opposition to other language groups, which are not only perceived as the 'others' but also as those that endanger the existence of 'us' and by implication, according to the one-state nationalist ideology, also 'our' states. Language appropriation and interaction across difference is thus hardly possible in the context of exclusive nation-building. Not only are nationalising policies fundamentally different from the post-modern

102 *Ibid.*, p. 112.

103 *Ibid.*, pp. 112–113.

104 J. Derrida, *Le monolinguisme de l'autre* (Paris, Éditions Gallilée, 1996) p. 121 ff.

practices and realities in contemporary societies, but they prevent the formation of language policies suitable to the different and changing societal needs and, consequently, they pose an obstacle to successful societal integration in the long-term.

Instead, states need to take seriously the speaker-centred approach, which corresponds to the FCNM's conception of minority rights as rights and freedoms of individuals interacting in social contexts. Language is closely tied to personal and collective experiences as well as to ideologies, discourses and power relations. When exploring relations between language and human rights, it is therefore necessary to take into account the multidimensionality of language in communication. Rethinking language rights from this perspective requires us to find ways to balance and fine-tune, according to the specific situation, language policies that take into account the dimensions of identification, of instrumentality and of social interaction.

Unlike approaches to linguistic rights that take languages or language communities as their point of departure, a speaker-centred approach as expressed in the FCNM aims at overcoming reified categorisations and making the constructedness of language categories apparent. Instead of thinking about linguistic rights in terms of particular 'languages', a speaker-centred approach focuses on the notion of language practices acknowledging the heterogeneity of individual linguistic resources and the heteroglossic character of language in interaction. Instead of taking the idea of collective identities to which individuals are ascribed to for granted, the speaker-centred approach focuses on situational acts of identification through which individuals signify distinction from or identification with others. Instead of assuming a quasi natural link between language and territory, the speaker-centred approach explores how speakers in their daily lives move through different social spaces characterised by and constituted through specific language practices.

In order to contribute to the overall goal of promoting social cohesion by guaranteeing the rights and freedoms of persons belonging to national minorities, language policies must be tailor-made to the situation of each minority within the specific context. As there is constant evolution, measures identified by states parties in response to certain circumstances will not necessarily ensure compliance with the standards of the FCNM in the future. Therefore, policies, legislative framework and implementation mechanisms directly or indirectly affecting the language rights of persons belonging to minorities must be continuously monitored, evaluated and amended, in close consultation with the communities concerned. It is in this context that legally non-binding instruments such as the Oslo Recommendations and the work of the High Commissioner on National Minorities complement the FCNM and the monitoring and advisory work of the Advisory Committee.

CHAPTER 11

The Right to Display Place Names in Regional or Minority Languages within the Council of Europe Legal Framework

Vesna Crnić-Grotić

Most of the European countries have linguistic minorities. The languages spoken (and written) present a rich cultural heritage of Europe but, at the same time, they present a challenge for States and their societies at large how to accommodate and reconcile the various and sometimes conflicting needs of the different groups.[1] At the same time States have to preserve the necessary integration of the society. It is well established that peaceful co-existence can be achieved by respecting fundamental human rights that have an impact on ethnic or linguistic interests.[2]

Special rights belonging to members of national minorities as well as their collective bodies today form an integral part of the human rights protection in international law. Among them the linguistic rights have a very prominent place since a different language often is one of the dominant characteristics distinguishing a minority from the majority population in a country, along with religion, ethnicity or other trait. At the same time, we have to be aware that members of minorities enjoy general human rights just like every other person. Starting with the Universal Declaration of Human Rights, adopted by the UN General Assembly in 1948 and continuing with the subsequent international law instruments, members of national, religious, ethnic and linguistic minorities are entitled to the same level of protection as the majority population. In that respect the most basic means of protection for speakers of minority languages is the principle of non-discrimination.[3] Non-discrimination principle is found in every human rights instrument that provide human rights

1 J. Packer, (editor's note): "Since European States have been largely organised around a dominant 'nation' which is typically defined by language more than any other trait, the situation and interests of linguistic minorities has become a central concern within and between States". 6 *International Journal on Minority and Group Rights* (1999) p. v.

2 F. de Varennes, 'Equality and Non-Discrimination: Fundamental Principles of Minority Language Rights', 6 *International Journal on Minority and Group Rights* (1999) pp. 307–318.

3 R. Dunbar, 'Minority Language Rights in International Law', 50 *Int'l & Comp. L.Q* (2001) p. 100.

© KONINKLIJKE BRILL NV, LEIDEN, 2018 | DOI 10.1163/9789004357754_012

protection "without distinction of any kind, such as race, colour, sex, language, religion, political or other opinion, national or social origin, property, birth or other status".[4]

The protection of minorities and their languages in international law, however, is still 'work in progress' and only some rules can be said to have general application and universal binding force as the rules of customary international law.[5] The International Court of Justice has repeatedly confirmed that the existence of a rule of customary international law requires the presence of two elements, namely State practice (*usus*) and a conviction that such practice is required, prohibited or allowed, depending on the nature of the rule, as a matter of law (*opinio juris sive necessitatis*).[6] In this context, *usus* can include any State practice, by action or by omission, by physical acts or by declaratory statements as long as it is accompanied by the *opinio juris* that such behaviour is required by international law. It is generally accepted that the relevant State practice has to be uniform and consistent.[7] When this is not the case, it is not possible to claim that a rule belongs to customary international law. Thus, in the Chapman case, even the principle that national minorities should be protected was considered too abstract by the European Court of Human Rights (ECtHR) to impact its judgment.[8]

4 Article 2, Universal Declaration of Human Rights, UN General Assembly resolution 217A, 10 December 1948. The European Convention on Human Rights, 1950, contains a similar clause in Article 14 with some additional tokens of discrimination: "The enjoyment of the rights and freedoms set forth in this Convention shall be secured without discrimination on any ground such as sex, race, colour, language, religion, political or other opinion, national or social origin, association with a national minority, property, birth or other status".

5 Article 38.1.b) of the Statute of the International Court of Justice describes customary international law as a 'general practice accepted as law'.

6 *North Sea Continental Shelf* cases, Judgment, 20 February 1969, *ICJ Reports 1969*, p. 3. *Continental Shelf* case (*Libyan Arab Jamahiriya v. Malta*), Judgment, 3 June 1985, *ICJ Reports 1985*, pp. 29–30, para. 27.

7 J. Crawford, *Brownlie's Principles of Public International Law* (Oxford, 2012) pp. 24–25.

8 *Chapman v. the United Kingdom*, 2001, para. 94. The ECtHR responded to the applicant's request "to take into account recent international developments, in particular the Framework Convention for the Protection of National Minorities". It observed that "there may be said to be an emerging international consensus amongst the Contracting States of the Council of Europe recognising the special needs of minorities and an obligation to protect their security, identity and lifestyle ... not only for the purpose of safeguarding the interests of the minorities themselves but to preserve a cultural diversity of value to the whole community". However, the ECtHR was "not persuaded that the consensus is sufficiently concrete for it to derive any guidance as to the conduct or standards which Contracting States consider desirable in any particular situation".

Another way of protecting minorities and their linguistic rights can be found in treaties concluded by States universally or regionally or, very often, bilaterally. Some of the instances of the treaty protection of religious or national and ethnic minorities can be traced back to the 1648 Peace Treaty in Westphalia. Many treaties dealing with protection of minorities were concluded after World War I. To a lesser degree specific treaties were also concluded after World War II. Nevertheless, the fact remains that today there are not that many specific treaty legal rules in force on this matter.

At the universal level, namely, within the United Nations, the development stopped at Article 27 of the 1966 International Covenant for Civil and Political Rights (ICCPR).[9] This article is the first and still the only treaty rule specifically speaking of the rights of the members of (linguistic) minorities at the level of the UN. According to it, among other rights, linguistic minorities "shall not be denied the right ... to use to use their own language".[10]

In 1992 the UN General Assembly adopted the Declaration on the Rights of Persons Belonging to National or Ethnic, Religious and Linguistic Minorities.[11] The declaration that listed basic minority rights was adopted in face of the new political situation in Europe. As regards the linguistic minorities, the declaration proclaims the right of the members of such minorities "to use their own language, in private and in public, freely and without interference or any form of discrimination" (Art. 2). In that respect, States "shall take measures to create favourable conditions" for minorities to develop and especially consider the field of education.[12] The General Assembly's declarations as such do not have a binding legal force[13] but one can claim that the rules in this one for a

9 Article 27: "In those States in which ethnic, religious or linguistic minorities exist, persons belonging to such minorities shall not be denied the right, in community with the other members of their group, to enjoy their own culture, to profess and practise their own religion, or to use their own language". International Covenant on Civil and Political Rights, UN Treaty Series, vol. 999, p. 171. In force since 1976. Today it has 169 States parties.

10 The Human Rights Committee in charge of monitoring the ICCPR application interpreted the phrase 'shall not be denied' as requiring also positive measures. General Comment No.23, 1994, para.6.2. More information available at <www.ohchr.org/EN/HRBodies/CCPR/Pages/CCPRIndex.aspx>, visited on 20 August 2017.

11 Adopted by General Assembly resolution 47/135 of 18 December 1992.

12 Art. 4. para. 2. In para. 4 of the same article the reference is made to education: "States should, where appropriate, take measures in the field of education, in order to encourage knowledge of the history, traditions, language and culture of the minorities existing within their territory".

13 *See* P. Daillier and A. Pellet, *Quoc Dinh Droit International Public* , 7th ed. (L.G.D.J. Paris, 2002) p.389.

bigger part reflect customary international law rules that are binding for all States as the rules adopted in practice.

The regional European approach has been more oriented to creating legal rules dedicated to the protection of minorities especially after the fall of the Berlin wall and the disintegration of the socialist federative States, such as Yugoslavia or the Soviet Union. The war in former Yugoslavia showed just how these processes are dangerous for the peace and stability in Europe. The then Conference for Security and Co-operation (later the Organisation for Security and Co-operation in Europe, OSCE) together with the Council of Europe worked together in an attempt to stabilize the situations in new States that had a potential to result in ethnic violence and war.[14] The early ideas about making a protocol to the European Convention on Human Rights were soon abandoned[15] and the two organizations continued their separate work. The results were different, reflecting the different nature of the two organizations and their respective mandates.

Two treaties adopted by the Council of Europe – the European Charter for Regional or Minority Languages (ECRML) adopted in 1992,[16] and the Framework Convention for the Protection of National Minorities (FCNM) in 1995,[17] came into force in 1998 and today are creating binding international obligations for their parties in the field of minority protection.

The OSCE, on the other hand, continued its preventive efforts through creation of the High Commissioner on National Minorities (HCNM) who subsequently adopted a series of recommendations relevant for the well-being of minorities, including the following: on education (The Hague, 1996), linguistic rights (Oslo, 1998) and on participation (Lund, 1999).[18] The recommendations,

14 *Comp.* R. Hofmann, 'The Framework Convention for the Protection of National Minorities: An Introduction', in M. Weller (ed.), *The Rights of Minorities* (Oxford, 2005) p. 2.

15 *See* the CoE Parliamentary Assembly Rec. 1201/EC of 1 February 1993.

16 ECRML has 25 States parties among the Council of Europe 47 member States. All information available at: <www.coe.int/en/web/european-charter-regional-or-minority-languages/home>, visited on 20 August 2017.

17 FCNM has 39 States parties among the Council of Europe 47 member States. Four more States signed, but have not ratified and four have never signed it (Andorra, France, Monaco and Turkey). All information available at: <www.coe.int/en/web/minorities/home>, visited on 20 August 2017.

18 Max van der Stoel was the first and probably the most prominent HCNM. *See* Zeller on his understanding of the HCNM recommendations: "He also shaped the institution of the High Commissioner in political terms. A good example of this is the HCNM's recommendations. Interpreting his mandate broadly, he introduced the HCNM's recommendations – both country-specific and issue-oriented – an instrument that has taken on tremendous

like the declarations, are not legally binding and they are "of political rather than legal commitment though they reflect consensus and repeat customary law on certain points".[19] Furthermore, if widely accepted in the practice of States, recommendations can help establish new rules of customary law if the rule in question is of 'norm creating character'.[20]

The Oslo Recommendations Regarding the Linguistic Rights of National Minorities, according to the introductory notes, "provide a useful reference for the development of State policies and laws which will contribute to an effective Implementation of the language rights of persons belonging to national minorities, especially in the public sphere". The recommendations elaborate linguistic rights with respect to names, religion, community life and NGOs, the media, economic life, administrative authorities and public services, independent national institutions, judicial authorities and deprivation of liberty. The Oslo Recommendations clarify how the principles of tolerance, coexistence and integration can be applied in relation to language use.[21]

The linguistic rights, however, are not absolute. By definition, the speakers of minority languages will be faced with the reality that most States have one or even more official languages.[22] An official language is a dominant language in education, administration, media and every other field of public life. A minority language, on the other hand is in a 'weaker' position in all these aspects and its speakers will not have the same opportunities to use it publicly as those who speak the official language. There is a rather rich case-law of the human rights monitoring bodies, such as the ECtHR or the UN Human Rights Committee, that treating these languages differently may be justified under the Convention or the ICCPR. One of the earlier ECtHR cases dealt with the problem of education in the minority language in Belgium. The applicants complained of the apparent discrimination for not being able to have education in their own language in the entire territory but the Court held that the right to education in Protocol to the Convention implied the right to be educated in the national language, and did not include the provision that the parent's linguistic

importance, but which is only tangentially based on the wording of his mandate...". W. Zeller, 'Max van der Stoel – Leveraging Academic Expertise for Conflict Prevention', 22:3 *Security and Human Rights* (2011) pp. 307–310, at p.308.

19 P. Thornberry and M.A.M. Estebanez, *Minority Rights in Europe* (Council of Europe Publ., Strasbourg, 2004) p. 18.

20 *See North Sea Continental Shelf* Case, *ICJ Reports* 1969, para 72: "[T]he provision concerned should, at alı events potentially, be of a fundamentally norm creating character such as could be regarded as forming the basis of a general rule of law".

21 F. de Varennes, *supra* note 2, p. 311.

22 Finland has two and Switzerland four national languages, three of which are official.

preferences be respected.[23] Furthermore, Article 6 of the Convention protects the right to hear charges in the language one understands. Since practically most members of a national minority understand the official language, there is no need to invoke the right to use their minority language.[24]

As stated above, most of the specific linguistic rights of the members of national minorities can be connected to some general human rights belonging to every person, such as the right to private and family life, freedom of expression, freedom of assembly, right to education or the prohibition of discrimination. The right to have one's name in one's own language can also be connected to the right to privacy. Most of these rights are enjoyed as individual human rights but some are enjoyed 'in community with others'.

However, there is one specific right belonging to national minorities as a collective that has no counterpart in the general human rights protection and that is the right to display place names in regional or minority languages.

The right to display place names in regional or minority languages is one of the most visible signs of presence of a particular linguistic minority in a certain territory.[25] It is a right guaranteed by the relevant international instruments for the protection of national minorities and their languages; however, it has no counter-part in the general human rights protection since it is not an individual right.

The right to display place names in regional or minority languages is specifically provided for in the above mentioned treaties on minorities concluded within the Council of Europe. States parties to the Language Charter or the Framework Convention *may* be under legal obligation to ensure this right under certain conditions in accordance with these conventions.

This obligation is further reinforced by the OSCE Oslo recommendations. Recommendation No. 3 provides that "[i]n areas inhabited by significant numbers of persons belonging to a national minority and when there is sufficient demand, public authorities shall make provision for the display, also in the minority language, of local names, street names and other topographical indications intended for the public". The recommendation is strongly grounded on

23 *Belgian Linguistic* case (No. 2), ECtHR 1968. The Court did, however, find discrimination on the basis that the legislation in question prevented certain children from having access to French-language schools in Brussels solely because of the residence of their parents.

24 *See also* G. Pentassuglia, 'Minority Issues as a Challenge in the European Court of Human Rights: A Comparison with the Case Law of the United Nations Human Rights Committee', 46 *German Y.B. Int'l L.* (2003) p. 401.

25 Some say that the display of the traditional place names in the minority language may be a sign of 'ownership' or at least association with a community other than the majority. F. de Varennes, *supra* note 2, p. 348.

the FCNM. It uses similar language as the FCNM. Furthermore, the Explanatory note to the Recommendations refers specifically to the corresponding article of the FCNM adding but a sentence: "Refusal to recognise the validity of historic denominations of the kind described can constitute an attempt to revise history and to assimilate minorities, thus constituting a serious threat to the identity of persons belonging to minorities".[26] The Recommendations should, however, also be interpreted in light of the introductory part covering all the linguistic rights. These rights must be seen in a balanced context of full participation in the wider society.

Although the three instruments may be similar in the objective they try to achieve, their requirements and conditions are different. Since the Recommendations rely on the corresponding article of the FCNM we shall look in detail in the provisions of the FCNM and the ECRML and the practice of their monitoring bodies.

1 Framework Convention for the Protection of National Minorities

The FCNM is specific for its programmatic and flexible nature: "Its provisions are designed to leave the States concerned a measure of discretion in the implementation of the objectives which they have undertaken to achieve, thus enabling them to take particular circumstances into account".[27] The convention provides for the monitoring of the Committee of Ministers of the Council of Europe with assistance of the Advisory Committee. In nearly 20 years of practice the Advisory Committee interpreted the FCNM in a way to "address unstable minority-majority relations that have a clear potential to destabilize peace and security in Europe".[28]

The linguistic aspects of minority protection play an important role in the FCNM and it deals with them in several articles. Among those we find Article 11.3 that speaks of the possibility to display traditional local names in the minority language. The provision is full of conditions, reflecting the fears and

26 The Oslo Recommendations Regarding the Linguistic Rights of National Minorities and Explanatory Note, 1998.

27 Explanatory Report to the FCNM, para. 11. <rm.coe.int/16800cb5eb>, visited 20 August 2017.

28 R. Hofmann, 'Framework Convention for the Protection of National Minorities: An Introduction', in M. Weller (ed.), *The Rights of Minorities* (Oxford U.P., Oxford, 2005) p. 6. State and monitoring reports by the Advisory Committee are available at <www.coe.int/en/web/minorities/country-specific-monitoring>, visited 20 August 2017.

doubts during the negotiations and making it clear that there is no absolute right to have it fulfilled:

> In areas traditionally inhabited by substantial numbers of persons belonging to a national minority, the Parties shall endeavour, in the framework of their legal system, including, where appropriate, agreements with other States, and taking into account their specific conditions, to display traditional local names, street names and other topographical indications intended for the public also in the minority language when there is a sufficient demand for such indications.

This is one of the least demanding provisions for authorities and it creates no individual right. Two of the conditions seem to be more important: (a) areas have to be traditionally (and still) inhabited by a substantial number of members of national minority, and (b) there has to be a sufficient demand for such signs although the convention does not explain how this demand is to be established. However, even when these conditions are met states can invoke 'specific conditions' or their legal framework which may speak against bilingual signs.[29] The Explanatory Report emphasises that this "provision does not imply any official recognition of local names in the minority languages" and that it aims to 'promote the possibility' of displaying toponymic bilingual signs when all the conditions are met. Even then, it is clear that the states are under an obligation to 'endeavour' to fulfil it but keeping a certain level of discretion. The drafting history shows that the drafters saw in this provision a potential for trouble going as far as separatist claims. This 'conditional' and cautious approach was meant to provide States with sufficient safeguards.[30]

Some States were not satisfied with that level of 'protection'. Upon ratification in 2015 Latvia made a declaration "that it will apply the provisions of Article 11, paragraph 3, of the Framework Convention without prejudice to the *Satversme* (Constitution) of the Republic of Latvia and the legislative acts governing the use of the State language that are currently into force". However, when the Advisory Committee examined the State report, it established that the Constitution and the State Language Law provide that place names shall be created and utilised (only) in the Latvian language. The Advisory Committee had to conclude, without much elaboration, that "[i]n so far as it does not

29 *See* F. de Varennes, *supra* note 2, p. 349.

30 Drafting took place within the expert group CAHMIN (Ad Hoc Committee for the Protection of National Minorities). Records are available at <www.coe.int/en/web/minorities/cahmin1>, visited 20 August 2017.

permit the use of minority languages alongside Latvian in local topographical indications, the Latvian legislation in force is not in conformity with the provisions of Article 11, paragraph 3 of the Framework Convention".[31]

In its monitoring the Advisory Committee has attempted to interpret para. 3 of Article 11 favouring the use of minority languages whenever the traditional presence of a particular minority was established. In the case of Slovakia and Romania the acceptable threshold was set at 20 percent, but in the Czech Republic the Advisory Committee was satisfied with the threshold of ten per cent.[32] It commended Austria for using ten per cent as a threshold presenting a 'substantial number' sufficient to demand bilingual signs.[33] However, in a subsequent opinion on Austria, the Advisory Committee had to conclude that despite the favourable legal framework, the overall approach taken by the Austrian authorities and the resulting denial of a possibility to seek an effective legal remedy for persons belonging to national minorities is not satisfactory.[34]

In its opinion on Estonia the Advisory Committee was very critical about the fact that in some places Russian was almost entirely absent from public spaces, even though over 90 per cent of the population were Russian-speaking. The Advisory Committee went on to emphasize that the display of the minority language has a significant symbolic value for integration: "Seeing the minority language, alongside the State language, in public spaces reaffirms that the minority belongs to the given region as an appreciated and welcome member of society and promotes a sense of trust among persons belonging to minorities".[35]

31 *Opinion on Latvia,* 2008 (made public in 2011, after receiving the communication from Latvia), para. 123.

32 The promotion of the regional or minority languages in the Czech Republic is partly dependent on local committees for national. Bilingual signs are to be installed if at least 10 per cent of the citizens of a municipality reported minority affiliation in the latest census and if the committee for national minorities requests it.

33 *Opinion on Austria,* 2002, para.50. The AC referred to the decision made by the Austrian Constitutional Court regarding Article 7, para. 3 of the State Treaty.

34 *Fourth Opinion on Austria,* 2016, para. 52. The amendment of the National Minorities Act in July 2011 produced a list of localities where the Slovenian, Croatian and Hungarian minority languages shall be displayed on topographical signs. The list contains 164 villages in 24 municipalities with respect to the Slovenian language, 28 municipalities with respect to Croatian and four with respect to Hungarian. However, the definition of 'signs and inscriptions of a topographical nature' refers exclusively to place names but not to street names or other topographical indications.

35 *Third Opinion on Estonia,* 2011, para.120. In the following monitoring round the AC does not seem to dedicate too much space to Article 11.3 other than establishing that "there have been no changes since the adoption of the Third Advisory Committee Opinion". The

Lithuania is one of the countries whose legislation does not allow bilingual topographical signs despite the continuous recommendations by the Advisory Committee and the Committee of Ministers of the Council of Europe. In the third monitoring opinion published in 2013 the Advisory Committee repeatedly established that the State Language Law demands that all public indications have to be in Lithuanian with an exception made only for the names of organisations of national minority communities and their information signs. If the local communities 'dared' to put up signs in the minority language they were fined and ordered to take them down even in areas that are densely populated by the particular minority.[36] The authorities even requested the removal of bilingual signs from private property.[37]

In many places the Advisory Committee confirmed that the gist of Article 11.3. is *bilingualism*. In the case of Italy it regretted that signposts and toponyms in South Tirol are not bilingual, irrespective of whether this is done to the detriment of minority or majority languages: "The Advisory Committee reiterates its view that on the contrary, the use of bilingualism in signposts conveys the message that a given territory is shared in harmony by various population groups".[38]

In another opinion, the Advisory Committee reiterated that:

> [T]he denial of the possibility of having local names, street names and other topographical indications in certain areas in minority languages alongside the official language not only violates the obligation of the State Party under Article 11.3, but also neglects the significant symbolic value for integration that such bilingualism carries for the minority as an affirmation of its presence as an appreciated and welcome part of society.[39]

---

rules in place remain very strict, but even when the Russian minority meets the strict criteria no signs in Russian have been displayed. *Fourth Opinion on Estonia*, 2015, para. 12.

36 The AC refers to examples of Šalčininkai and Vilnius District. In Šalčininkai district 77,75 per cent and in Vilnius 52.07 per cent of the population claimed Polish ethnicity in the 2011 census. *Third Opinion on Lithuania, 2013,* paras. 74–77.

37 Lithuania presented its latest report in 2017. It makes no reference to Art. 11.3. *The Fourth Report on the Implementation of the Council of Europe Framework Convention for the Protection of National Minorities in the Republic of Lithuania*, 2016, pp. 66–67. It is interesting to note that the municipality of Visagina keeps web pages also in Russian. The Russians make up 52 per cent of the population. <www.visaginas.lt/index.php?4069314576>, visited on 20 August 2017.

38 *Fourth Opinion on Italy*, 2015, para. 88.

39 *Third Opinion on Lithuania,* 2013, para.76.

2 European Charter for Regional or Minority Languages

The ECRML has two distinctive parts: one that brings objectives and principles to be observed by the State party (Part II) with respect to all languages spoken traditionally in (part of) the territory of the State.[40] The other part (Part III) is based on the 'menu system' and it allows States to choose from the offered undertakings with respect to all or some of the languages, depending on their political will and the actual situation at the time of ratification. So, Part II (Article 7.1.d) contains a more general reference to "the facilitation and/or encouragement of the use of regional or minority languages, in speech and writing, in public and private life" which could be interpreted broadly as including also the display of public signage in minority languages.[41] Part III, on the other hand, allows States parties to choose the specific undertaking under Article 10.2.g.:

> In respect of the local and regional authorities on whose territory the number of residents who are users of regional or minority languages is such as to justify the measures specified below, the Parties undertake to allow and/or encourage… the use or adoption, if necessary in conjunction with the name in the official language(s), of traditional and correct forms of place-names in regional or minority languages.

The 'size' requirement is typical for the ECRML and it refers to the community big enough "to justify the measures".[42] It does not mention any numbers or percentages.[43] In practice, however, many States parties opted for percentages

40 Article 1 of the ECRML defines regional or minority languages as languages that are: "*i* traditionally used within a given territory of a State by nationals of that State who form a group numerically smaller than the rest of the State's population; and are *ii* different from the official language(s) of that State".

41 So far, the Committee of Experts in charge of the interpretation of the Charter has refrained from a broad interpretation that this would include also place-names and traffic signs.

42 Article 1, para. b) of the Charter defines the phrase 'territory in which the regional and minority language is used' as the 'geographical area in which the said language is the mode of expression of a number of people justifying the adoption of the various protective and promotional measures provided for in the Charter'. This may also include some very small linguistic communities using the language at the verge of extinction, such as Saami in the Nordic countries as positive measures are necessary for its preservation.

43 *See* R. Dunbar, *supra* note 3, p. 112. He claims that "these formulae essentially link any State obligation to numerical criteria".

or relative numbers. Croatia demands that at least one third of the population of the local or regional unit belongs to a minority. This threshold was considered too high by the Committee of Experts.[44] Slovakia, Poland and Romania set the percentage to 20 per cent, Serbia to 15 per cent while the Czech Republic uses the threshold of 10 per cent. Most of these states also allow the local communities to use the language in signage regardless of the size of the community.[45] Although these percentages may seem favourable the Committee of Experts has not agreed with them.[46] On the one hand, it is possible that the relative size of the language community may in fact present a substantial number.[47] On the other hand, however, it happens that a particular group does not reach the threshold in any local community in which case the ratification does not ensure its protection in accordance with the Charter.[48]

44 The earlier legislation provided for 50 per cent threshold, but it was later changed to one third. *Application of the Charter in Croatia*, 2nd monitoring cycle, 2005, paras. 23–25. The old Ukrainian legislation of 1989 had the same threshold, but it was changed to 10 per cent by the 2012 Law of Ukraine on the Principles of State Language Policy (the 'Language Law'). *Application of the Charter in Ukraine*, 2nd monitoring cycle, 2012, para. 12. This report, however, was adopted by the Committee of Ministers only in January 2014, just before the events that will bring the annexation of Crimea to the Russian Federation. In a separate statement of 25 March 2014 the Bureau of the Committee of Experts reviewed the current situation of national minority languages in Ukraine concluding that the situation with Russian was still favourable from the point of view of the Charter. All State and evaluation reports are available at: <www.coe.int/en/web/european-charter-regional-or-minority-languages/reports-and-recommendations>, visited 20 August 2017.

45 The County of Istria in Croatia introduced Italian signage in its entire territory although the percentage of Italian speakers is far below the threshold. Italian was also introduced in 19 local units. Based on local statutes, additional local self-government units have introduced minority languages in equal and official use in accordance with national legislation. *Application of the Charter in Croatia*, 5th monitoring cycle, 2015, para. 23.

46 The Committee of Experts discussed the problem of thresholds in length in the case of Slovakia. *Application of the Charter in Slovakia*, 1st monitoring cycle, 2007, Ch. 1.5 (Particular issue concerning the 20 per cent threshold). The Committee of Experts concluded that "Article 10 of the Charter applies also to those municipalities where the regional or minority language speakers do not attain the 20 per cent threshold but represent nevertheless a sufficient number of speakers for the purpose of the undertakings entered into by Slovakia under Article 10…"

47 Finland's legislation recognizes bilingual character of a municipality when the Swedish minority makes up 8 per cent of the population or at least 3.000 people. For comparison, the total number of Ukrainian speakers in Croatia is below 1.500. *Application of the Charter in Finland*, 1st monitoring cycle, 2001, para. 28.

48 Ukrainian is not in official use in any of the municipalities or local settlements in the Republic of Serbia, since, for minority languages to be newly introduced in official use

The option to use names in minority language usually applies to the names of settlements (villages and towns), but it also covers other toponymic features. The accent of this provision is on traditional names and it proved to be a test of tolerance for the majority.[49] When signage in the Serbian Cyrillic appeared in Vukovar in Croatia it gave rise to public protests.[50] The sensitivity of the Croatian population is especially high in the parts of Croatia where the 1991–1995 war left deep scars but the negative sentiments spread across the country. In Poland the German speakers face all kinds of difficulties in their attempts to introduce bilingual signs due to opposition of the Polish majority. Many of the erected signs in German got sprayed and damaged.[51] Denmark, on the other hand, did not choose this obligation with respect to its only minority language, German, due to negative feelings against German signs of the majority based on, apparently, the Second Schleswig War of 1864.[52] In the United Kingdom the Irish language speakers have demanded the use of their traditional place names at least for the tourist signage in Northern Ireland with no success. They have also requested the bilingual street names but the authorities decided not to provide bilingual traffic signs. The decision also concerned signs in Ulster Scots that appears to suffer collateral damage.[53]

The ECRML holds a different kind of obligation than the FCNM or the Oslo Recommendations. States parties have to 'allow and/or encourage' the use or adoption of traditional place names. While 'allowing' would require the necessary legislative framework, 'encouragement' demands taking proactive positive

by the Statute of a municipality or local settlement, it is necessary that the members of the minority reach 15 per cent of the population in the municipality or local settlement. On the basis of the census results of 2011, members of the Ukrainian national minority did not reach the legally determined percentage in any of the municipalities or local communities in Serbia. *Application of the Charter in Serbia*, 3rd monitoring cycle, para. 690.

49 There is no requirement to translate the official name if the traditional name in the minority language does not exist.

50 In 2013, following war veterans' protests, the city of Vukovar refused to put up signs in Cyrillic after the census showed that the Serbian minority made up more than one third of the population. *Application of the Charter in Croatia*, 5th monitoring cycle, 2015, para. 83.

51 *Application of the Charter in Poland*, 2nd monitoring cycle, 2015, para. 258.

52 <www.thelocal.dk/20150317/danes-reject-german-town-names-in-southern-jutland>, visited 20 August 2017. The town of Haderslev had German name for about a week in 2015. <www.thelocal.dk/20150427/danish-town-is-german-no-more>, visited 20 August 2017.

53 *Application of the Charter in the United Kingdom*, 4th monitoring cycle, paras. 244–245.

measures with the aim of fulfilling the undertaking.[54] It is also significant that the ECRML does not insist on bilingual signage and the official name should be used 'if necessary'.

Spain is an example of good practice when it comes to bilingual signage in accordance with the Charter at least with respect to languages with 'co-official' status in several Autonomous Communities.[55] Bilingual signs are the competence of regional and local authorities and the support often depends on the political option in power. Nevertheless, the Committee of Experts concluded in the last monitoring cycle that the undertaking is overall fulfilled for all languages covered by Part III.[56] It shows that a persistent political work and co-operation between minority and majority population can bring good results even in this sensitive field.

3 Conclusion

In this short overview of the practical implementation of the right to display place names in regional or minority languages it is quite obvious that this right exists only as a treaty based right and even then only when meeting all the conditions and requirements. In that respect the Oslo Recommendations that are very close to Article 11.3 of the FCNM reinforce the conditionality of this right. It seems that the right has its strongest embodiment in the ECRML. When chosen by the State party under Part III of the Charter it is capable of reflecting the reality and the needs of the speakers of a minority language present in a certain part of the national territory. Nevertheless, one must keep in mind that the Oslo Recommendations are often the only source of, at least, political obligation for the countries that do not adopt the two Council of Europe conventions.

The issue of public display of traditional names in minority languages can indeed be a stumbling block in the minority-majority relations. The use of minority language place-names often brings out historic fears and even hostilities when taken as a 'mark' of ownership of the territory in question. The situation

54 In its practice the Committee of Experts considers the undertaking 'formally fulfilled' if the legislation does not result in any practical results.

55 Spain ratified Part III for Catalan in Catalonia and the Balearic Islands, Basque in the Basque Country and Navarra, Valencian in Valencia and Galician in Galicia. Due to a change in the Catalan Statute the Charter now applies also to Aranese.

56 *Application of the Charter in Spain*, 4th monitoring cycle, 2016.

is particularly complex in the wake of wars and conflicts. We have seen it in relations to more recent but also to (very) old wars and historic conflicts.

On the other hand, when taken as a part of historic and cultural heritage bilingual signs can help establish the sense of belonging of all inhabitants of that territory. In that context, as pointed out by the Advisory Committee of the FCNM, bilingualism must be used so as not to leave out anybody. When approached in this way the display of bilingual place names and other toponymic signs can fulfil their purpose.

CHAPTER 12

Protection of Linguistic Rights of Linguistic Minorities in the UN Context

Rita Izsák-Ndiaye

1 Introduction

After the escalation of the situation in the former Yugoslavia, the OSCE established the position of the High Commissioner on National Minorities. This office was called into existence in order to act as an instrument of conflict prevention at the earliest possible stage, and to play a role in establishing the peace and prosperity as envisaged in the Charter of Paris for a New Europe in 1990.

Already during the first years of the work of the High Commissioner on National Minorities, it became clear that restrictions on national minorities to freely use their language in the private and public spheres are potential drivers of conflict, deserving due attention and implementation guarantees. The Foundation on Inter-Ethnic Relations was requested to facilitate a series of consultations with experts from various pertinent disciplines in 1996, which resulted in the Oslo Recommendations Regarding the Linguistic Rights of National Minorities, whose 20th anniversary we celebrate this year.

The OSCE correctly recognised the link between minority rights protection and conflict prevention at an early stage and undertook significant efforts to establish legal guidance and appoint responsible personnel. The United Nations needs considerable strengthening if it is to respond effectively to emerging inter-ethnic and inter-religious tensions and conflict both in terms of its normative framework and the establishment of dedicated mechanisms. The only UN standard-setting document that is devoted to the rights of minorities is the 1992 Declaration on the Rights of Persons Belonging to National or Ethnic, Religious and Linguistic Minorities (UN Declaration on Minorities), which is not legally binding and has no monitoring or reporting mechanisms attached to it. The strongest instrument therefore remains the International Covenant on Civil and Political Rights and, specifically, its article 27 on the protection of minorities. This affirms that persons belonging to ethnic, religious or linguistic minorities shall not be denied the right, in community with the other members of their group, to enjoy their own culture, to profess and practice

© KONINKLIJKE BRILL NV, LEIDEN, 2018 | DOI 10.1163/9789004357754_013

their own religion, or to use their own language. Unfortunately, due to the wide portfolio and complexity of human rights concerns in front of it, the Human Rights Committee, which monitors the implementation of the Covenant, has considered issues regarding minority language use only to a limited extent.

One wonders why the UN until today has failed to establish a permanent office at the level of its senior management with a clear mandate of minority protection and conflict prevention despite the fact that almost every conflict situation we witness has clear ethnic, religious and linguistic identity dimensions at its heart. In some countries, the use of minority languages has been deemed a threat to national unity and an attempt by minorities to reinforce territorial or separatist claims, and has consequently been restricted or banned. Restrictions on language use have been reported alongside alleged prohibitions on aspects of cultural life, including song or theatre performances in minority languages, or political and civil society activities. In those contexts, minority languages may become highly emotive issues, and such prohibition is a significant cause of grievances for minority communities.

During my official country visits as Special Rapporteur, it was striking to see how language issues played an important role in the history of peaceful coexistence of various communities and how even attempted weakening of legislative guarantees of language rights have led to escalated tensions. In Sri Lanka, the various language policy changes made by successive administrations historically contributed to the ethnic tensions that exist today. The introduction of the 1956 Official Language Act, which declared Sinhala as the only official language, is said to have been the most devastating of all, fortifying the existing grievances and the ethnic and linguistic divide that eventually triggered the civil war.[1] In Ukraine, the use of minority languages is highly important and emotive and an essential aspect of individual and community identity. Steps in February 2014 to abolish the 2012 Law on the Principles of the State Language Policy, although vetoed in practice, created anxiety as minorities were concerned that new amendments would weaken their linguistic rights. This action further contributed to an environment of uncertainty and distrust that created fractures along national, ethnic and linguistic lines.[2] In the mainly French-speaking Cameroon, English speakers have long complained

1 Report of the Special Rapporteur on minority issues on her mission to Sri Lanka, A/HRC/34/53/Add.3 <ap.ohchr.org/documents/dpage_e.aspx?si=A/HRC/34/53/Add.3>, visited on 10 January 2018.

2 Report of the Special Rapporteur on minority issues, Rita Izsák, on her mission to Ukraine, A/HRC/28/64/Add.1 <ap.ohchr.org/documents/dpage_e.aspx?si=A/HRC/28/64/Add.1>, visited on 10 January 2018.

that they face discrimination and marginalization and are excluded from top civil service positions and public services. In 2016, protests have been organized, led by regional bar associations and teachers' unions, against the growing appointment of French-speaking civil servants in the Anglophone regions which have been responded to by excessive use of violence by security forces.[3]

Considering these past and current tensions and conflict situations, is it of utmost concern that minority issues still seem to be regarded as a marginal element of the UN's human rights agenda. Moreover, when discussions around it take place, they tend to be organized in Geneva and rarely in New York which sends the worrying signal that the UN still fails to consider minority rights protection as an important part of its peace and development work. The most relevant mandate in the United Nations system is the one of the Special Rapporteur on minority issues, which role I had the honour to fill between 2011–2017. The Special Rapporteur is mandated to promote the implementation of the UN Declaration on Minorities, to examine ways and means of overcoming existing obstacles to the full and effective realization of minority rights, to identify best practices, and to cooperate with the UN and NGOs. The Rapporteur prepares annual reports to the Human Rights Council and the General Assembly, issues communications to States concerning implementation of the Declaration on Minorities, and undertakes country visits at the invitation of Governments. However, it is an independent and volunteer position and the rapporteurs appointed by the Human Rights Council do not officially represent the views of the UN (or any other entity) itself. Moreover, at the moment, the only UN platform devoted to minorities is the Forum on Minority Issues, under the guidance of the Special Rapporteur on minority issues, where minorities can raise their voice directly and have a discussion with Member States and the UN. Unfortunately, it only takes place once a year and only for two days.

The main organizational unit within the UN system dealing specifically with minorities is the Indigenous Peoples and Minorities Section in the UN Office of the High Commissioner for Human Rights in Geneva, which is tasked to improve human rights protection for indigenous peoples and minorities at the international and national levels through strategies such as strengthening relevant legislations, policies and practices, as well as through undertaking capacity building activities. It also serves as the secretariat to coordinate the work of the UN Network on racial discrimination and the protection of

3 Report of the Independent Expert on minority issues, Rita Izsák, on her mission to Cameroon, A/HRC/25/56/Add.1 <ap.ohchr.org/documents/dpage_e.aspx?si=A/HRC/25/56/Add.1> and press release <www.ohchr.org/EN/NewsEvents/Pages/DisplayNews.aspx?NewsID=21054&LangID=E>, visited on 22 November 2017.

minorities, which was established in 2012. The Network is a welcome initiative as it gathers over 20 UN Departments, Agencies, Programmes and Funds and is was established to enhance dialogue and cooperation between relevant UN bodies. The Network has developed the Secretary General's Guidance Note on Racial Discrimination and Minorities, which provided key principles and advice on how to mainstream minority rights within the UN system. However, both the Section and the Network require massive strengthening, including increased staffing and budget, in order to fulfil their role and to be able to respond to emerging and actual situations.

The Universal Periodic Review (UPR) which is the most widely accepted and respected peer review mechanism at the UN could also pay stronger attention to minority issues. In the first and second cycles, minority-related recommendations made up 4 per cent and 5 per cent of total recommendations, respectively. During the first UPR cycle, there were forty-seven recommendations mentioning specific minority language groups and issues (made to Austria, Belgium, Bulgaria, Cambodia, China, Croatia, Estonia, Georgia, Greece, Kazakhstan, Latvia, Lithuania, FYR Macedonia, Moldova, Myanmar, Namibia, Nigeria, the Russian Federation, Slovakia, Turkey, Ukraine and Viet Nam) and sixteen addressed the situation of linguistic minorities (countries receiving such recommendations were Albania, Bosnia and Herzegovina, France, Georgia, Greece, Hungary, Iran, Iraq, Kyrgyzstan, Latvia, Lithuania, Nepal, Samoa, St Lucia).[4]

In my last reports to the Human Rights Council and the General Assembly, I recommended some concrete steps to be taken to strengthen the UN's work on minorities. It included that the UN in general should advocate more strongly for minority rights protection at both national and regional levels, to seek to ensure that States strengthen their legal, policy and institutional frameworks and that regional anti-discrimination and minority rights standards and mechanisms are put in place for the protection and promotion of minority rights, respectively. Equally, the UN should ensure that its staff in all offices and entities, particularly in the field, reflects the national, ethnic, religious and linguistic makeup of the societies in which they operate. There are good models to follow. The OHCHR office in the Republic of Moldova for example carried out an internal diversity mapping exercise through anonym questionnaires and, in the light of its results, established an internship and recruitment program for underrepresented communities, including members of Roma and Afro-Descendant groups, and persons with disabilities.

4 R. Izsák, *Minority Issues in the First Cycle of the Universal Periodic Review* (UPR), p. 11, <www.ohchr.org/EN/Issues/Minorities/SRMinorities/Pages/UPRProcess.aspx>, visited on 22 November 2017.

Existing mechanisms and platforms for minorities within the United Nations system should be strengthened, including the Forum on Minority Issues. The Forum plays a pivotal role as a unique and global platform to facilitate dialogue and address relevant issues pertaining to minorities. It should be provided with the necessary resources to fully implement its mandate. I encouraged consideration to be given to raising the Forum's profile at the regional and international levels, following up the implementation of its recommendations, fostering ownership of the Forum's agenda by minorities and promoting a more interactive dialogue and discussions during the Forum's sessions.

It would be important for the United Nations Network on Racial Discrimination and the Protection of Minorities to regularly update the Human Rights Council about its work. It would also be crucial that the UN considers appointing at least one high-level official on minority issues within the Secretariat as well as establish senior positions within United Nations departments and agencies to look into issues of minority rights protection, diversity management and safeguarding pluralistic societies. The designation of minority focal points in all United Nations field offices would be another great step forward.

The first Independent Expert on minority issues was Gay McDougall from the United States of America. Although she did not prepare a specific report on linguistic minorities, during all her official country visits she paid careful attention to the linguistic rights of minorities. When I took over the mandate in 2011 (which was renamed as Special Rapporteur on minority issues in 2014), it was clear that I must address language issues proactively and to draw clear attention to the importance of minority language use, including clarifying relevant State obligations. Therefore, in 2013, I prepared a specific report on the challenges of linguistic minorities to the Human Rights Council[5] and published a handbook in 2017 called "Language Rights of Linguistic Minorities: A Practical Guide for Implementation"[6] which aimed to provide practical guidance to all actors, mainly Governments, and to assisting them in considering and developing good practices of minority language use.[7]

5 Report of the Independent Expert on minority issues, Rita Izsák, A/HRC/22/49, <documents-dds-ny.un.org/doc/UNDOC/GEN/G13/100/19/PDF/G1310019.pdf?OpenElement>, visited on 22 November 2017.

6 United Nations Special Rapporteur on minority issues, R. Izsák-Ndiaye, Language rights of linguistic minorities, A practical guide for implementation, March 2017, <www.ohchr.org/Documents/Issues/Minorities/SR/LanguageRightsLinguisticMinorities_EN.pdf>, visited on 22 November 2017.

7 I wish to thank everyone who made important contributions to these reports, especially Graham Fox and Fernand de Varennes.

In this article, first I provide an overview of the general situation and challenges of linguistic minorities around the globe. Then I discuss the core human rights principles that must be considered when planning and implementing linguistic minority rights legislation, policies and programmes. In the final section, I discuss three specific linguistic minority rights. As this book contains several articles and case examples relevant to the OSCE area and the European continent, I highlight situations and good practices from other regions with the aim of drawing attention to common patterns and further inspire possible global, national and local solutions. Finally, I provide some final conclusions and recommendations on how to improve the situation of linguistic minorities and what further guarantees should be put in place to enable their equality in rights, dignity and opportunities. This article is largely based on my earlier HRC report and handbook on this subject and I wish to thank here once again my team, colleagues, consultants, editors and translators who contributed earlier to the preparations of these two important documents.

2 General Considerations

For minorities, language is a central element and expression of their identity and of key importance in the preservation of group identity. Language is often particularly important to non-dominant communities seeking to maintain their distinct group and cultural identity, sometimes under conditions of marginalization, exclusion and discrimination. Today significant challenges are faced by minorities in all regions who speak minority languages and wish to maintain and use them in public and private life. Linguistic minorities are frequently also national, ethnic or religious minorities and consequently the challenges they face may be exacerbated by discrimination on the grounds of their ethnicity, religion or nationality.

Historical factors such as colonialism have had a huge global impact on languages, resulting in the marginalization of indigenous and minority languages and a rapid decline in their use.[8] The introduction of colonial languages in Africa, Asia and the Americas initiated the marginalization of native and minority languages. Colonial languages were promoted in education, administration, political life and communications.[9] Minority and indigenous languages were often seen as backwards, a barrier to colonial hegemony, or as slowing national

8 I. Maja, *Towards the human rights protection of minority languages in Africa*, April 2008. <www.nyulawglobal.org/globalex/Minority_Languages_Africa.htm>, visited on 22 November 2017.

9 *Ibid.*

development. It can also be argued that today globalization is having a direct and detrimental impact on minority languages and linguistic diversity, as global communications and marketplaces require global understanding.

The phenomenon of minority language decline constitutes an urgent challenge worldwide. The UNESCO Endangered Languages Programme warns that half of the world's estimated 6,000 plus languages will likely die out by the end of the century.[10] In some cases, significant and urgent efforts are required to protect both the communities and their language heritage. More than 3,000 languages are reportedly spoken by fewer than 10,000 people each. For example, while over 20 languages are spoken in Cambodia, UNESCO has warned that 19 Cambodian languages are at risk of extinction over the coming decades.[11] National experts suggested that the number of endangered communities in Ethiopia, some of which have fewer than 300 members, could be as high as 16 out of some 80 identified communities. An unknown number of minority communities are believed to have already disappeared completely.[12] The decline in numbers of language speakers may be due to a combination of factors, including the result of processes of cultural dilution through interethnic marriage, voluntary relocation and decline in community numbers. However, some groups are vulnerable to factors beyond their control, such as policies of assimilation that promote dominant national or official languages, the impact of conflict, or forced displacement from their traditional lands. Some countries have aggressively promoted a single national language as a means of reinforcing sovereignty, national unity and territorial integrity.

The lack of domestic legal protection for minority languages in many regions remains a major concern. Legal recognition and legislative protection of minority languages create legal safeguards and a requirement for policy and programme measures to address the issues of linguistic minorities, and often result in institutional attention. Lack of such recognition and legal protections results in an environment where there is little or no formal legal commitment to promoting and protecting minority languages or the rights of linguistic minorities other than those required by international law. In such situations,

10 UNESCO's Endangered Language Programme, <www.unesco.org/new/en/culture/themes/endangered-languages/>, visited on 22 November 2017.

11 R. Carmichael, 'Cambodia's minority languages face bleak future', *Voices of America*, January 2010, <www.voanews.com/content/cambodias-minority-languages-face-bleak-future-82250487/165301.html>, visited on 22 November 2017.

12 Report of the Independent Expert on minority issues on her mission to Ethiopia, A/HRC/4/9/Add.3, para. 19., <documents-dds-ny.un.org/doc/UNDOC/GEN/G07/111/13/PDF/G0711113.pdf?OpenElement>, visited on 22 November 2017.

minority languages may remain largely in the private domain in terms of language use, transmission and education. Frequently, even where minority languages are officially recognized and legal provisions exist this does not result in implementation of rights in practice.

Some States assign official status to minority languages that may be historically present or are used by a significant proportion of the population,[13] while others establish broader constitutional and legal protection of all languages present in the State.[14] Some States with diverse linguistic communities have adopted specific laws on the use of minority languages. There is a strong legal and symbolic significance to such constitutional and legal recognition, which sends a positive message to minority communities that their language rights will be protected. Where there is no explicit legal recognition there may nevertheless be broader administrative recognition and policy relating to the use of minority languages that provide assurance and practical measures relating to language use, for example, where a linguistic minority is geographically concentrated.

Failure to recognize minority languages may stem from a broader lack of State recognition and acknowledgement of an ethnic or linguist minority group. This may be due to a number of factors, including historical, geographical and political factors and tensions over land and territory. Hence some minorities claim that a process of cultural assimilation may take place that constitutes a grave violation of their rights. In countries with federal structures, the imposition of local or regional languages as the official language of regional states has reportedly resulted in members of some linguistic communities being rendered functionally illiterate and excluded from participation in the public life of the regions in which they live, including on the basis of their lack of language proficiency.

A common problem faced by minorities is that minority languages are frequently not used in national or local administration or as the language of instruction in schools. Consequently, those belonging to minorities may face barriers to their full participation in public life and children from minorities may be disadvantaged in education from an early age. While accurate and detailed disaggregated data are scarce in most countries, evidence suggests that

13 There are more than 20 languages in Singapore. According to the Constitution of Singapore, the four official languages are English, Malay, Mandarin and Tamil.

14 The 2011 national census lists 123 Nepalese languages spoken as a mother tongue. According to Article 6 of the Constitution of Nepal, "all native languages spoken in Nepal are national languages of Nepal".

those belonging to linguistic minorities are at greater risk of experiencing poor socio-economic indicators relative to majority populations, poorer educational access and worse education outcomes, and consequently lower incomes and disproportionate levels of poverty.

For some who belong to linguistic minorities, including those who are not proficient in national languages and those who live in remote and rural localities where service provision and access are poor or difficult, the situation may be much worse and their economic, social and geographic mobility can be severely hampered. The situation of some minority women and girls can also be particularly problematic as they may face additional challenges, including relatively low levels of education and poor access to language learning opportunities relative to men and boys, that further restrict their ability to interact and benefit from opportunities outside their communities.

Each State can decide how it implements minority and linguistic rights in practice, and it is reasonable to consider that greater attention and resources will be dedicated to commonly spoken, traditionally present or geographically concentrated minority languages than is given to relatively newly arrived linguistic groups with few or dispersed members. Nevertheless, reasonable accommodation of smaller and less commonly used minority languages is required. Indeed, it may be the case that some highly marginalized minority groups require greater attention and stronger measures to support their linguistic and cultural rights. Modalities to support small or dispersed linguistic communities can include informal language classes within or outside public education structures, provision of key public information documents in such language, and consultation with cultural and national associations representing linguistic minorities to assess and respond to specific needs.

Minorities benefit immensely from proficiency in the official State or national languages, which enables them to integrate fully into and contribute to all aspects of society and enjoy the opportunities available to all. Without such proficiency minorities face severe barriers to their full participation in cultural, economic, political and social life. They may, for example, face barriers in gaining access to labour markets on the basis of their language skills or in establishing business enterprises. In terms of social life, minorities may be restricted in their interactions outside their own communities and consequently in their possibility to engage fully in the social and cultural life of the nation.

Minority language rights and language use have frequently been a source of tensions, both between and within States. Proponents of linguistic rights have sometimes been associated with secessionist movements or have been seen as a threat to the integrity or unity of a State. As the Working Group on

Minorities pointed out, it is often only when minorities assert their rights to identity and language that discrimination or persecution starts.[15] Fulfilling the rights of minorities, including their language rights, is an essential means to prevent tensions from emerging and is a key element of good governance and conflict prevention. If not appropriately addressed at an early stage, such tensions have led to protracted conflicts and deepening of divisions between linguistic groups. Where conflicts have ceased or peacebuilding initiatives are under way, it is essential that all groups in society play a full role in discussions, negotiations and decision-making processes.

The minority rights principles of non-discrimination, equality, participation and consultation must be respected, including with respect to language, to ensure that the issues and views of minorities are taken into account and their needs are adequately addressed. Linguistic minorities must be consulted and have a full and meaningful role in decisions affecting them, including relating to the shaping of language policy and practice, nationally and in the regions in which they live, in such key areas as education and official and administrative communications. Their views, perspectives and concerns should be fully taken into account to ensure that language issues do not become sources of grievances or conflict.

Centralized language policies may give primacy to the dominant national language, while decentralized policies can be more effective in responding to minority and regional language usage patterns and local conditions. Minority rights must also be considered in regional or local contexts. In some regions, such as autonomous minority regions, a particular linguistic minority may constitute the majority population and may have in place extensive provisions for the use of its language as the dominant language of the region in administration, education and service provision. In such cases it is important to ensure the language rights of those belonging to other communities who may find themselves de facto linguistic minorities in certain localities despite constituting a majority nationally.

It is essential to have accurate information and data that is disaggregated along language lines, in order to assess the number of minority language speakers, and to understand language issues and the need for measures to address the needs of linguistic minorities. Accurate data reveals issues that may otherwise remain hidden or neglected and allows language issues to be addressed in the localities where they are most present. Such data can reveal correlations between minorities and socioeconomic challenges such as low

15 Commentary of the Working Group on Minorities to the United Nations Declaration on the Rights of Persons Belonging to National or Ethnic, Religious and Linguistic Minorities, E/CN.4/Sub.2/AC.5/2005/2, para. 53.

incomes, poor education outcomes and problems facing minority women that may be connected to language issues and require targeted responses. Such data is rarely collected in census or social surveys, and the national picture of minority language issues and needs is incomplete.[16] Consequently, there is no strong statistical foundation for policy or programme formulation.

Issues relating to resources often feature in State considerations of support for minority languages and implementation of linguistic rights. Some States, facing limited resources, competing demands or times of economic difficulty, may give a low priority to expenditure on the protection of the linguistic and cultural rights of minorities. However, this can lead to tensions, for example where large or concentrated minority communities are denied their rights to education in minority languages. While some measures to implement the rights of minorities are relatively low cost and cost effective, where resource constraints are acute, inter-State cooperation and assistance may provide necessary opportunities, examples of good practices and practical assistance.

A number of conceptual issues continue to arise, and clarification would assist States in fulfilling their obligations. For example, while stronger entitlements may apply to traditionally present minorities and those that constitute a substantial percentage of a national or regional population, there is a lack of clarity regarding what the threshold should be in practice. Lack of clarity exists regarding the language rights entitlements of —new and dispersed minorities. In many countries with diverse language communities, understanding of the rights of linguistic minorities remains poor and implementation is consequently weak, inconsistent or neglected. Awareness-raising and technical assistance would improve the understanding of rights and duties as well as methodologies and technical and pedagogical modalities.

3 Core Human Rights Principles to be Considered

When designing and implementing legislation, policies and programmes for the protection of linguistic minorities and their right to use their language, the following core human rights principles must be respected:

16 This is unfortunately also often the case even when there is dedicated attention to linguistic minorities. The Commissioner on Linguistic Minorities in India for example publishes annual reports on the situation of linguistic minorities in each State of India but it does not contain any data or analysis of the actual socioeconomic status of the different linguistic minority groups.

3.1 *Dignity*

Article 1 of the Universal Declaration of Human Rights declares that all human beings are born free and equal in dignity and rights. This is a fundamental principle of international law. The commentary on the UN Declaration on Minorities states that good governance includes legal, administrative and territorial arrangements which allow for peaceful and constructive group accommodation based on equality in dignity and rights for all, and which allows for the necessary pluralism to enable people belonging to different groups to preserve and develop their identity.[17] Meeting the aspirations of minorities and ensuring their rights acknowledges the dignity and equality of all individuals, fosters participatory development and contributes to the lessening of tensions both within and among states.

3.2 *Liberty*

One of the most significant areas of language rights involves the private sphere where international human rights law is in place to guarantee linguistic freedom in private matters. These include private commercial and information-related activities,[18] civil society and private organizations,[19] staging a private theatre play in a minority language, private political and participatory activities or events, private publications, and even the linguistic form of a person's own name.[20] The language used in all private activities, including the medium of instruction in private educational activities or for broadcasting, is included in the area of language rights. Generally speaking, freedom of expression, including to use the language of one's choice cannot be prohibited, unless this is necessary on a strictly limited number of grounds which are exceptional and circumscribed by law such as for the protection of public order, or of public health or morals, or to ban incitement to hatred. Linguistic minority groups must also be free from persecution and threat against their identity as linguistic minorities. The authorities must therefore protect them

---

17 Commentary of the Working Group on Minorities to the United Nations Declaration on the Rights of Persons Belonging to National or Ethnic, Religious or Linguistic Minorities, para. 13, <documents-dds-ny.un.org/doc/UNDOC/GEN/G05/133/85/PDF/ G0513385 .pdf?OpenElement>, visited on 10 January 2018.

18 *Ballantyne, Davidson, McIntyre* v. *Canada*, UN Human Rights Committee, CCPR/C/47/D/ 359/1989 and 385/1989/Rev.1, 31 March 1993.

19 *Ouranio Toxo and Others* v. *Greece*, European Court of Human Rights, 74989/01, 20 October 2005.

20 *Raihman* v. *Latvia*, UN Human Rights Committee, CCPR/C/100/D/1621/2007, 28 October 2010.

against hate crime and other forms of prohibited intolerance, including in social media.

Individual liberty in the private sphere, including in terms of the language used, is a basic characteristic of free, inclusive and democratic societies. Private activities in areas such as education, family life, the names of individuals or localities, private printed and electronic media, songs and cultural events, religious ceremonies and commercial or political activities by private parties, are all subject to the general linguistic freedom of the parties involved.

3.3 *Equality and Non-discrimination*

All persons are entitled to equal and effective protection against discrimination on grounds of language. This means that language preferences that unreasonably or arbitrarily disadvantage or exclude individuals are a form of prohibited discrimination. This applies to differences of treatment between any language, including official languages,[21] or between an official and a minority language.[22] In any area of state activity or service, authorities must respect and implement the right to equality and the prohibition of discrimination in language matters, including the language for the delivery of administrative services,[23] access to the judiciary,[24] the regulation of banking services by authorities,[25] public education,[26] and even citizenship acquisition.[27]

The prohibition of discrimination on the ground of language and similar equality-based provisions lead to an obligation for the state to have in place reasonable and non-arbitrary language preferences. This does not affect a state's ability to determine its own official language(s), but entails that any language policy, preference or prohibition must conform with international human rights obligations. This human rights approach focuses on the differences in treatment between individuals, not languages. It is therefore the potential negative impacts, such as disadvantage or exclusion, on individuals rather than

21 *Kevin Mgwanga Gunme et al.* v. *Cameroon*, African Commission on Human and Peoples' Rights, Communication 266/2003, 27 May 2009.

22 *J.G.A. Diergaardt et al.* v. *Namibia*, UN Human Rights Committee, CCPR/C/69/D/760/1997, 25 July 2000.

23 J.*G.A. Diergaardt et al.* v. *Namibia* case (*supra* note 21).

24 *Bickel and Franz* v. *Italy*, European Court C-275/96, 24 November 1998.

25 *Kevin Mgwanga Gunme et al.* v. *Cameroon* (*supra* note 20).

26 Case relating to certain aspects of the laws on the use of languages in education in *Belgium* v *Belgium*, European Court of Human Rights, 1474/62, 1677/62, 1691/62, 1769/63, 1994/63, 2126/64, 23 July 1968.

27 Costa Rican Naturalisation Case, American Court of Human Rights, OC-4/84, Advisory Opinion of 19 January 1984.

languages that are considered in assessing the reasonableness of any language preference in the policies, support or services provided at all levels by state authorities and actions. A basic approach to determining reasonableness is to use as a starting point the principle of proportionality, as far as is practicable given local circumstances, in all language matters related to public services.

Issues of disadvantage, exclusion and reasonableness are central to the basis for a proportional approach to the use of minority languages in a state's public services and other activities. Using a minority language results in better, more efficient and more inclusive communication and exchange of information by public authorities. Employment and economic opportunities are also increased by making a minority language a language of public service to a fair and proportionate degree, and service delivery including in critical areas such as public health reaches individuals more directly and effectively in their own language. Individuals understand better information provided to them in their own language by public media.

In public education the consequences of the use of minority languages are even more far-reaching. Studies published by the World Bank,[28] UNESCO,[29] UNICEF,[30] and in different parts of the world,[31] confirm that the proportionate use of the language of minorities in education, combined with quality teaching of the official language:

1. Is more cost-effective in the long term.
2. Reduces dropout and repetition rates.
3. Leads to noticeably better academic results, particularly for girls.[32]

---

28 N. Dutcher and G.R. Tucker, The Use of First and Second Languages in Education: A Review of Educational Experience, World Bank, Washington DC, 1997.

29 L.E. Lopez, Reaching the unreached: indigenous intercultural bilingual education in Latin America, *Education for All Global Monitoring Report 2010, Reaching the Marginalized*, UNESCO, 2010.

30 UNICEF, 'Action Research on Mother Tongue-based Bilingual Education: Improving the equity and quality of education for ethnic minority children in Viet Nam', September 2012, <www.unicef.org/vietnam/Edu_Pro_Brief_3_-_8_pages.pdf>, visited on 22 November 2017.

31 UNESCO, K. Kosonen and K.R. Person, *Languages, identities and education in Thailand*, in P. Sercombe and R. Tupas (eds), *Language, Identities and Education in Asia*, Palgrave Macmillan, 2014; K. Baron, ACLU sues state over English-language instruction, April 2013, <edsource.org/today/2013/aclu-sues-state-over-english-lan-guage-instruction/30901#.UvsFZ_t_LSe>, visited on 22 November 2017.

32 C. Benson, *Girls, Educational Equity and Mother Tongue-based Teaching*, UNESCO, Bangkok, 2005, <unesdoc.unesco.org/images/0014/001420/142049e.pdf>, visited on 22 November 2017.

4. Improves levels of literacy and fluency in both the mother tongue and the official or majority language.[33]
5. Leads to greater family and community involvement and support.
6. The use of minority languages in a state's administrative and other public activities thus involves fundamental issues of inclusiveness, participation, access, quality and effectiveness.

3.4 *Identity*

In inclusive societies, both individual identity and national identity are important: neither excludes the other. This extends to the centrality of language as a marker of the identity of linguistic minorities as communities.

In addition to allowing an individual's own name to be used in private contexts, authorities should accept and use it in his or her language.[34] A non-discriminatory, inclusive and effective approach to language issues would also mean the use of topographical and street names in minority languages where minorities are concentrated or have been historically significant. Recognition and celebration of national identity should include an acknowledgment of the contributions of all components of society, including those of minorities and their languages.

The promotion of national identity and official languages is a legitimate objective from a human rights perspective. However, measures that seek to promote them must not be coercive or contrary to human rights obligations towards minorities, particularly where it affects their identity. The centrality of identity is emphasized in article 1 of the UN Declaration on Minorities.

Respecting language rights is of course generally conducive to the maintenance of identity, but the issue of names is often even more intimately connected to identity and dignity. The names of individuals, but also of communities and territories, are a link to tradition, culture, history and belonging, which can be deeply emotive and significant.

4 Specific Linguistic Rights

The Oslo Recommendations cover a broad area of linguistic rights in various fields of life and so does my Human Rights Council report and handbook on

---

33 J. Cummins, *Language, Power and Pedagogy: Bilingual Children in the Crossfire*, Clevedon, UK, 2000.

34 *Raihman* v. *Latvia*, UN Human Rights Committee, CCPR/C/100/D/1621/2007, 28 October 2010.

this subject. However, below I will only highlight three particular linguistic rights of minorities that seemed to concern minorities most during my term as Special Rapporteur. The rights and situation of national or ethnic, religious and linguistic minorities in the fields of education, public life and media have also been the annual themes of the UN Forum on Minority Issues and have resulted in numerous recommendations which are available at the Forum's website.[35]

4.1 *Education*

Restrictions on minority languages in the field of education are particularly sensitive and can be the cause of grievances. The UN Declaration on Minorities states that wherever possible minorities have the right to learn or to have instruction in their mother tongue (art. 4, para. 3). Indeed, the commentary to the Declaration states that denying minorities the possibility of learning their own language and of receiving instruction in their own language, or excluding from their education the transmission of knowledge about their own culture, history, tradition and language, would be a violation of the obligation to protect their identity.[36] When I visited Nigeria in 2014, one of the most ethnically and linguistically diverse country with over 350 ethnic groups and even more languages spoken within its territory, one of the Ogoni community representatives told me that "Once you lose the language, you lose your identity, and therefore who you are", and stated that between 80 per cent and 90 per cent of the children currently did not speak their local languages due to the lack of mother tongue education.

Where official State languages are the only languages used in schools, minority children whose first language is their minority language are placed at a disadvantage from the earliest years of school, since they are often less proficient in the State language and are likely to fall behind. UNICEF highlights evidence that bilingual education from the earliest years of schooling ensures that minority children become proficient in their mother tongue and the dominant language from an early age. Teaching children for a recommended six to eight years in their mother tongue and gradually introducing national languages has advantages, including the following: children learn better, they are more confident and are well equipped to transfer their literacy and numeracy skills

35 *See at* <www.ohchr.org/EN/HRBodies/HRC/Minority/Pages/ForumIndex.aspx> visited on 10 January 2018.

36 Commentary of the Working Group on Minorities to the United Nations Declaration on the Rights of Persons Belonging to National or Ethnic, Religious or Linguistic Minorities <documents-dds-ny.un.org/doc/UNDOC/GEN/G05/133/85/PDF/ G0513385.pdf?OpenElement>, para. 28.

to additional languages; children experience less frustration and failure and fewer drop out of school; and by including families and drawing on local cultural heritage, mother tongue–based education contributes to communities' social and cultural well-being and fosters inclusiveness within wider society. Moreover, quality public education in the mother tongue should 'be extended to as late a stage in education as possible'[37] up to and including public university education where practicable.[38] At the same time, the learning of the official language(s) of the country is crucial to enable minority children when they become adults to seek jobs or effectively participate in public life.

States can decide on approaches to ensure the enjoyment of language-related rights in practice, based on factors such as demand and the number and location of minority students. Where student numbers are higher it may be appropriate to provide formal classes in minority languages, while in other cases more informal approaches may be appropriate, including additional classes and out-of-school teaching options. Government motivation for restricting the teaching of minority languages and their use as a language of instruction may be based on such factors as a policy of promoting the use of one national language and national unity. Some consider it advantageous for the social and economic mobility of minorities to ensure that they are fully proficient in the national language and therefore to limit minority language use in education, however this is a violation of minority rights.

In Viet Nam, visited by my predecessor as Special Rapporteur in July 2010 (then Independent Expert),[39] many minority communities in isolated and remote locations do not frequently interact in Vietnamese. Many speak ethnic languages in almost all family and social interactions, and others, particularly older generations, speak and understand only a little Vietnamese. In Viet Nam, where there are 54 recognized distinct ethnic groups, only 24 ethnic minority languages have written scripts, which creates particular challenges for their preservation. UNICEF has been supporting the Ministry of Education and Training to address disparities in education outcomes between the majority and ethnic minorities. The mother tongue–based bilingual education programme has been implemented since 2008 in three provinces with three

37 UNESCO, The Use of Vernacular Languages in Education, *Monographs on Fundamental Education,* 1953, pp. 47–48.

38 OSCE HCNM, The Hague Recommendations Regarding the Education Rights of National Minorities, Recommendations 17 and 18.

39 Report of the independent expert on minority issues, Gay McDougall on her mission to Viet Nam A/HRC/16/45/Add.2, <documents-dds-ny.un.org/doc/UNDOC/GEN/G11/103/82/PDF/G1110382.pdf?OpenElement>, visited on 22 November 2017.

different ethnic minorities, the Mong, Jrai and Khmer, and shows very positive results.[40]

Mother tongue-based bilingual education requires resources and technical expertise for its practical delivery. This includes ensuring the recruitment and training of minority teachers and those proficient in minority languages, provision of minority language textbooks and teaching materials, and development of bilingual curricula. For example, in Cambodia, a Highland Children's Education Project included the recruitment and training of local teachers who speak minority languages in remote communities. The undertaking of classroom language mapping provides necessary information at the local level to identify requirements and possibilities for bilingual language approaches. Moreover, to promote tolerance and inclusion, all students should learn about each other: minorities must not be prevented from understanding the culture and language of the national community as a whole or from participating in its activities, and the majority must also be given similar opportunities in relation to minority cultures and languages.

4.2 *Participation in Public Life*

In Ethiopia, an estimated 89 different languages are spoken throughout the country. After her visit to Ethiopia in 2008, the former Independent Expert on minority issues raised serious concerns about increased tensions between communities that remained persistent due to the imposition of local or regional languages as the official language of regional states. As a consequence, some groups have been effectively excluded from participation in the public life of the regions in which they live, as they were not recognized as native to the region, or did not speak official local languages, and so could not hold certain public offices including regional president or cabinet member.

Indeed, one of the biggest challenges I encountered during my work as Special Rapporteur was the limited, or often complete lack of a minority presence in political and public offices, including in municipal and government structures, law enforcement bodies, the judiciary, legislative bodies, criminal justice systems and other relevant bodies and mechanisms, especially when their decisions affect minorities. Lack of provisions for minority language use in these bodies and minority's lack of proficiency in the country's official language(s) can both constitute a serious barrier in accessing these offices. Without the participation of minorities, such bodies are less able to take vital decisions for the benefit of the entire society and may be less trusted by minorities, who

40 UNICEF, Action research on mother tongue–based bilingual education: improving the equity and quality of education for ethnic minority children in Viet Nam, 2012. <www.unicef.org/vietnam/resources_19823.html>, visited on 22 November 2017.

may be reluctant to access them, or discouraged from doing so. Moreover, good and inclusive governance, which includes minorities and measures to ensure equality, are key conflict-prevention prerequisites.

In some national contexts Governments have imposed prohibitive restrictions on the use of minority languages in public spheres, including in political life. Under such circumstances minorities have even faced prosecution for exercising their right to use their language publicly, for example in the context of political campaigns. Such actions may be imposed in the context of efforts to stringently enforce the use of a single national language or assimilate minority communities via restrictions on their language use. In some cases, inter-ethnic or inter-religious conflict may motivate such restrictions designed to marginalize and exclude a particular population group. Few cases have been reported of restrictions on the use of minority languages in private life; however, aggressive promotion of a national language and restrictions on education in the mother tongue may be interpreted by members of a minority as attempts to assimilate them or eradicate minority language use in all spheres.

While it is legitimate to promote a common State language, certain factors should be taken into account to ensure that such promotion does not become discriminatory in practice. The OSCE High Commissioner on National Minorities has emphasized that an appropriate balance is required between strengthening the State language on the one hand, and protecting the linguistic rights of persons belonging to national minorities on the other.[41] In some situations, historical grievances relating to language use, including the previous imposition of non-native languages, have been reported; however, such issues do not constitute legitimate grounds for restrictions to be imposed on the use of any language in public or private or failure to fully implement minority rights relating to language.

Steps to encourage and facilitate the effective participation of minorities in public life include, where practicable, the use of their languages in electoral, consultative and other public participation processes. In areas where speakers of a minority language are concentrated and in significant numbers, electoral information, ballots and other public documents pertaining to elections or public consultation and participation events should be made available in that language. For example, in New Zealand, electoral information is provided in 27 other languages apart from English.[42]

---

41 Statement by OSCE Minorities Commissioner on Slovakia's State Language Act, 3 September 2009, <www.osce.org/hcnm/51272>, visited on 10 January 2018.

42 *See* website at <www.elections.org.nz/resources-learning/information-other-languages>, visited on 22 November 2017.

Linguistic requirements for voting or political participation must be non-discriminatory. Excluding individuals from voting or running for office because of their language, or lack of fluency in a state's official language, has extremely serious consequences. It precludes participation in public life and would generally be discriminatory. Consultation, participation, representation and meaningful influence of minorities on the decision-making bodies and processes that affect them must at all times be considered and facilitated, in order to best inform policymakers and foster cooperation between authorities and minority communities.

4.3 *Minority Languages in the Media*

The Oslo Recommendations set forth that minorities have the right to establish and maintain their own minority media. Moreover, minorities should have access to broadcast time in their own language on publicly funded media, appropriate with the size, concentration, the situation and needs of the national minority. For minority communities, the right to media in their language and appropriate to their cultural identity is particularly important and a vital vehicle for the preservation and transmission of minority cultures. Multilingual and multicultural public broadcasting can serve to mainstream the presence and participation of minorities and celebrate a state's diversity.

Nevertheless, restrictions on the free establishment and functioning of media in minority languages have been witnessed in a number of countries. Any unreasonable prohibition or restrictions of such rights in public or in private media could constitute a violation of minority rights and freedom of expression. Restrictions reported include barriers to the issuance of licenses and the adoption of legislation prescribing quotas for broadcasting time in a certain language. No undue restrictions, censorship or requirements for translation should be imposed on minority-language media.[43]

A lack of minority language programmes in publicly funded media is frequently a concern, and public media should review the extent to which its content caters to minority audiences. Where relatively large minority communities are dispersed throughout a country, minority language programmes broadcast nationally should be considered. In other cases, regional-based programming may be a more appropriate solution, catering to the needs of minorities concentrated in particular regions. Ultimately, access to public media in people's own languages is a communication, information and integration tool between

43 OSCE HCNM, Guidelines on the Use of Minority Languages in the Broadcast Media by the OSCE High Commissioner on National Minorities, October 2003, <www.osce.org/hcnm/32310?download=true>, visited on 22 November 2017.

state authorities and minorities. It gives governments a tool to prevent the isolation of minorities in public life, establishes a direct communication and information link between the state and minorities, and provides a particularly effective tool for ensuring their inclusion while promoting tolerance, cultural diversity, mutual respect, understanding and cooperation. The extent of programming depends on factors such as demand and, to some extent, the availability of private minority media sources. Nevertheless, minorities pay for public media via their taxes and consideration must be given to their content requirements.

Often problems relating to access to minority language media may stem not from State legislation or policy but from a lack of resources, skills and technical or journalistic training that limits capacity to establish minority language media. In such cases the State can play a valuable role in assisting minorities and, where necessary, financially supporting training and initiatives to create minority language media. For example, the authorities in Kosovo established a Minority Media Fund to provide financial and other assistance to electronic and printed minority language media. Minorities have the right to maintain cross-border relations, including with kin States, and these extend to the ability to receive language media and web-based information originating from abroad that conforms to international standards, for example with respect to the prohibition of incitement to ethnic or religious hatred.

From a practical point of view, authorities and policymakers should also consider that integration, communication and information need to be two-way processes: public media programmes and activities should target members of the majority as well. They should encourage the learning of minority and indigenous languages, as well as the setting up of multilingual and multicultural broadcasting facilities to mainstream minority concerns and promote programmes that celebrate a state's diversity rather than simply perpetuating a monolingual or single-culture vision of the state.

I wish to emphasize that while minority media can fulfil an important role in preserving language, culture and minority identity, it has very limited potential to balance negative stereotyping, stigmatization, and homogenization or fight back against hate speech emanating from mainstream media. This is partly due to the fact that minority media tends to be accessed by minority audiences and messages broadcast by them are often regarded as inferior by the society at large, compared to differing majority media viewpoints. Therefore, representation of minority groups in mainstream media is essential to ensure diversity in content and in the make-up and structures of media bodies themselves. However, minorities face numerous challenges both in their access to and representation in the media. Under-representation of minorities in the media means that their voices and influence are absent to counter negative expressions. One study in the United Kingdom confirmed a gross imbalance between white and ethnic minority journalists in relation to training and employment patterns and opportunities within the news media. Only 0.5 per cent of national newspaper journalists and only 0.2 per cent of provincial press journalists were Black or Asian. In the broadcasting industry, an estimated 2.7 per cent of editorial staff were Black or Asian. While equal opportunities policies, ethnic minority monitoring and training schemes of the BBC have helped, half of all Black staff work on black-only radio and television programs.[44]

5 Conclusions and Recommendations

Languages form an essential part of a nation's cultural and linguistic heritage and diversity. Factors such as voluntary and forced migration, conflict, climate change, and the opening of borders are creating ever more diverse ethnic and linguistic societies in which language rights and needs must be taken into account. The Declaration on the Rights of Persons Belonging to National or Ethnic, Religious and Linguistic Minorities and other international standards clearly establish the rights of linguistic minorities and the duties upon States. While they do not require that a State provide all activities and services in every language present within the State, in its assessment of how to fulfil its obligations, each State must take into account numerous factors relevant to linguistic minorities, including the number of language users and their distribution within the country. Each State can decide on approaches to how it implements the Declaration in practice, and it is reasonable to consider that greater attention and resources will be dedicated to certain traditionally present, commonly spoken, or geographically concentrated languages, for example, than are given to relatively newly established languages with few or dispersed users.

In many cases a strong community desire exists to maintain minority languages as a core and indispensable element of culture and identity. Sometimes this is viewed by Governments as divisive and counter to State ideologies and policies to promote national identity, national unity, integration and territorial integrity. In States in which historical, political and geographical factors have created highly diverse communities, disputes over territories and borders and tensions between different national, ethnic, religious and linguistic groups may exist. Irrespective of such factors States are obligated to respect, protect

44 S. Cottle, ed., *Ethnic Minorities and the Media: Changing Cultural Boundaries* (Berkshire, Open University Press, 2000).

and fulfil the rights of linguistic minorities, and restrictions must be in the public interest and proportional to the aims sought.

Globally, grievances and tensions relating to language rights and the rights of linguistic minorities have emerged and have even led to conflict. Restriction on the rights to use minority languages freely may be, or may be interpreted as, a threat to minority identity. It is important to acknowledge that issues relating to linguistic minorities and their rights may have implications for security and national stability. Protection of linguistic minority rights is a human rights obligation and an essential component of good governance, efforts to prevent tensions and conflict, and the construction of equal and politically and socially stable societies. To create unity in diversity requires dialogue with all stakeholders, including on how to appropriately accommodate the language needs and rights of all groups.

Laws, policies and processes must recognize language rights within a human rights framework. Working in the human rights paradigm and putting language issues in the context of international human rights instruments and standards, will help finding the right approach to managing linguistic pluralism. A regularly practiced, systematic human rights approach to language issues helps to identify potential issues and negative impacts, while also providing the ways and means to respond to and correct them. Core language rights contained in the various international treaties and standards contain four main principles: dignity; liberty; equality and non-discrimination; and identity.

On the national level, Governments must fulfil their obligations to the best of their ability for all linguistic minorities despite the often-existing financial challenges. Numerous cost-effective methods are available to fulfil language rights, including translation of key information, web-based resources targeted at minorities, and policies of promoting training of minorities and their recruitment at national and local levels in public institutions. The use of minority mediators is a positive practice utilized by some States to improve communication with minorities. It may also be appropriate to encourage and facilitate cross-border cooperation, for example where a linguistic minority has a neighbouring or kin-State with a shared language tradition.

The current Secretary-General of the United Nations has identified prevention as one of his main priorities. In his very first formal briefing in January 2017, he called on all sections of the society for greater political, cultural and economic investments in inclusivity and cohesion, so that people appreciate the benefits of diversity rather than perceiving it as a threat. In order for the UN to fulfil its vital conflict prevention role, its resources and mechanisms on minority rights protection must be strengthened, including the Forum on Minority Issues. It would be crucial that the UN considers appointing at least one high-level official on minority issues within the Secretariat as well as establish senior positions within United Nations departments and agencies to look into issues of minority rights protection, diversity management and safeguarding pluralistic societies. Focus and activities on minority rights protection and conflict prevention should be intensified not only in Geneva and in New York and by OHCHR but by all UN agencies, funds and programmes, especially on the field. The designation of minority focal points in all field offices is desirable. Moreover, UN offices should reach out to minority communities and include them into their consultations, as well as into the planning and implementation of programmes.

It is only through such strengthened efforts and commitments that a better social cohesion, peace and stability can be achieved where linguistic minorities feel that their identity is respected, that they belong to their society, and that the diversity they bring is viewed as a value and opportunity for all.

CHAPTER 13

Language Rights and the Work of the European Union

Bruno De Witte

1 Introduction: The Oslo Recommendations and the European Union, Worlds Apart?

The Oslo Recommendations regarding the Linguistic Rights of National Minorities, made by the OSCE's High Commissioner of National Minorities in 1998, do not seem greatly relevant to the operation of the European Union, for several reasons. Firstly, the Oslo Recommendations are addressed to governments of OSCE states rather than to the EU; as their introductory note states, they "will provide a useful reference for the development of State policies and laws".[1] And secondly, the legal status of national minorities (including their language rights) is one of the few remaining policy areas in which the role of the European Union continues to remain minimal and almost inexistent.

This does not mean that language issues, more broadly speaking, are irrelevant in the functioning of the European Union. Quite to the contrary: as a multilingual organisation, the European Union has had to deal with the question how to accommodate the linguistic diversity existing within its borders. It has responded to that challenge by affirming that linguistic diversity is a constitutional value that the EU institutions intend to 'respect'. This commitment is now contained in a very prominent place of the EU Treaties, namely in Article 3, paragraph 3, of the Treaty on European Union (TEU), as well as in Article 22 of the EU Charter of Fundamental Rights.[2] This constitutional mandate is reflected in policies that relate both to the operation of the European Union itself (including its relations with the citizens) and to the linguistic policies and rules of its member states. These EU policies have encompassed the development of a number of *language rights* under EU law; essentially, these

1 OSCE High Commissioner on National Minorities, *The Oslo Recommendations regarding the Linguistic Rights of National Minorities*, February 1998, Introduction (p. 4).

2 See X. Arzoz, 'The protection of linguistic diversity through Article 22 of the Charter of Fundamental Rights', in X. Arzoz (ed.), *Respecting Linguistic Diversity in the European Union* (John Benjamins, Amsterdam, 2008) p. 145.

© KONINKLIJKE BRILL NV, LEIDEN, 2018 | DOI 10.1163/9789004357754_014

are (a) the right to use any of the official languages of the European Union when dealing with its institutions; (b) the right of European Union citizens not to be discriminated on account of the language they speak; and (c) the right to interpretation and translation in criminal proceedings. The evolution and present scope of these rights will be discussed in Sections 2, 3 and 4, respectively. Yet, as we will see, these three rights are awarded to all EU citizens and not specifically to the members of linguistic minorities, who are the target group of the Oslo Recommendations. To that extent, the European Union's work remains far apart from the concerns that promoted the adoption, twenty years ago, of the Oslo Recommendations. The most one can say is that certain EU bodies, in certain circumstances, have taken a timid and intermittent interest in the language rights of national minorities, as we will describe in Section 5.

2 The Right to Use the Official Languages

The European Union institutions function in many languages. This institutional multilingualism embodies, in a symbolic and practical way, the equality between the Union's member states. It also reflects the value of democratic governance, since it guarantees that legislative, executive and judicial powers transferred from the member state level to the European level shall be exercised there in a manner which is comprehensible, literally speaking, for the citizens of all member states. Finally, this multilingualism is a precondition for the claim, made by the European Court of Justice and accepted by domestic courts, that large parts of EU law are directly applicable without the need to be transformed into national law; such a claim would not be tenable if Union law were not enacted in the languages of each member country.

This principled choice for multilingualism is not openly expressed in the text of the European Treaties. Indeed, the Treaty provision, mentioned above, according to which the EU shall respect linguistic diversity, does not necessarily imply the official status, in EU law, of any given language. However, a partial expression of the choice for multilingualism is laid down in Article 20 of the Treaty on the Functioning of the European Union (TFEU) which grants a right for citizens of the Union "to address the institutions and advisory bodies of the Union in any of the Treaty languages and to obtain a reply in the same language".[3]

3 Article 20 (2) (d). The 24 'Treaty languages' are listed in Article 55 TEU: Bulgarian, Croatian, Czech, Danish, Dutch, English, Estonian, Finnish, French, German, Greek, Hungarian, Irish,

This right was 'constitutionalised' relatively recently, namely by the Amsterdam Treaty in the late 1990's (coinciding in time with the Oslo recommendations), but it corresponds to the existing and much older practice of the European Union. Indeed, the rule was originally set out in the very first Regulation ever adopted under the EEC Treaty, namely Council Regulation 1/58 on the use of languages by the Community institutions.[4] The Council then adopted the principle, which is still valid today, that the national languages of the member states were to rank equally as official and working languages of the European Communities, subject to more detailed arrangements to be adopted by each institution separately. This rule was extended later on to the national official languages of all the states acceding to the Union.[5]

Still, the establishment of a *right* to use these languages, by the Treaty of Amsterdam, was not insignificant. It lent an entrenched constitutional status to the citizen-related dimension of a linguistic regime that hitherto was regulated by an act of secondary EU law. The language clause of the Amsterdam Treaty was also important because it renewed the original commitment of the member states to linguistic diversity, at a time when the cost of the language regime had become much higher than in 1958. Recommendations for a 'simplification' of the Union's linguistic regime were thus ignored and implicitly rejected. Also, the Treaty of Accession of April 2003 simply extended the existing linguistic regime to the European Union of 25 member states, modifying Regulation No 1 of 1958 so as to add no less than nine additional official languages, and the most recent Treaties of Accession also added Rumanian, Bulgarian and Croatian to the list. On each of these occasions, the exponential increase of translation and interpretation costs, and the growing danger of

Italian, Latvian, Lithuanian, Maltese, Polish, Portuguese, Romanian, Slovak, Slovenian, Spanish and Swedish.

4 *Journal Officiel des C.E.*, 1958, 385. The Regulation was adopted pursuant to Article 217 EEC Treaty (now Article 342 TFEU), which states: "The rules governing the languages of the institutions of the Union shall, without prejudice to the provisions contained in the Statute of the Court of Justice, be determined by the Council, acting unanimously by means of regulations".

5 An exception was made for Irish. There is an authentic version in Irish of the founding Treaties, but Irish was not included among the official and working languages when Regulation No 1 of 1958 was modified upon the accession of the UK, Ireland and Denmark (Section XIV of Annex I to the Act of Accession, OJ 1972, L 73/122). Irish became an official language more recently, from 1 January 2007, due to an amendment of Regulation No 1 (*Official Journal of the EU* 2005, L 156/3), but its use is more restricted than that of the other 23 official languages. As for Letzeburgesch, it became an official language of Luxembourg many years after that country helped found the European Communities, and this language was not subsequently added to the list of Regulation No. 1.

communication failures between actors in the European policy-making and implementation process, could not outweigh the commitment to linguistic diversity and equality among member states.

Between 1958 and now, the commitment to linguistic diversity has, in fact, radically changed in its tone and implications. In 1958, it was a pragmatic solution adopted by the EEC, in the same way as other international organisations decide on their language regime. The option chosen in 1958, which did not sacrifice any of its member states' national languages, was taken at a rather low cost, because it meant that a co-official status was being given to four languages only in the fairly limited range of activities covered, at the time, by the EEC. Today, the commitment to the equality of Europe's national languages has become a constitutional principle of paramount importance, which is extended to more than twenty languages, applies to a vastly expanded scope of EU activity and therefore lays a heavy (not only financial) burden on the Union's institutional machinery.

However, the principle does not guarantee full equality between all the EU citizens and residents irrespective of their mother tongue. Indeed, the right may well apply to all the *national* official languages of the member states, but it does not apply to their *regional* languages, even when these have official status in part of the country, such as Catalan or Welsh for example. Some of these regional languages count, of course, more speakers than a number of the national languages. To mitigate this differentiation, it was decided in 2005 that single member states could conclude administrative agreements with the various EU institutions in order to arrange for the use of regional languages in communications of these institutions with the citizenry. This resulted from a request by the Spanish government and was implemented, to a limited extent, for the benefit of Spain's regional official languages such as Catalan, Basque and Galician. However, these special arrangements do not provide for genuine *rights* to use those languages.[6]

Moreover, the leeway left to each of the institutions by Article 6 of Regulation 1/58, namely that they could make practical accommodations of the equality norm, has been used very extensively. The day-to-day reality of the European Union shows a rather different picture than the principles outlined above. Increasingly, policy documents emanating from the European institutions are placed on the websites of the EU in a few language versions only.

6 *See*, for the details, A. Milian Massana, 'Languages that are official in part of the territory of the Member States: Second-class languages or institutional recognition in EU law?', in X. Arzoz (ed.), *Respecting Linguistic Diversity in the European Union* (John Benjamins, Amsterdam, 2008) p. 191.

Furthermore, it is widely known that the internal working languages of the Commission services are English and French, to the almost total exclusion of the other languages (although German is formally the Commission's third working language, it is very seldom used). So, the right to use any of the 24 official languages does not apply to the EU citizens who work for one of the EU institutions.

3 The Right Not to be Discriminated on Grounds of Language

The EU Charter of Fundamental Rights contains, in its Article 21, a list of suspect grounds of discrimination, which corresponds to that of Article 14 of the European Convention of Human Rights and also includes 'language'. This right to non-discrimination on grounds of language is a judicially enforceable norm applying not only to the EU's own legislative and administrative activities, but also to the EU member states and to individual persons when they act within the scope of EU law. How does this European right affect the language policies and regulations of the EU member states?

In principle, EU law does not modify the power of the member states to determine their official language regimes and to differentiate between languages that may and may not be used in communications between citizens and public authorities. However, the national language regimes are not *entirely* immune from the impact of Union law. They may not be applied in a discriminatory way against the citizens of other EU countries. Thus, imposing proficiency in one or more particular languages for recruitment to public employment is allowed by Union law, but only if this requirement does not indirectly cause discrimination against EU citizens originating from other countries. This rule was recognised early on in the history of European Communities, namely in the text of Regulation 1612/68 on the free movement of workers (now replaced by Regulation 492/2011).[7] Article 2 of that Regulation prohibits indirect discrimination resulting from actions having as their exclusive or principal aim or effect to keep nationals of other member states away from the employment offered. To this rule, a qualifying statement is added, namely that the prohibition does 'not apply to conditions relating to linguistic knowledge required by reason of the nature of the post to be filled'. The question therefore is whether a particular requirement of linguistic proficiency is genuinely related to the

7 Regulation 492/2011 on freedom of movement for workers within the Union, *Official Journal of the EU* 2011, L 141/1.

public function concerned or, rather, is a condition whose aim or effect is to exclude foreigners, in particular EU citizens.

That question was addressed by the European Court of Justice in its high-profile *Groener* judgment of 1989.[8] Irish law imposed the requirement that candidates for a permanent post in public education should demonstrate an adequate knowledge of the Irish language. A Dutch applicant to such a job, Anita Groener, having failed the language test, alleged that this requirement effectively excluded EU citizens from applying for any of these jobs and was therefore a form of indirect discrimination falling under the prohibition of the (then applicable) Regulation 1612/68. Indeed, the job to which Ms Groener applied, that of teacher of painting in the College of Marketing and Design in Dublin, did not in fact require her to speak Irish at any time, and therefore knowledge of that language was not a functional necessity. However, the Court of Justice gave a remarkably wide interpretation to the language clause of Regulation 1612/68. Because Irish was an official language of the country, Ireland was allowed to require its knowledge from all teachers, even those who would not be called to use it in the course of their work, on condition that the required level was not set too high. The Court did not read Article 3 of the Regulation as laying down a purely functional test (namely: is knowledge of the language necessary for the day-to-day performance of the job?), but as leaving space for the broader constitutional background and the language policy priorities of the member states. Still, the Court was keen to insert a proportionality requirement. Based on this, the European Commission later stated that the condition, which is frequently used in announcements of recruitment, that candidates should be 'native speakers' of a particular language, is a prohibited form of indirect discrimination against citizens of other EU countries.[9]

This prohibition of discriminatory language conditions has been extended in two directions since 1968. Its substantive scope has been extended from public to private employment conditions and its personal scope is being extended, hesitantly still, from EU citizens to other categories of foreigners. The extension to private sector employment was clearly affirmed by the *Angonese* judgment of the European Court of Justice in 2000. That case concerned access to employment in a private bank in Bolzano that had been made dependent

8 ECJ, Case 379/87, *Groener* v. *Minister for Education and the Dublin Vocational Education Committee*, ECLI:EU:C:1989: 599.

9 *See* Commission Communication of 11 December 2002, *Free Movement of Workers – Achieving the Full Benefits and Potential*, COM (2002) 694, at p. 7: "The Commission considers that while a very high level of language may, under certain strict conditions, be justifiable for certain jobs, a requirement to be mother tongue is not acceptable".

upon a showing of adequate language knowledge of both Italian and German, the two official languages in South Tyrol. This, the Court found, was a direct and acceptable consequence of the minority protection regime enacted in that region of Italy (even though it concerned employment in a private bank), but the additional requirement that evidence of bilingualism could be provided *only* by means of an official local certificate was held to be an indirect discrimination against citizens from other EU countries, and hence in breach of EU law.[10] The judgment has become famous for its sweeping statement that the right to free movement has full horizontal application, i.e. that private persons are directly bound by this rule and must abstain from discrimination against EU citizens. So, the situation today is that, both in public and in private employment, language skills may only be imposed on citizens of other European Union countries to the extent that they are necessary for the good performance of the job.

The protection against language discrimination in recruitment and conditions of employment now arguably applies to *non-EU nationals* as well, on the basis of the European Union's Race Discrimination Directive of 2000.[11] Indeed, linguistic proficiency requirements that are not justified by the nature of the job could be considered, depending on the person, as an indirect form of racial or ethnic discrimination under the terms of this Directive. This duty of non-discrimination also applies horizontally; indeed, its main concern is to combat discrimination in private legal relations and in social life in general. So, the imposition of language conditions or requirements by private employers could amount to indirect discrimination on the grounds of race and ethnic origin, and thus be in breach of the Race Directive. Similarly, employment conditions unduly prohibiting the use of minority languages during work could be indirect discrimination on grounds of race. An example from practice is the decision of the Danish Board of Equal Treatment finding indirect discrimination on grounds of ethnic origin when a Taiwanese applicant for the position of organ player in a local church was rejected; according to the Board, the requirement of proficiency in the Danish language, which led to the rejection, was not sufficiently related to the performance of the job of organ player.[12]

All the cases mentioned so far relate to language discrimination in the field of employment. It is worth noting that, in all those cases, the relevant legal

10 ECJ, Case C-281/98, *Angonese* v. *Cassa di Risparmio di Bolzano*, ECLI:EU:C:2000:296.

11 Council Directive 2000/43 implementing the principle of equal treatment between persons irrespective of racial or ethnic origin, *Official Journal of the EU* 2000, L 180/22.

12 Danish Board of Equal Treatment, decision No. 9505 of 6 May 2016, summarized in *European Equality Law Review* (2017/1), p. 76.

norm was actually *not* the prohibition of language discrimination contained in Article 21 of the EU Charter of Fundamental Rights. Rather, linguistic requirements were struck down because they were seen as indirect forms of discrimination on grounds of (EU) nationality or on grounds of ethnic origin. Yet, discrimination 'purely' on grounds of language is clearly also prohibited. It extends not only to the field of employment (in which all the examples mentioned above are situated) but also to other domains that are within the scope of EU law, such as access to health services or education.

4 The Right to Interpretation and Translation in Criminal Proceedings

Whereas the two previously mentioned rights have constitutional status within the EU legal order, as they are laid down in the text of the European Union treaties, the third language right is contained in a piece of EU legislation, namely the Directive of 2010 on the right to interpretation and translation in criminal proceedings.[13] This text is part of a series of legislative initiatives of the EU to protect the defence rights of participants in criminal proceedings, as well as the rights of crime victims.[14] It can be seen as the detailed elaboration of the one language right that is expressly mentioned in the European Convention of Human Rights, namely the right to interpretation and translation for those who do not speak or understand the language of criminal proceedings, which is one of the fair trial rights in Article 6 of the Convention. Although the directive may have been primarily meant to improve the position of EU nationals finding themselves involved in criminal cases in EU countries other than their own, the right applies to all accused in all trials throughout the EU. The scope of the right extends beyond the existing case law of the European Court of Human Rights in a number of respects, but especially by including a right to the translation of all the essential documents of the trial, and not just the act of accusation. The rights of the Directive are also granted to non-EU nationals and to speakers of minority languages. In respect to the latter, the Directive elaborates on Oslo Recommendation number 17. In the unlikely case that a

13 Directive 2010/64 of 20 October 2010, *Official Journal of the EU* 2010, L 280/1. For a commentary, *see* S. Monjean-Decaudin, 'L'Union européenne consacre le droit a l'assistance linguistique dans les procédures pénales', *Revue trimestrielle de droit européen* (2012) p. 763.

14 For a complete presentation of these EU defence rights, *see* A. Klip, *European Criminal Law – An Integrative Approach*, 3rd edition (Intersentia, Cambridge, 2016), Chapter 6.

speaker of a minority language would not understand the official language of a court based in his/her own country, he or she could apply for interpretation and translation. However, a mere declaration by the accused is not sufficient; the directive rather requires the member states to put in place a mechanism to ascertain whether suspected or accused persons do speak and understand the language of the proceedings, or not.[15]

5 A Temporary Concern for the Language Rights of National Minorities

As was mentioned above, the three language rights recognised under EU law do not single out the rights of language minorities for special consideration; indeed, the first of the three rights even excludes minority languages from its scope. However, the European Union institutions were involved rather actively with the rights of minorities, including their language rights, in the external relations domain, in particular in the context of the preparation of new accessions to the EU. The heyday of the EU's involvement with minority languages was in the period 1993–2003, when a sufficient degree of minority protection was made into one of the political conditions for the accession of Central and Eastern European countries to the EU. In that context, the Commission produced annual progress reports in which it commented – in rather loose wording – on the performance of the candidate countries in relation to minority protection generally, including the protection of the language rights of minorities. In its annual reports, the Commission repeatedly referred to the minority protection instruments of the Council of Europe and to the advice given by the High Commissioner of National Minorities.[16] However, the EU institutions did not really adopt a fixed benchmark of minority protection standards, and the Oslo Recommendations, in particular, were not used as the benchmark for minority language rights. That period of minority protection activism of the EU institutions came to an end when the big-bang Accession Treaty of 2003 was adopted. Since then, the EU continues to examine minority protection in its assessment of the progress of the remaining candidates for accession, such as Turkey, Serbia and Macedonia, but the assessment has become rather more superficial than in the previous period, with little or no

15 Article 2 (4) of the Directive.

16 *See* G. Sasse, 'Minority Rights and EU Enlargement: Normative Overstretch or Effective Conditionality?', in G. Toggenburg (ed.), *Minority Protection and the Enlarged European Union: The Way Forward* (Open Society Institute, Budapest, 2004), 59, pp. 65–69.

reference to concrete external benchmarks and with no specific attention to the recognition of minority *rights*.

The claim has often been made that the European Union should correct this 'double standard', and start recognizing and guaranteeing the language rights of minorities situated *inside* the European Union, and not just those of minorities situated *outside*. In the course of the years, the European Parliament, in particular, adopted a number of non-binding resolutions advocating the adoption of a charter of minority rights of the EU, but this was never followed-up or turned into concrete legal projects by the Commission or the Council. On the last occasion in time, the European Parliament took a more narrow approach, by restricting its advocacy to the protection of *endangered* languages,[17] which is a less controversial stance since it echoes the commitments taken by the European Union when it ratified the UNESCO Convention on the diversity of cultural expressions. But even in this more narrowly focused text, no claim is made for the granting of genuine language *rights*; rather, the EP's request is that existing EU policies (especially its funding programmes) should be made more generously available to the endangered languages of Europe. More recently, the Citizens Initiative, the new participation instrument created by the Lisbon Treaty, was used for an initiative called Minority SafePack, which calls on the EU to undertake a number of new minority support initiatives but – again – without including the granting of minority language rights. The European Commission refused to act upon this Citizens Initiative, arguing that the European Union lacked the necessary competence to enact the kind of measures that were being proposed in the Initiative, but that refusal was in turn annulled by the General Court of the EU because the Commission had not given sufficient reasons for it.[18] The collection of one million signatures was started after that judgment. What is clear, though, is that there is little enthusiasm at the level of the European Commission, and at that of most member state governments, to let the European Union play the role of a standard-setter or major funder in relation to minority languages.

17 European Parliament resolution of 11 September 2013 on endangered European languages and linguistic diversity in the European Union (2013/2007(INI)).

18 General Court of the EU, Case T-646/13, *Bürgerausschuss für die Bürgerinitiative Minority SafePack – one million signatures for diversity in Europe v European Commission*, ECLI:EU:T:2017:59.

CHAPTER 14

'Taking Oslo Online': Minority Language Policy & the Internet

Jennifer Jackson-Preece

1 Introduction

The basic premise of this chapter is that 'language' is more than a category of analysis used by social scientists. It is first and foremost a set of lived practices, now increasingly performed online. Language *per se* constitutes social relationships, and is in turn shaped and conditioned by social relationships.[1] The context in which language operates is an 'intersubjective construct' embedded in specific practices of production, distribution and reception as well as in wider cultural, social, political, and economic practices.[2] As this chapter will demonstrate, technology is a crucial component of context precisely because it facilitates language production, distribution and reception. For this reason, technology matters for minority language rights. When technologies change, language practices change, and public policies directed at minority language speakers must respond accordingly.

This chapter will examine how new digital technologies have affected minority language speakers. Are persons belonging to minorities able to fully engage with the Internet using their minority languages? What, if any, obstacles may prevent the use of minority languages online? And how should states translate the *The Oslo Recommendations regarding the Linguistic Rights of National Minorities* (*Oslo Recommendations* or *Oslo*) into policies that support digital language diversity in cyberspace?

1 R. Wodak and N. Fairclough, 'Critical Discourse Analysis', in T. van Dijk (ed.), *Discourse as Social Interaction.* (Sage, London, 1997) p. 258.

2 V. Koller, 'How to Analyse Collective Identity in Discourse-Textual and Contextual Parameters'. *Critical Approaches to Discourse Analysis across Disciplines,* 5: 2 (2012), pp. 19–38.

© KONINKLIJKE BRILL NV, LEIDEN, 2018 | DOI 10.1163/9789004357754_015

2 Technology as a Context for Minority Languages

2.1 *Imagining Communities with Technology*

Technology is deeply implicated in practices of production, distribution and reception of language. For this reason, it has a profound effect on wider cultural, social, political and economic practices. Benedict Anderson in his seminal work 'Imagined Communities' argues that national identities, whether of majorities or minorities, emerged as a consequence of technological change, namely the invention of the printing press.[3] It was the printing press that enabled the mass production and (re)distribution of vernacular language which in turn created national audiences with commensurate and distinct national identities.

This explains why in their origins nations and indeed national minorities, were as much philological as political endeavours.[4] Thus, for example, nascent nationalisms in the nineteenth century were expressed and developed through literary efforts such as the production, printing and distribution of dictionaries, grammars, and folktales etc.

Once nation-states were created, national governments began to regulate the language used in the printing and distribution of laws, textbooks, and other sources of information.[5] These nascent national language policies were intended to ensure the continued pre-eminence of official languages over and above those of minority language speakers. They encouraged and in some cases even mandated processes of linguistic assimilation into the official language(s) of state, which were usually those of the titular (majority) nation.

Anderson claims that the rise of new technology such as radio and television supplemented print media's nationalistic influences.[6] When analogue radio and television technologies emerged, that same process of governmental regulation in support of official languages was applied to these mediums. Here, too, programming prioritised official (majority) languages over and above minority languages. The experience of minority language speakers during the nineteenth and twentieth centuries was thus one of increasing linguistic marginalisation and assimilation via majority control of the means of production, distribution and reception of language.

3 B. Anderson, *Imagined communities: Reflections on the origin and spread of nationalism* (Verso Books, London, 2006).

4 J. Jackson-Preece, *Minority Rights: Between Diversity and Community* (Polity, Cambridge, 2005), pp. 110–112.

5 Jackson-Preece, *supra* note 4, pp. 107–110.

6 Anderson, *supra* note 3, p. 135.

2.2 *Twentieth Century Technologies and the Oslo Recommendations*

The *Oslo Recommendations* were in their origins a response to a language context created and sustained by and through print, and analogue radio and television. Such technologies are clearly implicated across the full range of the *Oslo Recommendations*. In 1997, official documents, bills, receipts, and advertisements – not to mention laws, policies, and court judgements – all relied on print technology for their production, distribution and reception.

Minority language communities and their associated organisations also required printed materials (pamphlets, brochures, letters) and 'fair access' to radio and television broadcasting, including access to language broadcasts originating from kin-states across frontiers. Without access to print, radio and television technology, minority languages were unable to constitute those social relationships needed to sustain minority language communities in the late twentieth century.

Minority access to these technologies is explicitly discussed in the section of the *Oslo Recommendations* titled "THE MEDIA", where provisions stipulate that "state regulation of the broadcast media shall be based on objective and non-discriminatory criteria"[7] and "shall not be used to restrict enjoyment of minority rights".[8] In order to prevent the sort of linguistic marginalisation and assimilation described above, the *Oslo Recommendations* affirmed the desirability of linguistic diversity within states.

The *Oslo* provisions reiterate the duty of states to ensure that "persons belonging to national minorities have access to broadcast time in their own language on publically funded media".[9] Such access should include an "amount and quality of time" that was "commensurate with the numerical size and concentration of the national minority" and "appropriate to is situation and needs".[10] These 'fair access' requirements were to be overseen by public bodies that were 'independent' and "should include persons belonging to national minorities".[11] Finally, "access to media originating from abroad" should not "be unduly restricted".[12]

In short, *Oslo* provides the basic framework for a minority language policy well suited to the technological context of the time in which it was drafted.

7 OSCE High Commissioner on National Minorities, *The Oslo Recommendations regarding the Linguistic Rights of National Minorities & Explanatory Note*, 1998, paragraph 8.

8 *Ibid.*, *supra* note 7, para. 8.

9 *Ibid.*, para. 9.

10 *Ibid.*, para 9.

11 *Ibid.*, para 10.

12 *Ibid.*, para 11.

But can it also offer guidance on the sort of minority language policy relevant to the digital age? Is it possible to 'take *Oslo* online'?

3 Language Inequalities on the Internet

In the twenty years since the *Oslo Recommendations* were published, a digital revolution in communications has taken place. Analogue radio and television are being phased out in favour of new digital technologies. And everywhere the Internet is becoming an increasingly important medium for language based interactions: online shopping, online dating, online chat rooms and discussion boards, online newspapers, books and encyclopaedias, online music, online movies, and increasingly also online government. The methods of governance and commerce, the language of public and of private life, and the flow of information, are all changing in response to the widespread and regular use of the Internet and digital technology more generally. If persons belonging to minorities want to establish a community organisation today, they will probably require a web address, Facebook group and Twitter account before they require a street address.

3.1 *New Technologies and the FCNM Monitoring Process*

We can see the emergence of this technological context shift and its impact on minority languages in the monitoring process related to article 9 of the *Framework Convention for the Protection of National Minorities* (FCNM). FCNM article 9 minority language provisions are similar to those in the Oslo Recommendations, so its monitoring history may be expected to highlight developments relevant to this discussion. During the first cycle of FCNM monitoring (1999–2014), there were only a few references to the effects of new digital technologies on minority language speakers. But from 2004 onwards, minorities across Europe start to engage in a more sustained way with the language opportunities online.

For example, the Frisian broadcaster *Omrop Fryslân* launched Internet based Frisian language programming, including the live streaming of important cultural and sporting events, and a 24-hour channel with only Frisian music. The Advisory Committee for the Framework Convention (ACFC) singled out these Internet based initiatives as "keeping the Frisian language alive in the daily life of persons belonging to the Frisian minority in the Netherlands".[13]

13 Secretariat of the Framework Convention for the Protection of National Minorities, Compilation of Opinions of the Advisory Committee Relating to Article 9 of the Framework Convention, Second Cycle (Strasbourg, 2 February 2016), p. 35.

Similarly, an Internet radio service entirely run and financed by Roma associations began broadcasting out of Barcelona. *Rromane Glasură* (Roma Voices) sought to reverse the poor visibility and frequent stereotyping of Roma women in the mass media by giving Roma women a platform to have their voices heard.[14] It ran on the Internet for eight months, using a mixture of Catalan, Castilian and Romani languages.[15] It subsequently merged with *Voces Gitanas*, which retains an Internet presence at the time of publication

The various ACFC reports also show that new digital technologies can give rise to new inequalities. In Spain, for example, *Rromane Glasură* stands out as an innovative example in part because it is exceptional. Unfortunately, "few Roma in Spain have the training and resources needed to produce such programmes".[16] And even when minority language speakers are able to introduce Internet-based news and information initiatives, their sustainability is often uncertain due to limited funding prospects.

As the new digital technology becomes ever more a cornerstone of our daily lives, the effect of any such inequalities is likely to intensify. For example, the most recent ACFC reports (from the current fourth monitoring cycle) flag a lack of provision for high speed Internet in remote areas that are frequently inhabited by national minorities as an issue of growing importance.[17]

3.2 *Dominant Languages of the Internet*

The Internet promises an open space for communication that is without barriers to participation. The many-to-many broadcast structure of the Internet, as opposed to the few-to-many structure of previous mass media technologies, led to hopes that cyberspace would be a site of multiplicity and diversity. Indeed, early theorists assumed that the Internet would allow marginalized voices to share space equally with the mainstream, thus allowing "users to explore multiple subjectivities by providing opportunities for varied discursive production and consumption habits".[18]

14 J. Freire, 'A radio of 'Voces gitanas': Issues of media identity and self-representation in Barcelona', 28:1 *International Journal of Iberian Studies* (2015), pp. 83–104.

15 Freire, *supra* note 14, p. 91.

16 Secretariat of the Framework Convention, *supra* note 13, p. 49.

17 Secretariat of the Framework Convention for the Protection of National Minorities, Compilation of Opinions of the Advisory Committee Relating to Article 9 of the Framework Convention, Fourth Cycle (Strasbourg, 2 February 2016), p. 3 (Croatia), p. 5 (Cyprus), p. 17 (Italy).

18 C. Wei and B. Kolko, 'Studying mobile phone use in context: Cultural, political, and economic dimensions of mobile phone use', Proceedings of the Professional Communication Conference (2005), IEEE, p. 205.

But where minority languages are concerned, this may be a false promise. There is growing evidence that power inequalities between minority and majority languages persist online, and that state action may be required to overcome these.[19] Despite impressions to the contrary, language content online is not cost free, and the resulting economies of scale privilege majority languages – just as they did in the age of print, and analogue television and radio.

Computer software must be created to enable specific language interfaces, including character and word recognition etc. As a result, official state languages tend to have a greater online presence because of the national markets that they guarantee for software producers. At the same time, states are more likely to invest in or otherwise subsidise software production in their official language(s).

Consequently, speakers of official state languages are generally able to find, access, use, produce and share far more information online than are speakers of unofficial languages.[20] And even when more than one language is officially recognized by a state (*e.g.*, as part of their domestic language policy or as an undertaking with respect to the *European Charter for Regional or Minority Languages* (*ECRML*)), the majority language tends to disproportionately outperform the minority language online.

The only exception to this rule arises where the minority language is also a majority language in another (kin) state. In such cases, there will be more available digital language content online due to the economies of scale operating in the kin-state. But the kin-minority may still struggle to access this language content, due to access restrictions that privilege domestic over international users (e.g., many Internet TV broadcasters limit their broadcasts to certain countries) or a lack of technological infrastructure in those areas where the minorities are located (e.g., limited affordable and or high speed Internet connections).

These observations do not mean there is no minority language content on the Internet – far from it. Minorities are active and engaged on the Internet.

---

19 *See among others*: D. Cunliffe, and D. Roberts-Young. 'Online design for bilingual civil society: a Welsh perspective'. 17:1, *Interacting with Computers* (2004), pp. 85–104; A. Kornai, 'Digital language death', 8(10), *PloS one*, (2013), p.e77056; S. Wright, 'Regional or Minority Languages on the WWW', 5:2, *Journal of Language and Politics* (2006), pp. 189–216; Wei and Kolko, *supra* note 18; H. Wiggers, 'Digital Divide: Low German and other Minority Languages'. 8.2, *Advances in Language and Literary Studies* (2017), pp. 130–142.

20 United Nations Educational, Scientific and Cultural Organization, *Measuring Linguistic Diversity on the Internet*, 2005, p. 44.

As a result of this online activism, many minority languages have established an Internet presence. But the bulk of this online minority language content is either bilingual (appearing in both a minority and a majority language) or symbolic (mostly in a majority language but with a small portion in a minority language).[21] Meanwhile, official languages, especially those of titular nations, and global *lingua francas* – above all English – continue to predominate.

Facebook illustrates these online language dynamics. Facebook is now a core feature of twenty-first century life. In the first quarter of 2017, there were 2 billion Facebook users worldwide, with over 307 million of them in Europe.[22] Much like the market squares of medieval Europe, Facebook is where people today go to meet and exchange information. By 2016, more than half of all online users got their news from Facebook and other social media platforms.[23]

Until 2008, Facebook was only available in English. But since then Facebook has rapidly increased its language capacity.[24] It now offers not only multiple language interfaces but also built-in translation services. As of 2017, the following European languages are fully supported on Facebook: Albanian, Basque, Belorussian, Bosnian, Breton, Bulgarian, Catalan, Corsican, Croatian, Czech, Danish, Dutch, Estonian English, Faroese, Finnish, French, Frisian, Galician, German, Greek, Hungarian, Irish, Icelandic, Italian, Latvian, Lithuanian, Macedonian, Maltese, Norwegian, Polish, Portugese, Sardinian, Serbian, Silesian, Slovak, Slovenian, Spanish, Swedish, Romanian, Russian, Ukrainian, and Welsh.[25]

Official languages, especially those associated with so called titular nations (that form majorities within states) predominate within this Facebook language list. Of these fully supported European languages, only Silesian does not have a recognized or official status in a region where it is spoken.[26] Many other

21 Wight, *supra* note 19.

22 'The Top 20 Valuable Facebook Statistics', Zephoria Digital Marketing, <zephoria.com/top-15-valuable-facebook-statistics/>, visited on 15 August 2017.

23 M. Mis, 'More than half online users get their news from Facebook, Youtube and Twitter', Reuters, June 15, 2016, <uk.reuters.com/article/us-media-socialmedia-news/more-than-half-online-users-get-news-from-facebook-youtube-and-twitter-study-idUKKCN0Z02UB>, visited on 16 August 2017.

24 A. Lenihan, 'Join Our Community of Translators: Language Ideologies and/in Facebook', in C. Thurlow and K. Mroczek (eds.). *Digital Discourse: Language in the new media* (Oxford University Press on Demand, Oxford, 2011), pp. 48–50.

25 Facebook, Settings, 'Select Your Language', 2017.

26 The positive relationship between language vitality and jurisdictional status predates the rise of digital media. *See*, for example, J. Laponce, *Languages and their Territories* (Toronto: University of Toronto Press, 1987).

regional or minority languages are absent (and thus not fully supported on Facebook) – e.g., Cornish, Kashub, Manx, Occitan, Romani and Sami, to name only a few – despite having a recognized status under the *European Charter for Regional or Minority Languages* (ECRML). Speakers of these and other unsupported languages may be able to post some comments in their minority language on Facebook. But to navigate the Facebook site and make full use of its various features, they will need to use a fully supported language – most probably a national language or a global *lingua franca* such as English.

In sum, the Internet may create beneficial opportunities for some minority language speakers (e.g., the ability to create and participate in minority language social networks). But for many others, it may have an assimilationist effect with regard to their everyday online language use. Such minority language speakers may be attracted to dominant national and global languages in order to access and take full advantage of the opportunities that this new technology creates.

3.3 *Technology and Language Assimilation*

There is a precedent for technologically driven assimilative language effects of this kind. These same sort of minority language dilemmas also arose in the context of previous innovations in communications technology.

> While the printing press helped step up the exchange of information in Europe, it also led to the extinction of many European languages. Regional and minority languages were rarely printed and languages such as Cornish and Dalmatian were limited to oral forms of transmission, which in turn restricted their scope of use. Will the Internet have the same impact on our [minority] languages?[27]

The danger is that push (lack of language interfaces in the minority language) and pull (preponderance of easily accessible resources in national or global languages) factors online will make minority language speakers opt to use dominant languages in these new cyber spaces. The result of such push and pull factors may be a loss of language vitality online. Minority languages may find themselves with only a 'heritage' language status on the Internet. In such cases, minority language use will be mostly symbolic, and at the extreme 'digital death' may result.

---

27 European Commission Directorate-General Information Society and Media, 'User language Preferences Online', 313 *Flash Eurobarometer* (2011), p. 38.

> In the digital age, these signs of incipient language death take on the following characteristics. Loss of function *performed digitally* increasingly touches every functional area from day to day communication (texting, email) to commerce, official business, and so on. Loss of prestige is clearly seen in the adage *If it's not on the web, it does not exist*, and loss of competence boils down to the ability of raising digital natives in your own language.[28]

The following hypothetical scenario makes this danger clear. Let's suppose you are a native speaker of Northern Sami (*Davvisámegiella*) with some additional language proficiency in Finnish (*Duomi*), Norwegian (*Norsk*) or Swedish (*Svenska*). You want to use Wikipedia. As of 2017, there are 420,418 Wikipedia articles available in Finnish, 473,751 available in Norwegian, 3,788,998 Wikipedia articles available in Swedish, and 7311 Wikipedia articles available in Northern Sami.[29] Which language will you use?

For such a speaker, there would be obvious advantages to using Finnish, Norwegian or Swedish in this sort of online scenario. And if our native Sami speaker – or native Finnish, Norwegian or Swedish speaker for that matter – was also sufficiently proficient in English, the potential gain in Wikipedia resources would be even greater (a further 5,466,832 Wikipedia articles available in English).[30]

Language situations like these are commonplace online today. A 2017 Gallup survey of online preferences in the EU found that: 81% of respondents occasionally used another language when browsing for information or watching or reading the news online; 62% communicate online with people in another language; 57% use another language for searching and to purchase services and products online; and 53% would happily accept the English version of a site if it weren't available in their mother tongue.[31]

Similarly, a 2013 review of language presence online carried out by the mathematical linguistic Kornai concluded that the top sixteen thriving languages in this context were English, Japanese, French, German, Spanish,

28 Kornai, *supra* note 19.

29 Wikipedia, 'List of Wikipedias', <en.wikipedia.org/wiki/List_of_Wikipedias>, visited on 17 August 2017.

30 Wikipedia, *supra* note 28.

31 Travod International Blog, '55% of EU internet users use more than one language online. What languages do users prefer online?', August 25, 2017, <www.travod.com/55-of-eu-internet-users-use-more-than-one-language-online-what-languages-do-users-prefer-online/>, visited on 11 January 2017.

Italian, Portuguese, Dutch, Swedish, Norwegian, Danish, Finnish, Russian, Polish, Chinese, and Korean.[32] Conversely, at the other end of the spectrum, Kornai estimated that the number of languages with 'heritage' (only symbolic use) or 'still' (unused) status far exceed 'even the most pessimistic survey'.[33] Kornai predicted that by the start of the 21st century, there will be fewer than three hundred languages with an online presence.[34] In other words, it is not just speakers of unrecognized, small, regional or minority languages that may encounter push and pull factors towards more dominant languages online.

3.4 *Welsh on the Internet*

The Welsh (*Cymraeg*) language is a case in point. *The* UNESCO *Atlas of World Languages in Danger* currently lists Welsh as 'vulnerable' (the least endangered status in its ranking system).[35] The Welsh language has a good deal of institutional recognition and support. Welsh is an official language in Wales, and the devolved government for Wales actively promotes it. The UK government has also recognized Welsh under its ECRML and FCNM undertakings. Several leading Internet browsers have Welsh language interfaces, including Internet Explorer, and Mozilla Firefox, as does the Google search engine and the Gmail provider.[36] As already mentioned, Facebook fully supports Welsh language, and Wikipedia identifies Welsh as its 60th strongest content language (with 92,088 articles).[37]

A 2013 report commissioned by the Government of Wales found that almost three in four Welsh speakers were satisfied with the amount of information, material and services available to them in Welsh generally.[38] But the proportion satisfied with what is available in Welsh online was noticeably lower. "… [O]nly around six in ten were satisfied with the amount, accessibility and quality of Welsh language information, material and services on the Internet".[39]

32 Kornai, *supra* note 19.

33 *Ibid.*

34 *Ibid.*

35 UNESCO, *Atlas of World Languages in Danger,* 'United Kingdom of Great Britain and Northern Ireland', <www.unesco.org/languages-atlas/index.php>, visited on 6 August 2017.

36 J. Evas, *The Welsh Language in the Digital Age,* META-NET White Paper Series, 2013, pp. 50–51, <orca.cf.ac.uk/48988/1/10006110_4950.pdf>, visited on 1 September 2017.

37 Wikipedia, *supra* note 28.

38 Beaufort Research, *Exploring Welsh speakers' language use in their daily lives*, 2013, p. 14, <www.beaufortresearch.co.uk/BBQ01260eng.pdf>, visited on 5 September 2017.

39 *Ibid.*

Despite the provision of Welsh language interfaces, "fewer than one in five Welsh speakers always or usually used Welsh online in any way".[40] Welsh speakers surveyed for the report "displayed low levels of awareness of opportunities to use the language on the web" and "even some who were fluent, regular users of Welsh could not easily think of examples of sites with Welsh language content".[41] Instead, when using the Internet and especially as regards social media, English was found to have a distinct advantage over Welsh. Welsh speakers identified English as a more 'convenient language in online contexts'.[42]

In part, the 'convenience' of English online was a consequence of predictive text features on mobile devices that do not accommodate the Welsh language.[43] This software limitation disproportionately affects social media language usage. Mobile devices are a preferred medium for what are widely thought of as instant, spur of the moment social media communications of this kind. "The issue of awareness therefore combined with the notion that English was the default language online, to create a significant barrier to making more use of Welsh online..."[44]

3.5 *Basque on the Internet*

Similar push and pull factors have been noted with respect to the Basque (*Euskara*) language online. Like Welsh, Basque is also ranked as 'vulnerable' by UNESCO, which means it is in a good position relative to other languages on the endangered languages list.[45] Basque is also a recognized regional language in Spain (in the Basque Autonomous Community and in Northern Navarre) and with respect to Spain's obligations under the ECRML. The devolved government of the Basque Autonomous Community actively promotes it. There are Basque interfaces for Mozilla Firefox, YouTube, Google, Gmail, Twitter and of course Facebook.[46] Wikipedia identifies Basque as its 31st strongest content language, with 283,018 articles (three times more resources than are currently available in Welsh).[47]

40 Beaufort, *supra* note 37, p. 12.

41 Beaufort, *supra* note 37, p. 68.

42 Beaufort, *supra* note 37, p. 18.

43 Beaufort, *supra* note 37, pp. 63–64.

44 Bueafort, *supra* note 37, p. 68.

45 UNESCO, *supra* note 34, 'Spain', <www.unesco.org/languages-atlas/index.php>, visited on 1 September 2017.

46 I. Hernaez *et al.*, *The Basque Language in the Digital Age*, META-NET White Paper Series, 2012, p. 37, <www.meta-net.eu/whitepapers/e-book/basque.pdf>, visited on 5 September 2017.

47 Wikipedia, *supra* note 28.

Yet according to a 2012 Report by Meta-Net, only 22.9% of Basque language speakers online use the Basque language on the Internet.[48] Facilities for the use of Basque online at that time were reported as "still very limited when compared to the resources and tools for the Spanish language".[49] A further survey conducted in 2017 by the Digital Language Diversity Project found that respondents had "a strong desire to be able to use Basque on the Internet as part of their everyday life. There is a high level of agreement on not considering Basque as a spoken language that cannot be used on the Internet or not worth it".[50] However, "nearly a third part of the respondents feel that using Spanish is easier on the Internet".[51]

3.6 *Cornish on the Internet*

For less well supported regional or minority languages, the push and pull factors driving speakers towards national or global languages are likely to be even greater. The Cornish (*Kernewek*) language is instructive in this respect. Cornish does have a recognized status. In 2002, the UK recognized Cornish under the ECRML, and as of 2014 that recognition was extended to include the UK's obligations under the FCNM.[52] Cornish receives support from both regional and national governments in the UK. It also has an official administrative body responsible for its promotion, the Cornish Language Partnership.[53] Nevertheless, the *UNESCO Atlas of World Languages in Danger* currently lists Cornish as 'critically endangered' (second from the bottom in its language vitality ranking system).[54]

A 2015 report on the Cornish language strategy commissioned by Cornwall County Council identified the "digital media in particular ... as a potential

48 Hernaez, *supra* note 45, p. 47.

49 *Ibid.*, p. 62.

50 A Hernaiz et al., 'Basque – a digital language?', The Digital Language Diversity Project, p. 10, <www.dldp.eu/sites/default/files/documents/DLDP_Basque-Report.pdf>, visited on 6 September 2017.

51 *Ibid.*, p. 10.

52 Government of the United Kingdom, 'Cornish granted minority status within the UK', 24 April 2014, <www.gov.uk/government/news/cornish-granted-minority-status-within-the-uk>, visited on 6 September 2017.

53 'The Cornish Language Partnership', Cornish Culture, <cornishculture.co.uk/portfolio/the-cornish-language-partnership/>, visited on 6 September 2017.

54 UNESCO, *supra* note 34, 'United Kingdom', <www.unesco.org/languages-atlas/index.php>, visited on 1 September 2017.

growth area for the use of Cornish".[55] Cornish has some presence on the Internet and is used in social media.[56] For example, although Cornish is not a fully supported language on Facebook, there are several Facebook groups which promote it.[57] There are also several webpages dedicated to learning or promoting Cornish, such as the Cornish Language Fellowship.[58] But these various sites are almost all bilingual (Cornish / English). Experts suggest that Cornish speakers "learn to use the computer in English" and this limits online engagement in Cornish.[59] There are just 3791 Wikipedia articles in Cornish, almost half the number currently available in Northern Sami.[60] In sum, Cornish only (just) functions as a 'heritage language' online.

3.7 *Promoting Minority Language Rights Online*

Clearly, the Internet is not a straightforward context for minority language communications. As the Welsh, Basque and Cornish examples demonstrate, it is difficult (but not impossible) for minority languages to acquire and maintain an online presence. Conversely, it is much easier for minority languages to decline into 'digital obscurity' and even 'digital death'.

In the technological context of the twenty-first century, policy makers need to be thinking seriously about how minority language use can be promoted via new technologies, including online. How, in other words, might we be able to 'take the *Oslo Recommendations* online' in order to support digital language diversity? Are there any 'best practice' examples of minority language policy on the Internet that might offer guidance in this respect?

---

55 G. Ioan and M. Jones, *Cornish Language Strategy 2015–2025: Evaluation and Development Report*, p. 10, <www.cornwall.gov.uk/media/21486321/final-report-on-cornish-language-strategy-110315.pdf>, visited on 5 September 2017.

56 *Ibid.*, p. 14.

57 *See*, for example: MAGA – Sodhva an Taves Kernewek / Cornish Language Office, <www.facebook.com/magakernow/>, visited 6 September 2017; Kowethas: The Cornish Language Fellowship, <www.facebook.com/Kowethas/>, visited on 6 September 2017; and Gorsedh Kernow, <www.facebook.com/gorsedhkernow/>, visited on 6 September 2017.

58 Cornish Language Fellowship, <www.cornish-language.org/>, visited on 5 September 2017.

59 Indigenous Tweets, 'Not dead yet: John Gillingham on the Cornish Language', 1 May 2011, <indigenoustweets.blogspot.co.uk/2011/05/not-dead-yet-john-gillingham-on-cornish.html>, visited on 5 September 2017.

60 Wikipedia, *supra* note 28.

4 Case Study: 'Internet Bilingualism' in Canada

Canada is an interesting case to review in the context of digital language diversity because over the past two decades it has pioneered a policy of 'Internet bilingualism'. Canada is formally a bilingual state at the federal level, and its bilingual federal governance structures are both well developed and commensurate with much of the *Oslo Recommendations*.[61] Canadian federal policies to preserve and promote bilingualism on the Internet thus offer a unique insight into the kind of measures that might be required to 'take *Oslo* online'.

4.1 *Canada's Official Languages Policy*

Canada's *Official Languages Act* guarantees equality of status and equal rights and privileges for English and French in all federal institutions.[62] This equal status extends to parliamentary proceedings, legislative and other instruments, the administration of justice, the provision of communications and public services and the work of federal institutions. The act mandates federal government support for English and French linguistic minority communities as well as action to enhance the equality of status and use of the English and French languages within Canadian society. It details the powers, duties and functions of federal institutions with respect to the official languages of Canada.

The *Official Languages Act* also creates the Office of the Commissioner of Official Languages with a mandate to ensure that its objectives are fulfilled.[63] As an ombudsman, the Commissioner receives and reviews complaints, and where required investigates. He also conducts investigations on his own initiative, when appropriate. The Commissioner thus plays a key role in promotion and public awareness of the official languages.

61 The *Official Languages Act* does not apply to provincial or municipal governments or to private businesses. As a result, provincial language policies in Canada vary. Most Canadian provinces have laws that make either English or both English and French the official language(s) of the legislature and the courts, but may operate different policies in regards to education and the civil service. Nunevat and the Northwest Territories both recognise indigenous languages in addition to English and French. For more information on the *Official Languages Act*, see Office of the Commissioner of Official Languages, 'Understanding Your Language Rights', <www.officiallanguages.gc.ca/en/language_rights/act>, visited 5 September 2017.

62 Office of the Commissioner of Official Languages, 'Understanding Your Language Rights', <www.officiallanguages.gc.ca/en/language_rights/act>, visited 5 September 2017.

63 *Ibid.*, 'Mandate and Roles', <www.officiallanguages.gc.ca/en/aboutus/mandate>, visited on 5 September 2017.

In sum, although Canadian bilingualism pre-dates the *Oslo Recommendations*, it is nevertheless a good approximation of *Oslo*'s core content and general approach to minority languages. Canadian policies and practices adopted 'to take bilingualism online' are thus likely to be highly relevant to those efforts intended 'to take *Oslo* online'. They may stand as 'best practice' examples for other states wishing to develop and implement online minority language policies.

By the start of the new millennium, there was already evidence of an emerging 'digital divide' between Canada's language communities. Statistics Canada reported that French language speakers were less likely to use the Internet than English language speakers. While 58% of English speaking Canadians used the Internet in 2002, only 44% of French-speaking Canadians did likewise, and trends suggested that the digital divide between Anglophones and Francophones was likely to widen. Whereas almost all young English speakers who used the Internet believed there was sufficient online content in their language, only 59% of French speakers felt the same about their language.[64] The Canadian government therefore concluded that the "introduction of new technologies ... has the potential to create new inequalities in Canada, and we must be careful to minimize the negative impact of technological change".[65]

The starting point for Canada's 'Internet bilingualism' was its longstanding commitment to bilingualism at the federal level. 'Internet bilingualism' was a corollary of prior language policy pursued in the context of earlier technologies (print, and analogue radio and television). When the new digital technologies emerged, the Canadian government initiated a series of policy reviews intended to identify those measures need to transpose this longstanding bilingual policy onto cyber spaces.

As early as 1999, the Government of Canada recognised that the rise of digital technologies, including the Internet, must unavoidably affect Canadian language policies.

> The consequences of the digital revolution on the application of the *Official Languages Act* are enormous, because they directly affect the delivery of government services (Part IV of the Act) and the language of

64 Alain Clavet, *French on the Internet: Key to the Canadian Identity and the Knowledge Economy*, Follow-up Study by the Commissioner of Official Languages, 2002, p. 3, <publications.gc.ca/collections/Collection/SF31-60-2002E.pdf>, visited on 7 September 2017.

65 *Ibid.*, p. 3.

> work in the public service (Part V). But the most significant impact probably relates to Part VII of the Act, which states that the federal government is committed to promoting the full recognition and use of English and French in Canadian society. Clearly, then, the principle of linguistic duality applies and must be applied to the Internet.[66]

Accordingly, the Canadian federal government launched three strategic initiatives to address concerns raised with regard to bilingualism online.

Firstly, efforts were made to support the development of a critical mass of French language content on the Internet. Action concentrated upon four main areas: original French language content production, translation of existing digital resources into French, digitization of French print resources, and access related issues such as the availability of high speed Internet connections in minority communities.[67] This action was regarded as analogous to prior efforts made in respect of the provision of French language television.[68]

Secondly, the Canadian federal government undertook to ensure that norms and standards to encourage the use of French in information technologies and on the Internet were established and enforced. Efforts were also made to support the development of advanced technolinguistic tools in French.[69]

Finally, actions to support the development of French language on the Internet and connectivity and linguistic diversity online were incorporated within Canada's foreign policy related activities.[70] Canada's role as a member of La Francophonie (an international organization representing countries with significant French speaking populations) was particularly relevant in this context.[71]

By 2004, the Commissioner of Official Languages concluded:

> One can say now, with no hesitation, that Canada provides major support for the development and expansion of access to a critical mass of French-language content on the Internet, that it has taken measures to create conditions in which its language industry can structure itself strategically in order to meet the challenges posed by the increasing multilingualism of the Internet, and that its foreign policy helps to ensure that

66 *Ibid.*, p. 1.
67 *Ibid.*, p. 9.
68 *Ibid.*, p. 10.
69 *Ibid.*, p. 19.
70 *Ibid.*, p. 27.
71 *Ibid.*, p. 28.

> the international Francophonie is more firmly entrenched in the Information Society.[72]

There are a number of lessons to be learned from the Canadian case as regards the implications for applying the *Oslo Recommendations* in the new digital and online context. First, and most importantly, government action can improve the scope and content of minority languages online. With positive action measures, minority languages can establish a viable online presence sufficient to provide a reasonable basis for their continued use by minority language speakers. In other words, contrary to what Kornai (2013) has argued, 'digital death' is not necessarily a foregone conclusion for smaller, regional or minority languages.[73]

Secondly, the actions required in the new digital context are not radically different from those policies successfully implemented by governments in the age of print, and analogue radio and television broadcasting. In both contexts, the guarantee of minority access to the new technologies is essential.

Finally, if it is possible to 'take Canadian bilingualism online', then it is also possible to 'take the *Oslo Recommendations* online'. Canada's official languages policies, although developed in a different technological context, were nevertheless able to provide normative guidance to policy makers in the new digital context. By the same token, despite the passage of time and technology, the *Oslo Recommendations* remain a useful reference for state policies to ensure the effective implementation of minority language rights, including on the Internet.

5 How Should States Take Oslo Online?

Although much has changed in the twenty years since the *Oslo Recommendations* were launched, much also remains the same. Language continues to be a fundamental component of human identity. The context – be it online or offline – in which language interactions take place does not change this fundamental fact. Accordingly, respect for identity requires a respect for language use – *in both contexts*. Similarly, freedom of expression includes the right to

---

72 Government of Canada, *Final Report of the Government in response to the study by the Commissioner of Official Languages: French on the Internet: Key to Canadian Identity and the Knowledge Economy*, 2004, p. 29, <publications.gc.ca/collections/Collection/CH44-51-2004E.pdf>, visited on 7 September 2017.

73 Kornai, *supra* note 19.

impart or receive information and ideas of all sorts, regardless of frontiers, *in the medium or language of one's choice.* As the United Nations Special Rapporteur on the promotion and protection of the right to freedom of opinion and expression noted in 2011, "the Internet has become a key means by which individuals can exercise their right to freedom of opinion and expression, as guaranteed by article 19 of the Universal Declaration of Human Rights and the International Covenant on Civil and Political Rights".[74]

In terms of the *Oslo Recommendations*, the implications for minority language policy on the Internet are clear. *Minority language speakers have a right to access, produce and distribute information and ideas in digital media, including the Internet, in their minority language.* States, in their implementation of the *Oslo Recommendations*, should therefore take online contexts seriously.

With respect to community life and NGOs, minority organisations and associations may use the language of their choice online, and the state should not discriminate against these entities on the basis of their online language choice. If the state supports online activity in the social, cultural and sports spheres, then an equitable share of the total resources available from the state should be directed to minority language activity online.

The state should offer the same support to minority language content online as it does to minority language content in traditional media (such as print, television and radio). Persons belonging to minorities have the right to establish their own 'new media' (means of mass communication using digital technologies such as the Internet). Minority language speakers should have access to publically funded 'new media' content commensurate with the numerical size of the minority and appropriate to its situation and needs. State regulation of 'new media' should be based on objective and non-discriminatory criteria, and should not be used to restrict the enjoyment of minority rights.

Public bodies overseeing online content or the move to digitalization of radio and television should be independent and should include minority language speakers serving in their independent capacity. Such bodies should make every effort to ensure equal access to new digital technologies (such as affordable and high speed Internet) for minority language speakers who may be concentrated in remote or hard to reach areas. Due attention should also be

74 United Nations, *Report of the Special Rapporteur on the promotion and protection of the right of freedom of expression*, Frank La Rue, A/HRC/17/27, 16 May 2011, p. 7, <www2.ohchr.org/english/bodies/hrcouncil/docs/17session/A.HRC.17.27_en.pdf>, visited on 7 September 2017.

given to problems of hate speech online and cyber bullying, both of which may disproportionately affect persons belonging to minorities.

Access to online minority language content originating from abroad, e.g., a kin state, should not be unduly restricted. Instead, states should be encouraged to make respect for digital diversity a key component of their cross-border co-operation and cultural diplomacy.

Persons belonging to minorities also have the right to operate online businesses in the language or languages of their choice. The state should only require the additional use of the official language or languages in e-commerce where legitimate public interest can be demonstrated.

In regions and localities where minority language speakers are present in significant numbers, and where the desire has been expressed, states should ensure that all public services, laws and policies, court decisions and other information available online in the official language(s) is also available in the minority language(s). In other words, e-government in such areas should take into consideration the rights and interests of minority language speakers.

6 Conclusion

New digital technologies have enormous potential for minority language speakers. They can provide easily accessible platforms for social networking, and communications within minority language communities. They can bring together communities of language speakers who may otherwise be isolated from one another, either within or across frontiers. They can support minority language vitality in a number of areas, including education, culture and commerce. They can offer new ways for minorities to interact with their respective governments in the language of their choice.

But digital technologies will only have these beneficial outcomes for minority language speakers *if positive measures are taken to support the online presence of minority languages*. Accessibility is the key to ensuring minority language rights are respected online.

Minority language speakers must be able to access the new digital technology. This means that universal, affordable and high quality broadband Internet and digital networks should be universally available within states – including those regions where persons belonging to minorities reside. It also means that language interfaces online and in devices (e.g., mobile phones) used to access the Internet should be compatible with minority languages.

Minority language speakers should also be able to access sufficient online resources in their minority language. This means that e-government should be in minority languages where relevant. It also means that digital media available online (e.g., digital radio and television) should have sufficient minority language content.

Unless or until the *Oslo Recommendations* are taken seriously in the new digital context, persons belonging to minorities will not be able to realize the full potential of these new technologies in their minority languages. A clear commitment by states to 'take *Oslo* online' is therefore urgently required.

CHAPTER 15

Language Rights and Duties for New Minorities: Integration through Diversity Governance

Joseph Marko and Roberta Medda-Windischer

1 Introduction

Diversity governance is a challenging and complex matter that is at the forefront of the current political and public debate in almost all European countries. This is largely due to the increasing number of peoples – especially migrants and asylum seekers – with distinctive identities in terms of language, culture, or religion in urban as well as in more peripheral and rural contexts with varying degrees of permanence. Their reasons are partly political and humanitarian, partly a result of differing economic situations and the freedom of movement that growing migration to Europe, especially into the European Union, entails.[1]

Although economic actors and decision makers generally recognize the useful contribution to the labour force and the positive impact on the demographic structure of a steadily ageing population, the presence of large immigrant and refugee communities poses manifold challenges in the sphere of integration with regard to cultural and linguistic differences, protection of individual and group rights, and the preservation of social cohesion and unity. Identity claims, including linguistic claims, and economic rights however are not separate issues, as diversity claims very often arise precisely in labour and employment environments. Accommodation of diversity and labour market inclusion are indeed complementary and intimately intertwined, thus one cannot be solved without the other.

1 *See* Eurostat, *Migration and Migrant Population Statistics* (data from March 2017), <www.ec.europa.eu/eurostat/statistics-explained/index.php/Migration_and_migrant_population_statistics>; IOM, *World Migration Report 2018* (International Organization for Migration, Geneva, 2017); UNHCR, *Global Appeal – 2017 Update*, <www.reporting.unhcr.org/sites/default/files/ga2017/pdf/GA_2017%20Update%20Eng_Book_low-res.pdf>. The enlargement of the European Union, in particular, has made, and is likely to continue to make, these movements even more complex: new member states and acceding countries have not, in the past, focused on the integration of migrants or refugees as these countries have tended to be transit countries or even countries of origin.

© KONINKLIJKE BRILL NV, LEIDEN, 2018 | DOI 10.1163/9789004357754_016

The right to identity in diversity is also intimately linked to language.[2] Language is not only an important tool to communicate, but also for identity formation; language rights are thus based on a 'duality of structures'[3] in the form of the *multidimensionality* and *multifunctionality*: languages as an *instrumental medium* of communication as well as a substantial element for *personal and social identity formation* in the construction of 'meaning, trust and order'.[4] In this regard Kraus refers to language as a gate and as a tie.[5]

The *politics* of language have been always an ideological, political and legal contest for linguistic, and thus socio-cultural and political control, based on processes of language standardisation through selection of a particular language, usually that of the most powerful group, discouraging at the same time the use of other languages or even varieties (dialects) of the same language in the public sphere, thereby encouraging users to develop loyalty and pride in it.[6]

2 The Supreme Court of Canada has clarified this point in *Ford v. Quebec* (1988) by saying that "[l]anguage is not merely a means or medium of expression; […]. It is a means by which a people may express its cultural identity. It is also the means by which one expresses one's personal identity and sense of individuality".

3 A. Giddens, *The Constitution of Society: Outline of the Theory of Structuration* (University of California Press, Berkeley, 1984).

4 S.N. Eisenstadt, *Power, Trust, and Meaning. Essays in Sociological Theory and Analysis* (University of Chicago Press, Chicago, 1995). *See also*, S. Vertovec and S. Wessendorf, Centre on Migration, Policy and Society (COMPAS), *Migration and Cultural, Religious and Linguistic Diversity in Europe: An overview of issues and trends*, Working Paper No. 18 (University of Oxford, 2005) p.34,<www.compas.ox.ac.uk/media/WP-2005-018-Vertovec-Wessendorf_Religious_Linguistic_Diversity.pdf>.

5 P.A. Kraus and R. Kazlauskaite-Gürbüz, 'Addressing linguistic diversity in the European Union : Strategies and dilemmas', 14:4 *Ethnicities* (2014) pp. 517–538, p. 521. Kraus relates this approach to Ralf Dahrendorf's distinction between options and ligatures, according to which 'Options are possibilities of choice'; they provide us with 'structural opportunities for choice, thereby offering a template for our individual choices and decisions'. Ligatures, in contrast 'are allegiances; one might call them bonds or linkages as well'. R. Dahrendorf, *Life Chances: Approaches to Social and Political Theory* (University of Chicago Press, Chicago, 1979), *cit.* P.A. Kraus and R. Kazlauskaite-Gürbüz, 'Addressing linguistic diversity in the European Union: Strategies and dilemmas', *ibid.*, p. 521.

6 J. Marko *et al.*, *Minority Protection by Complex Diversity Governance. Law, Ideology, and Politics in European Perspective* (Routledge, London, New York, forthcoming 2018). Sonntag and Cardinal refer to 'language regimes' as concerning not only language practices but also "conceptions of language and language use as projected through state policies and as acted upon by language users". S.K. Sonntag and L. Cardinal (eds.), *State Traditions and Language Regimes* (McGill-Queen's University Press, Montreal, Kingston, 2015) p. 6.

Language standardisation and the creation of a 'monolingual habitus'[7] – with or without legally declaring the majority language the official language of the state – goes hand in hand with the need for standardized public education and literacy demands for the labour force which is thus postulated a 'normal', instrumental requirement. As a consequence, bi- or multilingual education and the use of languages other than the dominant or official language, i.e. minority languages or migrant languages, seem to require an exemption from this rule of monolingualism in public education, the economy, administration or politics.[8]

Language *policies* have thus political and social consequences; they can reinforce or diffuse conflicts, tensions or social unrest between language groups, they accelerate language loss or facilitate language revitalization, and they can be instruments of inclusion or exclusion.[9] Limitations on people's ability to use their native language – and limited facility in speaking the dominant or official national language – can in fact exclude people from education, political life and access to justice.[10]

But how to reconcile the demands for linguistic diversity and political unity, that is, how to create a political community that is both cohesive and stable and satisfies the legitimate aspirations of minorities, including new minorities?[11] Which public policies should be implemented to achieve this

7 *See*, I. Gogolin, *Der monolinguale 'Habitus' der multilingualen Schule.* (Waxman-Verlag, Münster, New York, 1994).

8 J. Marko *et al.*, *Minority Protection by Complex Diversity Governance. Law, Ideology, and Politics in European Perspective*, (Routledge, London, New York, forthcoming 2018).

9 S.K. Sonntag and L. Cardinal (eds.), *State Traditions and Language Regimes* (McGill-Queen's University Press, Montreal, Kingston, 2015) p. 3.

10 *See* OSCE High Commissioner on National Minorities, *Graz Recommendations on Access to Justice and National Minorities* (Organization for Security and Co-operation in Europe, The Hague, 2017); United Nations, *Human Development Report – 2004*, <www.hdr.undp.org/en/reports/global/2004>; T. Skutnabb-Kangas, 'Human Rights and Language Policy in Education', in S. May and N. Hornberger, *Encyclopedia of Language and Education* (Springer, New York, 2008) pp. 107–119.

11 On social cohesion, *see* the seminal study by R. Putnam, *Bowling Alone: the Collapse and Revival of American Community* (Simon & Schuster, New York, 2001); *and also* D. Stolle, S. Soroka and R. Johnston, 'When Does Diversity Erode Trust? Neighborhood Diversity, Interpersonal Trust and the Mediating Effect of Social Interactions', 56 *Political Studies* (2008) pp. 57–75; C. Kelser and I. Bloemraad, 'Does Immigration Erode Social Capital? The Conditional Effects of Immigration-Generated Diversity on Trust, Membership, and Participation across 19 Countries, 1981–2000', 42:2 *Canadian Journal of Political Science/Revue Canadienne de science politique* (2010) pp. 319–347; A. Portes and E. Vickstrom, 'Diversity, Social Capital, and Cohesion', 37 *Annual Review of Sociology* (2011) pp. 461–479.

aim?[12] And how to overcome thereby the risk of essentialisation of minority cultures by political mobilisation leading to the division of societies into us-versus-them antagonisms?[13] Hence, the theoretical as well as political challenge for diversity governance is the problem how to foster *multiple integration* into the host society, but simultaneously to allow for a remaining identification with the culture of the society of origin or minority group within this society and thereby to avoid institutional segregation from common institutions or sectors for living-together, in particular the public educational system and the labour market, possibly leading to socio-economic 'down-ward' assimilation within ethnic ghettos and complete cultural marginalization.[14]

Indeed, if it is certain from a human and minority rights perspective that *fundamental human rights and liberties* such as the right to existence, identity in diversity, freedom of expression and association must be accorded to all human beings, it is less certain, however, which are the *specific legal obligations of states* in language matters towards persons belonging to historical minorities and new minority groups stemming from migration. Moroever, these obligations are less clear when they are connected to claims vis-à-vis the state to adopt special measures to ensure appropriate conditions for the preservation and development of group identities. This question is, depending on the ideological positions adopted, hotly contested even within the context of human and minority rights protection.

In the following, this chapter discusses language rights and duties for new minorities originating from recent migration flows by relying on the analysis

---

12 *See among many*, J. Marko, *Multiple Diversity Governance through Law? Political Theory, Ideology and Norm Contestation in European Context: An Interdisciplinary Approach* (forthcoming, 2018); J. Marko, 'Ethnopolitics: The Challenge for Human and Minority Rights Protection', in C. Corradetti (ed.), *Philosophical Dimensions of Human Rights: Some Contemporary Views* (Springer, Dordrecht, Heidelberg, 2012); C. Joppke, *The Role of the State in Cultural Integration: Trends, Challenges, and Way Ahead* (Migration Policy Institute, Washington DC, 2012).

13 *See* J. Marko *et al.*, *Minority Protection by Complex Diversity Governance. Law, Ideology, and Politics in European Perspective* (Routledge, London, New York, forthcoming 2018); S. Vertovec and S. Wessendorf, Centre on Migration, Policy and Society (COMPAS), *Migration and Cultural, Religious and Linguistic Diversity in Europe: An overview of issues and trends,* Working Paper No. 18 (University of Oxford, 2005), p. 37, <www.compas.ox.ac.uk/media/WP-2005-018-Vertovec-Wessendorf_Religious_Linguistic_Diversity.pdf>.

14 For an analysis of the dualism of social integration, *see* J. Marko *et al.*, *Minority Protection by Complex Diversity Governance. Law, Ideology, and Politics in European Perspective* (Routledge, London, New York, forthcoming 2018) based on H. Esser, 'Integration und ethnische Schichtung', 40 *Mannheimer Zentrum für Europäische Sozialforschung* (2001) p. 19.

of legal and policy documents as well as previous literature and empirical studies conducted in this field. The chapter is structured in three sections: the first section provides the basis for the following parts by analyzing the alleged dichotomy between old and new minorities; the second section explores the normative framework pertaining to language rights and duties for new minorities, in particular as residence, family reunion and citizenship are concerned; in the third part, three major ambits in which language policies for new minorities have a particular relevance, namely education, the labour market and the law enforcement system, are analysed. The chapter concludes with some final remarks concerning future challenges and possible solutions.

2 Old and New Minorities: Setting the Grounds

In almost all European countries live communities whose members have a distinct language, religion, or socio-cultural practices as compared to the rest of the population and who have become minorities through the redrawing of international borders, having seen the sovereignty of their territories shift from one country to another. These are ethnic groups that have not achieved statehood on their own, for various reasons, and that have now become part of a larger country (or several countries): they are the so-called 'old minorities'.[15] In many, but not all cases, their co-ethnics may be numerically or politically dominant in another state, which they therefore regard as their 'external national homeland' or kin-state.[16]

Similar to the case of old minorities, in most European countries there are groups formed by individuals and families who have left their original homelands to emigrate to other countries: these are the so-called 'new minorities'.[17]

15 *See* R. Brubaker, *Ethnicity without Groups* (Harvard University Press, Harvard, 2004); A.D. Smith, *Nationalism: Theory, Ideology, History* (Polity Press, Cambridge, 2nd ed., 2010); M. Keating, *Nations Against the State* (Palgrave Macmillan, London, 2002); T.J. Mabry *et al.* (eds.), *Divided Nations and European Integration* (University of Pennsylvania Press, Philadelphia, 2013); J. Marko, *Minority Protection by Multiple Diversity Governance. Law, Ideology, and Politics in European Perspective* (Routledge, 2018 forthcoming).

16 See OSCE High Commissioner on National Minorities, *The Bolzano/Bozen Recommendations on National Minorities in Inter-State Relations* (Organization for Security and Co-operation in Europe, The Hague, 2008).

17 It is important to note that 'new minorities', as any other groupings of people, are communities based on fictitious constructions and narratives, or, following the classic Andersonian definition of national communities, they are 'imagined communities' resulting from the 'social construction of reality'. (B. Anderson, *Imagined Communities: Reflections*

In most cases, their reasons are economic, although political reasons play an increasingly important role as well. New minorities thus consist of migrants and refugees, and their descendants, who are living in a country other than that of their origin, on a basis that is more than merely transitional. They encompass multiple variations of situations ranging from acute refugee situations to economic migrants and their family reunification.

It must be acknowledged that the term 'new minorities' is subject to difficulties and criticism because it encompasses an enormous variation of situations. The use of the term is intended to refer to 'distinct' groups, and it by no means implies a weakening of their status. It aims to offer additional legal tools with which to respond to their specific needs for protection.[18] Moreover, the term 'new minorities' is broader than the term 'migrants', as it encompasses not only the first generation of migrants, but also their descendants, extending to include second and third generations of individuals with a background of migration, many of whom have been born in the country of immigration and who cannot objectively or subjectively be subsumed under the category of 'migrants'. Finally, the term 'new minorities' emphasizes the diversity of the individuals concerned, as well as their related individual and collective rights, whereas the term 'migrants' does not.[19]

According to Walzer, immigrants are regarded as having chosen to leave their original cultures, with the awareness that the success of their decisions depends upon integrating into the mainstream of their new societies.[20] In such

on the Origin and Spread of Nationalism (Verso, London, New York, 1983). New minorities then come into existence through processes of group formation in terms of social organisation such as family reunification, economic networks and forming civil and political associations. Commenting on Brubaker's definition of ethnic groups according to which "[ethnic groups] are collective cultural representation [...] that sustain the vision and division of the special world in racial, ethnic, or national terms" (R. Brubaker, *Ethnicity without Groups* (Harvard University Press, Harvard, 2004)), Marko clarifies that "(w)henever people define this situation as 'real' the consequences following from their actions are no less 'real' than the 'existence' of things". (J. Marko, *Minority Protection by Multiple Diversity Governance. Law, Ideology, and Politics in European Perspective* (Routledge, 2018 forthcoming).

18 *See* ACFC, *The Framework Convention: a Key Tool to Managing Diversity through Minority Rights*, Thematic Commentary no. 4, 2016; and ACFC, *Opinion on Cyprus, adopted on 6 April 2001*, ACFC/INF/OP/I(2002)004, para. 17.

19 For an analysis on new minorities, *see* R. Medda-Windischer, 'Integration of Old and New Minorities: Beyond a Janus-faced Perspective', 14 *European Yearbook of Minority Issues* (2017).

20 *See* M. Walzer, 'Pluralism: A Political Perspective', in W. Kymlicka (ed.), *The Rights of Minority Cultures* (Oxford University Press, Oxford, 1995) pp. 139–154.

cases, ethnic diversity arises from the *voluntary* decisions of individuals or families to uproot themselves and join another society. In contrast, Walzer argues, old minorities remain focused on their historic homelands. These groups find themselves in a minority position, not because they have uprooted themselves from their homeland, but because their homeland has been incorporated within the boundaries of a larger state. In most cases, this incorporation was *involuntary*, resulting from conquest, colonization or the ceding of territory from one imperial power to another. Under these circumstances, it is argued, minorities are rarely satisfied with models based on non-discrimination, individual rights and, eventually, integration. As proposed by Walzer, they desire 'national liberation' (i.e. some form of collective self-government) in order to ensure the continued development of their distinct culture. This differentiation could be called into question, however, largely because it is debatable whether migrants have truly made a voluntary 'choice' to migrate. This applies not only to refugees or those fleeing from wars or natural disasters, but also to 'labour migrants' escaping from economic distress.

A crucial issue in discussing language rights is that claims of minorities – old and new minorities alike – are often perceived as a challenge and antagonistic to the traditional model of culturally homogeneous nation states because both groups seek to increase, within this model, opportunities to express their identities and diversities at individual and group level. Moreover, old minorities and new groups stemming from migration are often perceived as 'foreigners' in the state where they live. Members of historical and new minorities are – even after generations – seen as loyal to their kin-state or to the original state whose citizens the first generation migrants had been as long as they are not absorbed into the national body through assimilation.

Historically, new minorities stemming from migration have reacted very differently than historical minorities to societies dominated by an ethnic majority. Unlike historical minorities whose cultural traditions may predate the establishment of the state that their members are now citizens of, in general few migrant groups object to the requirement that they must learn the official language of the host state as a condition of citizenship,[21] or that their children must learn the official language in school. Migrants usually accept that their life chances and those of their children depend largely on the participation in mainstream institutions operating in the majority language.[22]

21 *See* R. van Oers, *Deserving Citizenship: Citizenship Tests in Germany, the Netherlands and the United Kingdom* (Martinus Nijhoff Publishers, Leiden, Boston, 2014).

22 W. Kymlicka, *Politics in the Vernacular, Nationalism, Multiculturalism, and Citizenship* (Oxford University Press, Oxford, 2001) pp. 152–172.

Problems related to integration of second and third generations can be quite acute with regard to new minorities, though this also applies to a certain extent to traditional minorities, especially in the case of mixed marriages,. The children of second and third generations are in fact subjected to the decisions taken by their parents and their living with two cultures and languages can be perceived either as an enriching experience or, more frequently, as an excessive burden. This is due to the fact that often the second and third generations of new minorities' descendants have less cultural distance from the host society than their parents, but they have not reached a satisfactory degree of integration from a socio-economic viewpoint. In comparison to their parents, their expectations are as high as those of their 'pairs' without a migration background, and consequently, the risk of frustration and alienation from mainstream society may be very high.[23]

In the discussion on minorities and diversity, an ongoing debate is whether the scope of application of international treaties pertaining to minorities that are usually applied to historical, old minorities can be extended to new minority groups stemming from migration.[24] The positions in this regard are extremely diversified: among states, some have adopted rather narrow views firmly opposing the extension of minority provisions to new minorities,[25] others

23 *See* R. Alba and J. Holdaway, *The Children of Immigrants at School: A Comparative Look at Integration in the United States and Western Europe* (New York University Press, New York, London, 2013); C. Wihtol de Wenden, 'Second Generations: Citizenship and Transnationalism', 2 *Mondi Migranti* (2015) pp. 7–31.

24 R. Hofmann, *The Impact of International Norms on the Protection of National Minorities in Europe: The Added Value and Essential Role of the Framework Convention for the Protection of National Minorities*, Council of Europe Document DH-MIN(2006)18, 2006; W. Kymlicka, *Multicultural Odysseys: Navigating the New International Politics of Diversity* (Oxford University Press, Oxford, New York, 2007); R. Medda-Windischer, 'Integration of Old and New Minorities: Beyond a Janus-faced Perspective', 14 *European Yearbook of Minority Issues* (2017); R. Medda-Windischer, *Old and New Minorities: Reconciling Diversity and Cohesion* (Nomos, Baden-Baden, 2009); C. Joppke, 'Minority Rights for Immigrants? Multiculturalism versus Antidiscrimination', 43:49 *Israel Law Review* (2010) pp. 49–66; *and also*, J. Jackson-Preece, 'Positive Measures and the EU Equality Directives: Closing the Protection Gap Between 'New' and 'Old' Minorities Through the Reasonable Accommodation of Religion?', 9 *EYMI* (2010) pp. 519–550. Specifically on language rights for old and new minorities, *see* G. Poggeschi, *Language Rights and Duties in the Evolution of Public Law* (Baden-Baden, Nomos, 2013).

25 Council of Europe, FCNM, List of Declarations, Declaration by Germany, dated 11 May 1995, renewed on 10 September 1997, <www.conventions.coe.int>; Council of Europe, FCNM, List of Declarations, Declaration by Estonia dated 6 January 1997, <www.conventions.coe.int>.

have instead pragmatically applied some provisions to new groups,[26] while others have taken a more blurred position.

Most international bodies dealing with minorities have adopted in this regard an inclusive approach, especially the Advisory Committee on the Framework Convention (ACFC),[27] the European Commission for Democracy Through Law,[28] the UN Human Rights Committee,[29] the UN Working Group on Minorities,[30] and the OSCE High Commissioner on National Minorities which

26 ACFC, Opinion on the United Kingdom, 30 November 2001, ACFC/INF/OP/I(2002)006; ACFC, Second Report submitted by Finland, 10 December 2004, ACFC/SR/II(2004)012. In this regard, it has to be noted the proactive position of the Czech Republic that has officially recognized a new minority group as a national minority, namely the Vietnamese community, the third largest minority group in the Czech Republic. With the new status, Czech-Vietnamese receive support from the government's budget to preserve Vietnamese culture, tradition and language. In particular, the official minority status ensures them the right to use Vietnamese language at offices as well as courts, set up Vietnamese broadcast or TV programs, among others; *see* K. Kascian and H. Vasilevich, 'Czech Republic Acknowledgment of Belarusian and Vietnamese as New Minorities', 12 *European Yearbook of Minority Issues* (2013); L. Trlifajova, *Czech Republic: Vietnamese and Belarusian recognised as ethnic minorities*, 3 July 2013, <www.ec.europa.eu/migrant-integration/index.cfm?action=furl.go&go=/news/czech-republic-vietnamese-and-belarusians-recognized-as-ethnic-minorities>.

27 ACFC, *The Framework Convention: a Key Tool to Managing Diversity through Minority Rights*, Thematic Commentary no. 4, 2016; ACFC, *Opinion on Austria*, 16 May 2001, ACFC/INF/OP/I/009, paras. 19–20, p. 34; ACFC, *Opinion on Germany*, 1 March 2002, ACFC/INF/OP/I/008, paras. 17–18, p. 40; ACFC, *Opinion on Ukraine*, 1 March 2002, ACFC/INF/OP/I/010, para. 18.

28 Council of Europe Venice Commission, *Report on Non-Citizens and Minority Right*, CDL-AD(2007)001, 18 January 2007.

29 The UN Human Rights Committee clarified that the terms of Article 27 ICCPR indicate that individuals designated to be protected need not be citizens of a state party, and that a "State party may not therefore restrict the rights under Article 27 to its citizens alone". The UN HR Committee continues: "Just as they need not be nationals or citizens, they need not be permanent residents. Thus, migrant workers or even visitors in a State party constituting such minorities are entitled not to be denied the exercise of those rights". *See* UN, Human Rights Committee, General Comment No. 23, *The Rights of Minorities* (Art. 27), CCPR/C/21/Rev.1/Add.5, 8 April 1994, paras. 5.1–5.2. *See also* UN HRC, *Sandra Lovelace v. Canada,* Communication No. 24/1977, UN Doc. CCPR/C/13/D/24/1977, Views of 30 July 1981.

30 A. Eide, *Commentary to the UN Declaration on the Rights of Persons Belonging to National or Ethnic, Religious and Linguistic Minorities*, Working Paper submitted to the UN Working Group on Minorities, sixth session, 22–26 May 2000, UN Doc., E/CN.4/Sub.2/AC.5/2000/WP.1.

seems to have extended its mandate to new minority groups stemming from migration.[31]

The approach taken by the Advisory Committee on the Framework Convention with regard to new minority groups originating from immigration is particularly relevant in this regard. Due to the significant proportion of non-citizens – including migrant workers – in the total population of some countries, the Advisory Committee found that it would be possible to consider the inclusion of persons belonging to these groups in the application of the Framework Convention on an *article-by-article* basis, and noted that the authorities of the countries concerned should consider this issue in consultation with those concerned.[32] In particular, the ACFC emphasized that 'inclusive language policies should cater for the needs of everybody based on their different characteristics and needs, including persons belonging to national minorities living outside their traditional areas of settlement, immigrants and non-citizens'.[33]

It has to be acknowledged, however, that, as it will be further discussed in this chapter, any decision to bring minorities with a recent international mobility background within the scope of application of international and/or national instruments pertaining to minorities is bound to be mainly a political one.

31 OSCE, Parliamentary Assembly, Edinburgh Declaration, 2004; OSCE, High Commissioner on National Minorities, *Policies on Integration and Diversity in some OSCE Participating States*, Exploratory Study prepared by the Migration Policy Group, HCNM.GAL/6/06, 3 July 2006; R. Ekéus, *Statement to the OSCE Parliamentary Assembly*, Fifth Annual Winter Meeting, Vienna, 23 February 2006, HCNM.GAL/3/06, 24 February 2006; OSCE High Commissioner on National Minorities, *The Ljubljana Guidelines on Integration of Diverse Societies* (OSCE/HCNM, The Hague, 2012).

32 For instance, in 2007, the ACFC mentioned Turkish *Gastarbeiter* in Germany as a group that could benefit from certain rights covered by the Framework Convention for Protection of National Minorities (FCNM) (Second Opinion on Germany 2007). One year later, it welcomed the appointment by the Department for Intercultural and Integration Affairs of Vienna of "a person specifically in charge of dealing with problems facing the Roma, whether autochthonous or those with migrant background" (Second Opinion on Austria, 2008). Moreover, the ACFC pointed out that Austria would need to provide support for the preservation of the cultural and linguistic heritage of Czechs, Slovaks, and Hungarians living in Vienna (Second Opinion on Austria, 2008). These minority communities have a historical presence in Vienna, but nowadays they include among their number those who have moved to Austria in recent decades.

33 ACFC, *The Framework Convention: a Key Tool to Managing Diversity through Minority Rights*, Thematic Commentary no. 4, 2016, para. 62.

3 Normative Framework on Language Rights and Duties for New Minorities

The discourse around rights and duties in the linguistic sphere for new minorities raises a number of questions, in particular, whether the use of a particular language for either official or non-official purposes is a right or not,[34] and even if we can speak in terms of 'rights', what pragmatic limitations can legitimately be placed on the exercise of language choice. As seen earlier, rights are balanced against other (often relatively abstract) interests such as general societal interests – e.g. requirements of the 'common good' or of 'public policy' – or more specific economic or political interests as spelled out as possible 'substantive limitations' for state interference in the European Convention of Human Rights or the EU Fundamental Rights Charter.[35]

Hence, discussing language rights and duties for new minorities refers to the wider debate on *social integration*, that is the focus of this chapter, and *system integration* developed and conceptualized in scholarly literature.[36]

Language rights and duties for new minorities from international, European and national legislation can be classified around three categories: (1) Language rights necessary to preserve and maintain cultural ties with the country of origin, or that of the parents or minority group in case of second-third generations, and, (2) Language duties (or requirements) which are necessary to be able to

34 One vexing, yet unresolved question concerns whether minority rights have a collective or an individual dimension. As stated by Marko, "[t]hese two forms of rights not only can, but even must be used cumulatively when organising equality on the basis of difference". *See* J. Marko, 'Equality and Difference: Political and Legal Aspects of Ethnic Group Relations', in Franz Matscher (ed.), *Vienna International Encounter on Some Current Issues Regarding the Situation of National Minorities* (N.P. Engel Verlag, Kehl, Strasbourg, Arlington, 1997) p. 87; and R. Hofmann, 'Minority Rights: Individual or Group Rights? A Comparative View on European Legal Systems', 40 *GYIL* (1998), pp. 356–382. Ultimately, the true issue concerns whether the groups that human beings form are free and whether the members of these groups are able to live in dignity, including with regard to the maintenance and development of their identities.

35 N.N. Shuibhne, *EC Law and Minority Language Policy. Culture, Citizenship and Fundamental Rights*, (Kluwer Law International, The Hague, 2002) p. 189.

36 *See* J. Marko, *Minority Protection by Multiple Diversity Governance. Law, Ideology, and Politics in European Perspective* (Routledge, 2018 forthcoming); M. Gordon, *Assimilation in American Life* (Oxford Univeristy Press, New York, 1964); J.W. Berry, 'Immigration, Acculturation, and Adaptation', 46(1) *Applied Psychology: An International Review* (1997) pp. 5–68; H. Esser, 'Integration und ethnische Schichtung', 40 *Mannheimer Zentrum für Europäische Sozialforschung* (2001).

communicate and participate in the overall society, and (3) State obligations to protect and to promote both the preservation of the language of origin as well as the learning of the language of the host state which is not in every situation identical with the rights and duties under (1) and (2). Just to illustrate this with a not only hypothetical example: Shall parents have a right to home-schooling of their children (under 1) so that children (under the age of 14) would have no right to attend a public school with mandatory learning of the state language as language of instruction?

3.1 *Language Rights for New Minorities*

International norms dealing with language rights for new minorities are those foreseen, for instance, in the UN Convention on the Rights of the Child that extends the right to education far beyond equality of access to education and includes provisions concerning the development of the child's cultural identity, language and values of the child's country of origin.[37]

Most international instruments for the protection of migrants, such as the United Nation's 1990 International Convention on the Protection of the Rights of All Migrants Workers and Members of Their Families,[38] the Council of Europe's 1977 Convention on the Legal Status of Migrant Workers[39] or the EU Directive on the Status of Third-Country Nationals who are Long Term Residents (LTRD),[40] refer to the teaching of the migrant workers' mother tongue for their children. These instruments however contain also references to possible requirements of 'integration' that include linguistic training in the language of the settlement country.[41] Moreover, the aim of the provisions concerning mother tongue tuition is mainly the return of these children to the country

37 *See* art. 29 (1) (c) of the UN Convention on the Rights of the Child, Adopted by General Assembly Resolution 44/25, entered into force on 2 September 1990.

38 UN, International Convention on the Protection of the Rights of All Migrants Workers and Members of Their Families, adopted by General Assembly Resolution 45/158, entered into force on 1 July 2003.

39 Council of Europe, Convention on the Legal Status of Migrant Workers, adopted on 24 November 1977, entered into force on 1 May 1983, ETS No. 093.

40 EU Council Directive 2003/109/EC of 25 November 2003 concerning the status of third-country nationals who are long-term residents (LTRD), OJ L 16, 23 January 2004.

41 *See* art. 5(2) and 15(3) of the EU Council Directive 2003/109/EC of 25 November 2003 concerning the status of third-country nationals who are long-term residents (LTRD), OJ L 16, 23 January 2004; *and also* art. 14 of the Council of Europe European *Convention* on the Legal Status of *Migrant Workers*, European *Treaty* Series – No. 93, Strasbourg, 24 November 1977.

of origin of their parents rather than the protection and promotion of their identities.[42]

The sole EU legislative measure concerning new minorities' language education is Directive 486/EEC, entitled *On the Education of the Children of Migrant Workers*, which was adopted by the then European Community in 1977.[43] The Directive's scope is limited to children of workers who are nationals of other Member States (MSs) and it aims to ease the difficulties associated with the initial reception and integration of such children into the educational school system of the host state. The Directive 486/EEC requires EU Members to ensure, among others, the promotion of the teaching of the mother tongue and culture of the country of origin of such children, along with regular education and in cooperation with the country of origin; and ensure free tuition in their territory, adapted to the specific needs of such children, in particular the teaching of an official language of the settlement State. As said, Directive 486/EEC deals only with the education of children who are EU citizens, and it does not address a substantial part of the challenge posed by most recent migration, namely the education of children who are third-country nationals.[44]

In general, the role of the European Union in the field of education is limited to supporting and promoting the educational policies of its Member States. The latter retain full control in establishing their school systems and school curricula, provided that they apply the principle of equality and prohibit discrimination. At the EU level, however, the issue of education of children who are unable to speak the language of the host society has increasingly gained increased attention. The European Commission, in particular, facilitates the exchange of good practices on the integration of new minorities and funds

42 The Council of Europe Migrant Workers' Convention (Art. 15) reads specifically: "The Contracting Parties concerned shall take actions by common accord to arrange, so far as practicable, for the migrant worker's children, special courses for the teaching of the migrant worker's mother tongue, to facilitate, inter alia, their return to their State of origin". See also Artt. 1 and 67 of the UN *International Convention* on the Protection of the Rights of All *Migrant Workers* and Members of Their Families, signed on 18 December 1990 and entered into force on 1 July 2003.

43 Council Directive 77/486/EEC of 25 July 1977 on the education of the children of migrant workers, O.J. (L199) 32, <www.eur-lex.europa.eu/legal-content/EN/TXT/?uri=CELEX%3A31977L0486>.

44 European Union Agency for Fundamental Rights and Council of Europe, *Handbook on European law relating to the rights of the child* (Luxembourg: Publications Office of the European Union, 2015), <www.echr.coe.int/Documents/Handbook_rights_child_ENG.PDF>, p. 146.

relevant projects across the different levels of education.[45] This is being attributed to the transformation that the EU has undergone in the last years due to the greater mobility associated with the latest enlargements and the large influx of migrants and asylum seekers from non-EU countries.

3.2 *Language Duties for New Minorities*

Following the rise of migration in Europe, a growing number of European countries has been adopting norms and regulations providing and/or requiring language tests or courses for residence and, sometimes, even admission to residence, as well as for the acquisition of citizenship.[46]

In general, new countries of immigration, such as Greece, Ireland, Italy and Spain, are less concerned about proficiency in the national language than countries which have a longer history of immigration, particularly when these countries are former countries of emigration which in a very short lapse of time have become countries of immigration. The approach in these countries is quite on the opposite end of that in countries which have experienced a great deal of family-based immigration and have chosen to introduce a number of language requirements for the issue of many documents for migrants and their family members.[47]

3.3 *Residence*

The EU Directive on the Status of Third-Country Nationals who are Long Term Residents (LTRD)[48] provides that third-country nationals are entitled to the

---

45 For an overview of the activities of the European Commission in the field of education for migrants and refugees settled in EU MSs, *see* <www.ec.europa.eu/education/policy/migration_en>.

46 For a recent comparative overview *see* EU Agency for Fundamental Rights, *Together in the EU – Promoting the participation of migrants and their descendants*, (Publications Office of the European Union, Luxembourg, 2017), <www.fra.europa.eu/en/publication/2017/migrant-participation>, pp. 51–54; R. van Oers, E. Ersbøll and D. Kostakopoulou, *A Re-definition of Belonging? Language and Integration Tests in Europe* (Martinus Nijhoff Publishers, Leiden, Boston, 2010); S. Iglesias Sánchez, 'Free Movement as a Precondition for Integration of Third-Country Nationals in the EU', in E. Guild, Kees Groenendijk and S. Carrera (eds.), *Illiberal Liberal State: Immigration, Citizenship and Integration in the EU* (Ashgate, Farnham, Burlington, 2009); M. Jesse, *The Civic Citizens of Europe. The Legal Potential for Immigrant Integration in the EU, Belgium, Germany, and the United Kingdom*, (Brill-Nijhoff, Leiden, Boston, 2017).

47 Council of Europe, *Linguistic Integration of Adult Migrants: Policy and Practice – Final Report on the 3rd Council of Europe Survey* (Council of Europe, Strasbourg, 2014) p. 26.

48 EU Council Directive 2003/109/EC of 25 November 2003 concerning the status of third-country nationals who are long-term residents (LTRD), OJ L 16, 23 January 2004.

long-term resident status after residing legally and continuously for five years in the territory of a Member State before their application for status.[49] The status entitles long-term residents to equal treatment with nationals in a number of areas and enhanced protection against expulsion. As seen earlier, the Directive permits states to impose integration requirements as a condition for acquiring long-term resident status in the first place,[50] and to impose language requirements as a condition for access to education and training.[51] The integration requirements foreseen in the LTRD have a precise antecedent in the citizenship legislation of some MSs, which require 'integration' to be understood as a result-oriented process proven through language proficiency and knowledge of the country, for instance history, culture, tradition, legal system, Constitution, geography, etc. in order to obtain citizenship.[52]

As of residence permits and integration requirements, Italy, for instance, has introduced an integration agreement that must be signed by a third-country national entering Italy for the first time. According to the law a language test must also be passed in order to obtain the long-term residence permit.[53] There are exceptions for those who are under 14 years of age and those who suffer from limitations to learning languages due to their age or physical condition.[54]

49 *See* art. 4 (1), Council Directive 2003/109/EC of 25 November 2003 concerning the status of third-country nationals who are long-term residents (LTRD), OJ L 16, 23 January 2004.

50 Art. 5(2) LTRD (Conditions for acquiring long-term resident status) provides: "Member States may require third-country nationals to comply with integration conditions, in accordance with national law". and Art. 15 LTRD (Conditions for residence in a second Member State) reads: "Member States may require third-country nationals to comply with integration measures, in accordance with national law. This condition shall not apply where the third-country nationals concerned have been required to comply with integration conditions in order to be granted long-term resident status, in accordance with the provisions of Article 5(2). Without prejudice to the second subparagraph, the persons concerned may be required to attend language courses".

51 Art. 11(3)(b) LTRD.

52 *See* R. Bauböck *et al.*, 'Acquisition and Loss of Nationality,' 1–2 *Policies and Trends in 15 European Countries* (Amsterdam University Press, Amsterdam, 2006); D. Acosta Arcarazo, *The Long-Term Residence Status as a Subsidiary Form of EU Citizenship. An Analysis of Directive 2003/109*, (Martinus Nijhoff Publishers, Leiden-Boston, 2011) p. 164.

53 Law n. 94, 15 July 2009, *Disposizioni in materia di sicurezza pubblica; Decree of the President of the Republic* (D.P.R.) n. 179, 14 September 2011, *Regolamento concernente la disciplina dell'accordo di integrazione tra lo straniero e lo Stato.*

54 Italian Immigration Act, n. 286/1998 (*T. U. delle disposizioni concernenti la disciplina dell'immigrazione e norme sulla condizione dello straniero*), as revised by *Decree of the President of the Republic* (D.P.R.) n. 179, 14 September 2011 and *Regolamento concernente la disciplina dell'accordo di integrazione tra lo straniero e lo Stato,* art. 2 (8).

In other cases, such as the Flemish community in Belgium, newly arrived immigrants are required to take an officially provided language course, though the granting of a residence permit is not linked to the course. This is due to the fact that permission to enter the country and the granting of residence permits is dealt with at federal level, whereas the regional level is responsible for integration policies and their implementation.[55]

According to Bauböck, obligatory language requirements for the right to stay in the country of settlement are legitimate only 'when they assume a convergence of public interests and private interests of the immigrants themselves'.[56] Hence, mandatory language courses for adults would be justifiable 'as a form of benign paternalism'.[57] From this point of view, language courses can secure migrants' long-term interests regarding social-upward mobility as opposed to short-term interests in earning income in low-skilled jobs leading to forms of 'down-ward assimilation'.[58] However, the legitimacy of defining such interests 'from above', that is from outside migrant communities, remains questionable.[59]

3.4 *Family Reunification*

At European level family-based immigration has lately doubled in comparison to work-related immigration.[60] As a consequence, many countries have adopted measures to foster work-related immigration for skilled workers and *a contrario* to discourage family-based immigration in the case of unskilled migrants. In recent years, family-based immigration policies have been on the whole more restrictive, in particular, in the so-called 'interventionist' countries

55 Council of Europe, *Linguistic Integration of Adult Migrants: Policy and Practice – Final Report on the 3rd Council of Europe Survey* (Council of Europe, Strasbourg 2014) p. 9.

56 R. Bauböck, 'Public Culture in Societies of Immigration' in R. Sackmann, T. Faist, and B. Peters (eds.), *Identity and Integration. Migrants in Western Europe* (Ashgate, Avebury, 2003) pp. 37–57.

57 R. Bauböck, 'Public Culture in Societies of Immigration' in R. Sackmann, T. Faist, and B. Peters (eds.), *Identity and Integration. Migrants in Western Europe* (Ashgate, Avebury, 2003) pp. 37–57.

58 J. Marko, *Minority Protection by Multiple Diversity Governance. Law, Ideology, and Politics in European Perspective* (Routledge, 2018 forthcoming).

59 S. Vertovec and S. Wessendorf, Centre on Migration, Policy and Society (COMPAS), *Migration and Cultural, Religious and Linguistic Diversity in Europe: An overview of issues and trends,* Working Paper No. 18 (University of Oxford, 2005) p. 34, <www.compas.ox.ac.uk/media/WP-2005-018-Vertovec-Wessendorf_Religious_Linguistic_Diversity.pdf>.

60 Council of Europe, *Linguistic Integration of Adult Migrants: Policy and Practice – Final Report on the 3rd Council of Europe Survey* (Council of Europe, Strasbourg, 2014) p. 26.

of Northern Europe, such as the United Kingdom, Denmark, the Netherlands, Sweden, and France.[61]

As said earlier, former countries of emigration from Southern Europe, which are now countries of immigration, generally take few measures. As family-based immigration is in no way comparable to that in so-called 'interventionist' countries, work-related immigration is dominant and proficiency in the language is of less concern to the authorities than in Northern European countries.[62]

Most Eastern European countries, apart from the Czech Republic, which had a high rate of immigration in the mid-2000s, do not have to deal with much immigration and are not very 'interventionist'. According to a study conducted by the CoE, in these countries if the level of languages is stipulated by law, it is not very high and language courses are seldom proposed.[63]

In the frame of EU legislation, the Family Reunification Directive has been adopted with the main purpose to determine the conditions for the exercise of the right to family reunion by third-country nationals residing lawfully in the territory of a MS.[64] According to the Directive, a third-country national must fulfil several conditions to be able to exercise his/her right to family reunification, including an integration provision that MSs implemented in different ways. Some MSs bound by the Directive, in particular the Netherlands, France and Germany, apply integration conditions before entry for family members of third-country nationals. Under the terms of the Directive, MSs can offer language courses where available, although they cannot oblige third-country nationals to pass an examination in order to be admitted.[65]

---

61 The Organisation for Economic Co-operation and Development (OECD), *International Migration Outlook,* (OECD, Paris, 2013) p. 63; Council of Europe, *Linguistic Integration of Adult Migrants: Policy and Practice – Final Report on the 3rd Council of Europe Survey* (Council of Europe, Strasbourg, 2014) pp. 27–28.

62 Council of Europe, *Linguistic Integration of Adult Migrants: Policy and Practice – Final Report on the 3rd Council of Europe Survey* (Council of Europe, Strasbourg, 2014) pp. 28–29.

63 Council of Europe, *Linguistic Integration of Adult Migrants: Policy and Practice – Final Report on the 3rd Council of Europe Survey* (Council of Europe, Strasbourg, 2014) p. 30.

64 *See* K. Groenendijk, 'Legal Concepts of Integration in EU Migration Law', 6 *European Journal of Migration and Law* (2004) pp. 111–126, pp. 120–121; J. Apap and S. Carrera, *Towards a Proactive Immigration Policy for the EU?* (CEPS Working Documents, Brussels, 2003) p. 10; T. Kostakopoulou, 'Long-Term Resident Third Country Nationals in the European Union: Institutional Legacies and Evolving Norms', in R. Craufurd Smith (ed.), *Culture and European Union Law* (Oxford University Press, Oxford, 2004) pp. 299–323, p. 312.

65 K. Groenendijk, *Integration Tests Abroad as a Condition for Family Reunification in the EU?,* Immigration Law Practitioner's Association, European Update June 2007.

Nevertheless, the 2007 French Immigration law, for instance, requires that family members, who are being sponsored, have his/her knowledge of French and the values of the Republic evaluated. If the candidate fails the examination, the administrative authorities provide a course of a maximum of two months, after which the third-country national is evaluated again.[66] In Germany, legislation provides that a third-country national`s spouse must be able to communicate in basic German to be granted a residence permit.[67]

3.5 *Citizenship*

In the last decade, many European countries have increasingly introduced language tests and examinations on the knowledge of different aspects of the receiving country (history, traditions, etc.) as an unavoidable requirement for acquiring citizenship.[68] Sometimes, the conditions required in order to acquire a long-term residence permit are the same as those needed to acquire citizenship, but in general there has been a transition by which integration conditions to obtain citizenship have gradually also been adopted for the acquisition of permanent residence.[69]

For instance, according to the Austrian Nationality Act, it is a precondition for the acquisition of Austrian nationality that the applicant for naturalization demonstrates knowledge of the German language and a basic knowledge of the democratic legal order and the history of Austria and the respective federal state.[70] Also in Germany language is an important requirement for naturalization: the applicant for naturalization has to demonstrate ′sufficient` oral and written skills of the German language.[71] The ′sufficient` nature of the skills can be demonstrated in different ways, such as the participation of the applicant in a language course when applying for a residence permit.[72] In the UK applicants applying for naturalization must demonstrate that they have sufficient

66 D. Acosta Arcarazo, *The Long-Term Residence Status as a Subsidiary Form of EU Citizenship. An Analysis of Directive 2003/109* (Martinus Nijhoff Publishers, Leiden-Boston, 2011) p. 169.

67 *Ibid.*, p. 170.

68 *Ibid.*, p. 164.

69 *Ibid.*, p. 166.

70 Austrian Nationality Act, Bundesgesetz über die österreichische Staatsbürgerschaft, Nr. 311/1985, Revised version of 30 December 2017, § 10(a).

71 German Nationality Act (Staatsangehörigkeitsgesetz in der im Bundesgesetzblatt), Part III, Revised version of 11 October 2016 (BGBl. I S. 2218), §10.

72 See E. Guild, K. Groenendijk and S. Carrera, *Illiberal Liberal States. Immigration, Citizenship and Integration in the EU* (Farnham- Burlington, Ashgate, 2009) p. 63.

understanding of English (or Welsh or Scottish Gaelic), in addition to sufficient knowledge of life in the UK.[73]

Exceptions are applied in most countries, generally for mental, physical or intellectual diseases or handicaps, or age (for instance, in Austria, UK and Germany),[74] but also if the mother tongue of the person is already the language to be tested (Austria and Germany).[75]

4 Main Spheres of Life with Language Policy Implications for New Minorities

Language is, as noted earlier, a crucial identity marker and relevant for identity building, at individual and group level, and it is also a fundamental tool for integration. Various spheres of life are relevant when dealing with language and new minorities. There are, however, three dimensions that are particularly important, namely education, the labour market and the judicial system.

4.1 *Education*

While persons belonging to new minorities shall not be discriminated against in their access to education, a much larger and more complex issue is to what extent they can demand that their identity and culture, including language, be taken into account in the educational process. The process of education has a profound impact, positively or negatively, on a young person's sense of identity. Education has in fact been described as a 'powerful instrument for the achievement of social engineering'.[76] Education can help to strengthen

73 UK Nationality, Immigration and Asylum Act 2002, Chapter 41. Regarding the command of English for speakers of other languages, this implies "the ability to hold a conversation on an unexpected topic, which is workable, though not perfect, English" (E. Guild, K. Groenendijk and S. Carrera, *Illiberal Liberal States. Immigration, Citizenship and Integration in the EU* (Farnham- Burlington, Ashgate, 2009) p. 69). The main goal of the test is however not to assess the level of command of the English language but rather the knowledge of the candidate about the British society. In the UK therefore the level of command of the English language is only implicitly tested: the UK assumes that by passing the immigration test on the knowledge of British society the applicant has already demonstrated that his command of the language is sufficient (*Ibid.*, pp. 69 and 73).

74 E. Guild, K. Groenendijk and S. Carrera, *Illiberal Liberal States. Immigration, Citizenship and Integration in the EU* (Farnham- Burlington, Ashgate, 2009) p. 74.

75 *Ibid.*, pp. 73–74.

76 P. Thornberry and M. Amor Martín Estébanez, *Minority Rights in Europe: A Review of the Work and Standards of the Council of Europe* (Council of Europe, Strasbourg, 2004) p. 108.

and further develop that identity while creating awareness and tolerance of other cultures existing in the same society. Educational policies should therefore combine a focus on the universal values, the practical needs of children thereby facilitating their participation in socio-economic life, and the respect for their distinct cultural traditions and identities.

The political and legal progression from 'language as a problem' to 'language as a right'[77] is a difficult, hotly contested process. Indeed, states seem to see the granting of language rights to minorities as a highly divisive issue and ultimately leading to the disintegration of the state.[78] As Palermo has rightly pointed out: "Languages of the minorities are often seen as the main threat to the development of the state language, thus something against which the state language must be protected. This often creates a clash between laws aimed at protecting the minority languages and state language laws".[79]

In education there is thus a constant tension between these aspects: How to preserve, on the one hand, the distinctive identity of a minority and, on the other, how to contribute to social cohesion? How far does the teaching of and education in new minorities' languages lead to the retreat of minority members into their communities or encourages social integration beyond the family?

During the first waves of post-war immigration from post-colonial areas and from Southern Europe during the 1970s and 1980s, issues of language rights and education for new minorities have been largely dismissed.[80] However, proficiency in the language of origin of new minorities is increasingly considered to be of great importance for pupils.[81] Proficiency can make it easier for these

77 I. Gogolin, *Der monolinguale 'Habitus' der multilingualen Schule* (Waxman-Verlag, Miinster, New York, 1994).

78 *See* T. Skutnabb-Kangas, 'Human Rights and language Policy in Education', in S. May and N. Hornberger, *Encyclopedia of Language and Education* (Springer, New York, 2008) pp. 107–119; S. Vertovec and S. Wessendorf, Centre on Migration, Policy and Society (COMPAS), *Migration and Cultural, Religious and Linguistic Diversity in Europe: An overview of issues and trends,* Working Paper No. 18 (University of Oxford, 2005) p. 36, <www.compas.ox.ac.uk/media/WP-2005-018-Vertovec-Wessendorf_Religious_Linguistic_Diversity.pdf>.

79 F. Palermo, 'The Protection of Minorities in International Law. Recent Developments and Trends', in *Les minorités: un défi pour les État. Actes du colloque international, 22–23 May, 2011* (Academie royale de Belgique, Brussels, 2012) pp. 165–185, p. 8.

80 *See* D.E. Ager, *Language Policy in Britain and France: The Processes of Policy* (Cassell, London, 1996;); J. Twitchin and C. Demuth, *Multi-Cultural Education: Views from the Classroom* (British Broadcasting Corporation, London, 1985); G.K. Verma and C. Bagley (eds.), *Race, Education and Identity* (The Macmilla Press Limited, London, 1979).

81 Eurydice, *Integrating Immigrant Children into Schools in Europe* (European Commission, Bruxelles, 2009) p. 19, <www.eacea.ec.europa.eu/education/eurydice/documents/thematic_reports/101EN.pdf>.

pupils to learn the state language or language of instruction and thus stimulate their development and participation in various spheres of life. For some students, knowledge of the language of their parents might open up additional opportunities for their educational and professional development and could improve their chances on the job market, although the evidence supporting this assumption is unclear.[82] In addition, knowledge of the language of origin of their parents can contribute to secure the self-esteem and identity of children belonging to new minorities helping them to preserve and intensify their social ties with members of their community in the country of origin and in the settlement country.[83]

Nevertheless, it is also acknowledged that children who do not speak, read, or write the language of instruction to the level of their peers perform less well in school.[84] The programme of international students' assessment (PISA) has demonstrated that being of immigrant background still constitutes a disadvantage with respect to school success, putting the responsibility on public

---

82 K. Pendakur and R. Pendakur, 'Language knowledge as human capital and ethnicity', 36:1 *International Migration Review* (2002) pp. 147–177.

83 C.L. Bankston and M. Zhou, 'Effects of minority-language literacy on the academic achievement of Vietnamese youth in New Orleans', 68 *Sociology of Education* (1995) pp. 1–17; Eurydice, *Integrating Immigrant Children into Schools in Europe* (European Commission, Bruxelles, 2009) <www.eacea.ec.europa.eu/education/eurydice/documents/thematic_reports/101EN.pdf>.

84 Organization for Economic Cooperation and Development (OECD), *Knowledge and Skills for Life: First Results from the OECD Programme for Integrational Student Assessment (PISA) 2000* (OECD, Paris, 2001). On educational inequality *see* G. Baysu and H. de Valk, 'Navigating the school system in Sweden, Belgium, Austria and Germany, School segregation and second generation school trajectories', 12:6 *Ethnicities* (2012) pp. 776–799; A.F. Heath *et al.*, 'The second generation in Western Europe: education, unemployment and occupational attainment', 34 *Annual Review of Sociology* (2008) pp. 211–235; K. Phalet and A.F. Heath, 'Ethnic community, urban economy and second generation attainment: Turkish disadvantage in Belgium', in A.R. and M. Waters (eds.), *New Dimensions of Diversity: The Children of Immigrants in North America and Western Europe* (New York University Press, New York, 2011) pp. 135–165; specifically on test scores, *see* H. *Entorf* and N. *Minoiu*, 'What a Difference Immigration Policy makes: a comparison of PISA results in Europe and traditional countries of immigration', 6 *German Economic Review* (2005) pp. 355–376; M. *Levels and* J. *Dronkers*, 'Educational performance of native and immigrant children from various countries of origin', 31 *Ethnic and Racial Studies* (2008) pp. 1404–1425; Organization for Economic Cooperation and Development (OECD), *Where Immigrant Students Succeed: A Comparative review of Performance and Engagement in PISA 2003*, (OECD, Paris, 2006); and on dropout rates, M. *Kalmijn* and G. *Kraaykamp*, Dropout and downward mobility in the educational careers: an event-history analysis of ethnic schooling differences in the Netherlands, *Educational Research and Evaluation* (2003) pp. 265–287.

schools to establish equal chances for every citizen.[85] This argument has been defined as the 'institutionalised reproduction of inequality' and as a factor for new minorities' underachievement.[86]

Helping children of new minorities maintain and develop both languages – the state language or language of instruction and the language of the country of origin of their parents – is a worthwhile, though difficult, goal.[87] Regardless of the different attitudes that lead to education models and teaching methods, finding a balance between the three aims of education, namely universal values, practical needs of the child and respect for distinct cultural traditions and identities, is often described, especially by teachers, as difficult or problematic. The problems range from complications of the teaching assignment and decreased educational quality because of restricted linguistic competences of the children, to difficulties to convince parents and administrations that it is profitable to teach languages of countries of origin of new minorities like Turkish or Arabic, which for many seem to be largely irrelevant to European societies.[88]

85 *See* U. Mehlem, U. Maas and C. Schroeder, 'Mehrsprachigkeit und Mehrschriftigkeit bei Einwanderern in Deutschland', in K.J. Bade, M. Bommes, and R. Münz (eds.) *Migrationsreport 2004. Fakten – Analysen – Perspektiven.* (Campus, Frankfurt, New York, 2004) pp. 117–149; G. Christensen and P. Stanat, 'Language policies and practices for helping immigrants and second-generation students succeed', *Migration Policy Institute, Policy Briefs* (2007) <www.migrationpolicy.org/research/language-policies-and-practices-helping-immigrants-and-second-generation-students-succeed>.

86 J. Marko, 'Five Years After: Continuing Reflections on the Thematic Commentary on Effective Participation. The Interplay between Equality and Participation', in T.H. Malloy and U. Caruso (eds.), *Minorities, Their Rights and the Monitoring of the European Framework Convention for the Protection of National Minorities. Essays in Honour of Rainer Hofmann* (Martinus Nijhoff Publishers, Leiden, 2013); F.-O. Radtke and M. Gomolla, *Institutionelle Diskriminierung: Die Herstellung ethnische Differenz in der Schule* (Leske und Budrich Verlag, Opladen, 2002); S. Vertovec and S. Wessendorf, Centre on Migration, Policy and Society (COMPAS), *Migration and Cultural, Religious and Linguistic Diversity in Europe: An overview of issues and trends,* Working Paper No. 18 (University of Oxford, 2005) p. 32, <www.compas.ox.ac.uk/media/WP-2005-018-Vertovec-Wessendorf_Religious_Linguistic_Diversity.pdf>.

87 G. Christensen and P. Stanat, *Language policies and practices for helping immigrants and second-generation students succeed* (Migration Policy Institute, Policy Briefs, 2007) p. 3, <www.migrationpolicy.org/research/language-policies-and-practices-helping-immigrants-and-second-generation-students-succeed>.

88 S. De Carlo, 'Multilingualism as a Burden for the Educational System?', in S. Vertovec and S. Wessendorf, Centre on Migration, Policy and Society (COMPAS), *Migration and Cultural, Religious and Linguistic Diversity in Europe: An overview of issues and trends* (University of

Schools therefore often see the languages of new minorities as necessary but negative temporary tools while the child is learning the state official language.[89] As soon as he/she is deemed in some way competent in the language of instruction, the minority language can be left behind and the child has no right to maintain this language and develop it further in the educational system what usually is a one-way mechanism to assimilation.

The perceived burden of teachers to deal with bi-multilingualism reflects an ongoing transformation into a multilingual society. And this process takes place in one of the functional parts of society, the educational system, which has to deal with contrary requests: a state defined monolingualism and a multilingual reality.[90]

4.1.1 Models of Language Education for New Minorities

The debate around language education for new minorities focuses mainly on two spheres, namely public and private education, and two dimensions: teaching in a given language as language of instruction, and teaching the given language.

In relation to the first point, the question arises whether there is a right for new minorities for, at least partial, public schooling respecting and promoting their language and culture or whether this right should be implemented only in private schooling. As for the second point, teaching the language of new minorities is a more common case than teaching in the language of new minorities as language of instruction. This case is however often limited to voluntary, extracurricular activities organized within public (local) school institutions at the request of parents (with minimum thresholds) or, even more often, organized by NGOs, sometimes supported by public funding, outside the school (Sunday schooling – private initiatives); so mainly on a voluntary basis, at the local level based on the school autonomy, and upon parents' request. A number of exceptions are, however, noteworthy in this domain, as it will be discussed later in this section.

Oxford, 2005) p. 35, <www.compas.ox.ac.uk/media/WP-2005-018-Vertovec-Wessendorf_Religious_Linguistic_Diversity.pdf>.

89 T. Skutnabb-Kangas, 'Human Rights and language Policy in Education', in S. May and N. Hornberger, *Encyclopedia of Language and Education* (Springer, New York, 2008) pp. 107–119.

90 S. De Carlo, 'Multilingualism as a Burden for the Educational System?', in S. Vertovec and S. Wessendorf, Centre on Migration, Policy and Society (COMPAS), Migration and Cultural, Religious and Linguistic Diversity in Europe: An overview of issues and trends (University of Oxford, 2005) p. 35, <www.compas.ox.ac.uk/media/WP-2005-018-Vertovec-Wessendorf_Religious_Linguistic_Diversity.pdf>.

Educational systems vary widely across Europe but they fall usually within three main models that generally coexist within a given country:[91]

a. An assimilationist model, in which children of new minorities are included in mainstream education classes and taught the same curricula as students from majority groups. Classes are composed of children of the same age or occasionally younger children. Measures to offer support for the language of instruction or the state language are offered to individual children as needed during normal school hours;
b. A separatist model, which appears in two forms:
   - Transitional arrangements: Children of new minorities are grouped together separately from other children in school temporarily, in order to receive special attention suited to their needs; such children may attend some mainstream classes; and
   - Long-term arrangements: Children of new minorities are grouped together for several school years according to their competence level in the language of instruction.
c. An inclusive or pluralist model in which teaching the language of instruction or state language is complemented by an effort to keep children of new minorities in touch with the language and culture of the country of origin of their parents.[92]

---

91 These models are drawn and adapted from T. Papademetriou, *The Education of Non-Native Language Speaking Children: European Union* (2009) <www.loc.gov/law/help/non-native-education/european-union.php>. Analogous categorisation of educational systems has been suggested by A. Spiliopoulou Åkermark along the lines of *segregationist, assimilationist and inclusive models. See* Advisory Committee on the Framework Convention for the Protection of National Minorities (ACFC), *Commentary on Education under the Framework Convention for the Protection of National Minorities* (Strasbourg, 2006); A. Spiliopoulou Åkermark, 'Minority Education – Torn in Contradictions?', 9 *European Yearbook on Minority Issues* (2012). Specifically on the governance of linguistic diversity, Rainer Bauböck has suggested the following categories: *linguistic liberty, assimilation, accommodation and recognition.* R. Bauböck, 'Public Culture in Societies of Immigration' in R. Sackmann, T. Faist, and B. Peters (eds.) *Identity and Integration. Migrants in Western Europe* (Avebury, Ashgate, 2003) pp. 37–57. *See also* the taxonomy of group relations suggested by Joseph Marko based on the duality Unity-Diversity and Equality-Inequality with the possible combination of integration, assimilation, autonomy and separation. J. Marko *et al., Minority Protection by Complex Diversity Governance. Law, Ideology, and Politics in European Perspective* (Routledge, London, New York, forthcoming 2018).

92 T. Papademetriou, *The Education of Non-Native Language Speaking Children: European Union* (2009) <www.loc.gov/law/help/non-native-education/european-union.php>.

In terms of language support, EU legislation introduced in the 1970s following the Directive 1977/486/EEC requires MSs, as seen earlier, to provide supplementary language tuition for children of EU migrant workers, in both the host state language and in their minority language, with a view to facilitate their integration in the host state and in their country of origin should they subsequently return.[93] However, while this seems to offer quite generous and valuable supplementary support to children following their admission to a school in the settlement state, its implementation across different countries has been notoriously patchy and increasingly impractical given the range of different languages to accommodate.[94]

Policies and *practices* that countries use for language support can be divided into five different categories:[95]

1. Immersion: These programs provide no specific language support: students are 'immersed' in the language of instruction within mainstream classrooms.
2. Immersion with systematic language support: Students are taught in the mainstream classroom, but they receive specified periods of instruction aimed at increasing proficiency in the language of instruction over a period of time.
3. Immersion with a preparatory phase: Students participate in a preparatory program before making the transition to mainstream classes.[96]

---

93 European Union Agency for Fundamental Rights (FRA) and Council of Europe (CoE), *Handbook on European law relating to the rights of the child* (Publications Office of the European Union, Luxembourg, 2015) p. 46, <www.echr.coe.int/Documents/Handbook_rights_child_ENG.PDF>.

94 *Ibid.*, p. 146.

95 G. Christensen and P. Stanat, *Language policies and practices for helping immigrants and second-generation students succeed* (Migration Policy Institute, Policy Briefs, 2007) p. 4, <www.migrationpolicy.org/research/language-policies-and-practices-helping-immigrants-and-second-generation-students-succeed>.

96 Several countries have adopted programs to teach young children the language of instruction prior to attending compulsory education. For instance, Germany has such programs for children who were born in the country or came to Germany at a very young age. The Flemish community in Belgium as well as Lithuania, Luxembourg, and Norway provide reception classes to children to equip them with language skills prior to attending compulsory education. In addition, the Czech Republic, Finland, and some municipalities of Sweden offer pre-primary language instruction. *See* T. Papademetriou, *The Education of Non-Native Language Speaking Children: European Union* (2009), <www.loc.gov/law/help/non-native-education/european-union.php>.

4. Transitional bilingual schooling: Students initially learn in their minority language before teaching gradually shifts to the language of instruction.
5. Bilingual schooling *stricto sensu*: Students receive significant amounts of instruction in their minority language; programs aim to develop proficiency both in the minority and the state official language.[97]

In Europe, most countries offer monolingual programs that provide additional support for second-language learning. The most common approach in primary and secondary school is immersion with systematic language support.[98] According to Christensen and Stanat, it is difficult to determine the extent to which the different language support programs contribute to the relative achievement levels of immigrant students.[99] Studies conducted in this field indicate, however, that countries that tend to have long-standing language support programs with clearly defined goals and standards are those with relatively small achievement gaps between new minorities and students from majority groups, or smaller gaps for second-generation students compared to first-generation students.[100] In contrast, in countries where new minorities perform at significantly lower levels than their peers from the majority group, language support tends to be less systematic.[101]

Cross-country comparative studies in Europe provide examples of models for language support that seem to be effective. Some important recommendations can be drawn from best practices developed in these countries that have

97 Some Scandinavian countries, including Finland, Norway, and Sweden, as well as Cyprus, Estonia, and Latvia, offer bilingual instruction, where teachers teach in the new minorities' languages and the language of instruction. *See* T. Papademetriou, *The Education of Non-Native Language Speaking Children: European Union* (2009), <www.loc.gov/law/help/non-native-education/european-union.php>. In the United Kingdom, schools have always been able to offer languages spoken by their pupils within the modern foreign languages curriculum, if they so wish. For instance, in the UK a number of schools are offering classes in Polish language and culture. *See* Eurydice, *Integrating Immigrant Children into Schools in Europe* (European Commission, Bruxelles, 2009) p. 20; p. 26, <www.eacea.ec.europa.eu/education/eurydice/documents/thematic_reports/101EN.pdf>.

98 G. Christensen and P. Stanat, *Language policies and practices for helping immigrants and second-generation students succeed* (Migration Policy Institute, Policy Briefs, 2007) p. 8, <www.migrationpolicy.org/research/language-policies-and-practices-helping-immigrants-and-second-generation-students-succeed>.

99 *Ibid.*

100 Organization for Economic Cooperation and Development (OECD), *Where Immigrant Students Succeed: A Comparative review of Performance and Engagement in PISA 2003* (OECD, Paris, 2006).

101 *Ibid.*

both a significant immigrant population and relatively small achievement differences between students with and without migration background. In line with the inclusive or pluralist model described earlier, we find among these recommendations that countries should consider offering bilingual programs and heritage-language programs to foster multilingualism as a resource.[102]

4.1.2 New Minorities' Language Tuition: Some Examples

In Europe many countries have issued regulations or recommendations on public school-based provision of new minorities' language tuition.[103] In other countries, new minorities' language tuition mainly depends on voluntary and private initiatives, which sometimes are supported by central and/or local authorities. Lately, however, the diversified character of immigration has led to an increasing prioritisation of additional resources for teaching the state language rather than languages of new minorities.[104]

New minorities' languages tuition is offered to new minority pupils in a variety of institutional forms. European countries that have provisions for new minorities' language tuition implement these provisions on the following basis: organized under bilateral agreements, financed by the diplomatic missions of certain countries, organised and funded by the settlement country's educational system.[105]

Some countries have chosen a combination of approaches: tuition for new minority pupils organised under bilateral agreements together with tuition organised and funded by the national education system (e.g. Slovenia), or tuition for new minority pupils coupled with a closer correspondence between the provision of foreign languages and the languages spoken by the new communities established in the country (e.g. Estonia and France).[106]

Lastly, in several countries (e.g. Spain and Italy), new minorities' languages tuition can be offered outside the school framework, by voluntary and private initiatives, such as specific communities themselves.

As a general rule, no systematic correlation between national immigration profiles and the policies adopted in respect of languages of new minorities

102 *Supra* note 98, pp. 10–11.

103 Eurydice, *Integrating Immigrant Children into Schools in Europe* (European Commission, Bruxelles, 2009) pp. 21–26, <www.eacea.ec.europa.eu/education/eurydice/documents/thematic_reports/101EN.pdf>.

104 *Ibid.* p. 21.

105 *Ibid.* pp. 21–26.

106 *Ibid.*

tuition is apparent.[107] However, in all countries, the decision on whether to organise such tuition is ultimately dependant on demand and the availability of material and human resources.[108]

4.2 *Labour and Employment*

Also in the field of labour and employment, language is considered to have an eminent role as an instrument to assure the successful integration of new minorities in society. Language is however also relevant to guarantee that the economy of a state functions properly. As for education, language has then a bi-directional dimension or value: a tool for new minorities to integrate and a tool for the economy to function properly.

Considerable research has examined the relationship between language proficiency in the state language and labour market integration. It is acknowledged that new minorities with greater language proficiency in the state language earn more and work in more skilled occupations than those with low proficiency, even after controlling for differences in education and skill associated with language abilities.[109] In particular, for the highly skilled, language fluency allows new minorities to practice the profession in which they are trained, rather than being downgraded to less-skilled jobs. Finally, for those with low- to mid-level skills, language proficiency is the ticket to better-paying jobs and upward mobility.[110]

Insufficient knowledge of the state language is in fact one of the main grounds for exclusion of new minorities in the labour market as this factor is so relevant for improving their status and to achieve social mobility. There is however evidence that language competence is often used as a pretext by many employers to exclude some candidates on cultural or religious grounds, in particular Muslims, even if they have been living in the country for 2 or 3 generations.[111]

107 *Ibid.* p. 29; European Monitoring Centre on Racism and Xenophobia (EUMC), *Migrants, minorities and education. Documenting discrimination and integration in 15 member states of the European Union, Equality and diversity for an inclusive Europe.* EUMC *comparative study* (European Communities, Luxembourg, 2004) pp. 78–79.

108 *Supra* note 103 p. 25.

109 M. McHugh and A.E. Challinor, *Improving Immigrants' Employment Prospects through Work-focused Language Instruction* (Migration Policy Institute, Washington, D.C., 2011) p. 2.

110 *Ibid.*

111 *See* most recently, European Union Agency for Fundamental Rights (FRA), *Second European Union Minorities and Discrimination Survey* (2017); D. Dechief and P. Oreopoulos, 'Why do some employers prefer to interview Matthew but not Samir? New evidence from

Language-based discrimination in the labour market is a salient issue that links language policies and the equality principle. Language proficiency requirements and certification of language proficiency may indeed constitute a disproportionate obstacle for access to certain occupations for persons belonging to new minorities. In this regard, but only as far as EU nationals are corcerned, the European Court of Justice acknowledged that it is legitimate to require a job applicant to have a certain level of linguistic knowledge. However, the Court stated: "the right to require a certain level of knowledge of a language in view of the nature of the post must not encroach upon the free movement of workers. The requirements under measures intended to implement that right must not in any circumstances be disproportionate to the aim pursued and the manner in which they are applied must not bring about discrimination against nationals of other Member States".[112]

Various European countries have rather strict state language laws and apply rigid requirements of state language proficiency to access positions in the public service and even jobs in the private sector. In practice, this may lead to direct or indirect discrimination against those who have insufficient command of the state language.

In parallel with this trend, the awareness of the importance of language skills, including languages of new minorities, is increasingly gaining ground in the current economic context. A multilingual and multicultural labour force is indeed considered crucial for economic growth and better jobs, enabling businesses to be more competitive.[113] According to this view, languages, including languages of new minorities, are conceived as an opportunity for growth and prosperity.

4.3 *The Law Enforcement System*

The use of languages other than the state language in the law enforcement system has both an instrumental and an intrinsic value. Besides ensuring

---

Toronto, Montreal and Vancouver', Working Paper No. 95, *Canadian Labour Market and Skills Researcher Network* (2012).

112 ECJ, *European Commission* v. *Kingdom of Belgium*, para. 25 (2015).

113 *See* European Commission, *Communication on Multilingualism: an asset for Europe and a shared commitment*, COM/2008/0566 final, Brussels, 18 September 2008; T. Huddleston and A. Wolffhardt, *Back to School: Responding to the Needs of Newcomer Refugee Youth* (Migration Policy Group, Brussels, 2016) pp. 44–45; The European Network to Promote Linguistic Diversity's (NPLD), *The European Roadmap for Linguistic Diversity. Towards a new approach on languages as part of the European Agenda 2020*, (NPLD, Bruxelles, 2015). For an analysis, *see* M. Gazzola and B.-A. Wickström (eds.), *The Economics of Language Policy* (MIT Press, Cambridge (MA), London, 2016).

communication with the public authorities, using a language other than the state official in the public realm, shall guarantee, as emphasised earlier, the preservation and promotion of specific identities.

A number of safeguards in this field are set up by the European Convention on Human Rights (ECHR). Under Article 5 (2) ECHR, anyone arrested must be informed promptly and in a language that he/she understands of the reasons why he/she was arrested, so as to be able to seek judicial review of his/her arrest or detention.[114] Use of the terms 'arrested' and ′charge' in article 5(2) implies that the text belongs to a criminal law context.[115] The information referred to in Article 5(2) need not be related in its entirety by the arresting officer at the very moment of the arrest. Besides, there is no requirement that the reasons be in writing or in any special form.[116] This guarantee is applied in many cases of extradition and explusion.[117]

Human rights standards recognize also minimum guarantees in criminal prosecutions because it is clear that an accused person who is not familiar with the language used by the criminal tribunal is at a particular disadvantage. These guarantees include the right to receive information about the nature and cause of the charge in a language which he/she understands (art. 6 (3) (a) ECHR). This right is operative well before the trial and from the moment when the individual is ′charged'.[118]

The ECHR recognizes also the right of a person charged with a criminal offence to have free assistance by an interpreter if he/she cannot understand or speak the language used in court (art. 6(3)(e)). An evaluation of the linguistic abilities of the person charged with an offence is obviously vital to the application of this provision. Assessing the language skills of the accused person is primarily a matter for the domestic authorities, and, in principle, the ECHR will not intervene in such determinations. On occasion, however, the Court has made its own evaluation.[119] The right to an interpreter applies not only to oral statements at the trial, but also to documentary material in order to

114 In *Zamir* v. *the United Kingdom*, the Commission was of the opinion that free legal aid should have been made available to an illegal immigrant detained pending deportation because of his poor command of English and the complexity of the case. ECommHR, *Zamir* v. *the United Kingdom*, Appl. No. 9174/80, 11 October 1983.

115 W.A. Schabas, *The European Convention on Human Rights. A Commentary* (Oxford University Press, Oxford, 2015) p. 245.

116 *Ibid.*

117 *Ibid.*

118 *Ibid.*, p. 307; C. Ovey and R.C.A. White, *The European Convention on Human Rights* (Oxford University Press, Oxford, 2006) p. 327.

119 *See* ECtHR, *Katritsch* v. *France*, Appl. No. 22575/08, 4 November 2010.

have the benefit of a fair trial.[120] The right to a free interpreter only extends to the language used in court: an accused who understands that language cannot insist upon the services of an interpreter to allow him/her to conduct his/her defence in another language, including a language of an ethnic minority of which he/she is a member.[121]

In addition to human rights norms – the so-called 'hard law' – also 'soft law' can be of assistance to new minorities as in the case of the recent Graz Recommendations on the Access to Justice for National Minorities.[122] However the decision on whether the scope of application of these recommendations should also be extended to new minorities is bound to be political and therefore it is largely left to the discretion of each country.

5 Conclusions

As international mobility flows continue to increase in Europe as elsewhere at an unprecedented high level, the question of integration through diversity governance reveals unequivocal urgency for most European countries that consider themselves to be rather culturally homogenous and cohesive. As a result, the process of integration of new minorities is seen as an important and urgent strategy to be adopted by most countries in order to retain an adequate level of social cohesion and prosperity.[123]

In this chapter we have argued that in today's increasingly diverse societies it would be conceptually meaningful and beneficial in terms of diversity governance to widen the scope of minority rights traditionally conceived for old, historical minorities, such as those found in the Council of Europe Framework Convention on National Minorities, to new minorities originating from migration. This would fill a still existing gap. Especially in terms of rights related to identity and diversity, we have seen that most international instruments on migrants' rights contain only weak and ambivalent references. But the protection

120 *Supra* note 115. p. 315; C. Ovey and R.C.A. White, *The European Convention on Human Rights*(Oxford University Press, Oxford, 2006) pp. 327–328.

121 ECommHR, *K* v. *France*, Appl. No. 10210/82, 7 December 1983; ECommHR, *Bideault v. France*, Appl. No. 11261/84, 6 October 1986; ECtHR, *Lagerblom v. Sweden*, Appl. No. 26891/95, 14 January 2003.

122 OSCE High Commissioner on National Minorities, *Graz Recommendations on Access to Justice and National Minorities* (Organization for Security and Co-operation in Europe, The Hague, 2017).

123 E. Collett and M. Petrovic, *The Future of Immigrant Integration in Europe: Mainstreaming Approaches for Inclusion* (Migration Policy Institute, Brussels, 2014).

of identity and language rights, including those of new minorities, is one of the bases of a veritable process of inclusion[124] through which minority groups can develop a genuine sense of loyalty and common belonging with the rest of the population without the threat of being forcibly assimilated in the mainstream society which, as a result, can engender resistance and alienation.[125]

Accommodating diversity, including linguistic diversity, is a powerful tool to reduce tensions and prevent conflicts; language is an important factor of diversity and identity building at individual and group level, thus some forms of accommodation must be found with all communities in society that speak languages different from the state language. These communities also include

124 In this regard, the OSCE HCNM called on States Parties to include minority cultures and tolerance in the general curriculum in order to increase inter-ethnic understanding and dialogue and to "advance the important goal of sensitizing students to foreign cultures that do not qualify as national minorities, e.g., recent immigrants or refugees resident in the country" (OSCE HCNM, *Report on the Linguistic Rights of Persons Belonging to National Minorities in the OSCE Area*, p. 38, para. 4, <www.osce.org/hcnm/42060?download=true>, 1997). Likewise, article 6 FCMN calls on State Parties to encourage a "spirit of tolerance and intercultural dialogue" and promote "mutual respect and understanding", and the CSCE/OSCE Copenhagen Document invites State Parties to "promote a climate of mutual respect, understanding, co-operation and solidarity among all persons living on its territory, without distinction as to ethnic or national origin or religion" (CSCE/OSCE, *Document of the Copenhagen Meeting of the Conference on the Human Dimension of the CSCE* (1990) para. 36, <www.osce.org/odihr/elections/14304?download=true>). *See* also EU, Communication from the Commission, *A Common Agenda for Integration: Framework for the Integration of Third-Country Nationals in the European Union*, 1 September 2005, COM(2005) 389 final, Annex, CBP 1; EU, European Commission (DG Justice, Freedom and Security), *Handbook on Integration for Policy Makers and Practitioners* (Migration Policy Group, November 2004, 1st ed., May 2007, 2nd ed. and April 2010, 3rd ed.); EU, Council Meeting (2618), Justice and Home Affairs, *Common Basic Principles for Immigrant Integration Policy in the European Union*, Council Document 14615/04, 19 November 2004, Annex; OSCE, High Commissioner on National Minorities, *Policies on Integration and Diversity in some OSCE Participating States*, Exploratory Study prepared by the Migration Policy Group, HCNM.GAL/6/06, 3 July 2006. Among the vast literature on identity, *see* B. Parekh, *A New Politics of Identity* (Palgrave Macmillan, Basingstoke, 2008); E. Guild, *The Legal Elements of European Identity: EU Citizenship and Migration Law* (Kluwer International Law, The Hague, 2004); J.Y. Nazroo and S. Karlsen, 'Patterns of Identity among Ethnic Minority People: Diversity and Commonality', 26:5 *ERS* (2003) pp. 902–930.

125 On the politics of belonging, *see* A. Geddes and A. Favell (eds.), *The Politics of Belonging: Migrations and Minorities in Contemporary Europe* (Ashgate, Adelshot, 1999); N. Yuval-Davis, 'Belonging and the Politics of Belonging', 40:3 *Patterns of Prejudice* (2006) pp. 197–214.

new minorities who are increasingly the most relevant diverse communities in contemporary societies.

However, in order to spark solidarity and social trust, and thus social cohesion, recognition of diversity is not sufficient: states must also tackle social structures and mechanisms that result in systematic deprivation and exclusion of new minorities from their equal public standing.[126]

In addition, cultural attachment to a language other than the official state language neither competes with nor replaces the requirement of skills and fluency in the official language of the country. A common public language is indeed necessary for the state to function and proficiency in the state language is an important tool by which integration is assured.[127]

In conclusion, if a country is serious about the integration of new minorities, then it should not oppose the extension of the scope of application of minority provisions, including those pertaining to language rights to them. This would be an appropriate political gesture that underlines the importance of the country's integration policy and sends out a powerful message that populations of immigrans or asylum seekers are no longer seen as the 'legal Other',[128] but as an integral, though distinct, part of the nation.

---

126 P. Balint and S. Guérard de Latour (eds.), *Liberal Multiculturalism and the Fair Terms of Integration* (Palgrave Macmillan, Basingstoke, New York, 2013) p. 205.

127 *Ibid.* p. 209; G. Poggeschi, *Language Rights and Duties in the Evolution of Public Law* (Nomos, Baden-Baden, 2013) pp. 30–31.

128 D. Acosta Arcarazo, *The Long-Term Residence Status as a Subsidiary Form of EU Citizenship. An Analysis of Directive 2003/109* (Martinus Nijhoff Publishers, Leiden, Boston, 2011) p. 227. In a similar vein, Weiler notes: "Concern for the cultural, linguistic and ethnic integration of aliens may send a signal which accentuates both the otherness of the alien and an intolerance of the dominant culture towards such otherness". J.H.H. Weiler, 'Thou Shalt not Oppress the Stranger: On the Judicial Protection the Human Rights of Non-EC Nationals', 3:65 *European Journal of International Law* (1992) pp. 65–91, p. 67 (quoted by Arcarazo, *ibid.* p. 185).

APPENDIX

The Oslo Recommendations Regarding the Linguistic Rights of National Minorities & Explanatory Note – 1998

Introduction

In its Helsinki Decisions of July 1992, the Organization for Security and Co-operation in Europe (OSCE) established the position of High Commissioner on National Minorities to be "an instrument of conflict prevention at the earliest possible stage". This mandate was created largely in reaction to the situation in the former Yugoslavia which some feared would be repeated elsewhere in Europe, especially among the countries in transition to democracy, and could undermine the promise of peace and prosperity as envisaged in the Charter of Paris for a New Europe adopted by the Heads of State and Government in November 1990.

On 1 January 1993, Mr. Max van der Stoel took up his duties as the first OSCE High Commissioner on National Minorities (HCNM). Drawing on his considerable personal experience as a former Member of Parliament and Foreign Minister of The Netherlands, Permanent Representative to the United Nations, and long-time human rights advocate, Mr. Van der Stoel turned his attention to the many disputes between minorities and central authorities in Europe which had the potential, in his view, to escalate. Acting quietly through diplomatic means, the HCNM has become involved in the following States: Albania, Croatia, Estonia, Hungary, Kazakstan, Kyrgyzstan, Latvia, the Former Yugoslav Republic of Macedonia, Romania, Slovakia and Ukraine. His involvement has focused primarily on those situations involving persons belonging to national/ethnic groups who constitute the numerical majority in one State but the numerical minority in another (usually neighbouring) State, thus engaging the interest of governmental authorities in each State and constituting a potential source of inter-State tension if not conflict. Indeed, such tensions have defined much of European history.

In addressing the substance of tensions involving national minorities, the HCNM approaches the issues as an independent, impartial and cooperative actor. While the HCNM is not a supervisory mechanism, he employs the international standards to which each State has agreed as his principal framework of analysis and the foundation of his specific recommendations. In this relation, it is important to recall the commitments undertaken by all OSCE participating States, in particular those of the 1990 Copenhagen Document of the Conference on the Human Dimension which, in Part IV, articulates detailed obligations relating to national minorities. It is also important to

© KONINKLIJKE BRILL NV, LEIDEN, 2018 | DOI 10.1163/9789004357754_017

note that all OSCE States are bound by United Nations obligations relating to human rights, including minority rights, and that the great majority of OSCE States are also bound by the standards of the Council of Europe.

After five years of intense activity, the HCNM has been able to identify certain recurrent issues and themes which have become the subject of his attention in a number of States in which he is involved. The linguistic rights of national minorities, i.e. the right of persons belonging to national minorities to use their language in the private and public spheres, is such an issue. International human rights instruments refer to this right in a number of different contexts. On the one hand, language is a personal matter closely connected with identity. On the other hand, language is an essential tool of social organisation which in many situations becomes a matter of public interest. Certainly, the use of language bears on numerous aspects of a State's functioning. In a democratic State committed to human rights, the accommodation of existing diversity thus becomes an important matter of policy and law. Failure to achieve the appropriate balance may be the source of inter-ethnic tensions.

It is with this in mind that, in the summer of 1996, the HCNM requested the Foundation on Inter-Ethnic Relations to consult a small group of internationally recognised experts with a view to receiving their recommendations on an appropriate and coherent application of the linguistic rights of persons belonging to national minorities in the OSCE region. A similar request from the HCNM had previously resulted in the elaboration of **The Hague Recommendations Regarding the Education Rights of National Minorities and Explanatory Report.**[1] Insofar as The Hague Recommendations address comprehensively the use of the language or languages of national minorities in the field of education, it was decided to exclude this issue from consideration of the experts.

The Foundation on Inter-Ethnic Relations – a non-governmental organisation established in 1993 to carry out specialised activities in support of the HCNM – facilitated a series of consultations of experts from various pertinent disciplines, including two meetings in Oslo and one in The Hague. Among the experts consulted were jurists specialising in international law, as well as linguists, advocates and policy analysts specialising in the situations and needs of minorities. Specifically, the experts were:

> Professor Gudmundur Alfredsson, Co-Director, Raoul Wallenberg Institute (Sweden); Professor Asbjørn Eide, Senior Fellow, Norwegian Institute of Human Rights (Norway); Ms. Angelita Kamenska, Senior Researcher, Latvian Centre

1 Copies of The Hague Recommendations Regarding the Education Rights of National Minorities and Explanatory Report (October 1996) are available in several languages from the OSCE Office of the High Commissioner on National Minorities.

for Human Rights and Ethnic Studies (Latvia); Mr. Dónall Ó Riagáin, Secretary General, European Bureau of Lesser Used Languages (Ireland); Ms. Beate Slydal, Advisor, Norwegian Forum for the Freedom of Expression (Norway); Dr. Miquel Strubell, Director, Institute of Catalan Sociolinguistics, Government of Catalonia (Spain); Professor György Szepe, Department of Language Sciences at Janus Panonius University (Hungary); Professor Patrick Thornberry, Department of Law, Keele University (United Kingdom); Dr. Fernand de Varennes, Director of the Asia Pacific Centre for Human Rights and the Prevention of Ethnic Conflict (Australia); Professor Bruno de Witte, Faculty of Law, University of Maastricht (the Netherlands); Mr. Jean-Marie Woehrling, *Institut de droit local alsacien-mosellan* (France).

Insofar as existing standards of minority rights are part of human rights, the starting point for the consultations was to presume compliance by States with all other human rights obligations including, in particular, equality and freedom from discrimination, freedom of expression, freedom of assembly and of association, as well as all the rights and freedoms of persons belonging to national minorities.

It was also presumed that the ultimate object of all human rights is the full and free development of the individual human personality in conditions of equality. Consequently, it was presumed that civil society should be open and fluid and, therefore, integrate all persons, including those belonging to national minorities. Insofar as the use of language is also a fundamentally communicative matter, the essential social dimension of the human experience was also fully presumed.

The resultant Oslo Recommendations Regarding the Linguistic Rights of National Minorities attempt to clarify, in relatively straight-forward language, the content of minority language rights generally applicable in the situations in which the HCNM is involved. In addition, the standards have been interpreted in such a way as to ensure their coherence in application. The Recommendations are divided into sub-headings which respond to the language related issues which arise in practice. A more detailed explanation of the Recommendations is provided in an accompanying Explanatory Note wherein express reference to the relevant international standards is to be found. It is intended that each Recommendation is read in conjunction with the specifically relevant paragraphs of the Explanatory Note.

It is hoped that these Recommendations will provide a useful reference for the development of State policies and laws which will contribute to an effective implementation of the language rights of persons belonging to national minorities, especially in the public sphere.

Although these Recommendations refer to the use of language by persons belonging to national minorities, it is to be noted that the thrust of these Recommendations and the international instruments from which they derive could potentially apply to other types of minorities. The Recommendations which follow below are meant to clarify the existing body of rights. They are not meant to restrict the human rights of any person or groups of persons.

Recommendations

Names

1) Persons belonging to national minorities have the right to use their personal names in their own language according to their own traditions and linguistic systems. These shall be given official recognition and be used by the public authorities.
2) Similarly, private entities such as cultural associations and business enterprises established by persons belonging to national minorities shall enjoy the same right with regard to their names.
3) In areas inhabited by significant numbers of persons belonging to a national minority and when there is sufficient demand, public authorities shall make provision for the display, also in the minority language, of local names, street names and other topographical indications intended for the public.

Religion

4) In professing and practicing his or her own religion individually or in community with others, every person shall be entitled to use the language(s) of his or her choice.
5) For those religious ceremonies or acts pertaining also to civil status and which have legal effect within the State concerned, the State may require that certificates and documents pertaining to such status be produced also in the official language or languages of the State. The State may require that registers pertaining to civil status be kept by the religious authorities also in the official language or languages of the State.

Community Life and NGOs

6) All persons, including persons belonging to national minorities, have the right to establish and manage their own non-governmental organisations, associations and institutions. These entities may use the language(s) of their choosing. The State may not discriminate against these entities on the basis of language nor shall it unduly restrict the right of these entities to seek sources of funding from the State budget, international sources or the private sector.

7) If the State actively supports activities in, among others, the social, cultural and sports spheres, an equitable share of the total resources made available by the State shall go to support those similar activities undertaken by persons belonging to national minorities. State financial support for activities which take place in the language(s) of persons belonging to national minorities in such spheres shall be granted on a non-discriminatory basis.

The Media

8) Persons belonging to national minorities have the right to establish and maintain their own minority language media. State regulation of the broadcast media shall be based on objective and non-discriminatory criteria and shall not be used to restrict enjoyment of minority rights.

9) Persons belonging to national minorities should have access to broadcast time in their own language on publicly funded media. At national, regional and local levels the amount and quality of time allocated to broadcasting in the language of a given minority should be commensurate with the numerical size and concentration of the national minority and appropriate to its situation and needs.

10) The independent nature of the programming of public and private media in the language(s) of national minorities shall be safeguarded. Public media editorial boards overseeing the content and orientation of programming should be independent and should include persons belonging to national minorities serving in their independent capacity.

11) Access to media originating from abroad shall not be unduly restricted. Such access should not justify a diminution of broadcast time allocated to the minority in the publicly funded media of the State of residence of the minorities concerned.

Economic Life

12) All persons, including persons belonging to national minorities, have the right to operate private enterprises in the language or languages of their choice. The State may require the additional use of the official language or languages of the State only where a legitimate public interest can be demonstrated, such as interests relating to the protection of workers or consumers, or in dealings between the enterprise and governmental authorities.

Administrative Authorities and Public Services

13) In regions and localities where persons belonging to a national minority are present in significant numbers and where the desire for it has been expressed,

persons belonging to this national minority shall have the right to acquire civil documents and certificates both in the official language or languages of the State and in the language of the national minority in question from regional and/or local public institutions. Similarly regional and/or local public institutions shall keep the appropriate civil registers also in the language of the national minority.

14) Persons belonging to national minorities shall have adequate possibilities to use their language in communications with administrative authorities especially in regions and localities where they have expressed a desire for it and where they are present in significant numbers. Similarly, administrative authorities shall, wherever possible, ensure that public services are provided also in the language of the national minority. To this end, they shall adopt appropriate recruitment and/or training policies and programmes.

15) In regions and localities where persons belonging to a national minority are present in significant numbers, the State shall take measures to ensure that elected members of regional and local governmental bodies can use also the language of the national minority during activities relating to these bodies.

Independent National Institutions

16) States in which persons belonging to national minorities live should ensure that these persons have, in addition to appropriate judicial recourses, access to independent national institutions, such as ombudspersons or human rights commissions, in cases where they feel that their linguistic rights have been violated.

The Judicial Authorities

17) All persons, including persons belonging to a national minority, have the right to be informed promptly, in a language they understand, of the reasons for their arrest and/or detention and of the nature and cause of any accusation against them, and to defend themselves in this language, if necessary with the free assistance of an interpreter, before trial, during trial and on appeal.

18) In regions and localities where persons belonging to a national minority are present in significant numbers and where the desire for it has been expressed, persons belonging to this minority should have the right to express themselves in their own language in judicial proceedings, if necessary with the free assistance of an interpreter and/or translator.

19) In those regions and localities in which persons belonging to a national minority live in significant numbers and where the desire for it has been expressed,

States should give due consideration to the feasibility of conducting all judicial proceedings affecting such persons in the language of the minority.

Deprivation of Liberty

20) The director of a penal institution and other personnel of the institution shall be able to speak the language or languages of the greatest number of prisoners, or a language understood by the greatest number of them. Recruitment and/or training programmes should be directed towards this end. Whenever necessary, the services of an interpreter shall be used.

21) Detained persons belonging to national minorities shall have the right to use the language of their choice in communications with inmates as well as with others. Authorities shall, wherever possible, adopt measures to enable prisoners to communicate in their own language both orally and in personal correspondence, within the limitations prescribed by law. In this relation, a detained or imprisoned person should, in general, be kept in a place of detention or imprisonment near his or her usual place of residence.

Explanatory Note

General Introduction

Article l of the **Universal Declaration of Human Rights** refers to the innate dignity of all human beings as the fundamental concept underlying all human rights standards. Article 1 of the **Declaration** states "All human beings are born free and equal in dignity and rights [...]." The importance of this article cannot be overestimated. Not only does it relate to human rights generally, it also provides one of the foundations for the linguistic rights of persons belonging to national minorities. Equality in dignity and rights presupposes respect for the individual's identity as a human being. Language is one of the most fundamental components of human identity. Hence, respect for a person's dignity is intimately connected with respect for the person's identity and consequently for the person's language.

In this context, the **International Covenant on Civil and Political Rights** is of considerable importance. Article 2 of the **Covenant** requires States to ensure that the human rights of all individuals within their territory and subject to their jurisdiction will be ensured and respected "without distinction of any kind such as [...] language [...]." Article 19 of the **Covenant** guarantees freedom of expression which, as it is formulated in the **Covenant**, not only guarantees the right to impart or receive information and ideas of all sorts, regardless of frontiers, but also guarantees the right to do so in the medium or language of one's choice. The imparting and receiving of information also suggests people acting in community. In this context, Articles 21 and 22 of the **Covenant** guaranteeing the freedoms of peaceful assembly and association may be especially relevant.

Similarly, in Europe the freedom of expression stipulated in Article 10 of the **European Convention for the Protection of Human Rights and Fundamental Freedoms** shall be, according to Article 14 of the same convention, "secured without discrimination on any ground such as [...] language [...]." With expressed reference to both the **Universal Declaration of Human Rights** and the **European Convention for the Protection of Human Rights and Fundamental Freedoms**, the Council of Europe's **Declaration on Freedom of Expression and Information** affirms "that the freedom of expression and information is necessary for the social, economic, cultural and political development of every human being, and constitutes a condition for the harmonious progress of social and cultural groups, nations and the international community". In this connection, the freedoms of peaceful assembly and association as guaranteed by Article 11 of the **European Convention for the Protection of Human Rights and Fundamental Freedoms** are important.

Within the context of the Organization for Security and Co-operation in Europe (OSCE), the same fundamental ideas of freedom of expression, assembly and association are enumerated in paragraphs 9.1–9.3 of the **Document of the Copenhagen Meeting of the Conference on the Human Dimension.**

In the **Charter of Paris for a New Europe**, the Heads of State and Government of the OSCE participating States "affirm that, without discrimination, every individual has the right to: [...] freedom of expression, freedom of association and peaceful assembly, [...]."

Article 27 of the **International Covenant on Civil and Political Rights** is another key provision which has direct bearing on the linguistic rights of national minorities. It affirms that "persons belonging to [...] minorities shall not be denied the right, in community with the other members of their group, to [...] use their own language".

Similarly, Article 2(1) of the UN **Declaration on the Rights of Persons Belonging to National or Ethnic, Religious and Linguistic Minorities** proclaims the right of persons belonging to national minorities to "use their own language, in private and in public, freely and without interference or any form of discrimination". Article 10(1) of the Council of Europe's **Framework Convention for the Protection of National Minorities** stipulates that States will recognise the right of persons belonging to national minorities "to use freely and without interference his or her minority language, in private and in public, orally and in writing."

Although the instruments refer to the use of minority languages in public and in private, these same instruments do not precisely delimit the 'public' as opposed to the 'private' spheres. Indeed the spheres may overlap. This may well be the case, for example, when individuals acting alone or in community with others seek to establish their own private media or schools. What might begin as a private initiative may become the subject of legitimate public interest. Such an interest may give rise to some public regulation.

The use of minority languages 'in public and in private' by persons belonging to national minorities cannot be considered without making reference to education. Education issues as they relate to the languages of national minorities are treated in detail in The Hague Recommendations Regarding the Education Rights of National Minorities which were developed for the benefit of the OSCE High Commissioner on National Minorities by The Foundation on Inter-Ethnic Relations in collaboration with experts of international repute in the fields of both international human rights and education. The Hague Recommendations were developed with a view to facilitating a clearer understanding of the international instruments pertaining to the rights of persons belonging to national minorities in this area which is of such vital importance to the maintenance and development of the identity of persons belonging to national minorities.

International human rights instruments stipulate that human rights are universal and that they must be enjoyed equally and without discrimination. Most human rights, however, are not absolute. The instruments do foresee a limited number of situations in which States would be justified in restricting the application of certain rights. The restrictions permitted by international human rights law can be invoked in life-threatening emergencies and in situations which pose a threat to the rights and freedoms of others, or in situations which threaten public morals, public health, national security and the general welfare in a democratic society.[2] In human rights law, restrictions on freedoms are to be interpreted restrictively.

The rights of persons belonging to national minorities to use their language(s) in public and in private as set forth and elaborated in The Oslo Recommendations Regarding the Linguistic Rights of National Minorities must be seen in a balanced context of full participation in the wider society. The Recommendations do not propose an isolationist approach, but rather one which encourages a balance between the right of persons belonging to national minorities to maintain and develop their own identity, culture and language and the necessity of ensuring that they are able to integrate into the wider society as full and equal members. From this perspective, such integration is unlikely to take place without a sound knowledge of the official language(s) of the State. The prescription for such education is implied in Articles 13 and 14 of the **International Covenant on Economic, Social and Cultural Rights** and Articles 28 and

2 The above mentioned limitations are included, e.g., in the following provisions:
Art. 30 Universal Declaration of Human Rights.
Art. 19(3) International Covenant on Civil and Political Rights.
Art. 10(2) European Convention for the Protection of Human Rights and Fundamental Freedoms.

29 of the **Convention on the Rights of the Child** which confer a right to education and oblige the State to make education compulsory. At the same time, Article 14(3) of the **Framework Convention for the Protection of National Minorities** provides that the teaching of a minority language "shall be implemented without prejudice to the learning of the official language or the teaching in this language."

Names

1) Article 11(1) of the **Framework Convention for the Protection of National Minorities** stipulates that persons belonging to national minorities have the right to use their first name, their patronym and their surname in their own language. This right, the enjoyment of which is fundamental to one's personal identity, should be applied in light of the circumstances particular to each State. For example, public authorities would be justified in using the script of the official language or languages of the State to record the names of persons belonging to national minorities in their phonetic form. However this must be done in accordance with the language system and tradition of the national minority in question. In view of this very basic right relating closely to both the language and the identity of individuals, persons who have been forced by public authorities to give up their original or ancestral name(s) or whose name(s) have been changed against their will should be entitled to revert to them without having to incur any expenses.

2) Names are an important element of corporate identity as well, especially in the context of persons belonging to national minorities acting 'in community'. Article 2(1) of the **UN Declaration on the Rights of Persons Belonging to National or Ethnic, Religious and Linguistic Minorities** proclaims the right of persons belonging to national minorities to "use their own language, in private and in public, freely and without interference or any form of discrimination". Article 10(1) of the **Framework Convention for the Protection of National Minorities** stipulates that States will recognise the right of persons belonging to national minorities to "use freely and without interference his or her minority language, in private and in public, orally and in writing." Article 27 of the **International Covenant on Civil and Political Rights** declares that "persons belonging to [...] minorities shall not be denied the right, in community with other members of their group [...] to use their own language". A person's right to use his or her language in public, in community with others and without any interference or any form of discrimination is a strong indication that legal entities such as institutions, associations, organisations or business enterprises established and run by persons belonging to national minorities enjoy the right to adopt the name of their choice in their minority language. Such a corporate name should

be recognised by the public authorities and used in accordance with the given community's language system and traditions.

3) Article 11(3) of the **Framework Convention** states that "in areas traditionally inhabited by substantial numbers of persons belonging to a national minority, the Parties shall endeavour [...] to display traditional local names, street names and other topographical indications intended for the public also in the minority language when there is sufficient demand for such indications". Refusal to recognise the validity of historic denominations of the kind described can constitute an attempt to revise history and to assimilate minorities, thus constituting a serious threat to the identity of persons belonging to minorities.

Religion

4) Article 27 of the **International Covenant on Civil and Political Rights** affirms that "In those States in which ethnic, religious or linguistic minorities exist, persons belonging to such minorities shall not be denied the right, in community with the other members of their group [...] to profess and practice their own religion, or to use their own language." Article 3(1) of the **UN Declaration on the Rights of Persons Belonging to National or Ethnic, Religious and Linguistic Minorities** stipulates that "Persons belonging to minorities may exercise their rights [...] individually as well as in community with other members of their group, without any discrimination."

Religious belief and its practice 'in community' is an area of great importance to many persons belonging to national minorities. In this context it is worth noting that the right to one's own religion is unlimited and guaranteed by Article 18(1) of the **International Covenant on Civil and Political Rights** and Article 9(1) of the **European Convention for the Protection of Human Rights and Fundamental Freedoms.** However, the freedom to manifest one's religion and beliefs, including public worship, is subject to a number of limitations listed in subsidiary paragraphs of the same articles. These limitations must be prescribed by law and relate to the protection of public safety, order, health, morals and the protection of the fundamental rights and freedoms of others. They must be reasonable and proportional to the end sought, and States may not invoke them with a view to stifling the legitimate spiritual, linguistic or cultural aspirations of persons belonging to national minorities.

In minority contexts, the practice of religion is often especially closely related to the preservation of cultural and linguistic identity. The right to use a minority language in public worship is as inherent as the right to establish religious institutions and the right to public worship itself. Hence, public authorities may not impose any undue restrictions on public worship nor on the use of any language in public worship, be it the mother tongue of the national minority in question or the liturgical language used by that community.

5) Religious acts such as wedding ceremonies or funerals may also constitute legal civil acts determining civil status in certain countries. In such cases, public interest must be taken into consideration. Keeping in mind the principle that administrative considerations should not prevent the enjoyment of human rights, public authorities should not impose any linguistic restrictions on religious communities. This should apply equally to any administrative functions which religious communities assume and which may overlap with civil jurisdiction. The State may, however, require the religious community to record legal civil acts for which it has authority also in the official language or languages of the State so that the State may perform its legitimate regulatory and administrative tasks.

Community Life and NGOs

6) The collective life of persons belonging to national minorities, their acting 'in community' as stated by the international instruments, finds its expression in numerous activities and areas of endeavour. Not least of these is the life of their non-governmental organisations, associations and institutions whose existence is usually vital for the maintenance and development of their identity and is generally seen as beneficial and conducive to the development of civil society and democratic values within States.

Articles 21 and 22 of the **International Covenant on Civil and Political Rights** and Article 11 of the **European Convention for the Protection of Human Rights and Fundamental Freedoms** guarantee the right of persons to peaceful assembly and the freedom of association. The right of persons to act 'in community' with other members of their group – their right to establish and manage their own non-governmental organisations, associations and institutions – is one of the hallmarks of an open and democratic society. Article 27 of that same **Covenant** affirms that "Persons belonging to [...] minorities shall not be denied the right, in community with the other members of their group, to [...] use their own language". As a rule, therefore, public authorities should not be involved in the internal affairs of such entities 'acting in community', nor may they impose any limits on them, other than those permitted under international law. Article 17(2) of the **Framework Convention for the Protection of National Minorities** similarly engages States "not to interfere with the right of persons belonging to national minorities to participate in the activities of non-governmental organisations, both at the national and international levels".

Article 2(1) of the **International Covenant on Civil and Political Rights** stipulates that each State undertakes "to ensure to all individuals within its territory and subject to its jurisdiction the rights recognised in the present Covenant, without distinction of any kind such as [...] language". In line with this standard, States may not discriminate against NGOs on the basis of language nor impose any undue language requirements on them. This having been said, public authorities may require that such organisations, associations and institutions conform to the requirements of domestic law on the basis of a legitimate public interest, including the use of the official language(s) of the State in situations requiring interface with public bodies.

With regard to resources, paragraph 32.2 of the **Copenhagen Document** states that persons belonging to national minorities have the right "to establish and maintain their own educational, cultural and religious institutions, organisations or associations, which can seek voluntary financial and other contributions as well as public assistance, in conformity with national legislation." Accordingly, States should not prevent these entities from seeking financial resources from the State budget and from public international sources as well as from the private sector.

7) With regard to State financing of non-governmental activities in, among others, the social, cultural or sports fields, application of the principles of equality and non-discrimination requires that the public authorities provide an appropriate share of funding to similar activities taking place in the language of the national minorities living within their borders. In this context, Article 2(1) of the **International Covenant on Civil and Political Rights** stresses not only that there will be no distinction based on language in the treatment of individuals, but stipulates in Article 2(2) that States are required to "take the necessary steps [...] to adopt such legislative or other measures as may be necessary to give effect to the rights recognised in the [...] Covenant". Furthermore, Article 2(2) of the **International Covenant on the Elimination of Racial Discrimination**, (which seeks to eliminate any distinction, exclusion, restriction, or preference based on race, colour, descent, or national or ethnic origin) stipulates that "States Parties shall, when the circumstances so warrant, take, in the social, economic, cultural and other fields, special and concrete measures to ensure the adequate development and protection of certain racial groups or individuals belonging to them, for the purpose of guaranteeing them the full and equal enjoyment of human rights and fundamental freedoms [...]." Insofar as language is often a defining criterion of ethnicity as protected by the aforementioned convention, minority language communities may also be entitled to the benefits of such 'special and concrete measures'.

At the European level, paragraph 31 of the **Copenhagen Document** stipulates that "States will adopt, where necessary, special measures for the purpose of ensuring to persons belonging to national minorities full equality with the other citizens in the exercise and enjoyment of human rights and fundamental freedoms". Paragraph 2 of

Article 4 of the **Framework Convention for the Protection of National Minorities** obligates the States Parties "to adopt, where necessary, adequate measures in order to promote, in all areas of economic, social, political and cultural life, full and effective equality between persons belonging to a national minority and those belonging to the majority"; paragraph 3 of the same Article further specifies that such "measures adopted in accordance with paragraph 2 shall not be considered to be an act of discrimination." Moreover, Article 7(2) of the **European Charter for Regional or Minority Languages** stipulates that "the adoption of special measures in favour of regional or minority languages aimed at promoting equality between the users of the languages and the rest of the population or which take account of their specific conditions is not considered to be an act of discrimination against the users of more widely used languages." In this context, therefore, public authorities should provide an equitable share of resources from the State budget to the activities of persons belonging to national minorities in, among others, the social, cultural and sports related fields. Such support can be made available through subsidies, public benefits and tax exemptions.

The Media

8) Article 19 of the **International Covenant on Civil and Political Rights**, which guarantees the right to hold opinions as well as the right to express them, is a fundamental point of reference regarding the role and place of media in democratic societies. While Article 19(1) provides that "everyone shall have the right to hold opinions without interference", Article 19(2) proceeds to guarantee to everyone the freedom "to seek, receive and impart information and ideas of all kinds, regardless of frontiers, either orally, in writing or in print, in the form of art, or through the media of his choice." Article 10 of the **European Convention for the Protection of Human Rights and Fundamental Freedoms** guarantees the right to freedom of expression in a similar way. The member States of the Council of Europe reiterated in Article 1 of the **Declaration on the Freedom of Expression and Information** "their firm attachment to the principles of freedom of expression and information as a basic element of democratic and pluralist society". On this basis, States declared in the same instrument that "in the field of information and mass media they seek to achieve [...] d) The existence of a wide variety of independent and autonomous media, permitting the reflection of diversity of ideas and opinions".

Article 9(1) of the **Framework Convention for the Protection of National Minorities** states clearly that persons belonging to national minorities are free "to hold opinions and to receive and impart information and ideas in the minority language, without interference by public authorities and regardless of frontiers [...]." Further on, the same provision engages States to "ensure, within the framework of their legal systems, that persons belonging to a national minority are not discriminated against in their access to the media." Article 9(3) of the **Framework Convention** stipulates that States "shall not hinder the creation and the use of printed media by persons belonging to national minorities." The same provision requires that "in the legal framework of sound radio and television broadcasting, [States] shall ensure, as far as possible [...] that persons belonging to national minorities are granted the possibility of creating and using their own media." It is also to be noted that media may constitute entities of the kind foreseen in inter alia, paragraph 32.2 of the **Copenhagen Document** which provides for the right of persons belonging to national minorities to "establish and maintain their own educational, cultural and religious institutions, organisations or associations [...]" Even though the media are not cited expressly in this standard, the media often plays a fundamental role in the promotion and preservation of language, culture and identity.

Although there can be no doubt that persons belonging to national minorities have the right to establish and maintain private media, it is also true that this right is subject to the limitations provided by international law as well as such legitimate requirements of the State regarding the regulation of the media. Article 9(2) of the **Framework Convention** makes this very clear by underlining that the freedom of expression referred to in article 9(1) of the **Convention** "shall not prevent Parties from requiring the licensing, without discrimination and based on objective criteria, of sound radio and television broadcasting, or cinema enterprises." Regulatory requirements, where justified and necessary, may not be used to undermine the enjoyment of the right.

9) The issue of access to publicly funded media is closely linked with the concept of freedom of expression. Article 9(1) of the **Framework Convention** stipulates that the freedom of expression of persons belonging to national minorities includes the freedom to impart information and ideas in the minority language, without interference by public authorities, and goes on to say that "members of minorities shall not be discriminated against in their access to the media." Article 9(4) of the **Framework Convention** stipulates that "Parties shall adopt adequate measures in order to facilitate access to the media for persons belonging to national minorities." This implies that a national minority consisting of a substantial number of members should be given access to its fair share of broadcast time, on public radio and/or television, with the numerical size of the minority in question having a bearing on its share of broadcast time.

Numerical strength and concentration, however, cannot be seen as the only criteria when judging the amount of broadcast time to be allocated to any given national minority. In the case of smaller communities, consideration must be given to the viable minimum of time and resources without which a smaller minority would not meaningfully be able to avail itself of the media.

Moreover, the quality of the time allotted to minority programming is an issue that needs to be approached in a reasonable, non-discriminatory manner. The time-slots allotted to minority language programming should be such as to ensure that persons belonging to a national minority can enjoy programming in their language in a meaningful way. Hence, public authorities should ensure that this programming is transmitted at reasonable times of the day.

10) In an open and democratic society the content of media programming should not be unduly censored by the public authorities. The freedom of expression as guaranteed by Article 19(1) of the **International Covenant on Civil and Political Rights** and Article 10(1) of the **European Convention for the Protection of Human Rights and Fundamental Freedoms** is important in this regard. Any restrictions which might be imposed by the public authorities must be in line with Article 19(3) of the **Covenant** which stipulates that these restrictions "shall only be such as are provided by law and are necessary a) For the respect of the rights and reputations of others, b) For the protection of national security or of public order (*ordre public*), or of public health and morals." Article 10(2) of the **European Convention for the Protection of Human Rights and Fundamental Freedoms** stipulates almost identical restrictions on any interference by public authorities with the enjoyment of freedom of expression.

Mechanisms should be put in place to ensure that the public media programming developed by or on behalf of national minorities reflects the interests and desires of the community's members and is seen by them as independent. In this context, the participation of persons belonging to national minorities (acting in their private capacity) in the editorial process would go a long way in ensuring that the independent nature of the media would be preserved and that it would be responsive to the needs of the communities to be served.

In line with the principle of equality and non-discrimination, the composition of public institutions should be reflective of the populations they are designed to serve. This also applies to public media. Article 15 of the **Framework Convention** engages States to "create the conditions necessary for the effective participation of persons belonging to national minorities in cultural, social and economic life and in public affairs, in particular those affecting them." Article 2 of **International Labour Organisation Convention No. 111 Concerning Discrimination in Respect of Employment and Occupation** is more explicit in committing States to "pursue a national policy designed to promote [...] equality of opportunity and treatment in respect of employment and occupation, with a view to eliminating any discrimination in respect thereof". The non-discriminatory hiring of persons belonging to national minorities to work in the media will contribute to the representativity and objectivity of the media.

11) In keeping with the spirit of Articles 19(2) of the **International Covenant on Civil and Political Rights** and Article 9(1) of the **Framework Convention for the Protection of National Minorities** and of the principle of non-discrimination, access to programming in the language of persons belonging to a national minority, transmitted from another State or from the 'kin-State', should not justify a diminution of programme time allotted to the minority on the public media of the State in which its members live.

Transfrontier access to information and media networks is a fundamental element of the right to information which, in the context of accelerated technological progress, is of growing importance. Consequently, when cable licensing is involved, for example, it is not legitimate for a State to refuse to license television or radio stations based in a kin-State when the desire for access to these stations has been clearly expressed by the national minority concerned. This right applies not only to cable media but also to electronic information networks in the language of the national minority.

As a general matter, the member States of the Council of Europe resolved in Article III(c) of the **Declaration on the Freedom of Expression and Information** "to promote the free flow of information, thus contributing to international understanding, a better knowledge of convictions and traditions, respect for the diversity of opinions and the mutual enrichment of cultures". In relation to media contacts across frontiers, States should conform their policies to the spirit of this provision.

Economic Life

12) International instruments make little reference to the rights of persons belonging to national minorities in the field of economic activity. International instruments do, however, refer to the right of persons belonging to national minorities to use their language in public and in private, freely and without any form of discrimination, orally and in writing, individually and with others. Article 19(2) of the **International Covenant on Civil and Political Rights** and Article 10(1) of the **European Convention for the Protection of Human Rights and Fundamental Freedoms** guarantee freedom of expression with respect not only to ideas and opinions which may be transmitted to others (i.e. the content of communications), but also to language as a medium of communication. These rights, coupled with the right to equality and non-discrimination, imply the right of persons belonging to national minorities to run their businesses in the language of their choice. In view of the importance to private entrepreneurs to be able to communicate effectively with their clientele and to pursue their initiatives in fair conditions, there should be no undue restrictions on their free choice of language.

Article 11(2) of the **Framework Convention** stipulates that "every person belonging to a national minority has the right to display in his or her minority language, signs, inscriptions and other information of a private nature visible to the public." In the **Framework Convention** the expression 'of a private nature' refers to all that is not official. Hence, the State may not impose any restrictions on the choice of language in the administration of private business enterprises.

Notwithstanding the above, the State may require that the official language or languages of the State be accommodated in those sectors of economic activity which affect the enjoyment of the rights of others or require exchange and communication with public bodies. This follows from the permissible restrictions on freedom of expression as stipulated in Article 19(3) of the **International Covenant on Civil and Political Rights** and Article 10(2) of the **European Convention for the Protection of Human Rights and Fundamental Freedoms.** While the limited permissible restrictions expressed in the aforementioned articles could justify restrictions on the content of communications, they would never justify restrictions on the use of a language as a medium of communication. However, protection of the rights and freedoms of others and the limited requirements of public administration may well justify specific prescriptions for the additional use of the official language or languages of the State. This would apply to sectors of activity such as workplace health and safety, consumer protection, labour relations, taxation, financial reporting, State health and unemployment insurance and transportation, depending on the circumstances. On the basis of a legitimate public interest, the State could, in addition to the use of any other language, also require that the official language or languages of the State be accommodated in such business activities as public signage and labelling – as expressly stated in paragraph 60 of the **Explanatory Report to the Framework Convention for the Protection of National Minorities.** In sum, the State could never prohibit the use of a language, but it could, on the basis of a legitimate public interest, prescribe the additional use of the official language or languages of the State.

In keeping with the logic of legitimate public interest, any requirement(s) for the use of language which may be prescribed by the State must be proportional to the public interest to be served. The proportionality of any requirement is to be determined by the extent to which it is necessary. Accordingly, for example, in the public interest of workplace health and safety, the State could require private factories to post safety notices in the official language or languages of the State in addition to the chosen language(s) of the enterprise. Similarly, in the interest of accurate public administration in relation to taxation, the State could require that administrative forms be submitted in the official language or languages of the State and that, in the case of an audit by the public authorities, relevant records be made available also in the official language or languages of the State; the latter eventuality would not require that private enterprise maintain all records in the official language or languages of the State, but only that the burden of possible translation rests with the private enterprise.

This is without prejudice to the possible entitlement of persons belonging to national minorities to use their language(s) in communications with administrative authorities as foreseen in Article 10(2) of the **Framework Convention for the Protection of National Minorities.**

Administrative Authorities and Public Services

13/14/15) OSCE Participating States are committed to taking measures which will contribute to creating a dynamic environment, conducive not only to the maintenance of the identity of persons belonging to national minorities (including their language) but also to their development and promotion. As a consequence, these States have undertaken to respect "the right of persons belonging to national minorities to effective participation in public affairs" as outlined in paragraph 35 of the **Copenhagen Document.** Article 10(2) of the **Framework Convention for the Protection of National Minorities** expressly requires States to "make possible the use of minority languages in communications with administrative authorities." Paragraph 35 of the **Copenhagen Document** also makes reference to the possibility of creating an environment that would be conducive to the participation of national minorities in public affairs, in their own language, by establishing "appropriate local or autonomous administrations corresponding to the specific historical and territorial circumstances of minorities in accordance with the policies of the State concerned". Article 15 of the **Framework Convention** engages States to "create the conditions necessary for the effective participation of persons belonging to national minorities in cultural, social and economic life and in public affairs, in particular those affecting them." These provisions engage public authorities to enable persons belonging to national minorities to deal with local authorities in their language or to receive civil certificates and attestations in their own language. In line with the principles of equality and non-discrimination, these provisions also imply a dynamic participatory relationship wherein the language of the minority may be a full-fledged vehicle of communication in local political life and in the interface between citizens and public authorities including in the provision of public services.

The ethnic representativity of administrative institutions and agencies designed to serve the population is usually reflective of a pluralistic, open and non-discriminatory society. In order to counter the effects of past or existing discrimination within the system, Article 2 of **International Labour Organisation Convention No. 111 Concerning Discrimination in Respect of Employment and Occupation** requires States to "pursue a national policy designed to promote [...] equality of opportunity and treatment in respect of employment and occupation, with a view to eliminating any discrimination in respect thereof."

When designing and implementing programmes and services intended to serve the public, it is reasonable to expect that governments committed to the principles outlined above should take into consideration the expressed desires of persons belonging to national minorities as well as the principle of numerical justification. Where the need is expressed and the numbers are significant, equity requires that taxpayers belonging to national minorities have access to services also in their own language. This is particularly so in the case of health and social services which affect the quality of peoples' lives in an immediate and fundamental manner.

In line with the principles of equality and non-discrimination, administrative authorities are expected to deal with persons belonging to national minorities in an inclusive and equitable manner. States must recognise the demographic realities of the regions under their jurisdiction. Above all, States should not seek to avoid their obligations by changing the demographic reality of a region. Specifically Article 16 of the **Framework Convention** engages States to refrain from measures which might arbitrarily alter the proportion of the population in areas inhabited by persons belonging to national minorities with the objective of restricting the rights of these minorities. Such measures could consist of arbitrary expropriations, evictions, expulsions as well as the arbitrary redrawing of administrative borders and census manipulation.

Independent National Institutions

16) Human rights acquire real meaning for their intended beneficiaries when the public authorities of the State establish mechanisms to ensure that the rights guaranteed in international conventions and declarations, or in domestic legislation, are effectively implemented and protected. As a complement to judicial procedures, independent national institutions usually provide quicker and less expensive recourses and are as such more accessible.

Discrimination as referred to in the **Convention on the Elimination of Racial Discrimination** is not defined according to criteria relating strictly to race. Article 1(1) of the **Convention** stipulates that the concept of racial discrimination shall mean "any distinction, exclusion, restriction or preference based on race, colour, descent or national or ethnic origin which has the purpose or effect of nullifying or impairing the recognition, enjoyment or exercise, on an equal footing, of human rights and fundamental freedoms in the political, economic, social, cultural or any other field of public life." Article 6 of the Convention declares that "State Parties shall assure to everyone within their jurisdiction effective protection and remedies, through the competent national tribunals and other State institutions against any acts of racial discrimination which violate his human rights and fundamental freedoms contrary to this Convention […]" In this context, the establishment by States of independent national institutions that can act as mechanisms of redress and compensation, such as the institution of ombudsperson or a human rights commission is a measure of a given State's democratic and pluralistic nature. Accordingly, and with reference to **United Nations resolution**

48/134 of 20 December 1993, the Council of Europe has encouraged, in **Committee of Ministers Recommendation No. R(97)14 of 30 September 1997**, the establishment of "national human rights institutions, in particular human rights commissions which are pluralist in their membership, ombudsmen or comparable institutions." Such mechanisms of redress should be made available also to persons belonging to national minorities who consider that their linguistic and other rights have been violated.

Judicial Authorities

17/18) International law requires public authorities to ensure that all persons who are arrested, accused and tried be informed of the charges against them and of all other proceedings in a language they understand. If need be, an interpreter must be made available to them free of charge. This standard of due process of law is universal in its application and does not relate to the linguistic rights of national minorities as such. Rather, the underlying principles are those of equality and non-discrimination before the law. Respect for these principles is particularly vital in relation to criminal charges and proceedings. As a consequence, Article 14(3)(a) of the **International Covenant on Civil and Political Rights** requires that everyone charged with a criminal offense shall "be informed promptly and in detail in a language which he understands of the nature and cause of the charge against him". Article 6(3)(a) of the **European Convention for the Protection of Human Rights and Fundamental Freedoms** stipulates the same requirement in almost identical language. In addition, Article 5(2) of the aforementioned convention stipulates the same requirement in relation to arrest. Furthermore, Article 14(3) of the **International Covenant on Civil and Political Rights** stipulates the entitlement of everyone 'in full equality' [...] "(e) to examine, or have examined, the witnesses against him and to obtain the attendance and examination of witnesses on his behalf under the same conditions as witnesses against him". In this connection, Article 14(3)(f) of the **International Covenant on Civil and Political Rights** and Article 6(3)(e) of the **European Convention for the Protection of Human Rights and Fundamental Freedoms** guarantee the right of everyone "to have the free assistance of an interpreter if he cannot understand or speak the language used in court." While these guarantees concerning expressly the use of language are prescribed specifically in relation to criminal procedures, it follows from the fundamental guarantee of equality before courts and tribunals, as stipulated in the first sentence of Article 14(1) of the **International Covenant on Civil and Political Rights**, that legal proceedings of all kinds are to be considered more perfectly fair to the extent that the conditions are more strictly equal. This determination, which applies equally with respect to the choice of language for proceedings as a whole, should guide States in the development of their policies concerning the equal and effective administration of justice.

More generally, Article 7(1) of the **European Charter for Regional or Minority Languages** declares that States shall base their policies, legislation and practice on such objectives and principles as "the recognition of the regional or minority languages as an expression of cultural wealth [...]" and "the need for resolute action to promote regional or minority languages in order to safeguard them". Article 7(4) of the **European Charter** stipulates that "in determining their policy with regard to regional and minority languages, [...] Parties shall take into consideration the needs and wishes expressed by the groups which use such languages." Moreover, Article 15 of the **Framework Convention** engages States to "create the conditions necessary for the effective participation of persons belonging to national minorities in cultural, social and economic life and in public affairs, in particular those affecting them." If one considers the above-mentioned standards while taking into consideration the importance, in democratic societies, of effective access to justice, it is reasonable to expect that States should, so far as possible, ensure the right of persons belonging to national minorities to express themselves in their language in all stages of judicial proceedings (whether criminal, civil or administrative) while respecting the rights of others and maintaining the integrity of the processes, including through instances of appeal.

19) Insofar as access to justice is vital to the enjoyment of human rights, the degree to which one may participate directly and easily in available procedures is an important measure of such access. The availability of judicial procedures functioning in the language(s) of persons belonging to national minorities, therefore, renders access to justice more direct and easy for such persons.

On this basis, Article 9 of the **European Charter for Regional or Minority Languages** provides that, to the extent feasible and pursuant to the request of one of the affected parties, all judicial proceedings should be conducted in the regional or minority language. The Parliamentary Assembly of the Council of Europe, has come to the same conclusion in Article 7(3) of its **Recommendation 1201** which provides that "In regions in which substantial numbers of a national minority are settled, the persons belonging to a national minority shall have the right to use their mother tongue in their contacts with the administrative authorities and in proceedings before the courts and legal authorities." Accordingly, States should adopt appropriate recruitment and training policies for the judiciary.

Deprivation of Liberty

20) Rule 51, paragraphs 1 and 2, of the **United Nations Standard Minimum Rules for the Treatment of Prisoners** as well as Rule 60, paragraphs 1 and 2 of the **European Prison Rules of the Council of Europe** stress the importance of the right of the incarcerated to be understood by the prison administration as well as the importance for the prison administration to be understood by the inmate

population. These provisions do not relate to minority rights as such. However, taken into consideration along with the expressed desire of affected populations, their numerical strength and the principle of equality and non-discrimination, the aforementioned provisions are even more compelling in regions or localities where persons belonging to national minorities are present in significant numbers.

21) Rule 37 of the **United Nations Standard Minimum Rules for the Treatment of Prisoners** as well as Article 43(1) of the **European Prison Rules of the Council of Europe** uphold the right of prisoners to communicate with their families, reputable friends and persons or representatives of outside organisations. In view of the importance of such human rights as freedom of expression and the right to use one's language in public and in private, it is incumbent upon authorities to respect these rights within the limitations prescribed by law even in penitentiary institutions. As a rule, prisoners should be able to communicate in their own language both orally with other inmates and with visitors and also in personal correspondence. Nevertheless, certain human rights and freedoms of persons detained for criminal acts may legitimately be restricted or suspended for reasons of public security in conformity with the limitations prescribed by the international instruments. As a practical matter, enjoyment of the linguistic rights of detained persons may be best facilitated by their detention in a place where their language is usually spoken.

Index

Printed in the United States
By Bookmasters